Northeast India in the Vertical Gorge of Tsangpo: climate change and the crisis of Brahmaputra

KOILASHOR PORA TSANGPOR THIO GORAT UTTAL-PUB BHARAT, JALABAYU SALANI: BRAHMAPUTRAR SANKAT

কৈলাসৰ পৰা ছাংপোৰ থিয় গৰাত উত্তৰ-পূব ভাৰত

জলবায়ু সলনি, ব্ৰহ্মপুত্ৰৰ সংকত

A research book by Dr. Arati Baruah

Northeast India in the Vertical Gorge of Tsangpo: climate change and the crisis of Brahmaputra

KOILASHOR PORA TSANGPOR THIO GORAT
UTTAL-PUB BHARAT, JALABAYU SALANI:
BRAHMAPUTRAR SANKAT

কৈলাসৰ পৰা ছাংপোৰ
থিয় গৰাত উত্তৰ-পূৱ ভাৰত

জলবায়ু সলনি, ব্ৰহ্মপুত্ৰৰ সংকত

A research book by Dr. Arati Baruah

Coolgrove Press
Northeast Perspectives

Coolgrove Press, an imprint of
Cool Grove Publishing, Inc. New York.
512 Argyle Road, Brooklyn, NY 11218

www. coolgrove.com
For permissions and other inquiries write to
info@coolgrove. com

Originally published (2020) in the Assamese language as
KOILASHOR PORA TSANGPOR THIO GORAT UTTAL-PUB BHARAT: JALABAYUSALANI, BRAHMAPUTRARSANKAT

by Chandra Kalita Publication Zoo Road, Tiniali, Guwahati, Assam

This edition is a reproduction of the above mentioned Assamese language book with the English title

Northeast India in the Vertical Gorge of Tsangpo: climate change and the crisis of Brahmaputra

A research book by Dr. Arati Baruah

ISBN: 978-1887276-84-9

Media alchemy by Kiku

Coolgrove Press
Northeast perspectives

উছৰ্গা

নিজৰ ভৰিৰ ওপৰত থিয় হোৱা দেউতা,
অধ্যাপক চন্দ্ৰ কলিতা, জ্ঞানৰ প্ৰতীক আৰু মৰমীয়াল বৌটি
দুৰ্গেশ্বৰী বৰা আৰু ভৱিষ্যতৰ সপোন আৰম্ভ কৰা অঞ্জলি
আৰু এন্টনৰ হাতত অৰ্পণ কৰিলোঁ।

Publisher's note

NORTHEAST INDIA IN THE VERTICAL GORGE OF TSANGPO:
climate change and the crisis of Brahmaputra

For the benefit of Assamese readers outside India, Coolgrove Press is publishing (2021) Dr. Arati Baruah's book titled *Koilashor Pora Tsangpor Thio Gorat Utter-pub Bharat: Jalabayusalani, Brahmaputrarsankat* (with the English title: *Northeast India in the Vertical Gorge of Tsangpo: climate change and the crisis of Brahmaputra*). It was first published in India with favorable reviews in Assam in 2020. An English version of the above work by the author is being prepared at Coolgrove, provisionally titled, *Save the Tsangpo-Brahmaputra, Protect the Vertical Pole and Freeze Global Warming.* As the titles suggest, when it comes to international border crossing rivers, complex factors not limited to environmental, topographical and geological, affect the people who live in those river valleys.

However, when man-made disasters break upstream, problems cascades downstream where the people often pay the heavier price, though not always, in the long term. Treaties governed by international law need to be in place to enforce accountability for the responsible parties for such tragedies. Transcending national self-interest, the prevention of such disasters in mutual recognition of the loss of traditional lands and lives lost on both sides of the border need to be considered urgently. Such scenarios exist all over the world and require a closer look at the intentions and genuineness of the negotiating parties. Shifting the national aims from mindless and greedy exploitation of nature to mutual, good neighborly co-management of the ecosystems of such river valleys can instead support peace and prosperity on both sides of the river. Topographical geopolitics, historical perceptions and the good faith of the parties become crucial factors in the dynamics of negotiations. But governments come and governments go yet the lives, hopes and dreams of the people of valleys on both sides remain determined by the existence and absence of such guardrails.

From India to Tibet, from Mongolia to China to the nation states of Northeast India, indigenous peoples living on their ancestral lands, have straddled today's national boundaries in settlements predating the spreads of both, imperial Han Chinese and that of India's epic religious-mythologies which have historically justified the encroachment of tribal lands followed by the eventual displacement of tribal people, not unlike what happened in the Americas after the Europeans landed. What then do we mean by the 'rights' of indigenous people? While both books are written to raise awareness of the potentially catastrophic consequences of any giant hydro-electric dam projects to harness the energy of the waters of the Tsangpo—the headwaters of the Brahmaputra or any other river flowing south, this work also serves to illuminate the critical importance of Tibet not only to India, but to all of Asia on many levels.

Referring to Tibet as the 'Vertical Pole', the author reminds us that Tibet, also known as the 'Roof of the World', is actually and spectacularly, the source of all the great rivers of Asia. Let us not forget that both the Ganges and the Brahmaputra as well as other smaller rivers flowing south into India begin in Tibet, fed by glacial melt cascading down the numerous creases of the Himalayas. In the interest of identifying the long view for both sides of the border and the world by example, the works offer readers a localized and heartfelt perspective regarding the consequences of the topography and the geology of the long mountainous border region between India and Tibet-China, with an urgent appeal for both countries and the entire world, to pay closer attention to these issues and to take action to avoid catastrophes in the making.

Dr. Baruah reminds us that before China invaded Tibet in the mid 20th Century, there had never been a border conflict between Tibet and India. Not only was Tibet a buffer between India and China but from the 8th century onward, Tibet and India have been connected by the North-South trade routes for Indian and international goods and culturally, by the state sponsored importation and top down integration of Buddhism into Tibetan socety, overwhelmingly from Indian sources. But now we see a border conflict brewing between China and India in which voiceless indigenous people of the region are the helpless witnesses. How quickly people forget the difference between Tibetan and Chinese people? Dr. Baruah presents compelling arguments for Tibetans, Indians, Chinese and the international community to again ask the hard questions about what are the true boundaries and what if anything do they have to do with 'natural' boundaries and ancestral lands of the indigenous people of the area? Engaging in such deliberations can help all border sharing countries to elevate their policies to be more in keeping with realities on the ground. It is an opportunity for the parties to do something right and beneficial for everybody. What can India, China and the world do about it? What other significant changes, new directions and consequences are possible in the 21st Century?

— Tej Hazarika

কৈলাসৰ পৰা ছাংপোৰ থিয় গৰাত উত্তৰ-পূব ভাৰত

জলবায়ু সলনি, ব্ৰহ্মপুত্ৰৰ সংকত

মই এই কিতাপখনৰ প্ৰথম খণ্ডটো উত্তৰ-পূব ১০১ হিচাপে দাবী নকৰো, কিন্তু মই এইটো দাবী কৰিব বিচাৰিম যে এই কিতাপখন হাইস্কুলৰ সমাজ বিজ্ঞানৰ এটা অংশ আৰু উত্তৰ-পূব ভাৰতৰ ভূতাত্ত্বিক ১০১ৰ বাবে এখন সহায়ক পুথি হ'ব পাৰে।

—*লেখক*

কৃতজ্ঞতা

এই কিতাপখন যুগুত কৰাৰ ক্ষেত্ৰত বহুতো সুহৃদ ব্যক্তি, বন্ধু, অনুষ্ঠান-প্ৰতিষ্ঠান, সংবাদ মাধ্যম আৰু সাংবাদিক বন্ধুৱে সহায় কৰিছে। এই ছেগতে মই সকলোলৈকে মোৰ আন্তৰিক কৃতজ্ঞতা জ্ঞাপন কৰিলোঁ। এই ক্ষেত্ৰত মই কেইজনমান বিশেষ ব্যক্তিৰ লগতে অনুষ্ঠানৰ নাম বিশেষভাৱে উল্লেখ কৰিবই লাগিব। ইয়াৰ ভিতৰত ধেমাজি ভ্ৰমণত সহায় কৰা মুহি বৰগোঁহাই, বলিন কলিতা আৰু ডঃ চন্দন মহন্তক মই আন্তৰিক ধন্যবাদ জ্ঞাপন কৰিলোঁ। লখিমপুৰ ছোৱালী মহাবিদ্যালয়ত অনুষ্ঠিত কৰ্মশালাখনৰ বাবে মহাবিদ্যালয় পৰিয়ালক ধন্যবাদ জনালোঁ। ভাতৃপ্ৰতিম নৰজ্যোতি কলিতাৰ লগতে শিৱলোচন কলিতা, মুকুট কলিতা, ৰামণ বৰা আৰু তেওঁৰ সহযোগী বন্ধুবৰ্গক সম্পাদনাত সহায়-সহযোগিতা আগবঢ়োৱা বাবে অশেষ ধন্যবাদ জনালোঁ। মিনাক্ষী বৰুৱাৰ সৎ দিহা-পৰামৰ্শৰ বাবে তেওঁলৈও আন্তৰিক ধন্যবাদ জ্ঞাপন কৰিলোঁ।

অসমৰ প্ৰকৃতিৰ লগত খাপ খোৱাকৈ উন্নয়ন, সেউজ প্ৰকল্প, নদীবান্ধৰ যথোপযুক্ততাৰ ওপৰত মই 'আমাৰ অসম'ত দহ বছৰ আগৰ পৰাই লিখি আহিছোঁ। অসমীয়া লিখিবলৈ পাহৰি যোৱাৰ সময়ত মোক আৰু দেশক আগবঢ়াই নিবলৈ দিয়া উৎসাহ আৰু প্ৰচেষ্টাৰ বাবে হোমেন বৰগোহাঞিঙ ডাঙৰীয়াক কৃতজ্ঞতা জনালোঁ।

।। সূচীপত্ৰ।।

।। সূচীপত্ৰ।।

পৰ্ব দুই

পাতনি

এইখিনি অৱশ্যেই পঢ়ক

ব্ৰহ্মপুত্ৰক, ইয়াৰ অৰুণাচলত নাম ছিয়াং আৰু তিব্বতত য়াৰলুং ছাংপো বুলি জনা যায়, এইখন এখন সাধাৰণ নদী বুলিব নোৱাৰি। বৰ্তমানৰ কোনো নদীৰ লগত ই একে নহয়। যিখিনিৰ মিল আছে, তাৰে কিছুমান তুলনা উপৰুৱা, কিছুমান সাদৃশ্য মানৱসৃষ্ট আৰু কিছুমান প্ৰাকৃতিক। উদাহৰণস্বৰূপে পৃথিৱীত দুখন নদীয়েই আছে, আমাজান আৰু ব্ৰহ্মপুত্ৰ, যাক পুৰুষ নদী বোলা হয়। ব্ৰহ্মপুত্ৰই অসম্ভৱ গেদ আৰু পলস আনে, কিন্তু ই হোৱাংহো বা য়েল' নদীৰ সৈতে একে নহয়। ব্ৰহ্মপুত্ৰৰ বৈশিষ্ট্য; অৰ্থাৎ অসম্ভৱ গেদ-পলস অনা, কেনিয়নৰ পৰা আহিছে য'ত ই পাহাৰ কাটি নামিছে, যাক মই থিয় গৰা বুলিছোঁ। যদি বহুত লাভা, শিল বাব শিলাখণ্ড থাকিলহেঁতেন ব্ৰহ্মপুত্ৰ হয়তো জলপ্ৰপাতেদি এক মাইল নামি আহিলহেঁতেন। এই নদী উপত্যকাত নাব্য, মানে জাহাজ যাব পৰা কিন্তু লেহেমীয়া। এই কিতাপৰ প্ৰথম পৰ্বত নদীখনৰ হিমালয়ৰ আৰু তিব্বতৰ লগত সম্বন্ধ, হিমালয়ৰ গঠন আৰু উৎপত্তি, নদীৰ দিশ সলনিৰ বুৰঞ্জী, ভূতাত্ত্বিক বয়সত চালুকীয়া হিমালয়, হিমালয় আৰু ইয়াৰ আশপাশ, বৰ্ষাছায়া অঞ্চল আৰু মৰুভূমি, ভূতাত্ত্বিক চ্যুতি, চীনে তিব্বত লৈ লোৱাৰ পিচত নদীখন আৰু তিব্বত-উত্তৰ-পূব ভাৰত-ম্যানমাৰ নদী হাইৱে'ৰ বিলাই-বিপত্তি তথ্য হিচাবত দাঙি ধৰা হৈছে। দ্বিতীয় পৰ্বত ব্যক্তিগত পৰ্যবেক্ষণ-নিৰীক্ষণ আৰু কিছু মন্তব্যও আগবঢ়োৱা হৈছে।

জলবায়ু সলনি তথা গোলকীয় তাপৰ বৃদ্ধি (বেছি ক্ষেত্ৰতে তাপ বাঢ়িছে), সাগৰ পৃষ্ঠৰ উত্থান, বনজুই, ঘনাই ঘূৰ্ণীবতাহ-ধুমুহা, অসমত বজ্ৰপাত বৃদ্ধি, মিজোৰামত সঘনাই ভূমিকম্প, অসমত সঘনাই তৰাং পানীৰ বানপানী আদি সকলো যথাস্থানত অনা হৈছে। দুই মেৰু আৰু তৃতীয় মেৰু (অৰ্থাৎ তিব্বত)ৰ বৰফ আৰু হিমবাহ গলা, মধ্য এছিয়াৰ হিমবাহ গলা আৰু মধ্য এছিয়াৰ পানীৰ সংকট আৰু বাক-যুদ্ধ, কিমানলৈ হিন্দুকোষ, গোমুখী আৰু অৰুণাচলৰ পূবৰ পেমাকোৰ হিমবাহ গলিছে, তাৰ লগতে মুম্বাইৰ সাগৰ পৃষ্ঠ কিমান উঠিব, পশ্চিমবঙ্গৰ সুন্দৰবনত পানী বৃদ্ধি আৰু বাংলাদেশৰ সাহসিক সাগৰ পৃষ্ঠৰ উত্থান প্ৰত্যুত্তৰ তাৰ উল্লেখ পাব।

ব্লগটো কিয় দিয়া হ'ল? নদীখনৰ ওপৰত চীনদেশে কি প্ৰযুক্তি কৰিছে তাৰ খবৰ বিচাৰি বিচাৰি উলিয়াবলগা হৈছিল, সেইবাবে পৰিশিষ্টত দি ৰখা হৈছে। মানুহৰ স্মৃতি ক্ষন্তেকীয়া, প্ৰথম প্ৰতিক্ৰিয়া আৰু উত্তেজনা নাইকিয়া হ'লেই খবৰত থকা লোকসকলৰ অধিক স্বাধীনতা, তেওঁলোকৰ মতে সকলো কৰিবলৈ। সেইবাবে ব্লগটো সেই সময়ৰ স্নেপশ্বট হিচাবে ৰখা হৈছে। যিকোনো খবৰেই মানুহে পাহৰি যায়। এইটো সমস্যা সমাধান নকৰাৰ এটা ভাল অজুহাত হৈ পৰিছে। মই সেই সময়লৈ লৈ গৈছোঁ, য'ত আন এটা খবৰ দি নদীৰ দূষিত কৰা কথাটো ফাংফুং কৰা হ'ল। মনত পেলাই দিয়া যাওক যে, ২০০০ চনৰ ১১ জুনত ৩০ মহলাৰ সমান ঢৌ আহি য়িকিয়ঙৰ বাট বন্ধ হৈ যায়। পাচিঘাটত ৩০জন মানুহ মৰে। ৰাইজে নদীত কিবা হ'লেই কৃত্ৰিম উপগ্ৰহৰ ফটো চৰকাৰৰ পৰা দাবী কৰিব। ৰাইজ, ব্ৰহ্মপুত্ৰ অতি সঙ্কটত বুলি মোৰ দ্বাৰা চিঞৰি অহা হৈছে। পানীৰ ওপৰত এই অত্যাচাৰ অমাৰ্জনীয়। খবৰবোৰ পাহৰি গ'লেই সমস্যাৰ সমাধান নহয়, ব্ৰহ্মপুত্ৰ শুকাই যাবলৈ কিমান দিন? ব্লগটো এৰেলগে পঢ়িব বা skip কৰিব পাৰে। কিন্তু ব্ৰহ্মপুত্ৰৰ সংকটৰ কথা পাহৰি নাযাব।

চীনৰ ঠাইবোৰৰ অৱস্থান জানিবলৈ বৰ টান সেইবাবে মেপবোৰ দিয়া হৈছে।

দ্বিতীয় পৰ্বত মই মোৰ জীৱন সময়তে কেনেকৈ চীনে তিব্বত লোৱাৰ নামত অৰুণাচলৰ কিছু অংশ তেওঁলোকৰ বুলি হাস্যকৰ, কিম্ভুতকিমাকাৰ দাবী কৰিব পাৰে তাৰ প্ৰত্যুত্তৰ বুৰঞ্জী আৰু যুগ যুগৰ পৰম্পৰাৰ পৰা দিছোঁ আৰু ৰাষ্ট্ৰসংঘৰ বাবে এটা কাউণ্টাৰ প্ৰপ'জেলৰ কথা উনুকিয়াইছোঁ।

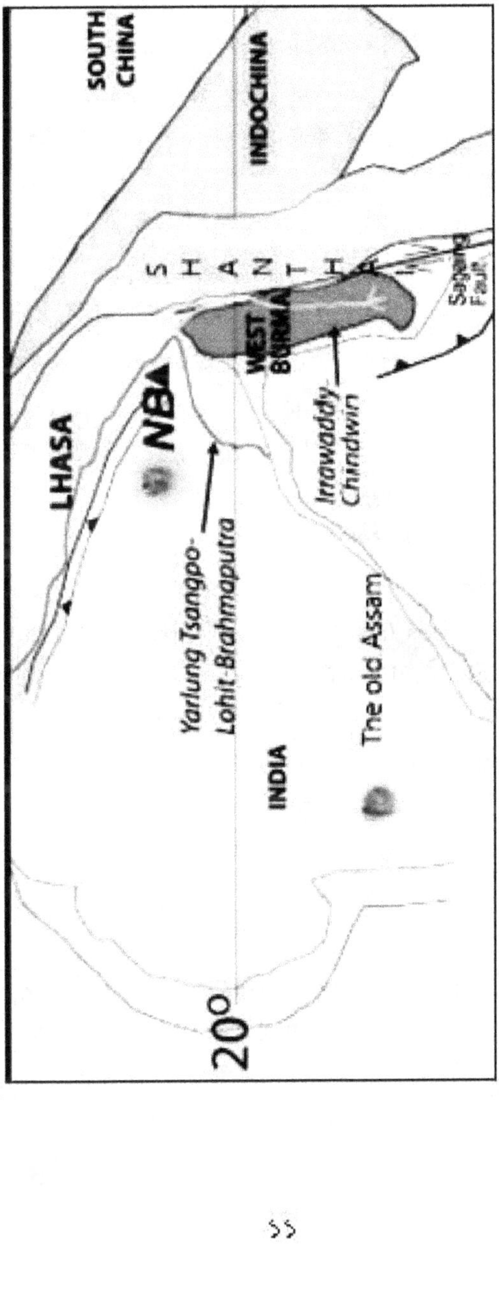

চিত্ৰ ঃ (১) পুৰণি জলমগ্ন ফটো

বৰ্তমান ব্ৰহ্মপুত্ৰ নদীৰ থাকিবলগীয়া 'U' বা 'V' আকাৰৰ কোনো আকাৰ নাই। ঠায়ে ঠায়ে কিছু দ ঠাই আছে তাত চাকনৈয়াও থাকিব পাৰে, কিন্তু নদীখনৰ পানী ৰখাৰ ধাৰণ ক্ষমতা হ্ৰাস পাইছে আৰু প্ৰায় কাঁহী এখনৰ দৰে হৈ গৈছে।

মানচিত্ৰসমূহ কষ্টেৰে যুগুত কৰা হৈছে যাতে লাগতিয়াল ঠাইৰ নামবোৰ একেখন ঠাইতে পায়, ছাংপোৰ ক'ত কি হৈছে তাক বুজিবলৈ, এতিয়া আৰু আগলৈও, ঠাইবোৰ বিচাৰি উলিওৱা হৈছে, কিছু ক্ষেত্ৰত চীনে তিব্বতীয় নামবোৰ সলনি কৰি দিছে। ৰাইজে যাতে ব্ৰহ্মপুত্ৰৰ হেডৱাটাৰত (উজনি নদী অংশত) কি হৈ আছে ভালকৈ বুজি পায় তাৰ বাবে যথেষ্ট মনোযোগ দিয়া হৈছে। ভূতাত্ত্বিক শব্দবোৰ পাবলৈ নাই, বিশেষকৈ suture-ক চিলাই-সীয়নি বোলা হৈছে। এই শব্দটো মূলতে চিকিৎসকে দিয়া চিলাইৰ সৈতে একে, দুই মাটিৰ খণ্ড লগলগাই প্ৰকৃতিয়ে কৰা চিলাই।

চীনে তিব্বত লোৱাৰ পিছৰে পৰা বিশেষকৈ ১৯৬২ চনৰ ভাৰতৰ ৰেজাং-লা আৰু বাম্-লা আক্ৰমণৰ পিছৰে পৰা ছিয়াঙত বহু অস্বাভাৱিক ঘটনা ঘটিছে, যাৰ কোনো উত্তৰেই চীনদেশে স্পষ্টকৈ দিয়া নাই। মই অৰুণাচলৰ ৰাইজক কথা দিছিলোঁ উৰহী গছৰ ওৰ উলিয়াম বুলিঙ্গ ছিয়াঙৰ পানী কিয় ক'লা হ'ল, তাৰ কোনো আনুষ্ঠানিক উত্তৰ নোপোৱাত এই পুথি লিখা হ'ল। তিব্বতৰ উচ্চতাত কি হৈছে অঞ্চলটোৰ নিম্নৰ ধ্বংসাত্মক কাৰ্যই প্ৰমাণ কৰেনে? এই প্ৰশ্নটো বিশ্বৰ সন্মুখত দাঙি ধৰা হ'ল। মোৰ আশা বিশ্বই নিৰ্ণয় কৰক যে এই সমস্যা অকল ভাৰতৰে নহয়, অকল দক্ষিণ-পূব এছিয়াৰে নহয়, ই বিশ্বৰ সমস্যাঙ্গ জলবায়ু সলনিয়ে কাকো নিস্তাৰ নিদিয়ে, কাকো মাৰ্জনা নকৰে, সংযোগিত বিশ্বত অকল অৰ্থনীতিৰ ওপৰত বিশ্ব নচলে। তিব্বতৰ মানুহে মাটিত খনন নকৰে, পাহাৰ, মালভূমি আলফুলে ৰাখে, সেই ভূমিপুত্ৰৰ দুৰ্দশাত বিশ্বই তথা ৰাষ্ট্ৰসংঘই মুখ ঘূৰালেই হ'বনে?

উত্তৰ-পূবৰ বিশেষকৈ অসমৰ প্ৰাকৃতিক দৃশ্য আৰুস্থলাকৃতি সলনি হৈ আহি আছে বুলি ভূতাত্ত্বিকসকলে স্বীকাৰ কৰিছে। পশ্চিমবংগ ভূতাত্ত্বিক স্কেলত পানীৰ পৰা উঠি অহা বেছিদিন হোৱা নাই। অসম উপত্যকাৰ সৃষ্টিৰ কাম আৰু উত্তৰ-পূবৰ পাহাৰ মসৃণ কৰা কাম একেলগে চলি আছে, লগতে আছে ভূমিকম্পৰ বিপদ, সুৰ মিলাই থকা প্ৰত্যাহ্বানটো গ্ৰহণ কৰিব লাগিবঙ্গ ইয়াৰ বাবে বিশ্বৰ

ভূতাত্ত্বিকৰ সহায় ল'ব লাগে।

এইখিনিতে আন এটা কথাৰ প্ৰসংগলৈ আহোঁ। বিদেশত থাকি অসমৰ পৰা অসমীয়া ভাষাত গ্ৰন্থ এখন প্ৰকাশৰ ক্ষেত্ৰত যথেষ্ট আহ্বানৰ সন্মুখীন হ'বলগীয়া হয়, যিটোৰ ক্ষেত্ৰত মই ভুক্তভোগী। এই ক্ষেত্ৰত শাৰীৰিক সংযোগ, দিহা-পৰামৰ্শৰ আদান-প্ৰদান তথা ছপা সম্পৰ্কীয় অন্যান্য প্ৰযুক্তিগত কথাবোৰ আছে। বিশেষকৈ ইউনিকোড মাধ্যমত আমি লিখা-মেলা কৰো কাৰণে সেইবোৰ পোনে পোনে ছপা কৰি দিব পৰা ব্যৱস্থাটো অসমত এতিয়াও উপলব্ধ হোৱা নাই, যাৰ বাবে সময় আৰু শাৰীৰিক শ্ৰম দুয়োটাই অধিক হৈছে। লগতে ভুলৰ পৰিমাণ সৰহ হোৱাৰো সুবিধা থাকে। বৰ্তমান সময়ত ইউনিকোড ষ্টেণ্ডাৰ্ড অসমীয়াত উপলব্ধ হ'ব লাগে যাতে আমাৰ দৰে প্ৰৱাসী অসমীয়াসকলে কিবা এটা চিন্তা কৰিলে তাক বাস্তৱ ৰূপ দিয়াৰ বাবে ভাবিবলগা নহয়। এই ক্ষেত্ৰত প্ৰযুক্তিগত উন্নয়নৰ লগতে অসমীয়া ভাষাৰ বিশ্বমানৰ লিপিৰ ক্ষেত্ৰত সংশ্লিষ্টসকলে চিন্তা-চৰ্চা কৰিব বুলি আশা কৰিলোঁ। লগতে অসাৱধানতাবশতঃ হৈ যোৱা ভুল-ত্ৰুটিৰ বাবে সকলোৰে ওচৰত মাৰ্জনা বিচাৰিলোঁ।

০০০

।। পৰ্ব এক।।

সূচনা

তিবৃতৰ উচ্চতাত কি হৈছে অঞ্চলটোৰ নিম্নৰ ধ্বংসাত্মক কাৰ্যই প্ৰমাণ কৰে

ইয়াত 'ওপৰ' (উচ্চ) আৰু 'তল' (নিম্ন) এই সৰল শব্দ দুটা ব্যৱহাৰ কৰিব বিচৰা হৈছে, আমাৰ বৰ্তমান বিশ্বত সংঘটিত হোৱা বিভিন্ন ঘটনাৱলী, বিশেষকৈ 'জলবায়ু পৰিৱৰ্তন', 'গোলকীয় উষ্ণতা' আৰু পানীৰ সংকট ব্যাখ্যা কৰিবৰ বাবে।

আৰম্ভণিৰ বাবে, ভৌগোলিক উত্তৰ মেৰুক 'ওপৰ' বুলি ধৰক। মানচিত্ৰত উত্তৰ সদায়ে ওপৰত। আমি শুনিবলৈ পাইছোঁ যে উত্তৰ মেৰুৰ গোট মাৰি থকা

বৰফৰ নৈসমূহ বা হিমবাহসমূহ গলাৰ বাবে সমগ্ৰ বিশ্বতে প্ৰভাৱ পৰিছে। পৃথিৱীৰ ঘূৰ্ণনৰ বাবে আৰু মেৰু কেইটা সূৰ্যৰ পৰা বহু দূৰত্বত অৱস্থিত হৈ অহাৰ বাবে, সূৰ্যৰ পৰা এনেয়েও কম শক্তি লাভ কৰে। ফলত দুয়োটা মেৰুৱেই ঠাণ্ডা অৱস্থাত আৰু বৰফৰে পৰিপূৰ্ণ হৈ থাকে। অৱশ্যেই গোলকীয় উষ্ণতাৰ প্ৰভাৱ মেৰু দুটাত অতি গুৰুত্বপূৰ্ণ। গোলকীয় উষ্ণতাৰ চাক্ষুস প্ৰভাৱ বিষুৱ অঞ্চলৰ ফালে ক্ৰমান্বয়ে হ্ৰাস প্ৰায় গৈ থাকে। গোলকীয় উষ্ণতাৰ বাবে হোৱা সালসলনি যদি মেৰুত ২.৫ ডিগ্ৰী হয়, বিযুৱত শূন্য ডিগ্ৰী। অৰ্থাৎ বিষুৱৰ ঠাইবোৰে উষ্ণতাৰ সলনিৰ প্ৰভাৱ নাপালেও মেৰুত দেখা যায়। হিমবাহ (Glaciers) আৰু বৰফ গলিবৰ বাবে ২.৫ ডিগ্ৰী চেলচিয়াছৰ সলনিয়েই যথেষ্ট। মেৰু দুটাত হিমবাহসমূহ গলাটোৱেই গোটেই বিশ্বত সাগৰ পৃষ্ঠৰ উচ্চতা বৃদ্ধিৰ কাৰক। যেতিয়া সাগৰ পৃষ্ঠৰ উচ্চতা বৃদ্ধি পায় তেতিয়া লুণীয়া পানী উপকূলৰ ভিতৰলৈ সোমাই আহে আৰু ভূমিপৃষ্ঠই লোণ শুহিবলৈ ধৰে, ডাঙৰ গছসমূহৰ পাতবোৰ সৰিবলৈ আৰম্ভ কৰে, ফলত গছবোৰ ক্ৰমান্বয়ে মৃত্যুৰ মুখলৈ আগবাঢ়ে। গেদ পৰি সৃষ্টি হোৱা অস্থায়ী নদীদ্বীপসমূহৰ বালিচৰত কৰা ধান, সৰিয়হ আদিৰ খেতিসমূহত নিমখ বিয়পি পৰাৰ বাবে শস্যৰ বৃদ্ধি বন্ধ হয়। কাৰ্বন-ডাই-অক্সাইডৰ বৃদ্ধিয়ে গোলকীয় উষ্ণতা বৃদ্ধিত অৰিহণা যোগায়। উষ্ণতা পৰিৱৰ্তনৰ প্ৰভাৱ মেৰু অঞ্চলত সৰ্বাধিক আৰু বিষুৱ অঞ্চলত সৰ্বনিম্ন। এইটো এক প্ৰকাৰ আঁতুৰা-ভৰাৰ দৰে, কিয়নো মানুহে তেওঁলোকৰ অৱস্থানৰ ওপৰত নিৰ্ভৰ কৰি ইয়াৰ প্ৰভাৱ নাজানিব পাৰে। আচলতে এইটো এটা দুৰ্ভাগ্যজনক কথা। ১৮ বছৰীয়া গ্ৰেটা থুৰ্নবাৰ্গে যিমান বুজিছে, উত্তৰ-পূবৰ ল'ৰা-ছোৱালীয়ে সিমান বুজা টান, গ্ৰেটা থাকে নৰৱে'ত। নৰৱে'ৰ অৱস্থান উত্তৰ মেৰুৰ কাষতে। কিন্তু উত্তৰ-পূবৰ ল'ৰা-ছোৱালীয়ে কাষৰ হিমালয় বা তিব্বতত কি হৈ আছে নজনাটো অমাৰ্জনীয়। আমি মেৰুসমূহত হিমবাহ গলাৰ ছবি প্ৰত্যক্ষ কৰিব পাৰো, বৰফৰ পৰ্বতসমূহ ভাঙি যোৱাৰ প্ৰত্যক্ষ কৰিব পাৰো আৰু আনকি এইবোৰ ধ্বংস হৈ সাগৰত পৰাও প্ৰত্যক্ষ কৰিবলৈ পাওঁ; এইবোৰ চাবলৈ আমি মেৰু অঞ্চললৈ যাব নোৱাৰিব পাৰো, কিন্তু ইয়াক অনুধাৱন কৰাৰ প্ৰয়োজন। হিমবাসমূহ গলা, সেউজগৃহ প্ৰভাৱ, পানীৰ বাষ্পীভৱন এই সকলোবোৰ সাগৰ পৃষ্ঠৰ বৃদ্ধি ঘটাৰ কাৰক।

আমাজনৰ বন ধ্বংস কাৰ্বন-মনোক্সাইড বৃদ্ধিৰ কাৰক, যিটোৱে সমগ্ৰ বিশ্বতে

উষ্ণতা পৰিৱৰ্তনৰ প্ৰভাৱ পেলাইছে। প্ৰতি মুহূৰ্ততে গছ-গছনি কাটি থকা হৈছে। ইয়াৰ পৰিৱৰ্তনৰ কথা মাথোঁ চিন্তা কৰাৰে প্ৰয়োজন নহয়, ইতিমধ্যে ইয়াৰ পৰিৱৰ্তনৰ বাবে পৰিকল্পনা কৰাৰো প্ৰয়োজন অত্যাৱশ্যকীয়। অতীতত গৃহ নিৰ্মাণ, ফাৰ্ণিচাৰ আৰু খৰিৰ বাবে বন ধ্বংস কৰা হৈছিল। বিলাসী ফাৰ্ণিচাৰ নিৰ্মাণৰ বাবে বিষুৱীয় অৰণ্যত কাঠৰ গছসমূহ কাটি অহা হৈছে আৰু সম্পদসমূহ লোপ পাব ধৰিছে। আমি কাৰক আৰু প্ৰভাৱৰ সম্পৰ্ক অনুভৱ কৰিব আৰম্ভ কৰিব লাগে। ইয়াৰ বাবে ইতিমধ্যেই বহু পলম হৈ গৈছে। বৰ্ষাৰণ্য ধ্বংস আৰু বিশ্বৰ যিকোনো ঠাইতেই নিৰ্বনানিকৰণ প্ৰাকৃতিক ভাৰসাম্যহীনতাৰ কাৰক হৈ পৰিছে আৰু ইয়াৰ প্ৰভাৱসমূহ অপৰিৱৰ্তনীয়।

জলবায়ু পৰিৱৰ্তন, গোলকীয় উষ্ণতাৰ প্ৰভাৱ বিশ্বৰ সীমিতসংখ্যক সম্পদসমূহৰ ওপৰত স্পষ্ট হৈ পৰিছে। জলবায়ু পৰিৱৰ্তন আৰু ইয়াৰ প্ৰভাৱৰ শক্তিশালী সম্পৰ্ক বৰ্তমান অধ্যয়নত প্ৰমাণ হৈছে। ভাৰতত এক ডিগ্ৰী চেলিচয়াছ উষ্ণতা বৃদ্ধিয়ে ২০ শতাংশ ঘেঁহু উৎপাদন কমাইছে। ইয়াৰ কাৰণ হ'ল ঘেঁহুৰ বৃদ্ধি স্তৰত নিশাবোৰ যিমান পৰিমাণৰ ঠাণ্ডা হ'ব লাগে সিমান পৰিমাণৰ নোহোৱা বাবে। আমেৰিকাৰ উত্তৰ-পূবৰ মেইন প্ৰদেশৰ শীতৰ সময়ত ঠাণ্ডা কমি অহা বাবে গছৰ পোকবোৰ বেছি দিন জীয়াইছে আৰু গছ ধ্বংস কৰিছে।

বৰ্তমান আপোনালোকক অন্য এক 'উচ্চতা'ৰ সৈতে চিনাকি কৰাই দিবলৈ সময় হ'ল। এই ভৌগোলিক অৱস্থান আক্ষৰিকভাৱেই উচ্চ— সাগৰ পৃষ্ঠতকৈ ৩.৫ মাইল উচ্চতাত আৰু ইয়াক জনপ্ৰিয়ভাৱে কোৱা হয়— 'পৃথিৱীৰ মুধচ'। এয়া হ'ল তিব্বত, অকল যোৱা শতিকাত চীনে জোৰেৰে লৈ লৈছে। তিব্বত হ'ল সমভূমি কিন্তু অসাধাৰণ উচ্চতাত অৱস্থিত আৰু ইয়াত থকা মানেই পৰ্বতৰ শৃংগত বাস কৰাৰ দৰে। তুলনামূলকভাৱে 'মাউণ্ট মেককিনলি', ডেনালি আলাস্কা হ'ল আমেৰিকাৰ সৰ্বোচ্চ পৰ্বত, ৩.৮ মাইল উচ্চতাৰ। পৃথিৱীৰ মুধচ তিব্বতক তৃতীয় মেৰু হিচাপেও জনা যায়। তিব্বতক আৱৰি আছে দক্ষিণত হিমালয়কে ধৰি প্ৰকাণ্ড পৰ্বতমালাই, তিব্বত ক্ৰমান্বয়ে পূবৰ ফালে এঢলীয়া, পেমাকোলৈ (পেমাকো, পেমাকোড বা পমা কো) ১১,৯৯৫ ফুট (২.২ মাইল) উচ্চতাৰ, পেমাকো অৰুণাচলৰ উত্তৰত। তিব্বতৰ উচ্চতাত যি ঘটে তাৰ প্ৰত্যক্ষ প্ৰভাৱ পৰে অঞ্চলটোৰ নিম্ন অংশত, প্ৰথমতে উত্তৰ-পূব ভাৰতৰ প্ৰদেশসমূহত প্ৰভাৱ

পৰে আৰু তাৰ পৰা দক্ষিণ-পূব এছিয়া, ভাৰতৰ বাকী অংশ আৰু পৰ্যায়ক্ৰমে বিশ্বৰ বাকী অংশত প্ৰভাৱ পৰে। য়াৰলুং ছাংপো/জাংবো ব্ৰহ্মপুত্ৰৰ তিব্বতৰ নাম, অৰুণাচল প্ৰদেশত ছিয়াং বা আনে, অসমত ব্ৰহ্মপুত্ৰ, বাংলাদেশত যমুনা আৰু পদ্মা— এই নদীখনৰ কাহিনী অতি মনোগ্ৰাহী আৰু বিগত তিনি বছৰৰ অধিক কাল এই গ্ৰন্থখনৰ মূল বিষয় হিচাপে আছে। এখন চালুকীয়া পৰ্বত, এখন গেদ-পলস অনা নদী প্ৰকৃতিৰ ইচ্ছা আৰু মানুহ দ্বাৰা সৃষ্ট টনা-আঁজোৰা জৰী যুদ্ধত। তিব্বতৰ তৃতীয় মেৰু বা জলস্তম্ভৰ সম্পূৰ্ণ বিৱৰণৰ বাবে 'তিব্বত তৃতীয় মেৰু আৰু কিছু কথা' সেই অধ্যায়লৈ ৰ'ব লাগিব।

'২০৫০ চনত পৃথিৱী' (The World in 2050) গ্ৰন্থৰ প্ৰণেতা লৰেন্স চি স্মিথে (Laurence C. Smith) তেওঁৰ গ্ৰন্থত 'California Browning, Shanghai Sinking', 'কেলিফ'ৰ্ণিয়া ৰঙচুৱা, ছাংহাই ডুবা' নামে এটা অধ্যায় লিখিছে। আমি ইতিমধ্যে কেলিফ'ৰ্ণিয়া ৰঙচুৱা হোৱা আৰু ছাংহাইৰ পানীৰ স্তৰ বৃদ্ধিৰ সাক্ষী হৈ আছোঁ। কেলিফ'ৰ্ণিয়া ৰঙচুৱা হোৱা মানে জুইৰ কথা কোৱা হৈছে, ২০১৯ত কেলিফ'ৰ্ণিয়া এমাহ শিৰোনামত থাকিল বনজুইৰ বাবদ। দক্ষিণ ফ্ল'ৰিডাৰ উপকূলীয় সম্প্ৰদায়সমূহত সাগৰ পৃষ্ঠ বৃদ্ধিৰো সাক্ষী হৈ আছোঁ। একে সমস্যাৰ ভুক্তভোগী হৈছে বাংলাদেশো; অৱশ্যে মই সেইসমূহৰ শেহতীয়া অধ্যয়নৰ ফলাফল অৰ্থাৎ ক'ত কিমান ইঞ্চি পানী উঠিছে তাৰ তথ্য পঢ়া নাই। চীনা চৰকাৰৰ বাবে বিস্ময়ৰ কাৰণ, চীনৰ গোবি মৰুভূমিৰ আকাৰ কিয় বাঢ়িহে গৈছে সেইটো এতিয়াও অবিদিত, আৰু জলবায়ু সলনিৰ এটা ৰূপ। এইটোৱেই কিছু মনোযোগ আকৰ্ষণ কৰে নিকটৱৰ্তী টাকলা মাকান নামৰ অন্য এখন সৰু মৰুভূমিলৈ। উল্লেখযোগ্য যে, এই স্থানলৈকে চীনে য়াৰলুং ছাংপোৰ পৰা এক সুৰংগ খান্দি পানী বোৱাই নিয়াৰ অভিযোগ উঠিছে। ছাংপোৰ উচ্চতা আৰু টাকলা মাকানৰ উচ্চতা সুৰংগৰ বাবে সুচল হয়। ছাংপো যে টাকলা মাকান সেউজকৰণৰ বাবে নহয়, কিন্তু সমগ্ৰ মানৱ জাতিৰ মংগল সাধন কৰিব পৰাকৈ তাক প্ৰকৃতভাৱেই ৰখাৰ বাবেহে সেইটো কোনে চীনক ক'ব? তিব্বতৰ সেই উচ্চতাত অতি বেছি পৰিমাণে উদ্ভিদৰ উৎপাদান হ'ব নোৱাৰে, হ'ব পাৰে মূলা, শাক, আলু, গাজৰ আৰু ঔষধি প্ৰজাতিঙ্গ 'হালধীয়া সোণ' হিচাপে পৰিচিত ঔষধি গুণবিশিষ্ট উচ্চ মূল্য সম্পন্ন ঔষধি উদ্ভিদ তাত হয়।

চিত্ৰ ঃ (২) 'হালধীয়া সোণ' একবিধ ভেকুৰজাতীয় শাক

তিব্বতে এই ধৰণৰ যদি ঔষধি প্ৰজাতি পায় সেইটো ভালৰেই কথা। কিন্তু আমি আৰম্ভণিতে বিশ্বৰ জলস্তম্ভ (Water Tower) আৰু হিমবাসমূহৰ আলোচনা কৰিব লাগিব। তলত তিব্বতৰ দক্ষিণৰ পৰা ওলোৱা নদীসমূহ দেখুওৱা হৈছে।

হিমালয়ক এখন ১০০০ মাইল দীঘল আৰু চাৰে পাঁচ মাইল ওখ ভাৰতৰ উত্তৰত বিশাল প্ৰাচীৰ বুলি ধৰি তাৰ পিছফালে তিব্বতক চাৰে তিনি মাইল ওখ জলস্তম্ভ বুলি অনুমান কৰা যাওক। ভাগীৰথী আৰু অলকানন্দা লগ হৈ গংগা এই প্ৰাচীৰৰ দক্ষিণৰ পৰা আহিছে। চম্বল আৰু সোণে (ইংৰাজীত son) গংগাত দক্ষিণৰ পৰা মিলিত হৈছে। যমুনাই গংগাত প্ৰয়াগত মিলিত হৈছে আৰু উত্তৰৰ বহু উপনদীও যোগ হৈছে। তাৰ পিছত গংগা বংগোপ সাগৰলৈ বৈ আহিছে। গংগা সেইকাৰণেই উত্তৰ ভাৰতৰ আটাইতকৈ ভিজিবল নদী। প্ৰাচীৰৰ পিচৰ তিব্বতৰ জলস্তম্ভৰ পৰা সিন্ধু আৰু ব্ৰহ্মপুত্ৰ আহিছে। সিন্ধু পশ্চিমলৈ গৈছে আৰু চটলেজে যোগ কৰাৰ পিছত জম্মু-কাশ্মীৰ পাৰ হৈ পাকিস্তান হৈ আৰবিয়ান সাগৰলৈ গৈছে। সিন্ধুৰ বিপৰীত ফালৰ পৰা ব্ৰহ্মপুত্ৰ প্ৰাচীৰৰ পিছফালৰ পৰা পূবলৈ আহিছে। এই তিব্বতৰ জলস্তম্ভৰ পৰা চলউইন, মেকং, য়াংছি আৰু য়াৰলুং নদীও আহিছে। এই গোটেই নদীসমূহ এছিয়াৰ প্ৰধান নদী। ব্ৰহ্মপুত্ৰ পূবলৈ গৈ ঘূৰি আহি অৰুণাচলত ভাৰতত সোমাল। তাৰ পিছত ই বংগোপ সাগৰলৈ বৈ গৈছে।

বিশ্বজুৰি বহুতো নদী দেশসমূহৰ সীমান্ত অতিক্ৰমি প্ৰবাহিত হয়। পানীৰ ব্যৱহাৰৰ লগতেই পৰিৱেশ সম্পৰ্কত প্ৰশ্ন উত্থাপিত হৈছে। আমি উত্থাপিত কৰিব বিচৰা প্ৰশ্নটো হৈছে যে, নৈপৰীয়া লোকসকলে তেওঁলোকে বাস কৰা আৰু নিৰ্ভৰ কৰা নদীৰ উপত্যকাৰ পৰিৱেশতন্ত্ৰ, যাক তেওঁলোকে ব্যৱহাৰ কৰে তাৰ অধিকাৰৰ ওপৰত লগতে সীমামূৰীয়া ৰাজ্যসমূহৰ সৈতে থকা চুক্তি সন্দৰ্ভত ৰাজ্যসমূহে কেনে ধৰণৰ সন্মান কৰে? কেনে ধৰণৰ উত্তম সীমান্ত আইনৰ প্ৰয়োজন? উচ্চাংশত এখন নদীৰ ওপৰত সংঘটিত কৰি অহা কাৰ্যবোৰে নিম্নাংশৰ লোকসকলৰ ওপৰত কেনেদৰে প্ৰভাৱ পেলাই আহিছে, নিম্নাংশত অৱস্থিত লোকে যাতে ভুগিব নালাগে। আমি এনেকুৱা এটা সময়ত বাস কৰিছোঁ যে যেতিয়া দেশসমূহক ক্ৰমবৰ্ধমান শক্তিৰ প্ৰয়োজনীয়তাই পৰিচালিত কৰিছে আৰু

উচ্চাংশৰ নদীসমূহে জলশক্তিৰ বান্ধৰ সম্ভাৱনীয়তা বহন কৰিছে যিয়ে নিম্নাংশৰ লোকসকলৰ বাবে সমস্যাৰ সৃষ্টি কৰিছে। চুবুৰীয়া ৰাজ্যসমূহৰ ব্যৱহাৰৰ বাবেই মাথোঁ নহয়, নৈৰ দুয়োপাৰে বসবাস কৰা লোকসকলৰ সুবিধাৰ বাবে আন্তঃৰাষ্ট্ৰীয় আইন প্ৰণয়ন কৰি তাক বলৱৎ কৰাৰ প্ৰয়োজন আছে। এই বিষয়সমূহৰ শান্তি আৰু বাণিজ্যক ত্বৰান্বিত কৰাৰ সম্ভাৱনীয়তা আছে, যিসকলে নদীসমূহক আশীৰ্বাদ হিচাপে ভাগবতৰা কৰি আহিছে। নিকটাত্মক ব্যৱহাৰ আৰু সভ্যতাৰ মাজত বেঞ্চমাৰ্ক কি? বোধকৰো কেৱল সেই দেশসমূহৰ মাজত দ্বি-পাক্ষিক চুক্তিয়েহে এইটো নিৰ্ধাৰণ কৰিব যাতে নদীসমূহ সীমান্তৰ দুয়োপাৰে সঠিকভাৱে সুবিধা আৰু লাভসমূহ বিতৰণ কৰা হয়। য়াৰলুং ছাংপো-ছিয়াং-ব্ৰহ্মপুত্ৰ নদী ব্যৱস্থাত কেনেধৰণৰ চুক্তি ভাৰত আৰু চীনৰ মাজত কৰিবৰ বাবে উপযুক্ত হিচাপে গ্ৰহণ কৰিব পৰা যায়। যদিও সীমান্তসমূহ বিবদমান, এটা নদী উপত্যকাত সীমান্তৰ দুয়োপাৰে সুৰক্ষা, শান্তি আৰু উন্নয়নৰ বাবে চুবুৰীয়াসকলে সহযোগিতাৰ ভিত্তিত কাম কৰা প্ৰয়োজন। ভাৰতৰ ছিয়াঙৰ লোকসকলে সন্মুখীন হৈ অহা অসুৰক্ষা আৰু ভোগ কৰি অহা বিভিন্ন সমস্যাসমূহৰ ওপৰত নিশ্চিতভাৱে আলোচনা কৰা প্ৰয়োজন। উত্তৰ-পূৰ্বাঞ্চল আৰু হিমালয়ৰ গঠনত সন্নিবিষ্ট মহা আন্তঃদেশীয় সংঘাতৰ ওপৰত আমি প্ৰথম স্তৰতে কিছু ভৌগোলিক বাস্তৱিকতা আৰু বিস্তৃতিৰ ওপৰত আমাৰ পুনৰ দৰ্শনৰ প্ৰয়োজন আছে।

এই কিতাপখনত লেখকৰ উদ্বিগ্নতা ব্যাখ্যা কৰাত সহায় কৰিবৰ বাবে গুৰুত্ব দিবলগীয়া বিষয়সমূহৰ ওপৰত মানচিত্ৰ আৰু ছবিৰ সৈতে কিছু পটভূমি প্ৰদান কৰা হৈছে। হাতেৰে অংকিত মানচিত্ৰসমূহ এটা নিৰ্দিষ্ট অঞ্চলৰ ওপৰত কোৱা কথাবোৰ কেনেদৰে এখন বগা বোৰ্ডত অংকন কৰিম তাৰ লগত একে কিন্তু মানচিত্ৰখন স্কেল মাপত নহয়।

মানচিত্ৰ সিপিঠিত

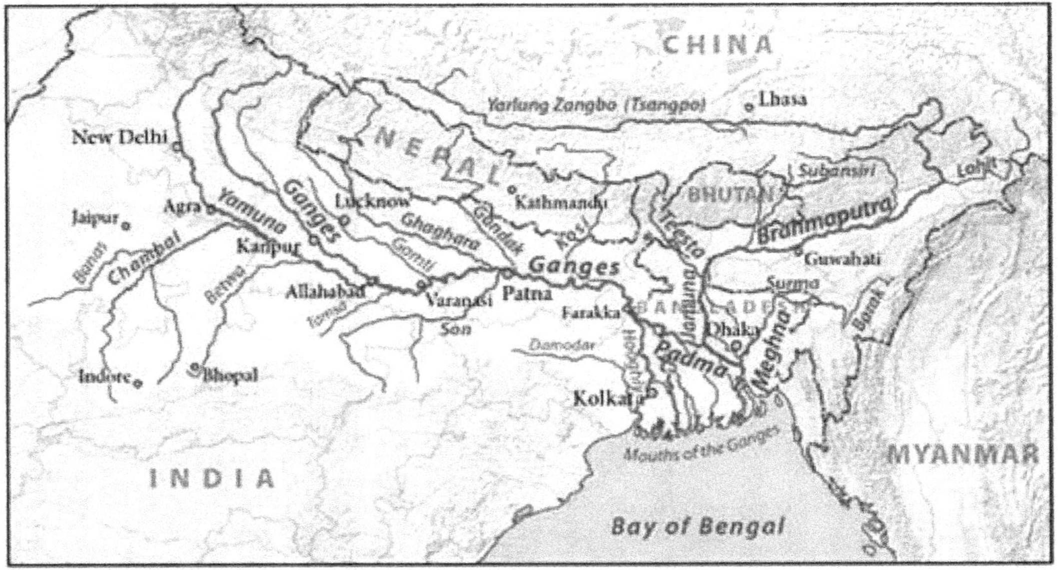

মানচিত্ৰ ঃ (১) উত্তৰ ভাৰতৰ নদীসমূহ, তিব্বত নামে পৰিচিত চীনৰ দক্ষিণ-পশ্চিম অংশৰ মানচিত্ৰত দেখুৱা হৈছে (ফটো ঃ ইণ্টাৰনেটৰ পৰা)

এই কিতাপখনে চীনে য়াৰলুং ছাংপোৰ পানী এটা সুৰংগৰ জৰিয়তে টাকলা মাকান মৰুভূমিলৈ গতিপথ সলনি কৰি বোৱাই নিব বিচৰা ভয়ংকৰ বাতৰিটোৰ ওপৰতো আলোকপাত কৰিব। বেলেগ ঠাইত বেলেগ নামেৰে কোৱা য়াৰলুং ছাংপো বা ব্ৰহ্মপুত্ৰৰ গতিপথ সলনি বা দূষিত পানীৰ ঘটনাই এই গ্ৰন্থৰ মূল বিষয়। জলবায়ু সলনি, চালুকীয়া হিমালয়ৰ গঠন, বিলিয়ন বছৰৰ সলনি ৪০ মিলিয়ন বছৰৰ পাৰ্থক্য এই সকলোবোৰেই সংলগ্ন বিষয়। লগতে পামিৰ নাটৰ পৰা হেংডুৱান পাহাৰলৈকে গোটেই অঞ্চলৰ ভৌগোলিক বিশ্লেষণ কৰা হৈছে। ২০১৭ চনৰ অক্টোবৰ মাহৰ পৰা ২০১৮ চনৰ মাজভাগলৈ সেই বাতৰিসমূহে কেনেদৰে তেতিয়াৰে পৰা এতিয়ালৈকে প্ৰভাৱিত কৰিছে, সেই বাতৰিসমূহ মোৰ ব্লগিং আৰু পৰ্যালোচনাৰ পিছত তাৰ চাৰিটা মূল অৰ্থৰ তলত দিয়া ধৰণে ভগাইছোঁ।

(১) এইটো অভিযোগ উঠিছে যে চীনে য়াৰলুং ছাংপোৰ পৰা পানী টাকলা মাকানলৈ পৃথক কৰি বোৱাই নিবৰ বাবে প্ৰায় এক হাজাৰ মাইলজোৰা এক সুৰংগ নিৰ্মাণ কৰিব পাৰে, যেনেদৰে ইজৰাইলে জৰ্ডানত উপস্থিত হোৱাৰ পূৰ্বে জৰ্ডান নদীৰ পানী বোৱাই নিবৰ বাবে এটা সুৰংগ নিৰ্মাণ কৰিছে। প্ৰথম স্থানত কিয় টাকলা মাকানলৈ পানীৰ গতিপথ সলনি কৰিব? এই কাহিনীটোৰ সত্যতা আছেনে? টাকলা মাকান কি, ক'ত কোৱা হ'ব।

(২) মই সমগ্ৰ মধ্য এছিয়াৰ পানীৰ ভয়ংকৰ অৱস্থা ব্যাখ্যাৰ প্ৰয়োজন আছে বুলি অনুভৱ কৰি চীনৰ উত্তৰ-পশ্চিম 'স্তান' দেশখিনিৰ ভৌগোলিক অৱস্থা বৰ্ণনা কৰিছোঁ। পামিৰত গলি যোৱা হিমবাহৰ সমস্যাই হিমালয় চুইছেনে?

(৩) মধ্য এছিয়াত হিমবাহ/বৰফ বিগত দহ বছৰ ধৰি গলা আৰু টুটা, আৰু ছোভিয়েট দেশৰ দ্বাৰা আৰাল সাগৰলৈ যোৱা চিৰ দৰিয়া আৰু আমুদৰিয়াৰ জল প্ৰকল্পৰ ঘটনাৰ বাবে ইতিমধ্যে অতি বেয়া পৰিস্থিতিৰ উদ্ভৱ হৈছে। তাৰ বিৱৰণ ইয়াত পাব।

(৪) টাকলা মাকানৰ টাৰিম অৱবাহিকা হ'ল এটা কঁপাহ উৎপাদন অঞ্চল। হিমবাহসমূহ গলাৰ ফলত তাত কেনেকুৱা বেয়া প্ৰভাৱ পৰিছে/পৰিব? হিমালয়ৰ হিমবাহসমূহতো সেয়া সংঘটিত হ'ব নেকি?

লগতে বৰযুণৰ পানীৰ সংৰক্ষণৰ উপায় আলোচনা কৰা হৈছে। অসমৰ

বানপানী, যাক মই তৰাং পানী বুলি কওঁ, গেদ আৰু পলসৰ বাবে ইয়াৰ নিজা চিহ্ন আছে, যি নিজেই এখন গ্ৰন্থ হ'ব তাক ইয়ালৈ সম্পূৰ্ণকৈ অনা নাই, কিছু অনা হৈছে। চীনা মানুহ, সভ্যতা আদিক সন্মান কৰি অবিশ্বাস্য প্ৰশ্ন আৰু বিষয়ত 'চীনা মহাৰজা' বাক্যাংশ ব্যৱহাৰ কৰা হৈছে। চীনৰ পলিচিৰ সন্দেহৰ ওপৰত গুৰুত্ব দিবলৈ পঞ্চশীলক উপেক্ষা কৰা 'চীনা মহাৰজা'ৰ নৈপৰীয়া ৰাইজৰ কথা ভাবিবলৈ অন্তৰ আছেনে? নৈপৰীয়া লোকসকলৰ অধিকাৰলৈ সন্মান নাই যদিওবা সেই অনুভূতিও নাই, গ্ৰাস কৰাই যদি কাৰোবাৰ মানসিকতা ভাৰতে প্ৰতিৰক্ষাৰ কি খেল খেলা উচিত?

প্ৰদূষণ আৰু গোলকীয় উষ্ণতাৰ কাৰক আৰু ইয়াৰ প্ৰভাৱে ভৌগোলিক সীমা নাজানে। চীন আৰু ভাৰত দুখন প্ৰদূষিত দেশৰ মাজত ম্যানমাৰ হ'ল এখন দেশ। সেই পৰিস্থিতিটোৰ পৰা উত্তৰ-পূৰ্বাঞ্চলো বেছি দূৰৈত নাই। অৱশ্যে, যদি সঠিকভাৱে পৰিকল্পনা কৰা হয় উত্তৰ-পূৰ্বাঞ্চলে বায়ু পৰিষ্কাৰ কৰি ৰাখিব পাৰি, জলবায়ুক সহায় কৰিব পাৰে। তিব্বত আৰু উত্তৰ-পূৰ্বাঞ্চল ইটোৰ ওপৰত সিটো নিৰ্ভৰশীল আৰু এইটো হ'ল আন্তঃসীমান্ত প্ৰসংগ।

পৃথিৱীৰ গোলকীয় উষ্ণতাৰ কাৰকৰ ক্ষেত্ৰত সুমেৰু, কুমেৰু আৰু তৃতীয় মেৰু (অৰ্থাৎ তিব্বত) সমানেই অৱশ্যকীয়। তিনিওটা মেৰুৰো পৰিৱেশত সজাগ হ'বলৈ এই গ্ৰন্থই আহ্বান জনাইছে। মোৰ মতে পৃথিৱীৰ পৰিৱেশতন্ত্ৰ থূলমূলতে হৈছে সুমেৰু, কুমেৰু, তৃতীয় মেৰু, আমাজন হাবি আৰু পৃথিৱীয়ে ধৰি থকা বায়ুখিনি।

টোকা ঃ

ব্ৰহ্মপুত্ৰৰ অন্যান্য নাম

য়াৰলুং ছাংপো (তিব্বতত)

জাংৰ' (তিব্বতত)

ছিয়াং, আনে (অৰুণাচলত)

লুইত (এসময়ত লোহিতেই লুইত আছিল, এতিয়াৰ লোহিতৰ সৈতে খেলিমেলি নকৰিব)

দিহাং বা দিহিং (দিবাঙৰ লগত খেলিমেলি নকৰিব)

যমুনা (বাংলাদেশত)

উত্তৰ-পূৰ্বাঞ্চল ঃ বাংলাদেশৰ পুব আৰু উত্তৰ প্ৰান্তত অৱস্থিত ভাৰতৰ আঠখন ৰাজ্য, অসম, অৰুণাচল, মিজোৰাম, মেঘালয়, নাগালেণ্ড, ছিকিম, মণিপুৰ আৰু ত্ৰিপুৰাক একেলগে উত্তৰ-পূৰ্বাঞ্চল বোলা হৈছে।

তিবৃতীয় ভাষাত 'লা' মানে গিৰিপথ 'ছ' (Pso) মানে হ্ৰদ আৰু 'ছু' (Chu) মানে সৰু নদী।

০০০

।। প্ৰথম অধ্যায় ।।

ছিয়াঙৰ পানী ক'লা হ'ল

ভাৰতৰ অৰুণাচলৰ অৰণ্যসমূহ আৰু ওখ ঠাইসমূহৰ গাঁওসমূহৰ সীমান্তত শেষ বাসস্থান হ'ল বিশ্বিং, যাৰ অৱস্থিতি তলৰ মানচিত্ৰত ডাঙৰ ফুট এটাৰে নিৰ্দেশ কৰা হৈছে। এই ঠাই ভাৰত-চীন সীমান্তৰ কাযতে অৱস্থিত নহয়, ইয়াতে ব্ৰহ্মপুত্ৰ নদী, স্থানীয় নাম ছিয়াং, ভাৰতৰ অৰুণাচল প্ৰদেশত প্ৰৱেশ কৰিছে। ২০১৭১ৰ ৯ নৱেম্বৰত বিশ্বিঙৰ পৰা প্ৰায় দহ মাইল দূৰত্বত তেওঁলোকৰ বাসস্থানৰ ওচৰৰ পাহাৰৰ দুজন আদিবাসীয়ে বেতৰ খাং বনাবলৈ বেত বিচাৰি ছিয়াং নদীৰ ওচৰে-পাজৰে ঘূৰি ফুৰিছিল। এইসমূহ ঠাই সহজতে গাড়ী-মটৰ চলা পথেৰে ঢুকি পোৱা নহয়। একেখন নদী, যাক তিব্বতত য়াৰলুং ছাংপো বোলা হয়, যি ব্ৰহ্মপুত্ৰ নদীৰ মূল পানী উৎস আৰু ইয়াক ছিয়াং নদীও বোলা হয়, ই মহাভাঁজত থিয় গড়াই দি, তাৰ গতিপথ পূবৰ পৰা দক্ষিণলৈ পৰিৱৰ্তন কৰি এই ঠাই পায়হি। তেওঁলোকে লক্ষ্য কৰে যে ছিয়াঙৰ স্বচ্ছ পানী লেতেৰা আৰু ক'লা হৈছে। পাহাৰৰ ওপৰৰ নৈৰ পানী সদায় স্ফটিকৰ দৰে স্বচ্ছ হয়, তাৰোপৰি বালি আৰু শিলৰ মাজেৰে অহা বাবে প্ৰাকৃতিক পদ্ধতিৰে শোধন হৈ থাকে।

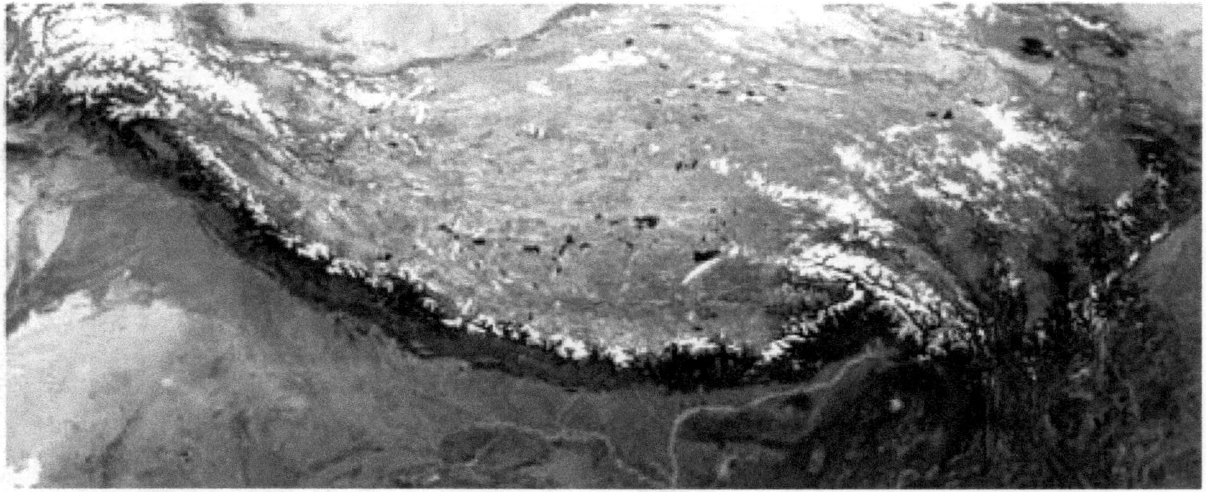

মানচিত্ৰ(২) ঃ অৰুণাচল, অসম আৰু নগালেণ্ডৰ কিছু অংশ। সীমান্তৱৰ্তী দেশসমূহ হ'ল ভূটান, চীন আৰু ম্যানমাৰ। পাহাৰত ছিয়াং নদী আৰু ভূপৃষ্ঠত ব্ৰহ্মপুত্ৰ নদী ইয়াত পৰিষ্কাৰকৈ দেখা গৈছে।

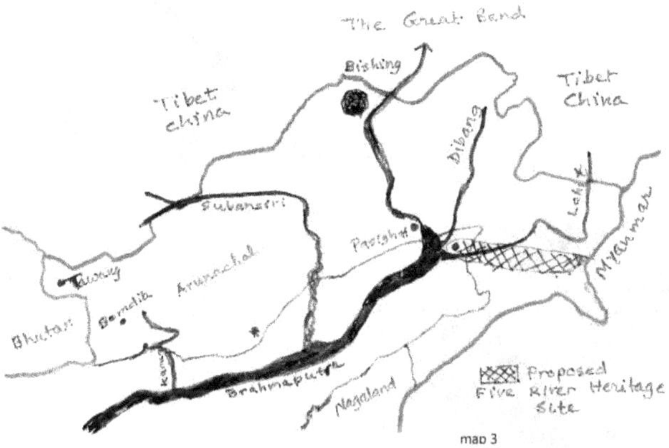

map 3

আদিবাসীসকলে স্থানীয়ভাৱে নদীখনক 'আনে' বুলি কয়। ইয়াৰ অৰ্থ হ'ল মাতৃ। ছিয়াং নেপৰীয়া সম্প্ৰদায়ৰ বাবে আনে হ'ল জীৱন ৰক্ত আৰু দৈনন্দিন জীৱন-ধাৰণৰ বাবে অতি আৱশ্যকীয়। তেওঁলোকৰ দৈনন্দিন জীৱন-নিৰ্বাহৰ বাবে প্ৰয়োজনীয় মূল আধাৰসমূহ আনেই যোগান ধৰে। পৰৱৰ্তী পৰ্যায়ত নদীখনক ভিত্তি কৰি চলা প্ৰত্যেকজন ব্যক্তিয়ে প্ৰত্যক্ষ কৰে যে, নিকটৱৰ্তী সকলো স্থানতে ছিয়াং নদীৰ পানী ক'লা হৈ পৰিছে। প্ৰবাদ মতে, ছিয়াঙৰ পানী চাৰি সপ্তাহলৈকে ক'লা হৈ আছিল। এইটো জনজাতিসকলৰ বাবে এক ভয়ংকৰ অভিজ্ঞতা হৈ পৰে, যি অনস্বীকাৰ্য। যেতিয়া আপোনাৰ দৈনন্দিন ব্যৱহাৰৰ বাবে যোগান ধৰা পানী প্ৰদূষিত হৈ পৰে আপুনি পানী বিচাৰি ক'লৈ দৌৰিব। সাধাৰণতে, এখন পাহাৰীয়া নদীৰ পানী তেনেকুৱা উচ্চতাত সদায় সতেজ, পৰিষ্কাৰ, স্বচ্ছ আৰু সেৱনৰ বাবে সদায় উপযোগী, যিহেতু ই প্ৰাকৃতিক শোধন প্ৰক্ৰিয়াৰে আহে। অৰুণাচল এখন প্ৰদেশ য'ত প্ৰতিখন জিলা নদীৰ নামেৰে দিয়া হৈছে আৰু সেই নদীখন সেই জিলাৰ মুখ্য নদী। মোৰ যাত্ৰা ইয়াতে আৰম্ভ হয়। উল্লেখ্য যে আদিসকল বাঁহৰ ওলোমা দলং নিৰ্মাণত অতিকৈ পাৰ্গত।

চিত্ৰ ঃ (৩) আদি বণুৱা ঃ ফটো সৌজন্য অমিত পাঠক

এই বাতৰিসমূহ ততালিকে বিস্তৃতভাৱে বিয়পি পৰে, প্ৰথমে অৰুণাচল প্ৰদেশত আৰু পাহাৰত, তাৰ পিছত পাচিঘাটত, শেষত বিশ্বত। অৰুণাচলীসকল হতবাক, ভীতিগ্ৰস্ত আৰু হতচকিত হৈ পৰিছিল। অৱশেত, ক'লা বস্তুটোৱে অশান্ত কৰি তোলে অসমৰ ব্ৰহ্মপুত্ৰ নদী, ভাৰত আৰু বিশ্বব্যাপী বাতৰি তৈয়াৰ কৰি। পানী ক'লা হোৱাৰ কোনো বিশ্বাসযোগ্য উত্তৰ নাছিল আৰু মই প্ৰতিটো বাতৰি বিচাৰি উলিয়াইছিলোঁ, বিভিন্ন প্ৰান্তৰ পৰা— অৰুণাচল, অসম ভাৰতৰ পৰা চীনলৈ, চৰকাৰী বাতৰি এজেন্সীসমূহৰ পৰা।

পাহাৰৰ শীৰ্ষত ছিয়াং ক'লা হোৱা আৰু লাহে লাহে উপত্যকাটোত তলৰ ফালে ক'লা হোৱা, য'ত ইয়াক ব্ৰহ্মপুত্ৰ বুলি কোৱা হয়, এক আশ্চৰ্যকৰ ঘটনা। চলমান সোঁতত প্ৰচুৰ মাত্ৰাত অজ্ঞাত পদাৰ্থ মিহলাই নিদিলে ইমান ক'লা হ'ব নোৱাৰে। অতি সৰু ঢালেৰে অসম উপত্যকাটোৰ মাজেৰে বৈ অহা ব্ৰহ্মপুত্ৰ হ'ল এখন লেহেমীয়া গতিৰ নদী। কাৰক সম্বন্ধত চাৰি সপ্তাহ যথেষ্ট সময়। অৱশেষত এই পানী পৰিষ্কাৰ হোৱাটোৱে এই দিশটো প্ৰমাণ কৰে যে, য়াৰলুং ছাংপোৰ মূল পানীৰ দ্বাৰা হোৱা অস্থায়ী স্থানীয় প্ৰভাৱ আছিল। এইটো পৰ্যবেক্ষণ কৰা হৈছিল যে কিছুমান প্ৰকাৰৰ ছুপাৰফাইন ক'লা সামগ্ৰী পানীত বোৱাই দিয়া হৈছিল, কিন্তু অৱশেষত খমলা বান্ধিছিল আৰু ডুবিছিল আৰু তেতিয়াও পানীৰ সৈতে প্ৰৱাহিত হৈ আছিল। কি কৰা হৈ আছে তাত ওপৰত, উচ্চ তিব্বতৰ পানীৰ উৎসৰ কাষত? তেনেকুৱা বহু ধৰণৰ প্ৰশ্নই আহিছিল মনলৈ।

নদীসমূহ বিভিন্ন দেশবোৰৰ মাজেৰে বোৱাৰ কাৰণে আৰু নদীৰ দুয়োপাৰৰ উপত্যকাত বাস কৰা লোকসকলক প্ৰভাৱিত কৰাৰ বাবে এইটো গুৰুত্বপূৰ্ণ যে, ওচৰ-চুবুৰীয়া দেশসমূহে নৈপৰীয়া লোকসকলৰ অধিকাৰক কেনেদৰে সন্মান কৰে। 'নীলা নীল' আৰু 'বগা নীল' নীল নদী গঠনৰ বাবে ইথিওপিয়াত মিলিত হৈছে যিয়ে ছুডান আৰু ইজিপ্তৰ মাজেৰে বৈ ইয়াৰ চূড়ান্ত লক্ষ্য লৈ ভূমধ্যসাগৰলৈ আহিছে। একেদৰে ডেনুব আৰু ৰাইন, যি খুব বেছি দূৰত্বত আৰম্ভ হোৱা নাই, বিভন্ন গতিপথেৰে বহু কেইখন দেশৰ মাজেৰে বৈ আহিছে। আমেৰিকাত কিছু নদী মহা বিভাজনৰ পৰা আহিছে বা কানাডাৰ পৰা আহিছে। বিশ্বৰ মানুহে কিছু ক্ষেত্ৰত মূৰপোলোকা মাৰি থাকিব ভাল নাপায় বিশেষকৈ যেতিয়া এইটো পানীৰ উৎস লৈ উদ্বিগ্ন হ'বলগীয়া বিষয় হয়। ই আনৰ কাৰণে এক বেয়া দৃষ্টান্তৰ সৃষ্টি

কৰে।

ব্ৰহ্মপুত্ৰৰ উজনি-উৎসৰ মালিক কোন? আপুনি নিজে বিচাৰক হওক। চীন আৰু ভাৰতে তেওঁলোকৰ নিজৰ বিচাৰধাৰা এক ৰাজহুৱা ফ'ৰামত উত্থাপন কৰিবলৈ সাজু হ'বনে? ছিয়াং পুনৰ স্বাস্থ্যকৰ হ'বনে? নেপৰীয়া লোকসকলে এইটো বিশ্বাস কৰিবলৈ সক্ষম হ'বনে যে নদীৰ বিশুদ্ধতা পূৰ্বৰ দৰে ব্যৱহাৰযোগ্য হ'ব? ক'লা পানীৰ পাছত, আন অন্য আমোদজনক ঘটনা সংঘটিত হৈছিল, যেনে ডাঙৰ ঢৌ, পৰ্যায়ক্ৰমে শুকাই যোৱা। এইক্ষেত্ৰত ছিয়াং নদীৰ মানুহে সুধিছে, নামনিৰ লোকসকলে আশ্চৰ্য প্ৰকাশ কৰিছে, আৰু মই আমি ধাৰাবাহিকভাৱে ঘটনাটোৰ পম খেদিছোঁ। অসহায় আনে (অৰ্থ মা)ই কান্দিছে।

ক'লা পানীৰ ঘটনা সংঘটিত হোৱাৰ মাত্ৰ এমাহ পূৰ্বে য়াৰলুং ছাংপো সম্পৰ্কে অন্য এক কষ্টদায়ক সংবাদ ওলাইছিল, ২০১৭ৰ ৩০ অক্টোবৰত। চীনে য়াৰলুং ছাংপো (ব্ৰহ্মপুত্ৰ)ৰ পানীৰ গতিপথ সলনি কৰাৰ বাবে এক দীৰ্ঘ সুৰংগ নিৰ্মাণ কৰিছে। এই দুটা কষ্টদায়ক ঘটনাৰ বাতৰিৰ মাজত কিবা এক সম্বন্ধ আছেনে? নিশ্চয়, দুয়োটাৰ মাজত সম্পৰ্ক আছে। 'তিব্বতৰ উচ্চত কি ঘটিছে'ৰ বিষয়ে ক'বলৈ আমি দুয়োটা ঘটনাই সংযোগ ঘটাব লাগিব। তদুপৰি, সুৰংগ খন্দাটো হ'ল মূৰৰ বিকৃতি। তেতিয়াই মই এটা ব্লগ লিখিবলৈ আৰম্ভ কৰো। ভংগুৰ সন্ধি অঞ্চলত এটা সুৰংগই তলৰ সমগ্ৰ উপত্যকাটোলৈ ধ্বংস মাতি আনিব। মোৰ ব্লগ, 'দ্য ব্ৰহ্মপুত্ৰ, য়াৰলুং ছাংপো, জাংবো, ছিয়াং, দিহিং, লোহিত' ইয়াত মোৰ প্ৰথম প্ৰৱেশ। তাৰ কিছু উদ্ধৃতি তলত দিছোঁ।

মোৰ ব্লগ 'দ্য ব্ৰহ্মপুত্ৰ, য়াৰলুং ছাংপো, জাংবো, ছিয়াং, দিহিং, লোহিত'।

সুৰংগ এটাৰ বিষয়ে এয়া কি শুনিছোঁ?

উত্তৰ-পূব ভাৰত আৰু ভাৰতৰ স্থানীয় সংবাদ-পত্ৰসমূহত ২০১৭ৰ ৩১ অক্টোবৰত প্ৰস্তাৱিত দীঘল সুৰংগ, ১,০০০ কিলোমিটাৰ দীঘল জিনজিয়াঙৰ য়াৰলুং ছাংপোৰ পৰা টাকলা মাকান (মানচিত্ৰ চাওক) মৰুভূমিলৈ নিৰ্মাণৰ বাতৰি প্ৰকাশ পোৱাই চৰম বিৰক্তিৰ সৃষ্টি কৰিছে। য়াৰলুং ছাংপো (ব্ৰহ্মপুত্ৰৰ) পানীৰ গতিপথ সলনি কৰাটো অস্বস্তিকৰ আৰু সহজভাৱে গ্ৰহণ কৰিব পৰা নহয়।

নৈপৰীয়া লোকসকলে ব্ৰহ্মপুত্ৰক দান দিয়া হিচাপে ধৰিব নোৱাৰে। চীন চৰকাৰে প্ৰতিবেদনখন অস্বীকাৰ কৰিছে কিন্তু তাত এটা ঐতিহাসিক প্ৰমাণ আছে যে চীনে কৰিব পৰা এইটো এটা পথ। সূত্ৰ মতে, চীনৰ পানীৰ গতিপথ সলনি কৰাটো এক ধাৰাবাহিক কাৰ্য, প্ৰচেষ্টা আৰু ভুল পদ্ধতি আৰু প্ৰকৃত ঘটনা কেতিয়াও চৰকাৰীভাৱে প্ৰকাশ নাপায়। চীনৰ সংবাদ প্ৰতিষ্ঠানসমূহৰ বাতৰি মতে, চীনে য়ুনান প্ৰদেশতো এক 'প্ৰট'টাইপ' সুৰংগ নিৰ্মাণ কৰিছে। এইটো ক'ত সংযোগ কৰা হ'ব মাত্ৰ সময়েহে ক'ব। এইটো দক্ষিণ সাগৰীয় প্ৰকল্পৰ দৰে নেকি য'ত চীনে সম্পূৰ্ণ নোহোৱা পৰ্যন্ত সুবিশাল নিৰ্মাণকাৰ্য অস্বীকাৰ কৰিছিল? মই বৰ্তমান ব্ৰহ্মপুত্ৰৰ প্ৰসংগ বিগত বাৰ বছৰ ধৰি অনুসৰণ কৰি আহিছোঁ, যেতিয়াৰে পৰা 'ব্ৰহ্ম টুইন' প্ৰকল্প আৰম্ভ হৈছিল। অন্তত চীনৰ পূৰ্বৰ প্ৰচেষ্টা, প্ৰায় ১০-১২ বছৰ পূৰ্বে মহাভাঁজৰ পৰা পানীৰ গতিপথ সলনি কৰা যিটো বাতৰি ওলাইছিল, তাৰ কাম কৰা হোৱা নাই। The International Rivers নামৰ এটি আন্তৰ্জাতিক নদী সংস্থাইও এইক্ষেত্ৰত স্পষ্টীকৰণ দিছে আৰু কৈছে যে চীনৰ পূবলৈ গতিপথ সলনি কৰাৰ পূৰ্বৰ প্ৰচেষ্টা ভুল হিচাপে প্ৰমাণিত হ'ল। তথাপিও, একে সময়তে, চীনে দক্ষিণ-পূব তিব্বতৰ ভাঁজৰ ওপৰত ছিয়াঙত (ভাঁজত বা ভাঁজৰ কাষত) পাঁচটা নদী বান্ধো নিৰ্মাণ কৰিছে। ভাঁজটো হ'ল য'ত নদীখন ১.৫ মাইল এঢলীয়া হৈ বৈছে। তিব্বত মালভূমি প্ৰায় ৩-৩.৫ মাইল উচ্চ। এটি যাযাবৰ জানজাতিয়ে তাত বসবাসৰ বাবে ব্যৱহাৰ কৰিছিল য'ত তেওঁলোকে কম অক্সিজেন পৰিৱেশৰ সৈতে অভিযোজিত হ'বলগা হৈছিল। অক্সিজেন হ্ৰাস পায় প্ৰতি ১০,০০০ ফুটত। এই উচ্চতাত অভ্যাস নোহোৱা লোকসকলৰ বাবে ইয়াত গুৰুতৰ অক্সিজেনৰ সমস্যা হয়। সেই সময়ত গুজৱ আছিল যে চীনে ইয়াত কেলিফৰ্ণিয়া বা লছ ভেগাছ নিৰ্মাণ কৰিব নোৱাৰে। অন্য এটা উদ্দেশ্য আছিল য়ুনান সুৰংগৰে পানী গ্ৰহণ কৰা। তেনেধৰণৰ বহুতো বিভ্ৰান্তিমূলক কাহিনী হ'ব যিবোৰ তেওঁলোকে অংশ হিচাপে নিৰ্মাণ কৰিব। এই সুৰংগ কাহিনীবোৰ আহি থাকিব। সেইটোৰ কাৰণতেই মই এই ব্ল'গ আৰম্ভ কৰিছোঁ।

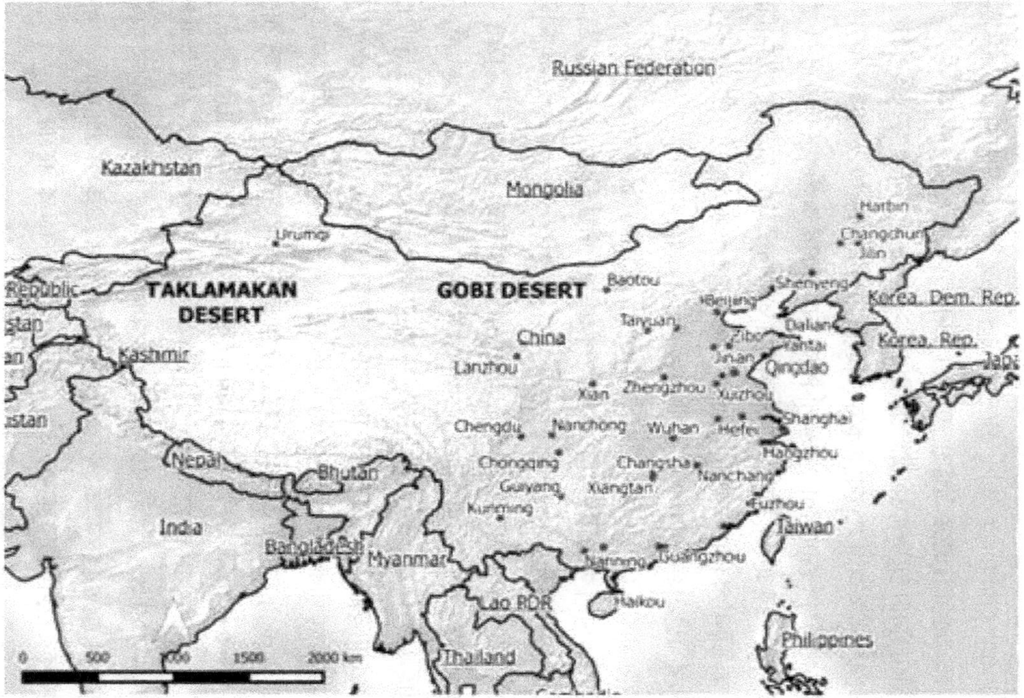

মানচিত্র (৪) ঃ টাকলা মাকান মরুভূমি

তাৰ পিছত তৃতীয় সংবাদ বিষয় আছিল যিটোৰ নদীৰ পানী কিয় ক'লা হৈছে তাক বৰ্ণনা কৰিবলৈ কৰা প্ৰয়াস। এইটো এটা আছিল এটা স্থানীয় ভূমিকম্পৰ বিষয়ে আৰু সেইটো বিশ্বাসযোগ্য নাছিল। বাতৰিটোত প্ৰতিবেদন প্ৰকাশ পাইছিল যে ১৭ নৱেম্বৰ, ২০১৭ত সংঘটিত সৰু ভূমিকম্পটোৰ ফলত হোৱা ভূমিস্খলনৰ বাবে য়াৰ্লুং ছাংপোৰ পথ বন্ধ হৈছিল। 'আছাম ট্ৰিবিউন'ত National Centre of Biological Sceinces-ৰ চিতৰ শেঠ আৰু Askhok Trust of Reasearch in Ecology and the Environment-ৰ অনিৰ্বাণ দত্ত ৰায়ৰ LANDSATৰ বিশ্লেষণ প্ৰকাশ পাইছিল। আনহাতে, বাতৰিটো আছিল যে অতি সোনকালে বিস্ফোৰক হ'বলগা বান্ধ এটা তাত আছে বা পিছত এইটো সত্য প্ৰমাণিত হৈছিল, অৱশ্যে ইয়াত নদীত থকা ক'লা পদাৰ্থসমূহৰ বিষয়ে ব্যাখ্যা নাছিল। কিন্তু এই হ্ৰদটো সোনকালে বা পিছত বিস্ফোৰণ হ'ব সেইটো অৰুণাচলবাসীৰ বাবে এতিয়াও এটা সতৰ্কবাণী বাতৰি হ'ব পাৰে। লোকসকলে দুৰ্যোগ নিয়ন্ত্ৰণ আৰু সকলো প্ৰকাৰৰ সুৰক্ষাৰ বিষয়ে সুধিবলৈ আৰম্ভ কৰে।

চিত্ৰ ঃ (৪) ব্ৰহ্মপুত্ৰৰ মহাভাঁজৰ নিকট চিত্ৰ

ভূমিকম্পৰ বাতৰিটোৰ সৈতে এইটোৱে সমস্যা। কেৱল চীনেহে যে ভূমিকম্পৰ খবৰ পালে ওচৰৰ আন আন অঞ্চল যেনে অৰুণাচল আদিয়ে কিয় নাপালে? এইটো কি মানৱসৃষ্ট ভূমিকম্প আছিল? মোৰ দৃষ্টিত, হয় অতি কমেও ৯০ শতাংশ সম্ভাব্য। এটা সম্ভাৱনীয় কাৰক হ'ব পাৰে চিমেণ্ট ফেক্টৰী য'ত ব্ৰহ্মপুত্ৰ নদীৰ তীৰৱৰ্তী নদীৰ পাথৰসমূহ বৃহৎ মাত্ৰাত ভঙাৰ ফলত। এই মেচিনসমূহ তাত নাই। উল্লেখ্য যে য়াৰলুং ছাংপো দুখন টেক্টʼনিক প্লেটৰ সৈতে ঢিলা কপলিঙেৰে মূৰৰ ফালে জোৰা লাগি আছে। তাত ফাঁট আছে য'ত গভীৰ পৃথিৱীৰ পৰা খনিজসমূহৰ দ্বাৰা আগুৰি আছে। এইটো হ'ল এটা অত্যন্ত ভংগুৰ ভূ-ব্যৱস্থা। উপৰোক্ত নিবন্ধ দুটাত আগবঢ়োৱা প্ৰাথমিক ব্যাখ্যাৰ পৰা এইটো ক'ব পৰি যে স্থানীয়ভাৱে মানৱসৃষ্ট 'ভূমিকম্প' ধৰণৰ বিস্ফোৰণ সহজেই ঘটিব পাৰে। এইটো অতি আশ্চৰ্যকৰ যে নামচা বাৰৱা আৰু গিয়ালা পেৰি নামৰ দুটা যমজ শৃংগৰ পৰা মাত্ৰ কিছু পূবত অৱস্থিত কাংগ্ৰি গাৰ্পোত থকা লোহিত নদীত কিন্তু তেনেধৰণৰ এটা ঘটনা সংঘটিত হোৱা নাছিল। উপগ্ৰহীয় পৰিদৰ্শনৰ পৰা কাৰকসমূহ লুকুৱাবৰ বাবে সুৰংগসমূহ হ'ল উত্তম পন্থা। কোনো ধৰণৰ অস্বীকাৰ নাই বা সুৰংগৰ ওপৰত হোৱা বাতৰিটো সম্পূৰ্ণ বিশ্বাসযোগ্য। মনত ৰাখিব যে এইটো সত্য যে চীনে কুনমিঙত এক 'ডেম'নষ্ট্ৰেটিভ' সুৰংগ নিৰ্মাণ কৰিছে। যিকোনো লোকে আশ্চৰ্য প্ৰকাশ কৰিব যে এই সুৰংগটোৱে কিহৰ সংযোগ কৰিবলৈ গৈ আছে? কোনে ইয়াৰ ভূগৰ্ভৰ পথ পৰীক্ষা কৰিব?

(বাকীখিনি ব্লগ পৰিশিষ্টত পাব)

০০০

।।দ্বিতীয় অধ্যায়।।

অসম আৰু অৰুণাচলৰ হিমবাহ নদীসমূহ আৰু ব্ৰহ্মপুত্ৰৰ উজনিৰ নদী অংশ

পূৰ্বে আৰম্ভণি কৰাৰ দৰে, য়াৰলুং ছাংপো যাক অৰুণাচলত ছিয়াং নামে জনা যায়, হৈছে ব্ৰহ্মপুত্ৰৰ উজনিৰ নদী অংশ। সোৱণশিৰি, লোহিত আৰু ছিয়াং হৈছে তিনিখন হিমবাহ নদী যিকেইখন অসমৰ মাজেৰে বৈ গৈছে আৰু ব্ৰহ্মপুত্ৰত মিলিত হৈছে। এই অঞ্চলটোত গ্ৰীষ্মৰ চাৰিটা মাহত বাৰিষাৰ প্ৰবল বৃষ্টিপাত হয়। আনহাতে, শীতৰ সময়ত কেইবা মাহো ধৰি ইয়াত বৰষুণ নহয়। হিমবাহ নদীসমূহেই হৈছে আমাৰ শক্তিশালী ব্ৰহ্মপুত্ৰই সমগ্ৰ শীত ঋতু ধৰি পানী ধাৰণ কৰি ৰখাৰ কাৰণ।

চিত্ৰ (৫) ঃ বিদ্যালয়লৈ যোৱাৰ প্ৰত্যাহ্বান

সাধাৰণতে ভাৰতীয়সকলৰ মাজত এক আচৰিত ধৰণৰ ভুল ধাৰণা আছে আৰু দুৰ্ভাগ্যজনকভাৱে অসমীয়াসকলৰো মাজত বিশেষকৈ অসমৰ সীমান্তৰ ভিতৰত 'পৰ্যাপ্ত পানী'ৰ ওপৰত। হয়, এইটো সত্য যে সমগ্ৰ উত্তৰ-পূৰ্বাঞ্চল মৌচুমী অঞ্চলত অৱস্থিত, ইয়াত মে', জুন, জুলাই আৰু আগষ্ট মাহত প্ৰচুৰ বৰষুণ হয়। মৌচুমী বায়ু সংঘটিত হয় কাৰণ ভাৰতৰ নিম্নাংশৰ সমুদ্ৰৰ পৰা বলা বতাহ হিমালয়ত খুন্দা খায়, ওপৰলৈ উঠে আৰু বৃষ্টিপাত হয়। তিব্বত তিনি মাইল উচ্চতাত অৱস্থিত, গ্ৰীষ্মত বৰ গৰম আৰু ইয়েই কাৰণ তলৰ উপত্যকাত বৰষুণ হোৱাৰ। ই নিয়মিত গোলকীয় বায়ুৰ গতিপথ সলনি কৰে। সেয়েহে কেৱল এখন ওখ দেৱালে নহয় কিন্তু এটা তাপৰ উৎসও। সেয়েহে, হিমালয় আৰু তিব্বত ভাৰতৰ অংশ বিশেষ আৰু দক্ষিণ-পূব এছিয়াৰ বৰ্ষা ঋতুৰ কাৰণ। ইয়াৰ উপৰি এইটো সঁচা যে বিশ্বৰ সৰ্বাধিক বৰষুণ হোৱা ঠাই মেঘালয়ৰ চেৰাপুঞ্জীত বছৰি গড় বৰষুণৰ পৰিমাণ ৪৬৩.৭ ইঞ্চি হয়। পিছত মৌছিনৰাম

নামৰ এখন দাঁতিকাষৰীয়া ঠাইৰ দ্বাৰা চেৰ পেলাইছে যাৰ বাৰ্ষিক গড় বৰষুণৰ পৰিমাণ ৪৬৭.৪ ইঞ্চিঙ্গ যদিও ইয়াত হোৱা অবিৰাম বৰষুণৰ বাবে গ্ৰীষ্মৰ সময়ত বিভিন্ন স্থানত বানপানীৰ সৃষ্টি কৰে, সেইটো নিশ্চিতি দিব নোৱাৰি যে চিৰদিন ধৰি অসমে অপৰ্যান্ত পানী লাভ কৰিবঙ্গ ইয়াৰ এটা কাৰণ হ'ল, ব্ৰহ্মপুত্ৰ আৰু ইয়াৰ উপনৈসমূহ প্ৰতি বছৰে উপচি পৰে কাৰণ সেইবোৰ তৰাং হৈ গৈ আছে, অতিৰিক্ত পানীৰ বাবে নহয়। প্ৰতিটো গ্ৰীষ্মৰ সময়ত বৰ্ষা ঋতুত ওপৰৰ পাহাৰৰ পৰা অত্যধিক পৰিমাণে পলস আৰু শিল-বালি নামি অহাটো নৈসমূহ উপচি পৰাৰ মুখ্য কাৰক। বৰ্তমান, শীতকালত ব্ৰহ্মপুত্ৰৰ মাজভাগত যথেষ্ট পৰিমাণৰ খোলা বালিচৰৰ বাবে ফেৰীৰে যাত্ৰা কৰাটো কঠিন কৰি তোলে। কিছুমান ঠাইত নদীখন এক মাইল পৰ্যন্ত বহল, কিন্তু বেছিভাগতেই তৰাং যিটো ফেৰী চালকসকলৰ বাবে জনাটো প্ৰয়োজন নদীৰ গভীৰতাৰ ভিন্নতা সম্পৰ্কে আৰু কাৰণবশতঃ তৰাং ঠাইৰ কাযেৰে জাহাজ চলাবৰ বাবে নতুন পথ বিচাৰি লয় আৰু জাহাজ ৰখাবৰ বাবেও নতুন ঠাই বিচাৰি লয়। ছিয়াং (দিহাং আৰু দিহিং নামেও জনাজাত) হ'ল ব্ৰহ্মপুত্ৰৰ মুখ্য পানীৰ উৎস। ই পাচিঘাটত ব্ৰহ্মপুত্ৰক ২৯ শতাংশ যোগান ধৰে। কিয় এইটো গুৰুত্বপূৰ্ণ? ইয়াৰ কাৰণ হ'ল ছিয়াং যিখন উত্তৰৰ পৰা প্ৰবাহিত হৈছে আচলতে মহা ছাংপো বা য়াৰলুং জাংবো যি মানস সৰোবৰৰ হিমবাহৰ কাষৰ পৰা গতি কৰিছে যিটো ভাঁজৰ পৰা ১,০০০ মাইল পশ্চিমত। অৰুণাচল প্ৰদেশ ছিয়াং (এনি) আৰু কিছুমান সৰু সৰু হিমবাহ নদীৰ দ্বাৰাও সুস্থঙ্গ লোহিত, পৰৱৰ্তী সময়ত পূবে হিমবাহত আৰম্ভ হৈছে আৰু সেয়েহে গোটেই ঋতু ধৰি পানী থকাৰ কাৰণসমূহৰ ভিতৰত এটা।

দিবাঙৰ বৰঙনি হ'ল প্ৰায় ৫ শতাংশ, আনহাতে লোহিতৰ বৰঙনি ৯ শতাংশ। বাকী ব্ৰহ্মপুত্ৰৰ উত্তৰ আৰু দক্ষিণৰ উপনদীসমূহৰ অৱদান হৈছে মাত্ৰ ৩৫ শতাংশলৈকে। সোৱণশিৰিয়ে অৱদান আগবঢ়াইছে প্ৰায় ১৯ শতাংশৰ পৰা ২০ শতাংশ। সোৱণশিৰি, লোহিত আৰু ছিয়াং নদীকেইখনৰ আটাইকেইখনৰে উৎসত হিমবাহ আছে। সোৱণশিৰিয়ে বেছিভাগ উত্তৰ-দক্ষিণেৰে বৈ আহিছে, আনহাতে লোহিত ব্ৰহ্মপুত্ৰ উপত্যকাত প্ৰৱেশ কৰিছে পূব দিশৰ পৰা। পেমাকোত নামচাক বুৰৱা পৰ্বতৰ ওচৰত ব্ৰিটিছ কাৰ্টোগ্ৰাফাৰসকলে মহাভাঁজ (গ্ৰেট বেণ্ড) দেখাৰ পূৰ্বে তেওঁলোকে জনা নাছিল ক'ৰ পৰা তেনে এক শক্তিশালী নদী নামি আহিছে।

মহাভাঁজত, ছাংপোৱে এক নাটকীয় ভাঁজ লৈছে দক্ষিণলৈ। ভাৰতে জানিবলৈ আৰম্ভ কৰে ছিয়াং/দিহাং হিচাপে। আৰম্ভণিতে ব্ৰিটিছ এজেণ্টে এটা জলপ্ৰপাতৰ সন্ধান কৰিছিল এই নদীখনক ব্যাখ্যা কৰিবৰ বাবে। সংযোগ প্ৰমাণ কৰিবৰ বাবে এইটো কঠিন আছিল য়াৰলুং ছাংপোৰ পূব দিশ আৰু ছিয়াঙৰ দক্ষিণ দিশৰ বাবে। কিন্তু অঞ্চলটোৰ সেই অংশত কোনো ডাঙৰ জলপ্ৰপাত পোৱা নাছিল যিহেতু পৰ্বতসমূহ টিলা মাটিৰে তৈয়াৰী কাৰণে এটা ডাঙৰ জলপ্ৰপাত অসম্ভৱ। তেওঁলোকে ৰামধেনু জলপ্ৰপাত আৱিষ্কাৰ কৰিছিল কিন্তু এইটো তেতিয়াও ব্ৰহ্মপুত্ৰলৈ সংযোগ হোৱা নাছিল। এইটো মহাভাঁজত গতিপথত যে নদীখনে কেৱল গতিপথেই সলনি কৰা নাই কিন্তু মহা উচ্চতাও হেৰুৱাই চীনৰ বাবে বান্ধৰ জৰিয়তে পৰিচালিত জলবিদ্যুৎ প্ৰকল্পৰ বাবে বহু স্তৰীয় বান্ধ নিৰ্মাণৰ বাবেও বহু মূল্যৱান ঠাই হিচাপে নিৰ্মাণ কৰিছে।

চিত্ৰ ঃ (৬) মহাভাঁজ ঃ এই থলেই ঠাই য'ত যাৰলুং ছাংপো নদীখনে ১৮০ ডিগ্ৰী এক নাটকীয় ভাঁজ লৈছে আৰু নদীৰ পুবৰ পথ দক্ষিণলৈ পৰিবৰ্তন কৰিছে। পূৰ্বতে, এইটো ধাৰণা কৰা হৈছিল যে তাত কেইবাটাও ডাঙৰ জলপ্ৰপাত আছে ক্ৰমাগত উচ্চতা হ্ৰাস আৰু দিশ পৰিৱৰ্তন ব্যাখ্যা কৰিবলৈ, কিন্তু কোনো ডাঙৰ জলপ্ৰপাত আৱিষ্কাৰ হোৱা নাছিল। ভাঁজটোৰ পিছত নদীখনক ছিয়াং নদী হিচাপে জনা যায়।

যদিও তিনিওখন নদী, ছিয়াং (দিহিং), দিবাং আৰু লোহিত অসমত মিলিত হৈছে (ওপৰৰ মানচিত্ৰ চাওক) বিশাল পুৰুষ নদী ব্ৰহ্মপুত্ৰ গঠন কৰিবলৈ পুৰণি শদিয়াৰ ওচৰত, এইখন ছিয়াং যিয়ে তাৰ পথ নিৰ্ধাৰণ কৰিছে। ছাংপো-ছিয়াং হ'ল ব্ৰহ্মপুত্ৰৰ মুখ্য পানী। যদি ছিয়াঙৰ পৰা পানীৰ গতিপথ সলনি কৰা হয়, ব্ৰহ্মপুত্ৰ helter-skelterলৈ গতি কৰিব। ইয়াৰ উপৰি ই অৰুণাচল প্ৰদেশত বিপৰ্যয়ৰো সৃষ্টি কৰিব। এইটো ভবাটো এটা চূড়ান্ত ভ্ৰান্ত ধাৰণা হ'ব যে ব্ৰহ্মপুত্ৰই মাত্ৰ ২০ শতাংশ পানীহে গ্ৰহণ কৰে আৰু অসম আৰু অৰুণাচলে উত্তৰৰ পৰা পানী নোহোৱাকৈয়ে জীয়াই থাকিব পাৰে। আমি কি জানো, সেইটো এটা অযৌক্তিক প্ৰত্যাশা হিচাপে আমি উৎসৰ বিষয়ে কৈ আছোঁঙ্গ মূৰ হ'ব পাৰে মানৱ দেহৰ কেৱল ২০ শতাংশঙ্গ তাৰ মানে এইটো নহয় যে আমি আমাৰ মূৰটো কাটি বাচি থাকিব পাৰিম। কোনোৱে এখন নদী আৰু এজন মানুহৰ মূৰৰ মাজত তুলনা কৰিব বিচৰাটো অযুক্তিকৰ, কিন্তু নদী এখন হ'ল জীৱন্ত মানুহৰ বাবে জীৱন্ত শৰীৰ নদীৰ দ্বাৰা। মনত ৰাখিব যে মই অসমৰ তুলনাত নদীসমূহৰ অৱদান উল্লেখ কৰিছোঁ, চীনৰ সীমান্তত নহয়। অনুগ্ৰহ কৰি উপত্যকাটোৰ তলত বাস কৰাসকলৰ বাবে ছিয়াং কিমান গুৰুত্বপূৰ্ণ তাক প্ৰত্যক্ষ কৰিবলৈ সংখ্যাসমূহ আভ্যন্তৰীণ কৰক আৰু পৰ্বতসমূহ আৰু অৰুণাচল প্ৰদেশৰ উপত্যকাসমূহৰ বাসিন্দাৰ বাবে।

ছিয়াং নদীখন য'ত অৰুণাচলত সোমাইছে সেইখিনিত আদি (আগতে আবৰ বুলিছিল) সম্প্ৰদায়ৰ লোকে বাস কৰে। পাচিঘাটৰ পৰা বিচমাৰ্কলৈ ঠাইখিনি আবৰ কাণ্ট্ৰি বুলি জনা যায়। এই সীমান্তৰ লাডাখৰ লগত এটা সামঞ্জস্য আছে। এই দুই ঠাইতে সীমান্তৰ দুয়োপাৰে যুগ যুগ ধৰি মানুহে বসতি কৰিছে। অৰুণাচলৰ সীমান্তত মেমব্ৰা বোলা বৌদ্ধ সম্প্ৰদায়ৰ মানুহে বসতি কৰি আহিছেঙ্গ অৰুণাচলৰ এই সীমাত মেকমোহন লাইনে তেওঁলোকক দুভাগ কৰিলে। দুয়োপিনে পাঁচখনকৈ গাঁও পৰিছে। ১৯৬২ চনৰ চীনৰ ভাৰত আক্ৰমণৰ পিচত তেওঁলোক বিচ্ছিন্ন হৈ পৰিছে, লগ পাব নোৱাৰে। পশ্চিম ছিয়াঙৰ য়াৰ্গমছু উপত্যকাৰ মেচুকাত মেমব্ৰা সম্প্ৰদায়ৰ চাৰি-পাঁচ হাজাৰমান লোক আছে, বাকীখিনি মেডগ কাউণ্ট্ৰিতঙ্গ আদিসকল অৰুণাচলৰ এটা প্ৰধান সম্প্ৰদায়। এওঁলোকৰ মতে ২০১৭ত নদীৰ পানী ক'লা হোৱাৰ পিচত বহুবাৰ নদীখন মাজে মাজে শুকাই গৈছে। ফলত মাছ

তেতিয়া মৰি গৈছে আৰু বাৰিষাৰ সময়ত চীনে নজনা নোকোৱাকৈ ওপৰৰ পৰা পানী নদীত এৰিছে।

চিত্ৰ ঃ (৭) চিয়াং নদীৰ ওপৰত ৮খন গাঁৱৰ প্ৰায় ৯ হাজাৰ গাঁওবাসীৰ নিকটৱৰ্তী চহৰ পাচিঘাটলৈ যাতায়াতৰ বাবে একমাত্ৰ বিপদসংকুল ওলোমা ফুট ব্ৰীজ।

ফটো সৌজন্য ঃ সনত দত্ত

উত্তৰ-পূবৰ আন এখন প্ৰধান নদী তিস্তাঙ্গ ৰংগীত আৰু তিস্তা পশ্চিমবঙ্গ প্ৰদেশৰ উপত্যকাত মিলিত হৈছে। কাঞ্চনজংঘাৰ তলৰ অংশৰ মাউন্ট কাব্ৰুৰ হিমবাহৰ পৰা ৰংগীত ওলাইছে, তিস্তা ছিকিমৰ পৰা আহিছেঙ্গ তিস্তা দাৰ্জিলিং মহকুমা আৰু ছিকিমৰ প্ৰান্তইদি বৈছে।

অসমৰ আটাইতকৈ ডাঙৰ মহানগৰ গুৱাহাটীৰ আকাশমাৰ্গত এতিয়াও হাই-ৰাইজ মানে স্কাই-স্কেপাৰ হোৱা নাই। স্কাই-স্কেপাৰে পানীৰ ছাপ্লাইৰ সক্ষমতা আৰু ধাৰণ ক্ষমতাৰ ভাল পৰীক্ষা কৰে। এটা স্কাই-স্কেপাৰত এটা পিন কোডৰ মানুহ ধৰিব পাৰে। ওপৰৰ তলালৈকে পানীৰ প্ৰেছাৰ বজাই ৰখাৰ বাবে উপযুক্ত পাইপ আদিৰ উৎপাদান হোৱা নাই বুলি শুনিছোঁ। মুঠতে পানীৰ আচল ব্যৱহাৰ এতিয়াও হোৱা নাই। কাপোৰধোৱা মেচিন আদিতো বহুত পানী লাগে।

○○○

।।তৃতীয় অধ্যায়।।

হিমালয়ৰ গঠন আৰু তিব্বতৰ ঊৰ্ধ্বগতি

পূৰ্ব্বোত্তৰ পাহাৰসমূহৰ ভঙ্গুৰ গঠনক বুজিবৰ বাবে তিব্বতৰ দক্ষিণ অংশৰ লগত উত্তৰ-পূব ভাৰতৰ ভূবিজ্ঞান, ভূতত্ত্ব, ভুগোল আৰু প্ৰাকৃতিক তত্ত্ব জনাটো অতি গুৰুত্বপূৰ্ণ। মই এই পাহাৰসমূহৰ কিছু পাহাৰক ছফ্‌ট বা শিথিল পাহাৰ নামাকৰণ কৰিছোঁ যাৰ অৰ্থ আৰু উদাহৰণ এই পুথিত যথেষ্ট পাব। চিলাই, সিয়নি আৰু চ্যুতিসমূহে এই অঞ্চল ভূমিকম্পপ্ৰবণ কৰিছে। ইয়াৰ টেকটনিক প্লেটসমূহ, পৰিবেশতন্ত্ৰ, ভূগোল আৰু জৈৱ-বৈচিত্ৰ্য ভালকৈ নাজানিলে এই অঞ্চল সুৰক্ষিত আৰু সংৰক্ষিত সহজ নহ'ব। উত্তৰ-পূবত বহুত প্ৰাকৃতিক বিচিত্ৰতা আছে, উচ্চ অঞ্চল, নিম্ন অঞ্চল, সুন্দৰ প্ৰাকৃতিক পৰিদৃশ্য, খনিজ সম্পদ আৰু বহু নদীয়ে এই অঞ্চল পৰিপূৰ্ণ কৰিছে।

বহুতো অঞ্চল বিশেষকৈ য়াৰলুং ছাংপো অঞ্চলৰ ওপৰত পাৰিবেশিক আৰু পৰিস্থিতি তত্ত্ব বিষয়ক গৱেষণা আৰু অধ্যয়ন হোৱাৰ প্ৰয়োজন আছে। মোৰ লক্ষ্য এই গুৰুতৰ বিষয়টোলৈ আপোনালোকৰ ধ্যান অনা আৰু উত্তৰ-পূব তথা ভাৰতীয় মূলৰ ইচ্ছুক নতুন প্ৰজন্মক এই সম্পৰ্কে সচেতন কৰা। এই যে পৰ্ব্বতমালা ভূতাত্বিক স্কেলত তেনেই চালুকীয়া, ইয়াৰ পৰা কি আশা কৰিব পাৰি তাক অধ্যয়ন আৰু হৃদয়ংগম কৰা।

সাধাৰণতে স্কুলবোৰত মহাদেশীয় গতিৰ বিষয়ে শিকায়, বহু যুগৰ আগতে যে পাঞ্জীয়া নামৰ এখন মহাদেশেই আছিল, সেইটো কোৱা হয়। পাঞ্জীয়া কেনেকৈ ভাগিল ইয়াত থুলমূলকৈ কোৱা হৈছে।

হিমালয়ৰ সৃষ্টি, সুউচ্চ তিব্বতীয় মালভূমিৰ উত্থান আৰু অতীত তথা বৰ্তমানত ইয়াৰ গতিশীল প্ৰভাৱৰ বিষয়ে নজনাকৈ এই অঞ্চলত কোনো থাকিব নোৱাৰে। ভাৰতবৰ্ষ দক্ষিণৰ পৰা (যেতিয়া অষ্ট্ৰেলিয়াৰ ওচৰত আছিল) অহা কাৰ্য পৰ্যায়ক্ৰমে

হৈছিল আৰু এইটো আশ্চৰ্যজনক নহয় যে ভাৰতীয় কিংবদন্তিসমূহ সৃষ্টি, ধ্বংস, পালন আৰু জীৱনৰ অস্তিত্ব সম্পৰ্কে যথেষ্ট চিন্তিত। হিমালয়ৰ পৰ্বতমালা পৃথিৱীৰ বাকীবোৰ পৰ্বতমালাতকৈ নৱতম আৰু ই এতিয়া বিভিন্ন সালসলনিৰ পৰিক্ৰমা কিছু পাৰ কৰি গৈছে— এটা বিশেষ তথ্য এই যে, প্ৰত্যেক বছৰে এভাৰেষ্ট শৃংগৰ উচ্চতা এক ইঞ্চিকৈ বৃদ্ধি পাইছে আৰু নামচা বৰৱা আধা ইঞ্চিকৈ ডুবি গৈ আছে। নাভাগাস্কাৰৰ পৰা আঁতৰি অহাৰ পিছত আৰু সংঘৰ্ষৰ আগত ভাৰতবৰ্ষই মহাদ্বীপসমূহৰ ভিতৰত, বা মহাদেশীয় টেকটনিক প্লেট হিচাবে সকলোতকৈ দীঘলীয় যাত্ৰা কৰিছে। মাভাগাস্কাৰৰ পৰা আঁতৰি অহাৰ পিছতেই ভাৰতীয় ফলকৰ গতি যথেষ্ট বাঢ়িছিল। ইউৰেছিয়া ফলকৰ লগত খুন্দা আৰু প্ৰচণ্ডভাৱে সংযুক্ত হৈ হিমালয় পৰ্যায়ক্ৰমে গঠিত হোৱা আৰু ওপৰপিনে ভাঁজ লোৱা পৰ্বতমালা। মই থকা আমেৰিকাৰ পশ্চিমীয়া ৰাজ্য ৱাশ্বিংটন প্ৰদেশৰ কাস্কাড পৰ্বতমালাও জুৱান দ্য ফুকা ফলক আৰু উত্তৰ আমেৰিকান ফলকৰ ক্ৰমাগত সংঘৰ্ষৰ দ্বাৰা গঠিত হৈছিল। এই পৰ্বতৰ পৰিক্ৰমাটো উত্তৰ-কেলিফৰ্ণিয়াৰ পৰা অ'ৰিগন আৰু ৱাশ্বিংটনৰ মাজেৰে পাৰ হৈ কানাডালৈকে এটা দীঘল বাট অতিক্ৰম কৰি আহিছে। কাস্কাড পৰ্বতমালাৰ ক্ষেত্ৰত ই সক্ৰিয় আৰু সুপ্ত উভয় আগ্নেয়গিৰিৰে গঠিত। কাস্কাডও হিমালয়ৰ দৰে ভাঁজ লোৱা পৰ্বতমালা কিন্তু অন্যতম পাৰ্থক্য এই যে হিমালয়ত জ্বালামুখী বা সক্ৰিয় ভলকেনো নাই। আচৰিতভাৱে আমেৰিকাৰ পশ্চিমতম ৰাজ্য ৱাশ্বিংটন, প্ৰশান্ত মহাসাগৰৰ পাৰত, এখন বিস্ময়কৰ জলবায়ুৰ প্ৰদেশ। কাস্কাড পৰ্বতমালাই পশ্চিম আৰু পূব অংশ দুভাগ ওলোটা জলবায়ুৰ অংশত ভাগ কৰিছে। পশ্চিমত এখন মৃদু শীতকালীন অঞ্চল আৰু পূবত শীতত শীত আৰু গ্ৰীষ্মত উত্তপ্ত আৰু শুকান অৱস্থাই মোক ভূতত্ত্ব অধ্যয়ন কৰিবলৈ আগ্ৰহী কৰি তুলিলে। মই বহু বছৰ ধৰি ৱাশ্বিংটনত বাস কৰি আছোঁ।

ত্ৰয়াসিক আৰু ভুৰাচিক যুগত পাঞ্জীয়া নামৰ এখন মহাদেশেই আছিল (বিভিন্ন আখৰ জোঁটনি বিদ্যমান)। দীৰ্ঘ মহাদেশীয় প্ৰৱাহৰ সময়ত আফ্ৰিকা আৰু দক্ষিণ আমেৰিকা পৃথক হৈ যায়। ইয়াত আচৰিত হ'বলগীয়া একো নাই যে আফ্ৰিকাৰ পশ্চিম উপকূল ৰেখা দক্ষিণ আমেৰিকাৰ উপকূল ৰেখাৰ লগত খাপ খাই পৰে। মনত ৰাখিবলগীয়া কথা, পাঞ্জীয়া ভাঙিবলৈ আৰম্ভ কৰাৰ আগতে ভাৰতীয়

ফলক এণ্টাৰ্কটিকাৰ সৈতে আৰু পিছত অষ্ট্ৰেলিয়াৰ সৈতে সংযুক্ত আছিল। অনুগ্ৰহ কৰি তলৰ চিত্ৰখনলৈ লক্ষ্য কৰক। ইয়াৰ পিছত ভাৰতীয় ফলক পৃথক হৈ যায় আৰু ভাৰতীয় মহাদেশীয় ফলক উত্তৰলৈ গতি কৰে। প্ৰায় স্থিৰ ইউৰেছিয়া ফলক আৰু ভাৰতীয় ফলক বহু যুগৰ পৰিক্ৰমাত সংঘৰ্ষ হয়। গঠিত হিমালয় আৰু উত্তৰ-পূব অঞ্চলৰ সৈতে সংঘৰ্ষত টেথিছ সাগৰৰ চৰত যি ইউৰেছিয় ফলক আছিল সেয়া তিনি মাইল উচ্চতালৈ ফুটি উঠিছে আৰু টেথিছ সাগৰ ছিটিকি অদৃশ্য হৈ হ্ৰদ হিচাপে লুকাইছে। এই সংঘৰ্ষ প্ৰক্ৰিয়াৰ মাজতে হিমালয়ে তিব্বতক পৃথিৱীৰ সৰ্বোচ্চ আৰু বৃহত্তম মালভূমি হিচাপে গঢ়ি তুলিবলৈ আৰম্ভ কৰিছিল। ইয়াত এই সংঘৰ্ষ প্ৰক্ৰিয়া থুলমূলকৈ দিয়া হৈছে, বিশদভাবে জানিবলৈ বা বিতৰ্ক কৰিবলৈ ভূতত্ত্ববিদ হওকঙ্গ

সিন্ধু আৰু য়াৰলুং ছাংপো দুইখন নদীয়েই ইউৰেছিয়া আৰু ভাৰতীয় ফলকৰ মাজেৰে পাৰ হৈ গৈছে। সংঘৰ্ষ সীমাৰ (ITSZ, Indus Tsangpo Suture Zone, সিন্ধু, ছাংপো চিলাই ক্ষেত্ৰ) দক্ষিণ অঞ্চলৰ হিমালয় পৰ্বতমালা উচ্চতাৰ বৃদ্ধি আৰু কিছু শিথিলিক শৃংগৰ বৰ্তমান ৰূপ বহুবোৰ যুগৰ ফলাফলঙ্গ চিলাই অঞ্চলসমূহ, পৰ্বতসমূহ, সিয়নিসমূহ আৰু চ্যুতিসমূহ গোটেই উত্তৰ-পূব অঞ্চলৰ বাবে অসাধাৰণ বিষয়, আৰু কৈলাস এখন অসাধাৰণ পৰ্বতঙ্গ লক্ষ্য কৰা হৈছে যে, পৃথিৱীৰ মহাসাগৰীয় ভূত্বক আৰু অন্তৰ্নিহিত উপৰিভাগৰ আৱৰণৰ উপৰিভাগৰ শিলসমূহক হিমালয়ৰ কিছু অংশত পোৱা যায় (ভূত্বক শলিসমূহ পৃথিৱীত ২.৫ মিলিয়ন বছৰৰ আগতে কঠিন আৱৰণৰ ফলত গঠন হোৱা শিল) উত্তৰ-পূবৰ বহুতো অঞ্চলত প্ৰচুৰ পৰিমাণ সৰ্পিল খনিজ আছে— সেউজ শিলসমূহৰ নানা সাগৰ তলিত পোৱা সৰ্প বা সাগৰ সেউজীয়া ৰঙৰ লগত মিলাই ৰখা হৈছিল- পোৱা যায়। (নগাসকলে কিয় সাগৰৰ কাষৰ মানুহ আছিল বুলি ভাবে? নিশ্চয় মোৰ কল্পনা নহয়ঙ্গ) হিমালয়ৰ নিৰ্মাণৰ সময়ত প্ৰদান কৰা এটা তথ্য এই যে কাৰাকোৰাম উথাপনৰ পিছত হিমালয়ৰ উত্থান তিনিটা স্তৰত হৈছিল ক্ৰিটেচাছু কালত। প্ৰথম আৰু সকলোতকৈ পুৰণি উচ্চ হিমালয়ৰ আন্তঃগাঁঠনি হৈছিল অলিগচিন কালত। দ্বিতীয় স্তৰত হিমালয়ৰ মধ্যভাগ গঠন হৈছিল, মায়'চিন কালত। তৃতীয় আৰু সকলোতকৈ শেষৰটো স্তৰত হিমালয়ৰ বহিঃগাঁঠনি বা শিবালিক হৈছিল পূৰ্ব পাইল'চিয়ান কালত। মোৰ চিন্তাদৃষ্টিত হিমালয়ৰ বৈচিত্ৰ্য

নজনাকৈ ইয়াত বিশাল প্ৰয়োগ (construction) কৰিব নাপায়, তলৰ মাটিৰ গঠন জনাটো সাধাৰণ প্ৰচেষ্টা।

উল্লেখযোগ্য বিষয়টো হ'ল, ইউৰেছিয়া আৰু ভাৰতীয় ফলক দুয়োটাই প্ৰায় একেই ঘনত্বৰ আছিল। এখন ফলক আনখনৰ ওপৰত উঠি গৈছিল আৰু হিমালয়ৰ শৃংগসমূহৰ সৃষ্টি হৈছিল, এইটো ভূ-বৈজ্ঞানিকৰ ভাষাত 'ভাঁজ' বা 'Fold' হিচাপে ব্যাখ্যা কৰা হয়। তেনেদৰেই চ্যুতিসমূহ এই ভাঁজৰ ফলত সৃষ্টি হয়। হিমালয়ৰ উপবিভাগত গ্ৰেণাইট চ্যুতি ৰেখাসমূহ স্পষ্টভাৱে পৰিলক্ষিত হয়। যিয়ে এই চ্যুতিসমূহ প্ৰকাশ কৰে। লাডাখ অঞ্চলৰ সিন্ধু চ্যুতি অঞ্চলত ইয়াৰ চাপ অতি গভীৰ। কিন্তু উত্তৰ-পূবত ইয়াৰ চাপ দুৰ্বল আছিল। ফলস্বৰূপে ফলকসমূহ পশ্চিমত ভালদৰে যুক্ত হৈ আছে, য'ত উত্তৰ-পূবৰ য়াৰলুং-চাংপো অঞ্চল শিথিল যুক্ততা পৰিলক্ষিত হয়। তাৰ ফলত, ছিকিম আৰু অৰুণাচল অঞ্চলৰ পাদদেশসমূহত টেথিছ সাগৰৰ কেঁচা মলি বা বালি পোৰা গৈছিল। এই পাহাৰৰ কিছু অংশ কেৱল 'কোমল' বা 'শিথিল' মাটিৰ, যি দীৰ্ঘ সময়জুৰি কোনো চাপৰ মাজত নহি আৰু খুব সহজেই ভাঙি যায় আৰু ক্ষয় হয়।

মানচিত্ৰ ঃ (৫) ইউৰেছিয়া ফলকৰ সৈতে সংঘৰ্ষৰ বাবে ভাৰতীয় মহাকাশীয় ফলকৰ উত্তৰীয় প্ৰৱাহ।

অৰুণাচল প্ৰদেশত কোনো পিৰামিডীয় বা গোলাকাৰ আধাৰ নোহোৱাকৈ বেৰৰ দৰে পাহাৰসমূহ আছে আৰু ইয়াৰ ভিতৰত অধিকাংশ শিথিল মাটিৰ দ্বাৰা গঠিত হৈছে। পথ নিৰ্মাণৰ বাবেও পাহাৰ কটা হয়। পাহাৰৰ কোনো নগ্ন এটা অংশই ভূমিস্খলন কৰি পাহাৰৰ স্থিৰতাৰ বিপদ আনিব পাৰে। সেই কাৰণেই অৰুণাচল প্ৰদেশৰ বহুত অঞ্চলৰ পাহাৰসমূহত ডাঙৰ জলপ্ৰপাত নাই, কাৰণ জলপ্ৰপাতসমূহক দীৰ্ঘজীৱী হ'বলৈ স্থিৰ কঠিন শিলৰ প্ৰয়োজন। ইয়াৰ পৰিৱৰ্তে আমি কেৱল উচ্চ আৰু সুন্দৰ নিজৰাসমূহ দেখিবলৈ পাওঁ যি হাজাৰ ফুট ওপৰৰ পৰা তলৰ উপত্যকাত পৰিছেহি। সেইবিলাকে ইয়াকে সত্য বুলি উপস্থাপন কৰে যে কোনো কোনো ঠাইত ডাঙৰ শিলৰ গঠন হোৱা নাই (ভূতত্ত্ববিদসকল, যিমান ব্যাখ্যা কৰিবলৈ আছে কৰক, মই সাধাৰণ জ্ঞান হিচাবেহে আলোচনা কৰিছোঁ)। এই শিথিল মাটিসমূহত কোনো চাপ বা তাপমানৰ প্ৰভাৱ বহু সময়জুৰি নাই আৰু সেয়েহে ক'ব পাৰি ইয়াত কোনো ডাঙৰ কঠিন শিলাখণ্ড বা সুগঠিত মাটি গঠন হোৱাৰ সময় হোৱা নাই। কিছুমান ঠাইত কিছু আগ্নেয় শিলৰ চিহ্ন পালেও অধিক বৃষ্টিপাত আৰু নিৰ্মাণৰ পিছত উত্তৰ-পূবৰ কিছু পাদদেশ অস্থিৰ হৈ পৰিব পাৰে। নদীবান্ধ নিৰ্মাণ কিছুমান ঠাইত শুদ্ধ হ'ব নোৱাৰে আৰু পাহাৰৰ দাঁতিকাষৰীয়া অঞ্চলসমূহৰ ভূমিস্খলন হোৱাৰ উচ্চ সম্ভাৱনা আছে। এই বৈশিষ্ট্যসমূহে অঞ্চলটোক বৃহৎ নদীবান্ধৰ বাবে অনুপযুক্ত কৰি তুলিছে। কেনেবাকৈ এনে বান্ধ নিৰ্মাণ কৰিলেও এটা পাহাৰে ৰিখটাৰ স্কেলৰ ৫.০ ভূমিকম্পক সহ্য কৰিব নোৱাৰিব যদি ভূমিকম্পৰ কেন্দ্ৰস্থল পাহাৰ বা পাহাৰৰ আশেপাশে আৰু পৃষ্ঠৰ আশেপাশে অৱস্থিত হয়। অসমৰ এটা অংশ ঘন ভূমিকম্প আশংকিত অঞ্চল।

চিত্ৰ সিপিঠিত

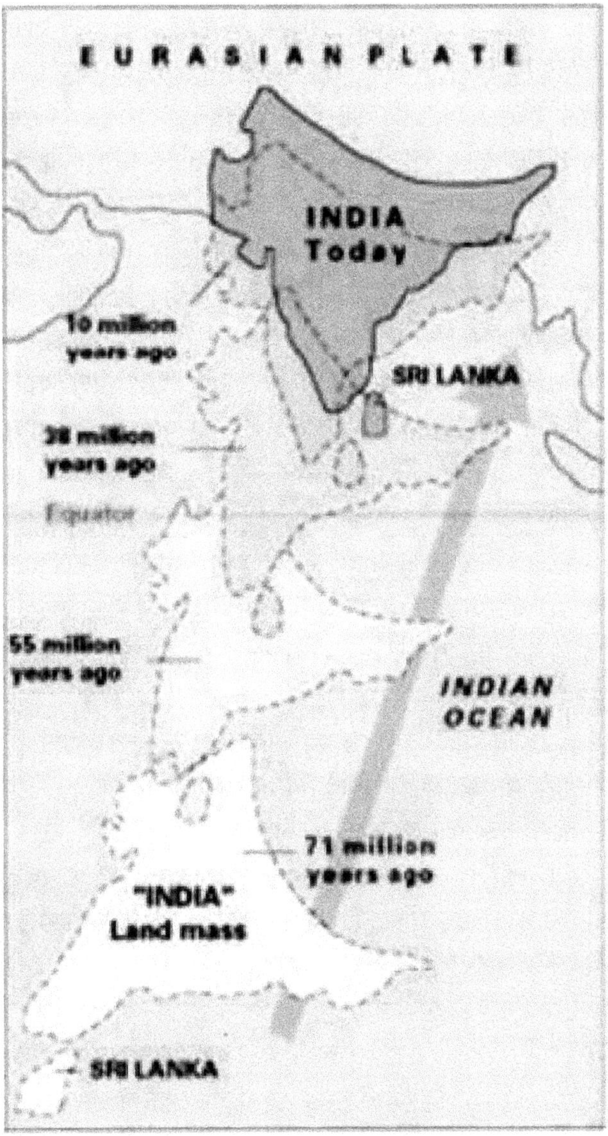

মানচিত্ৰ ঃ (৬) ভাৰতীয় মহাকাশীয় ফলকৰ উত্তৰীয় গতিৰ সৰল চিত্ৰ

নামচা বাৰৱা আৰু অৰুণাচল প্ৰদেশৰ পাহাৰসমূহৰ শিথিল সংযোজনে বেছলটিক লৱণ, আৰ্ছেনিক আৰু সীহক উন্মোক্ত কৰে, যাৰ দ্বাৰা সেইবিলাক পদাৰ্থ বৰযুণৰ পানী, নিজৰা আৰু নদীৰ পানীত সংমিশ্ৰণ হ'ব পাৰে। যদি কোনোৱে ইণ্টাৰনেটৰ পৰা লোৱা তলৰ চিত্ৰখন লক্ষ্য কৰে এই ক্ষেত্ৰত সাধাৰণ ধাৰণা এটা পাব পাৰিব যে ভাৰতীয় ফলক কেনেকৈ আগবাঢ়িছিল আৰু এতিয়া আমি য'ত দেখিছোঁ তাত কেনেকৈ সংযোজিত হ'ল। তথাপিও আপোনালোকক অৱশ্যেই সতৰ্ক কৰিব লাগিব যে এইখন কেৱল শিল্পীৰ চিত্ৰকলা আৰু ভাৰতীয় ফলকৰ প্ৰকৃত আকাৰ ইয়াত নিৰ্ভুল বা বিশদ নহয়। লাহে লাহে পৰিৱৰ্তনসমূহ হৈছিল। প্ৰকৃততে ভাৰতীয় ফলকসমূহৰ লগত কি ভাঁহি আহিছিল, ইয়াৰ ভাঁহি অহাৰ লগত কি সংযোগ হ'ব আৰু কি সংযোজন নহ'ল ইয়াৰ বৈজ্ঞানিক অধ্যয়ন কৰা হোৱা নাই। পূৰ্বোত্তৰ বৰ্তমানৰ স্থিতিত নাছিল তেতিয়া। সময় সাপেক্ষিক কিংবদন্তিসমূহে আৰু পৌৰাণিক কাহিনীসমূহে উত্তৰ-পূবৰ অন্য এক আমাৰ আকাৰ আৰু গঠন হিচাপৰ বৰ্ণনা কৰিছিল। একমাত্ৰ এটা বস্তুৱেই নিশ্চিত আছিল আৰু সেইটো হ'ল ডেক্কান অঞ্চলটো একেলগে আছিল, ইয়াৰ খণ্ড খণ্ড হোৱাৰ পথ নাছিল। এইটো এটা আশ্চৰ্যজনক কথা নহয় যে লাছা এলেকাত, তিব্বতৰ দক্ষিণত, এক বিশেষ শিল বা শিলৰ সমষ্টি পোৱা হয়, যি নিশ্চিতভাৱে অষ্ট্ৰেলিয়াৰ পৰা আহিছে।

এই বিষয়টো আকৰ্ষণীয় যে মহাভাৰতত উত্তৰ-পূবৰ গঠন বেলেগ ৰূপত আছিল বুলি অনুমান কৰিব পাৰি, কিন্তু মানচিত্ৰ বা প্ৰমাণ নোহোৱাকৈ দিয়া এইটো সন্দেহযুক্ত বক্তব্য, কিন্তু বিভিন্ন গুহা, ফলক আদি ডিজিটেলী পোৱা গ'লে কোনোবাই পূৰ্বৰ কথাসমূহৰ বিষয়ত অধ্যয়ন কৰিব পাৰিব বুলি এই কথা উল্লেখ কৰা হ'ল। এই অঞ্চলৰ ক্ৰমাগত পৰিৱৰ্তনসমূহ কিংবদন্তি আৰু লোক-কাহিনীৰ দৃষ্টিকোণৰ পৰাও অধ্যয়ন কৰিব পাৰি। কোনোবাই ক'ব পাৰিব নেকি মহাকাব্য, মহাভাৰত আৰু ৰামায়ণৰ সময়ত উত্তৰ-পূবৰ আকাৰ কি আছিল? একেদৰে, যদিও হেৰাই যোৱা সৰস্বতী নদী বৰ্তমান ৰাজস্থানৰ শুকান এলেকাত পোৱা গৈছে, কিন্তু কোনেও সময় ৰেখা বা স্পষ্টীকৰণ দিব নোৱাৰিব যে শতিকাজুৰি কি হৈছিল আৰু পাহাৰৰ ওপৰত কি ঘটিছিল তাৰ ব্যাখ্যা আৰু অসম্ভৱঙ্গ তদুপৰি, সিন্ধু আৰু য়াৰলুং ছাংপো দুখন বেলেগ নহয় বুলি প্ৰশ্ন কৰা

হৈছে, দুয়োখন মানস সৰোবৰৰ ওচৰৰ। দুখন বিপৰীতমুখী নদী একেখন ঠাইৰ পৰা কেতিয়াও নাহে (হয়, এঢলীয়া ঠাইৰ ফালৰ পৰা চাবলৈ গ'লে সেইটো শুদ্ধ হয়)। সি যি কি নহওক, হিমালয়ৰ মাজেৰে বৈ অহাৰ পিছত পাহাৰৰ পৰা নামি পাঁচখন নদীৰে মিলি সিন্ধুৰে নদী বেছিনৰ সৃষ্টি কৰিছে। সেইদৰে য়াৰলুং ছাংপোৱে বিৰাট নদী অৱবাহিকাৰ সৃষ্টি কৰিছে।

য়াৰলুং ছাংপো চিলাই-সিয়নি অঞ্চলে আকৰ্ষণীয় গঠন দেখুৱাইছে। ছিয়াং নদীৰ সন্ধিস্থলৰ পিছৰ পৰা য়াৰলুং ছাংপো চিলাই-সিয়নি অঞ্চল ম্যানমাৰৰ ছংগাইং চ্যুতিৰ মুখামুখি নহয়। ১৮৮৫ চনৰ এংগল-বাৰ্মিজ যুদ্ধৰ পিছত, বাৰ্মাৰ উপৰি অংশক ভাৰতীয় ৰাজত্বৰ অন্তৰ্গত কৰা হৈছিল। সম্পূৰ্ণ ম্যানমাৰ ব্ৰিটিছ নিয়ন্ত্ৰণৰ অধীনত আছিল। চিলাই-সিয়নি অঞ্চলৰ ধাৰাবাহিকতাৰ ওপৰত ব্ৰিটিছৰ ৰাজত্বৰ অধীনত এক সামগ্ৰিক ভূতাত্ত্বিক গৱেষণা হৈছিল। ম্যানমাৰৰ চাগাইং চ্যুতি ৬ কিঃমিঃ দৈৰ্ঘ্যৰ চাপৰ শৈলশিৰা। এই সক্ৰিয় চ্যুতিয়ে আয়াৰবেদী (ইৰাৱতী) নদীক পোনে পোনেই বৈ যাবলৈ বাধ্য কৰিছিল। এইটো পশ্চিম আমেৰিকাৰ চান আদ্ৰিয়াচ চ্যুতিৰ অনুৰূপ অনুভূমিক চ্যুতি। অনুভূমিক চ্যুতি (strike-slip fault)সমূহ সাধাৰণতে সমান্তৰাল, যেন ভূত্বকৰ মাজেৰে চুৰিকাঘাত কৰি দুভাগ কৰা হৈছে। ছিয়াঙৰ পূব অংশত lesser Himalay ব্লক আৰু ব'মডিলা শ্ৰেণীৰ crystalline আছে। শিলৰ চেলা শ্ৰেণী MCT (Main Central Thrust) ওপৰত আছে। হিমালয়ৰ ওপৰৰ অংশ অঙ্কিতন'লাইটৰ মিশ্ৰৰ টিউটিং-টিডিং তৰাই অঞ্চল আৰু LPC (Lohit Plutonic Complex) বুলি দুই ভাগত বিভক্ত। নাগা দিচাং চাপ MBT (মূল সীমাবদ্ধতা)ৰ সমান। এই চাপ আৰু চ্যুতি পৰৱৰ্তী অধ্যয়নত আকৌ এবাৰ আলোচনা কৰা হ'ব।

উত্তৰ-পূবৰ জলবায়ুৰ ওপৰত ইয়াৰ প্ৰভাৱ অন্য জলবায়ুৰ তথ্য তুলনা কৰিবলৈ নাথাকিলে জানিব পৰা নাযাব। এই তথ্য খণ্ডসমূহৰ পৰা তৈয়াৰ কৰিব লাগিব আৰু পৰৱৰ্তী সময়ত ইয়াৰ অধ্যয়ন কৰিব লাগিব। মই নতুন প্ৰজন্মক আঠ ভাই-ভনী ৰাজ্যকেইখনৰ ভিন্ন দৈহিক আৰু ভৌগোলিক প্ৰকৃতি সম্পৰ্কে আৰু দাঁতিকাষৰীয়া অঞ্চলৰ বিষয়ে শিকিবলৈ অনুৰোধ কৰিলোঁঙ্গ ভূবিজ্ঞানী আৰু পৰিৱেশিকসকলে তাত অধ্যয়ন আৰু গৱেষণাৰ লগত জড়িত হোৱা উচিত। এই অঞ্চলত এনে বহুতো পাৰিৱেশক আৰু পাৰিস্থিতিক সমস্যা আছে যাক সমাধান

কৰাটো প্ৰয়োজনীয়। নতুন আৱিষ্কাৰ হ'ব পাৰে আৰু নতুন ধাৰণাও উদ্ভৱ হ'ব পাৰে। বৰ্তমান বাংলাদেশে কিছু ভূতাত্ত্বিক গৱেষণা কৰি আছে। পশ্চিমবংগৰ সুন্দৰবনত গেদ জমা হোৱা আৰু সাগৰৰ পৃষ্ঠ উঠি অহা দেখা গৈছে। সুন্দৰবনৰ পশ্চিমবংগৰ অংশ গোলকীয় উষ্ণতাৰ বাবদ বেছি ডুব গৈছে বুলি জনা গৈছে।

০০০

।। চতুৰ্থ অধ্যায় ।।

হিমালয়ৰ প্ৰাকৃতিক নদী হাইৰে’

অৰুণাচলত য়াৰলুং ছাংপোক ছিয়াং বা দিহিং নামেৰে জনা যায়। চীনৰ তিব্বতত য়াৰলুং ছাংপোক জাংবো বুলিও কোৱা হয়। ব্ৰহ্মপুত্ৰ বুলিলে সাধাৰণতে অসমত শদিয়াৰ ওচৰত তিনিওখন নদীৰ মিলনৰ পিচৰখিনি বুজা যায়। ছাংপোৱে প্ৰথমতে লোহিতেদি বৈছিল। সেয়ে পৰশুকুণ্ডৰ কাহিনী কালজয়ী কৰা হৈছে। ব্ৰহ্মপুত্ৰ যে বিভিন্ন পথেৰে বৈছিল তাৰ পুৰা প্ৰমাণ আছে, আৰু এতিয়া আমি বৰ্তমান যিটো পথ জানো সেইফালেৰে কেতিয়া আহিল তাৰ আচল সময়টোহে জনা নাযায়। এখন সংবাদ-পত্ৰত আঠ মিলিয়ন বছৰৰ আগতে বুলিছে। চুতীয়া ৰজাৰ ৰাজধানী পাচিঘাট বুলি জনা যায়। শংকৰদেৱ আৰু মাধৱদেৱৰ জীৱনী ‘গুৰু-চৰিত’ত প্ৰমাণিত হৈছে দিহিং এতিয়াৰ পথেৰে প্ৰৱাহিত হোৱা নাছিল। কিন্তু সেইবোৰ সৰু-সুৰা সলনি, আৰু বুৰঞ্জীৰ সময়ৰ ভিতৰত। ভূতাত্ত্বিক তথ্যৰে প্ৰমাণ হোৱা ঘাই সলনিবোৰ প্ৰমাণসহ (কাকতৰ নামসহ) ইয়াত বিতংকৈ কোৱা হ’ব।

হিমালয় যে পৃথিৱীৰ আটাইতকৈ চালুকীয়া পাহাৰ আৰু আমি এই পৰ্বতমালাৰ লগত সহবাস কৰিবলৈ জানিব লাগিব সেইটো মোৰ লক্ষ্য। পৃথিবীৰ ফলকবোৰো বছৰত এক ইঞ্চিমানকৈ প্ৰৱাহিত হৈছে। চেন অড্ৰিয়ান চ্যুতিৰ বাবদ হয়তো ত্ৰিশ হাজাৰ বছৰৰ পিচত হলিউড হিল আৰু ছান ফ্ৰান্সিস্কো ওচৰা-ওচৰি হ'ব। চ্যুতি অধ্যয়ন কৰা হয় ভূমিকম্পৰ সঘনতাৰ বাবেও। হিমালয়ৰ চ্যুতি আৰু ফলকবোৰৰ অধ্যয়ন অবিহনে আমি ব্ৰহ্মপুত্ৰৰ প্ৰাকৃতিক সলনি আৰু পৰিকল্পনা, পদাৰ্থ বিজ্ঞানৰ আঁচনিৰ ভূমিকাই নাজানিম।

য়াৰলুং ছাংপো বা ব্ৰহ্মপুত্ৰ নদীক জীৱ বিকাশৰ বাবে উত্তৰ-পশ্চিম-দক্ষিণ হাইৱে' বুলি ভাবিব পাৰি। আদিম কুকুৰনেচীয়া বাঘ আৰু মাছৰ প্ৰব্ৰজন আৰু ক্ৰমবিকাশ, বিশেষকৈ ইউৰোপ, চাইবেৰিয়াৰ পৰা ম্যানমাৰলৈ, এই পথেদি হৈছে। তিব্বত, অৰুণাচল, অসম, ম্যানমাৰৰ এই হাইৱে' হিমালয়ৰ সমান পুৰণি যদিও বাটটোৰ সলনি সময়ত হৈছে। য়াৰলুং ছাংপোৰ ডাউনহিল গতিয়ে এই হাইৱে'ৰ প্ৰাধান্য বঢ়াইছে। এই নদী হাইৱে'ৰ তথ্য এই দুখন কাকতৰ পৰা লোৱা হৈছেঃ

Yu-Hsual Liang et.al., "Detrital zircon Evidence from Brahmaputra for Reorganization of the East Himalayan Rivers", American Journal of Science, April 2008.

Ruth A.J.Robinson et.al., "Large rivers and orogens : The evolution of the Yarlung Tsangpo–Irrawaddy system and the eastern Himalayan syntaxis".

প্ৰথম কাকতখনত য়াৰলুং ছাংপোৱে তিনিবাৰ দিশ সলোৱা বুলি দিছে, তলত তাৰ চিত্ৰ দিয়া হ'ল। প্ৰথমে ছাংপোৱে ৰেড ৰিভাৰৰ লগত সংযোগ কৰিছিল, তাৰ পিচত আয়াৰবৰ্দী (ইৰাৱতী) আৰু তৃতীয়তে ব্ৰহ্মপূত্ৰৰ লগত। সময়, পূৰ্ব মায়চিন। পাচত মই পঢ়িবলৈ পাইছোঁ যে এসময়ত ছলউইন, মেকং আৰু য়াচিংও একেখন নদীয়েই আছিল। পঢুৱৈক সেই তত্ত্বৰ সন্ধান নিজকে ল'বলৈ দিয়া হ'ল। তিনিওখনৰে উৎস তিব্বতত অলপ দূৰে দুৰে দেখুওৱা হয়, কিন্তু কথা হ'ল এই নদীসমূহ শদিয়াৰ পৰা পশ্চিমত, অলপ পাহাৰ উঠি গ'লেই অতি ওচৰে ওচৰে সমান্তৰালকৈ বৈছে। ইটো দৰকাৰী কথা হ'ল ছাংপোৱেহে অৰুণাচলৰ পশ্চিম সীমাত যথেষ্ট পৰিবৰ্তনৰ মাজেৰে গৈছে।

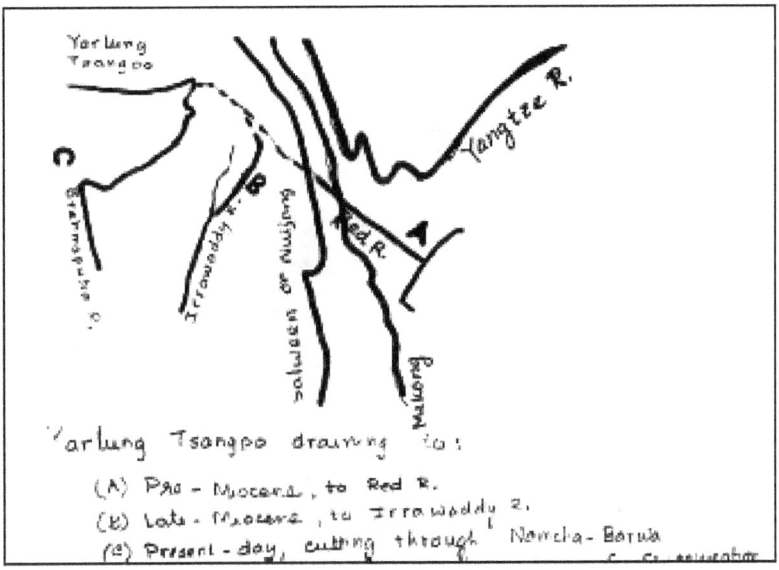

মানচিত্ৰ ঃ (৭) মহা গঠন আৰু মহা গলনিৰ ক্ষেত্ৰত ছলউইন-মেকং-য়াচিং এটা গোট আছিল। ছাংপোৱে আনহাতে ইৰাৱতী, ছিণ্ডউইন, লোহিত, দিবাং, ছিয়াং এই অনুক্ৰমত ঘড়ীৰ কাঁটাৰ গতিত নদীবোৰৰ লগত সংলগ্ন হৈ আহিছে।

দ্বিতীয়খন কাকতত লিখা ছাংপো-ইৰাৱতী-ছিণ্ডউইন কৰিডৰৰ ঘটনা ওঠৰ মিলিয়নমান বছৰৰ আগৰ। ইয়াত কোৱা হৈছে যে ছাংপোৱে প্ৰথমে ছাংপো-ইৰাৱতী-ছিণ্ডউইন কৰিডৰৰ সৃষ্টি কৰিছিল। অৰ্থাৎ প্ৰথমতে ছাংপো, ইৰাৱতী আৰু ছিণ্ডউইন নদীৰ লগত সংলগ্ন আছিল ।ইৰাৱতী নৈলৈকে উত্তৰ-পূব ভাৰত, ম্যানমাৰৰ জীৱ-জন্তুৰ সামঞ্জস্য আছে বুলি ফ্ৰান্‌ক কিংডন ৱাৰ্ডে লিখি গৈছে।

ছাংপোৱে কাম্বী গাৰপো পাহাৰৰ লোহিত এৰি নামচা বাৰৱাৰ পাহাৰ কটা প্ৰায় আঠ মিলিয়ন বছৰৰ আগৰ কথা আৰু ছিয়াং হোৱা কম প্ৰাকৃতিক বিপৰ্যয় আছিলনে? জীৱ-জন্তুৰ বাবে ই আকস্মিক দুৰ্ঘটনা আছিল যদিও নদীখনে পদাৰ্থ বিজ্ঞানহে মানিছে। মানুহে পৰশুকুণ্ডক কালজয়ী কৰি এই ঘটনা অমৰ কৰিছে। তিব্বতীয়সকলে পেমাকো, তথা ব্ৰজযোগিনী বা ডাকিনী সূত্ৰৰে ছাংপোৱে নামচা

বাৰম্বাৰ কাটি নামি অহা প্ৰকৃতি মাতৃৰ শক্তিক হৃদয়ংগম কৰিবলৈ শিকাইছে। সেই বিষয়ে এতিয়া বহলাই আলোচনা কৰিম।

তিব্বতৰ লগত অৰুণাচল আৰু অসমৰ সম্বন্ধ ওতপ্ৰোতভাৱে জড়িত আৰু ই যুগ যুগৰ। অৰুণাচলৰ বাহিৰেও অসমৰ বহু শতাংশ মানুহৰ উপৰি পুৰুষে গিৰিপথবোৰৰ মাজেৰে চুবুৰীয়া ঠাইৰ লগত সংযোগ ৰাখিছিল, সেই পথেৰে অসম পাইছিলহি। অৰুণাচলৰ পূবৰ দুৰ্গম ঠাইবোৰত মাজে মাজে তিব্বতীয়সকল আছিল। য়ুনানৰ উত্তৰ-পশ্চিম অংশত এনে ওখ থিয় পৰ্বত আৰু দ উপত্যকা আছে য'ত মানুহৰ ভৰি নপৰিছিল। এনেকুৱা বেছি অংশই তিব্বতত পৰিছিল। চীনৰ পৰা এইবোৰ ঠাইলৈ অহাৰ বাট নাছিল। ভাৰতৰ উত্তৰৰ নিকটৱৰ্তী তিব্বতৰ ঠাইখিনিৰ লগত ইমান ভাল সম্পৰ্ক আছিল যে তেওঁলোকে শান্তিৰে সহবাস কৰিছিল। তিব্বতৰ উত্তৰ আৰু পূবহে ছিল্ক ৰোডৰ বাবদ বাহিৰৰ বিশ্বৰ লগত যোগাযোগ আছিল। তিব্বতীয়সকলৰ এটা বৈশিষ্ট্য হৈছে তেওঁলোকে প্ৰকৃতিক সন্মান কৰে আৰু প্ৰকৃতিৰ লগত শান্তিপূৰ্ণ সহবাস কৰে। গুৰু ৰিপনছে বা পদ্মস্মভাৱাৰ বেউল নীতিও অতি উত্তম। তেওঁলোকে খনিজ পদাৰ্থৰ বাবে খনন নকৰে পৃথিৱীয়ে দুখ পাব বুলি।

পেমাকো ঠাইখিনি তেওঁলোকৰ বাবে অতি পবিত্ৰ। পেমাকো ৰামধেনুৰ ঠাই, ইয়াত সঘনে অৰ্ধ ৰামধেনু দেখা যায়। বৈজ্ঞানিক ফালৰ পৰা পেমাকোৰ জিঅমিত্ৰি যথাযথ, নিৰ্ভুল আৰু নিখুঁতঙ্গ নামচা বাৰৱাৰ মহাভাঁজ পেমাকোৰ পৰাহে দেখা যায়। তেওঁলোকে এই পাহাৰ যে আলফুলকৈ ৰাখিব লাগে তাৰ মূল্য ভালকৈ বুজিছিল। পেমাকোৰে মহাভাঁজৰ ওপৰৰ পাহাৰীয়া ঠাই এডোখৰ ত্ৰিবিমিত্ৰীয়ত প্ৰকাশ কৰিছে এগৰাকী মহিলাৰ ৰূপত। বৰ্জযোগানী বোলা এই পবিত্ৰ শৰীৰৰ শিৰ কাংগৰী গাৰপোৰ শিখৰ, নামচা বাৰোৱা আৰু গায়লা পেৰী দুই স্তন, এই শৰীৰৰ নাভিৰ পৰা তলৰ গোটেই অংশ অৰুণাচলত পৰে। নাভিটো উজনি ছিয়াঙৰ য়িকিয়ঙত বুলি কোৱা হয়। য়িকিয়ঙৰ পৰা নামচা বাৰৱাৰ বৰফাবৃত শিখৰ চাবলৈ বৰ সুন্দৰ। পেমাকোলৈ উত্তৰ চিয়াঙৰ পৰাহে যাব পাৰি। তিব্বতৰ কিছু অংশ আবৰ, ডফলা আৰু মিচিমি পাহাৰেদিহে যাব পাৰি। চীনৰ পৰা আহিবলৈ প্ৰায় অসম্ভৱ।

পেমাকোক least interference policy মানে কোনো হস্তক্ষেপ নকৰাকৈ

ৰক্ষা কৰা অতি আৱশ্যক। এয়া ব্ৰহ্মপুত্ৰৰ বাবদ, তিব্বত-উত্তৰ-পূব ভাৰত-ম্যানমাৰ-বাংলাদেশৰ বাবদ, এই কৰিডৰৰ জন্তু, বিশেষকৈ চৰাই (অৰ্থাৎ গোটেই পৰিবেশতন্ত্ৰ) আৰু ৰাইজৰ জীৱন ৰক্ষাৰ বাবদ। মই কথাটো আৰু অলপ বহলাইছোঁ। নামচা বাৰৱা পাহাৰখন কাটি অহাৰ বাবদ ব্ৰহ্মপুত্ৰই বহুত গেদ-পলস আনে। তাতে যদি ছাংপোৰ ওপৰত বান্ধ আদি কৰি, বিশেষকৈ নামচা বাৰৱাত গধুৰ মেচিনেৰে প্ৰকল্প আৰম্ভ কৰে ই অসমৰ বাবে মৃত্যুৰ ৰায়। চীনা মহাৰজাই নামচা বাৰৱাৰ শিখৰত এটা কৃত্ৰিম হ্ৰদ কৰি জলবোমা হিচাবে ব্যৱহাৰ কৰিবলৈ প্ৰস্তুত হৈছে বুলি এটা অভিযোগ আহি আছে। মই এই খবৰটোৰ পম খেদিবলৈ আৰম্ভ কৰিছোঁ। ব্ৰহ্মপুত্ৰই ইমানেই গেদ আনিছে আৰু ঠায়ে ঠায়ে ইমান খহনীয়া হৈছে যে প্ৰকৃতিয়ে এই অঞ্চলৰ বাবে কি পৰিকল্পনা কৰিছে? ব্ৰহ্মপুত্ৰৰ দিশ সলনিৰ বুৰঞ্জীয়ে কি কয়?

চালুকীয়া পাহাৰৰ কামেই হৈছে, পৰ্বতৰ শিখৰবোৰ মসৃণ কৰা। এইক্ষেত্ৰত উত্তৰ-পূব ভাৰতেই তাৰ পূৰা ফল পাইছে। চীনৰ সামৰিক আগ্ৰাসন প্ৰৱণতাই অকল তিব্বতৰে বিলাই-বিপত্তি কৰা নাই, ই এতিয়া তিব্বত-উত্তৰ-পূব ভাৰতলৈও আহিছে। ১৯৫০ত চীনে তিব্বত সহজে লৈলোৱাৰ এটা সুযোগ আছিল, তিব্বতৰ এটা ডাঙৰ সৈন্যবাহিনী নাছিল। ভাৰতে তিব্বতক স্বীকাৰ কৰাৰ কথা ভাবিবৰ হ'ল। ভূমিপুত্ৰইহে ভূমিৰ মূল্য জানেঙ্গ অন্তত উৎচান, বাৰিগা হিমবাহসমূহ আৰু পেমাকো তিব্বতৰ নহ'লে ছাংপো-ছিয়াং-লোহিত-দিবাং-ব্ৰহ্মপুত্ৰ ৰক্ষা কৰিব নোৱাৰি। ভৌগোলিক ক্ষেত্ৰত তিব্বতীয়সকলে অতি উত্তম তথ্য ৰাখিছিল। হিমালয় পৰ্বতমালাৰ জ্ঞান আমাক লাগে, ভূমিকম্প আৰু প্ৰাকৃতিক বিপৰ্যয়ৰ বুৰঞ্জী আমাক লাগে। তিব্বতৰ মাটিৰ প্ৰতি অকণো মূল্য নিদিয়া চীনে মাত্ৰ সৰ্বোচ্চ ভূমিখিনি তললৈ মিছাইল টোঁৱাই থাকিবলৈ উচিত প্ৰতিপাদন কৰিব নোৱাৰে। চীনাই আগতে তিব্বতৰ চুকৰ পাহাৰীয়া ভূমিখিনি, অৰুণাচল আদিলৈ কেৰেপেই নকৰিছিল। সকলো সলনি হ'ল দ্বিতীয় মহাসমৰত। জাপানক বাধা দিবলৈ চীনৰ প্ৰয়োজনত চীনে এয়াৰ'প্লেন দেখিলে। চীনে হেংডুৱান আৱিষ্কাৰ কৰিলে অ'ভাৰ দ্য হাম্প এয়াৰ'প্লেন ছাৰ্ভিচৰ বাবে। চীনে তিব্বতৰ ভিতৰুৱা গিৰিপথবোৰ লাহে লাহেহে জানিছে। যুৱক দালাই লামা কি বাটেৰে তেজপুৰ পালেহি চীনৰ তেতিয়া সেই জ্ঞান অকণো নাছিল।

তিব্বতীয়সকলে খনিজ খনন নকৰিছিল। তেওঁলোকে খনন কৰা মানে ধৰিত্ৰী আইক আঘাত কৰা বুলি বাবে। এইটো এটা সঁচা কথা প্ৰযুক্তিগত কথাবোৰ, যদিহে যথেমধে কৰা হয়, ই ৰাইজৰ অতি অপকাৰ কৰে। খনন ঠিকমতে নকৰিলে নদী-নলাবোৰ বহুত অনিষ্টকাৰী হৈ পৰে। তলৰ ছবিত 'অপেন পিট মাইনিং' দেখুওৱা হৈছে। এই ক্ষেত্ৰত পানীৰ দূষিত হোৱাৰ কাৰণ দেখদেখকৈ ধৰিব পাৰি। খননৰ বাবদ ছালফিউৰিক এচিড পানীত মিহলি হয়। চীন মহাৰজাই তিব্বতত যথেষ্ট খনন প্ৰকল্প কৰিছে, বিশেষকৈ সোণৰ।

চিত্ৰ ঃ (৮) কয়লাৰ পৰা ছালফাৰ পানীত মিহলি হৈ ছালফিউৰিক এচিড সৃষ্টি কৰি পানী দূষিত কৰিছে।

ঢাকা আৰু আইজল (মিজোৰাম)ৰ মাজৰ টেক্টনিক ফলক অৱৰুদ্ধ হৈ গৈছে বুলি খবৰ আহিছে। ইতিমধ্যে সঘনে সৰু সৰু ভূমিকম্প হৈ আছে। সোনকালেই এই অঞ্চলত এটা ভূমিকম্প হ'ব। কোনোবাই অধ্যয়ন কৰিবলৈ বা অনুমান কৰিবলৈ চেষ্টা কৰিছে নেকি? মিজোৰামত সঘনাই হোৱা ভূমিকম্পই মোৰ উদ্বেগ বঢ়াইছে।

আকৰ্ষণীয় কথাটো হ'ল, ১৮৯৭ চনৰ আগৰ অসমৰ ভূমিকম্পৰ অত্যাধিক অধ্যয়ন কৰা হৈছিল। যি কি নহওক, ১৯৫০ চনৰ ভূমিকম্পৰ পিছত চিলাই-সীয়নি ভূমিৰ ওপৰত কোনো বিশেষ অধ্যয়ন কৰা হোৱা নাছিল। ১৮৯৭ চনৰ ভূমিকম্প ইমানেই প্ৰবল আছিল যে বৃহৎ আকাৰৰ শিলাখণ্ডবোৰো খহি পৰিছিল। এইটো গুৰুত্ব দিয়া প্ৰয়োজন যে এভাৰেষ্ট শৃংগ এতিয়াও বাঢ়ি গৈ আছে আৰু নামচা বাৰৱাৰ শৃংগ ডুবি গৈ আছে। নামচা বাৰৱাত ছাংপোৰ 'U' বক্ৰৰ গতি লৈছে আৰু ই অৰুণাচল সীমাৰ পৰা বৰ বেছি দূৰত্বত নাই। ভাঁজ আৰু চ্যুতিৰ পৰা হিমালয়ৰ গঠন বুলি গ্ৰহণ কৰা হৈছে। কিন্তু চ্যুতিসমূহ ভয়ানক। স্থানীয় আৰু আন্তৰ্জাতিক পণ্ডিতসকলৰ সৈতে নিকটৱৰ্তী অঞ্চলত এটা গৱেষণাৰ প্ৰয়োজনীয়তা সম্পৰ্কে কৈ থকা হৈছে আৰু উত্তৰ-পূৰ্বৰ মানুহক সচেতন কৰি দিয়া হৈছে। আইআইটি ৰুড়কী আৰু চীনৰ অংশগ্ৰহণো অতি সমালোচিত।

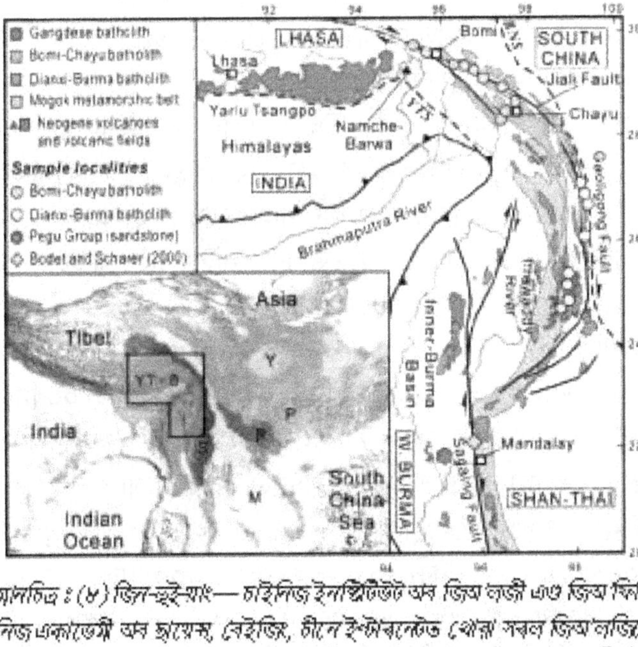

মানচিত্ৰ ঃ (৮) জিন-হুই-যাং— চাইনিজ ইনষ্টিটিউট অব জিঅ'লজী এণ্ড জিঅ' ফিজিক্স, চাইনিজ একাডেমী অব ছায়েন্স, বেইজিং, চীনে ইন্টাৰনেটত থোৱা সৰল জিঅ'লজিকেল মেপ। পূব হিমালয়ৰ বাথলিট, চ্যুতি আৰু নদী ব্যৱস্থা, YTS, যাৰলুং ছাংপো চিলাই সীয়নি

০০০

।। পঞ্চম অধ্যায় ।।

শিৱালিক আৰু ছফ্‌ট পাহাৰ কি ?

শিৱালিক বা বহিৰ্হিমালয়, হিমালয় পৰ্বতৰ তিনিটা শাৰীৰ সবাতোকৈ দক্ষিণৰ ফালে পৰ্বত শাৰী যাৰ উচ্চতা ৬০০ৰ পৰা ১৫০০ মিটাৰ (০.৪ৰ পৰা প্ৰায় এক মাইল)। হিমালয়ক যে এক পৰ্বতমালা বোলা হয় এই কথা অৰ্থপূৰ্ণ আৰু তাৎপৰ্যপূৰ্ণ। ভাৰতৰ উত্তৰে ই উত্তল তিনিলানি মালা, তিনিসৰী (সাতসৰীত সাতডাল মালা, তিনিসৰীত তিনিডাল) বুলিলে ভুল নহ'ব। মই উত্তল তথ্যটো বিভ্ৰান্তিকৰ পাওঁ কাৰণ উত্তলখিনি অকল জম্মু আৰু কাশমীৰতহে। নংগা পৰ্বত আৰু নামচা বাৰৱালৈ হিমালয়ৰ কাঁচিজোন তিনিসৰী (তলৰ দুয়োখন চিত্ৰ চাওক) মালা বুলি ভাবিলে বাস্তৱিকভাবে অনুভৱ কৰিবলৈ আৰু মনত ৰাখিবলৈ উপযোগী। এই তিনিসৰী, অৰ্থাৎ উচ্চ হিমালয়, মধ্য হিমালয়, শিৱালিক— এই তিনিওৰ মাজত শিবালিক কনিষ্ঠ আৰু ইয়াৰ কিছুমান পাহাৰ শিথিল মাটিৰ। মই শিথিল মাটিৰ পাহাৰবোৰক চফ্‌ট পাহাৰ নাম দিছোঁ আৰু ইএটা বিচাৰ্যৰ বিষয় বুলিছোঁ। ফল্ট বা চ্যুতি, দুই ভূভাগৰ চিলাইৰ লাইন বা ছুচাৰ, টেকটনিক প্লেটৰ সীমা— এই গোটেই বিষয়বস্তু হিমালয় আৰু নিম্নভাগৰ সুৰক্ষাৰ বাবে অত্যাৱশ্যকীয়।

উত্তৰৰ উচ্চ হিমালয় বা হিমাদ্ৰীৰ উচ্চতা গড় হিচাবত ৬১০০ মিটাৰ (৩.৮ মিটাৰৰ পৰা পাঁচ মাইল) আৰু ২৫ কিলোমিটাৰ প্ৰস্থৰ আৰু সম্পূৰ্ণ বছৰ বৰফৰে আবৃত হৈ থাকে। হাতেৰে অকা মানচিত্ৰত ইয়াক নংগা পৰ্বতৰ পৰা নামচা বাৰৱালৈকে দেখুওৱা হৈছে। মধ্য হিমালয় বা মহাভাৰত শ্ৰেণীৰ গড় উচ্চতা ৩৭০০ৰ পৰা ৪,৫০০ মিটাৰ (১২,০০০ৰ পৰা ১৫,০০০ ফুট)। ইয়াত ভাৰতবৰ্ষৰ হিল ষ্টেচনবোৰ আছে, গছৰ ভিতৰত পাইন, অ'ক আৰু ফলৰ বাগান আছে। এই পৰ্বতমালা তিব্বতৰ পিনে বৰ ঠিয়। আনহাতে, ভাৰতৰ ফালে ক্ৰমশঃ এঢলীয়া হোৱাত ৰে'ল আৰু ৰাস্তাৰ যোগাযোগ হ'ব পাৰিছে।

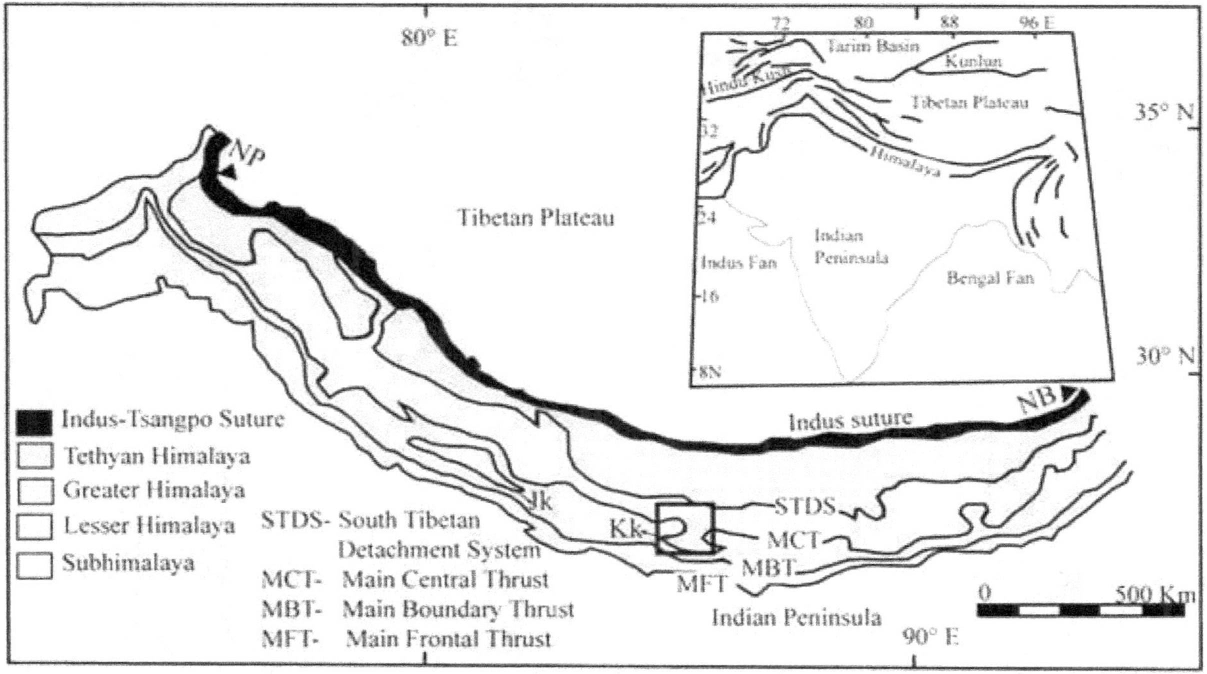

মানচিত্ৰ ঃ (৯) উচ্চ, মধ্য, আৰু শিবালিক হিমালয় আৰু মুখ্য চ্যুতিসমূহ

বিশাল কাৰাকোৰাম পৰ্বতমালা ভাৰতৰ উত্তৰ-পশ্চিম দিশৰ পৰা আফগানিস্তানৰ পৰা তাজিকিস্তানলৈ প্ৰসাৰিত হৈ ভাৰত, চীনৰ সীমাত আৰু পাকিস্তানত বিস্তৃত হৈ আছে। চীনৰ দ্বাৰা নিয়ন্ত্ৰিত আকচাই চিনো ইয়াতে, কাৰাকোৰাম হাইৱে' আৰু কে২, পৃথিৱীৰ দ্বিতীয় ওখ শৃংগও ইয়াতে। মেৰু অঞ্চলক বাদ দিলে পৃথিৱীৰ সৰ্ববৃহৎ হিমবাহ ইয়াতে আছে। তলত গিলগিটৰ ওচৰৰ কাৰাকোৰম, হিন্দুকোষ, আৰু হিমালয়ৰ মিলন স্থান দেখুৱা হৈছে।

চিত্ৰ ঃ (৯)

এসময়ত ভাৰতৰ পৰা ক্ৰীতদাস মধ্য এছিয়ালৈ হিন্দুকোষেদি নিয়া হৈছিল আৰু পাহাৰীয়া কঠোৰ বাট আৰু জলবায়ুত বহুত মৰিছিল, হিন্দুকোষ বা 'হিন্দুক মাৰে' নামটো তাৰ পৰা হৈছিল। কাৰাকোৰম, লাডাখ আৰু লাডাখৰ বিস্তৃতি কৈলাস, ঝস্কাৰ পৰ্বতমালাক একেলগে ট্ৰেন্স হিমালয়ান বুলি কোৱা হয়। হিন্দুকোষ বা 'হিন্দুক মাৰে' পাহাৰৰ নামটোৱে আন এটা তথ্যলৈ লৈ আহে। আপুনি যদি ইউৰোপৰ পৰা ভাৰতৰ ফাললৈ উৰাজাহাজেৰে দিনৰ পোহৰত আহে, ভাৰত পোৱাৰ আগতে বহুত পাহাৰ পাব, তাৰ পাচতে হঠাতে সাগৰৰ লেভেলৰ উপত্যকা

পাব, প্ৰথমে পাঁচখন নদীৰ পঞ্জাব, আৰু তাৰ পাচত গঙ্গা উপত্যকা। অৰ্থাৎ আগতে আক্ৰমণকাৰীসকল পশ্চিমৰ পৰা নামি আহিছিল, উত্তৰ-পশ্চিমৰ পৰা আহিলে পাহাৰ নামি ভাৰতবৰ্ষ পায়। আনহাতে, ভাৰতৰ পৰা গ'লে পাহাৰ কাব লাগে। 'পামিৰ মালভূমি', য'ত মধ্য এছিয়াৰ পাহাৰবোৰ আৰম্ভ হৈছে বুলিলে পাহাৰবোৰ মনত ৰাখিবলৈ সহজ। হিন্দুকোষ সদায়ে বৰফৰে ঢকা আছিল, কিন্তু ১৯৭০ৰ ৰিপৰ্ট মতে, ইয়াত ১৫ শতাংশ বৰফ গলিছে। এই হাৰত বৰফ গলিলে হিন্দুকোষৰ গোটেই বৰফ ২১০০ লৈ গলি যাব আৰু তেতিয়ালৈ শৃংখল প্ৰতিক্ৰিয়া হৈ বহুত জীৱ ধ্বংস হ'ব। দুহেজাৰ বছৰৰ আগতে এই 'পামিৰ মালভূমি' গোটেইবোৰ ওচৰৰ দেশৰে, ৰাছিয়া, চীন, পাৰ্চিয়া, ভাৰত ইত্যাদি, যোগসূত্ৰ আছিল। কিম্বা ভূমিকম্প বা সৰস্বতী নদী লুকোৱাৰ বাবদ হয়তো ভৌগোলিক সাসলনি হ'ল। ইয়াৰ কোনো প্ৰমাণ নাহি, কিন্তু জনা গৈছে যে ভৌগোলিক সলনিৰ কোনো মেপ বুৰঞ্জীত নাই।

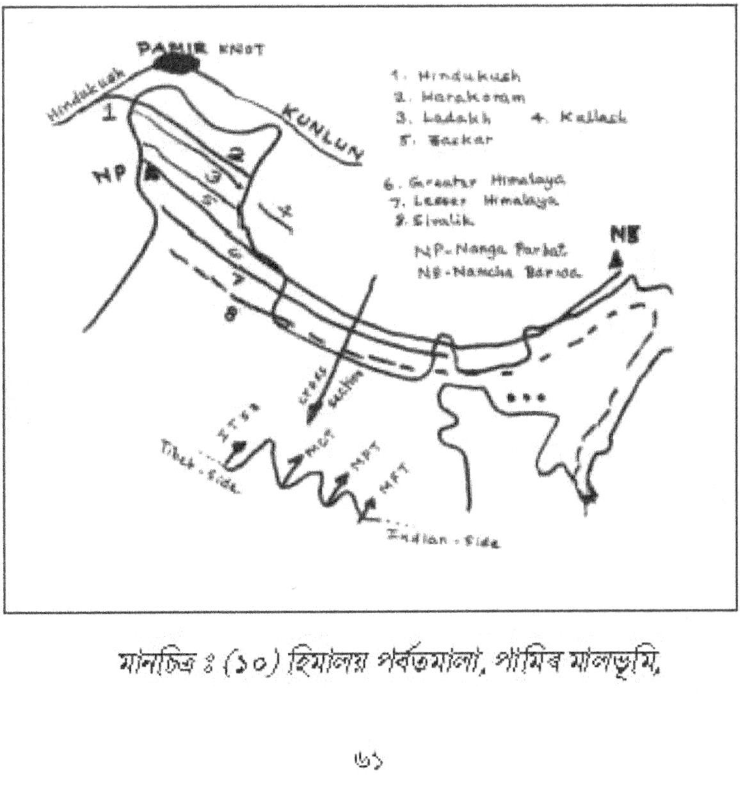

মানচিত্ৰ ঃ (১০) হিমালয় পৰ্বতমালা, পামিৰ মালভূমি,

ছিকিমত, পৃথিবীৰ তৃতীয় উচ্চ পাহাৰ কাঞ্চনজংঘাৰ পূব অংশডোখৰ আছে, কিন্তু ছিকিমৰ কিছু পাহাৰতো শিথিল মাটি আছে। পশ্চিম কাঞ্চনজংঘা নেপালত। ভূটানত উচ্চ হিমালয়, আৰু শিবালিকৰ বাহিৰেও উপ-হিমালয় আছে, এই পাহাৰবোৰৰ লগত অসমৰ যোগাযোগ বহুত দিনৰ। নেপালত উচ্চ হিমালয়ৰ আটাইতকৈ ওখ শৃঙ্গ মাউণ্ট এভাৰেষ্ট, দ্বিতীয় ওখ শৃঙ্গ লটচেৰ বাহিৰেও অন্নপূৰ্ণা, কালি গন্দকী আৰু ঢোলাগিৰি শৃঙ্গ আছে।

অৰুণাচলৰ পাহাৰখিনি বেছিভাগেই শিবালিকত পৰে, শিবালিক শ্ৰেণীটো যথেষ্ট ভগা-ছিগা, সম্পূৰ্ণ ধাৰাবাহিক নহয়। ডফলা, মিৰি, মিচিমি মানচিত্ৰত দেখুওৱা হৈছে। পূৰ্বাঞ্চল বা পূব পাৰ্বত্য অঞ্চল আন এটা পাহাৰৰ শ্ৰেণী। মানচিত্ৰত পাঁটকাই পৰ্বত, নাগালেণ্ড, মণিপুৰ, আৰু মিজোৰাম দেখুওৱা হৈছে। ব্ৰহ্মপুত্ৰ উপত্যকাৰ হিমালয়ৰ অংশসমূহো বেছিভাগেই শিবালিক, উচ্চতা জুম খেতিৰ বাবে উপযোগী। অৰুণাচলৰ শিবালিকৰ কিছু পাহাৰ শিথিল মাটিৰে গঠিত যিটো লক্ষ্য কৰিবলগীয়া কথা।

মানচিত্ৰ ঃ (১১) শ্বিলং মালভূমিত পশ্চিম আৰু পূব গাৰো পাহাৰ, পশ্চিম আৰু পূব খাচী পাহাৰ, জয়ন্তীয়া আৰু কাৰ্বিআলং অন্তৰ্ভুক্ত হৈছে।

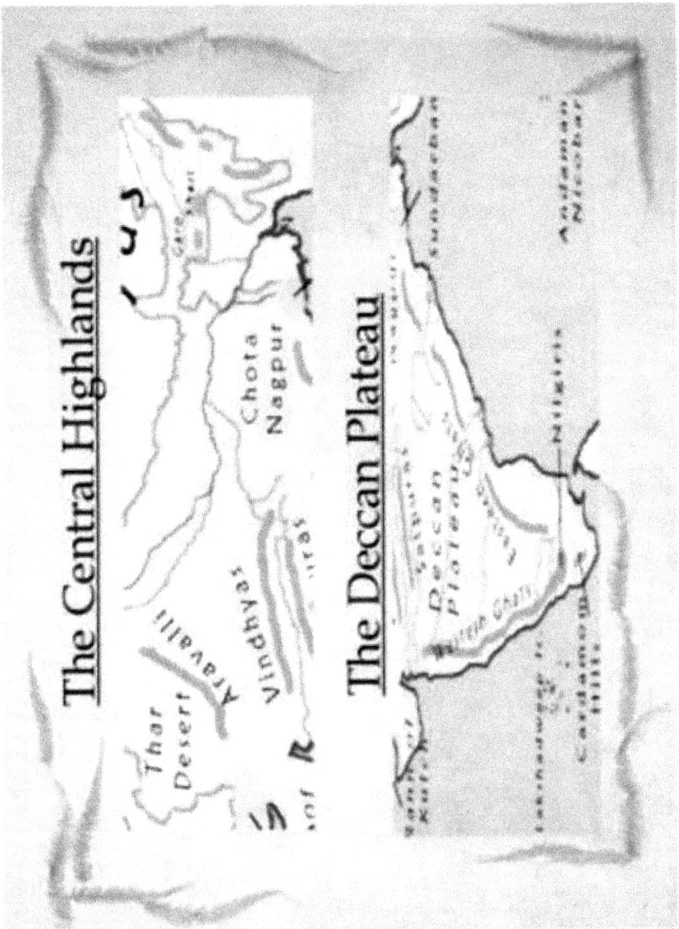

মানচিত্ৰ ঃ (১২) শ্বিলং মালভূমি ভাৰতৰ মধ্য উচ্চাঞ্চলৰ সৈতে জড়িত

অসম বা উত্তৰ-পূব ভাৰতৰ ভালকৈ উল্লেখ নকৰা তথ্য হৈছে শ্বিলং ভাৰতৰ মধ্য উচ্চাঞ্চলৰ এটা বিস্তাৰিত অংশ। ভাৰতৰ মধ্য উচ্চাঞ্চলৰ মেপ তলত দিয়া হৈছে। আৰাৱলী, বিন্ধ্য, মালোৱা, বগেলখণ্ড, চোটা নাগপুৰ মালভূমি ভাৰতৰ মধ্য উচ্চাঞ্চলৰ ভিতৰত পৰে। শ্বিলং মালভূমি মধ্য উচ্চাঞ্চলৰ পৰা এতিয়া অসলগ্ন, এই বিষয় লৈ আকৌ অহা হ'ব। এই বিচ্ছিন্নতাৰ অধ্যয়নে বুৰঞ্জী, ভূমিকম্প আৰু অনেক কথা জনাত সহায় কৰিব।

চিত্ৰ ঃ (১০) গছৰ শিপাৰে কৰা চেৰাপুঞ্জীৰ কাষৰীয়া অঞ্চলৰ এখন দলং, জৈৱিক প্ৰযুক্তিৰ এক দক্ষতাৰ উদাহৰণ। ডিমৰু জাতীয় গছৰ উবি থকা শিপাবোৰক লক্ষ্য কৰি বন্ধা হয়। তামোল গছৰ খোঁপোলা টুকুৰাত এই শিপাবোৰ সুমুৱাই দিয়া হয়। অৰুণাচলত যদি ডিমৰু গছ হয় সৰু জুৰিৰ ওপৰত এই দলং পৰিবেশতন্ত্ৰক সহায় কৰা ফুট ব্ৰিজ হ'ব।

সম্পূৰ্ণ হিমালয়ৰ ভূতত্ত্ব সম্পৰ্কীয় গৱেষণাৰ বিশদ বিৱৰণ সহজলভ্য নহয়, বিশেষকৈ চিলাই-জোৰাৰ যি এটা মুৰৰ পৰা সিমুৰলৈ যায় সেই চিলাই-জোৰা ম্যানমাৰত শেষ হৈছে। ITSZ – Indus Tsangpo Suture zone চিলাই-জোৰাৰ সম্পূৰ্ণ মেপ এখন দিবলৈ পোৱা নগ'ল। চিলাই-জোৰাও এটা fault বা চ্যুতি।

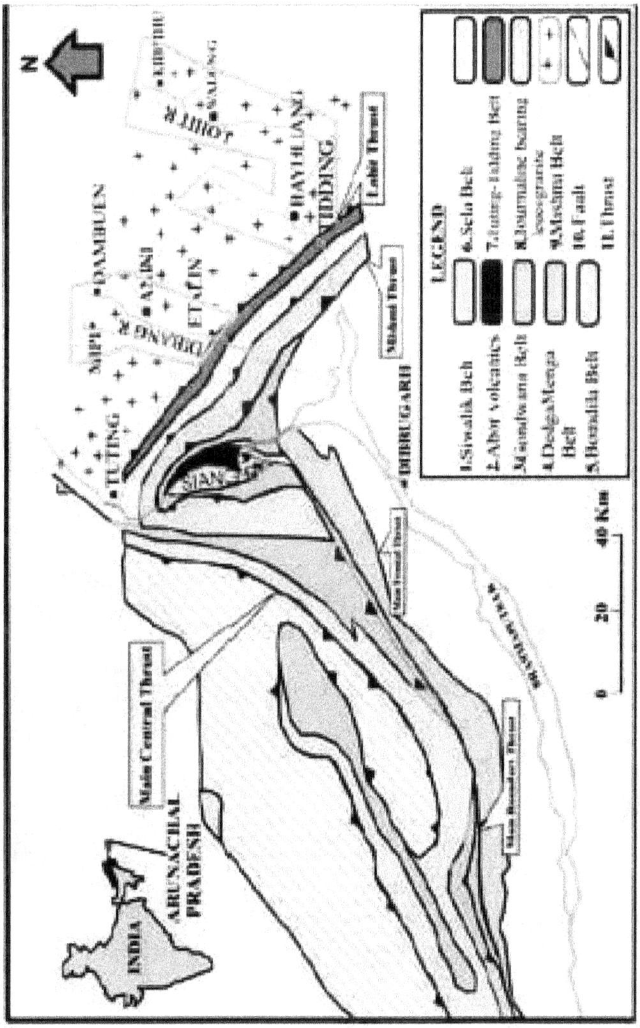

মানচিত্ৰ ঃ (১৩) গুৰুত্বপূৰ্ণ ভিতৰ-থুৰুৰ চ্যুতি, অৰ্থাৎ থ্ৰাষ্ট আৰু অৱস্থিতিৰ

মোৰ কৌতুহল আৰম্ভ হয় ছফ্‌ট পাহাৰৰ বাবদ। সাধাৰণতে পাহাৰত টান কম্পেক্ট মাটি আশা কৰা যায়।অন্ততঃ পাহাৰৰ অন্তৰৰ মাটি ওপৰৰ মাটিৰ হেঁচাত কম্পেক্ট হ'ব লাগে। ভূতাত্ত্বিক বা জিঅ'লজিকেল স্কেলত হিমালয় ইমান নতুন যে যত টেথিছ সাগৰৰ মাটি উঠিল সি এতিয়াও শিথিল হৈয়েই আছে। ৰাস্তা নাভাঙিবৰ বাবে পৰিবহণ ব্যৱস্থা বিশেষকৈ কৰাৰ আৱশ্যক।

১৯৫০ চনৰ ভূমিকম্পৰ অভিকেন্দ্ৰ আছিল পৰশুৰামকুণ্ডৰ ওচৰত। পৰশুৰামকুণ্ড লোহিত নদীৰ মাজত। ইয়াতে কিংবদন্তি মতে পৰশুৰামৰ কুঠাৰ হাতৰ পৰা খহি পৰিছিল। অৱশ্যে কেৰালাতো এটা এনে কুণ্ড আছে। বিজ্ঞানমতে ইয়াত প্ৰচণ্ড দুৰ্যোগ হোৱাৰ সম্ভাৱনা আছিল। ব্ৰহ্মপুত্ৰৰ আন নাম লুইতৰ পৰা জনা যায় এসময়ত লোহিতেই ব্ৰহ্মপুত্ৰ আছিল।ব্ৰহ্মপুত্ৰ নামটো বাৰম্বাৰ কাটি মহাভাঁজ হোৱাৰ আচল তাৰিখ জনা নাযায়। কিন্তু এইখিনি নদীৰ গতিপথ সলনি পূৰ্বতে হৈছে। ছফ্‌ট পাহাৰ, ভূমিস্খলন, আৰু faults and foldৰ পৰা বহু কথাত সাৱধানতা ল'ব লাগে। হিমালয়ৰ নিচিনা চালুকীয়া পৰ্বতমালাত বহুত প্ৰত্যাহ্বান আছে। অৰুণাচলৰ পূবত এতিয়া তিনিখন নদী হোৱা মেকং, চলউইন আৰু য়াচিং এসময়ত বেড ৰিভাৰৰ লগত একেখন হৈ আছিল।

চিত্ৰ ঃ (১১) পৰশুৰামকুণ্ড

চিত্ৰ ঃ (১২) হুস্কট পাহাৰ ভূমিস্খলন, ১১ জুলাই, ২০২০

অতি প্ৰয়োজনীয় আৰু বিচাৰ্যৰ বিষয় হৈছে ছিকিম-অৰুণাচলৰ শিথিল মাটিসমূহ চিহ্নিত কৰা। ভৈয়ামত যেনেকৈ জলাশয়বোৰ সংৰক্ষিত কৰিব লাগে, ছফ্‌ট পাহাৰবোৰো বিশেষভাৱে সংৰক্ষিত আৰু ৰক্ষণাবেক্ষণ হ'ব লাগে। পথ বনোৱাৰ সলনি কিছুমান ঠাইত ৰোপৱে' আৰু স্কাই লিফ্‌ট দিব লাগে। ইয়াৰ বাবে ২৪ ঘণ্টাজুৰি সৌৰশক্তিৰ ব্যৱস্থা অতি উত্তম হ'ব। য'ত পাৰি ডাঙৰ লিফ্‌ট আৰু কণমানি সুৰঙ্গৰ দ্বাৰা গাড়ী, মটৰচাইকেল আৰু বোজা কঢ়িওৱাৰ কথা ভাবিব পাৰি। ছফ্‌ট পাহাৰত নদীবান্ধৰ কথা নভবাই ভাল। ফিলিপিনছত ব্যৱহাৰ হোৱা স্কাই চাইকেল অৰুণাচলৰ বাবে অতি উপযোগী।

চিত্ৰ ঃ (১৩) স্কাই চাইকেল

আৰু এটা গৱেষণাৰ বিষয় হ'ব লাগে, মহাভাৰতৰ বা ৰামায়ণৰ দিনত উত্তৰ-পূৱ ভাৰত কেনে আছিল। তিব্বতীয়সকলে বহুত ভৌগোলিক তত্ত্ব লিখি থৈছিল। হিউৱেন চাঙৰ ভ্ৰমণৰ লিপিৰ পৰাও নতুন কথা অনুমান কৰিব পাৰি। গুৰু দুজনাৰ দিনতো কিছু নদী বেলেগভাবে বৈছিল যেন লাগে।

উত্তৰ-পূবৰ পৰিবেশতন্ত্ৰৰ সংৰক্ষণ আৰু সুৰক্ষিত কৰা ভাৰতৰ বাবে অতি প্ৰয়োজনীয়। এইটো নিশ্চিত কৰিব লাগে যাতে অনুপযুক্ত ঠাইত ডাঙৰ নিৰ্মাণ নহয়। উত্তৰ-পূবে ভাৰতৰ অক্সিজেন যোগানত আৰু প্ৰদূষণ কমোৱাত সহায় কৰিব। ছিকিম প্লাষ্টিকৰ ব্যৱহাৰ বন্ধ কৰা প্ৰথমখন ৰাজ্য, প্ৰথম জৈৱিক ৰাজ্য, আৰু নিজ ৰাজ্যৰ জোখতকৈ অতিৰিক্ত বিজুলী শক্তি উৎপাদনৰ সক্ষম। ছিকিমৰ অনন্য কাৰ্যসমূহে ইয়াকে প্ৰমাণ কৰে যে উন্নত বিচাৰ-বিবেচনা আৰু প্ৰকৃতি আৰু প্ৰযুক্তিৰ ভাৰসাম্য ৰক্ষা কৰিবৰ বাবে আকৃতিত ডাঙৰ নহ'লেও হ'ব। এই ক্ষেত্ৰত ছিকিমৰ পৰা ভবিষ্যতলৈ আৰু আশা ৰাখিলোঁ।

○○○

।। ষষ্ঠ অধ্যায় ।।

বিশুদ্ধ পানী আৰু পৰিষ্কাৰ নদী

নদী আৰু বিশুদ্ধ পানীৰ হ্ৰদসমূহ এখন দেশৰ বাবে অতি গুৰুত্বপূৰ্ণ সম্পদ। যদিও পৃথিৱীত জলপৃষ্ঠ অধিক, তাৰ ৯৭ শতাংশ পানীয়েই লুণীয়া, বাকী ৩ শতাংশ পানীহে সেৱনযোগ্য বিশুদ্ধ পানী। নিমখীয়া পানীত বিভিন্ন খনিজ দ্ৰব্য থাকিব পাৰে আৰু লোণমুক্ত নকৰিলে ই খোৱাৰ অনুপযুক্ত। বিশুদ্ধ পানীৰ ৩ শতাংশ হিমবাহ বা বৰফ ধৰা হোৱা নাই। লোণমুক্ত কৰা পদ্ধতিটো সহজ আৰু সুলভ দুয়োটাই নহয়, আচলতে ই অতি খৰচী। তদুপৰি, বিশুদ্ধিকৰণৰ লগত আন এটা সমস্যা যোগ হয়। এই প্ৰযুক্তি যিকোনো ঠাইতে কৰিব নোৱাৰি, সাগৰৰ বা ডাঙৰ হ্ৰদৰ দাঁতিকাষৰীয়া অঞ্চলসমূহহে ইয়াৰ উপযুক্ত। কাৰণ বিশুদ্ধকৰণ কৰাৰ পিচত হোৱা লোণৰ পাহাৰটো জমা কৰিব ক'ত? য'তেই নাৰাখক বৰষুণে লোণবোৰ বোৱাই নি ভূমি গছ-গছনিৰ অযোগ্য কৰিব। বিশুদ্ধ পানী ওখ ঠাইলৈ পাম্পেৰে আৰু দূৰ চহৰলৈ পাইপেৰে পঠিওৱা দুয়োটাই ফলপ্ৰসূ নহয়। নিশ্চিতভাৱে সিদ্ধান্ত ল'ব পাৰি যে পৃথিৱীৰ বহুবোৰ দেশতে পানীৰ চাহিদা

পানীৰ যোগানতকৈ বেছি। উন্নত দেশসমূহ পানীৰ ক্ষেত্ৰত যথেষ্ট প্ৰতিক্ৰিয়াশীল, আনহাতে উন্নয়নশীল দেশবোৰে যেন একোৱে হোৱা নাই তেনে ভাবত আছে। কানাডা যথেষ্ট বিশুদ্ধ পানী থকা দেশ এখন, অথচ ভেনকুভেৰ, কানাডাত ইতিমধ্যে পানী সংৰক্ষণৰ ব্যৱস্থা গ্ৰহণ কৰিছে। হিমালয় পৰ্বতমালাত হিমবাহবিলাক গলিবলৈ আৰম্ভ কৰাটো, বিশেষকৈ বৰফাবৃত হিন্দুকোষৰ হিমপ্ৰবাহ গলন ভাৰতবৰ্ষৰ দৰে উন্নয়নশীল দেশবোৰৰ বাবে সজাগ আৰু সাৱধানবাণী, সেউজ গৃহ গেছ কিন্তু আশাকৰাৰ দৰে কমা নাই। আগেয়ে আমেৰিকাৰ গাড়ীৰ নিৰ্গমনক বিলাসিতা প্ৰদূষণ বোলা চীনদেশত গাড়ীৰ ৰাস্তা আৰু গাড়ীৰ সংখ্যা দহগুণৰ বেছি হৈ দূষিতকৰণ অতি বাঢ়িছে। তলত ভাৰতৰ ওচৰ-পাজৰৰ এছিয়াৰ কিছু দেশৰ জল সমস্যা আৰু বাস্তৱমুখী জল সংৰক্ষণৰ উদাহৰণ দিয়া হ'ল।

যদিও ছিংগাপুৰ ১৯৬৫ চনত মালয়েছিয়াৰ পৰা বিভক্ত হৈ স্বাধীন ৰাষ্ট্ৰ হ'ল, প্ৰথমাৱস্থাত মালয়েছিয়াই ছিংগাপুৰৰ কাৰণে পানীৰ গুৰুত্বপূৰ্ণ উৎস হৈ আছিল। অথচ যথেষ্ট বুদ্ধিদীপ্ততাৰে পানীৰ বিকল্প উৎসৰ গৱেষণা কৰি পানীৰ নিজৰ উৎসতে আত্মনিৰ্ভৰশীল হোৱাৰ উপৰি মালয়েছিয়াকে কিছু শতাংশ বিক্ৰী কৰিব পৰা হ'ল। বৰষুণৰ জমা পানী ছিংগাপুৰৰ বাবে বৰ্তমান পানীৰ এটা ডাঙৰ উৎস। ২০১১ চনৰ পৰা মাৰিনা পুৰংগল আৰু চেৰাংগুন জলাশয় পূৰ হোৱাৰ লগতে পানী সংৰক্ষণৰ ঠাইসমূহৰ সীমা বহলোৱা হৈছে। ছিংগাপুৰৰ পানীৰ আত্মনিৰ্ভৰশীলতা চিত্তাকৰ্ষক আগ্ৰাসক অথচ এটা বাস্তৱবাদী সফল উদাহৰণ। জলসংৰক্ষণৰ আৰু drip irrigationৰ পৰামৰ্শৰ বাবে ইজৰাইলী বিশেষজ্ঞ আনিছিল।

ইজৰাইল আন এখন দেশ যি পানীৰ ক্ষেত্ৰত যথেষ্ট সক্ৰিয় আৰু চিন্তাশীল। সমগ্ৰ বিশ্বই স্বীকাৰ কৰে যে ১৯৬৭ চনৰ ছয়দিনীয়া যুদ্ধখন ইজৰাইলৰ মূল খোৱাপানীৰ উৎস জৰ্দান নদীক অন্য দিশে গতি কৰাৰ জলযুদ্ধ আছিল। ইজৰাইলে কেৱল পানীৰ বাবেই গোলান হাইট দখল কৰিছিল। ইজৰাইলে জৰ্ডান নদীৰ পানী জৰ্ডান দেশ পোৱাৰ আগতেই পাইপেৰে নিজৰ বাবে দখল কৰি লয়। পানীৰ পাইপবিলাক অতি সুৰক্ষিতভাৱে সংৰক্ষিত কৰা হৈছে, গৃহযুদ্ধ বা যিকোনো অস্থিৰতাৰ পৰা। জল সুৰক্ষা আৰু জল সংৰক্ষণৰ গৱেষণা আৰু বিকাশ ইজৰাইলৰ বাবে সদায়ে সৰ্বোচ্চ গুৰুত্বপূৰ্ণ বিষয়।

মানচিত্ৰ ঃ (১৪) আৰল সাগৰ

মধ্য এছিয়াৰ আৰল সাগৰ অতি দ্ৰুতগতিত শুকুৱাটো কৃত্ৰিম মনুষ্যসৃষ্ট সমস্যা। এই সমস্যাটোৰ অৱগত হোৱা, খোৱাপানী যে টুটি আহিব পাৰে, এই সকলো নদীৰ উৎসত বা হেড ৱাটাৰত হোৱা অযোগ্য প্ৰকল্পৰ বাবদ, এই বিষয়ে সতৰ্ক নহ'লে ৰাইজে বেয়া ফল ভুগিব। গণতন্ত্ৰত সজাগ জনতা লাগে। বৰ্তমান কাজাকাস্তান আৰু উজবেকিস্তানৰ পৰা আৰল সাগৰ অদৃশ্য সদৃশ হোৱাৰ কাৰণ পূৰ্বতে ছোভিয়েট ৰাছিয়াই আমুদৰিয়া আৰু চিৰদৰিয়া নামৰ নদী দুখন কঁপাহৰ খেতিৰ বাবে পথাৰত পানী যোগান আৰম্ভ কৰাৰ পিছতেই। আমুদৰিয়া বা আমুৰ ঐতিহাসিক লেটিন নাম অক্সাছ। মেপত দেখাৰ দৰে আফগানিস্তান আৰু তাজিকিস্তানৰ সীমাৰ উত্তৰ-পশ্চিমৰ পৰা আৰল সাগৰৰ দক্ষিণ সীমালৈ বোৱা

এইখন মধ্য এছিয়াৰ এখন মুখ্য নদী। চিৰদৰিয়া নদীখন কিৰ্গিস্তানৰ টিয়েনচান পৰ্বতমালাৰ পৰা উৎপত্তি হৈছে। আৰল সাগৰ সংকুচিত হোৱা তথ্যটো পৃথিৱীৰ অতি বেয়া প্ৰাকৃতিক দুৰ্যোগ আৰু অতি দুখজনক মানৱসৃষ্ট সমস্যা।

ইৰাণৰ ইস্তাফানত অৱস্থিত ৩৩ গোলাকাৰ গাঁঠনিৰ চি-অ'-চেহ প'ল নামৰ ৪০০ বছৰীয়া পুৰণা দলং এখনৰ তলেৰে এসময়ৰ ভৰপূৰ জায়েণ্ডা নদীখন এতিয়া বৈ নাযায়। ইৰাণৰ আন কিছু ঋতুকালীন নদীৰ নিচিনা আগতে সকলো সময়তে প্ৰৱহমান হোৱা জায়েণ্ডা বৰ্তমান ইস্তাফান পোৱাৰ আগতেই জল নিষ্কাশনৰ ফলত শুকাই যায়। ২০১০ চনৰ প্ৰথম ভাগত নদীখন তলীলৈকে সম্পূৰ্ণভাৱে শুকাই যায় বহু বছৰ ঋতুকালীন হৈ থকাৰ পিচত।

চিত্ৰ ঃ (১৪) এতিয়াৰ জায়েণ্ডা নদী

চিত্ৰ ঃ (১৫) পূৰ্বৰ জায়েণ্ডা নদী

হিমালয়ৰ অঞ্চলসমূহত নদীবান্ধৰ পৰা হোৱা সমস্যাসমূহ

নদীবান্ধৰ সাধাৰণ সমস্যাটো হ'ল জলাশয় বা ৰিজাৰ্ভাৰটোৱে কৰা অপ্ৰাকৃতিক পৰিবেশ। যিখিনি ঠাই প্লাবিত কৰা হয়, তাত গছ-গছনি, বন্যপ্ৰাণী মৰে আৰু জঁকাবোৰ থাকি যায় ফলত পচা গেছ, অৰ্থাৎ মিথেন গেছ উৎপন্ন হয়। অৰ্থাৎ বোকা, বালি, পলস, মৰা উদ্ভিদ, মৰা বণ্যপ্ৰাণীৰ জঁকা, অপৰিষ্কাৰ পানী আদি সকলো বেয়া ব্যৱস্থাৰে নদীখনক স্থৱিৰ কৰি দিয়া হয়। আন এটা সমস্যা হ'ল অসময়ত পানী এৰি দিয়া।

নদী কেৱল স্থানীয় গছ-গছনি বা জীৱ-জন্তুৱে বিচিত্ৰতা নাশৰ বাবেই দায়ী নহয়, ই স্থানান্তৰ কৰা ৰহিজৰ দুৰ্দশাৰ বাবেও দায়ী যদিহে লোকসকলক শুদ্ধ মতে বাসস্থান দিয়া নহয়। ভূঁইকপ, সামাজিক অস্থায়ীতা, অসামৰিক যুদ্ধই বান্ধৰ বিস্তৰ ক্ষতিৰ সম্ভাৱনা আনে। যেতিয়া বহু উচ্চতাৰ পৰা বহু পানী একেলগে তললৈ এৰি দিয়া হয়, নদীৰ শিহু, মাছসমূহো মৃত্যুমুখত পৰে। যদি প্লাৱিত কৰা ঠাইবোৰ আগ্নেয়গিৰিৰ লাভা বা টান শিল থকা ঠাই হয় মিথেইন গেছ বৰকৈ হ'বলৈ নাপায়। হিমালয়ৰ পাদদেশ নিশ্চিতভাৱে নদীবান্ধৰ, বিশেষকৈ বৃহৎ নদীবান্ধৰ বাবে উপযোগী ঠাই নহয়।

ডিক্ৰং নদীত এৰি দিয়া হৈছিল বাবদ ৰঙা নদী শুকাই গ'ল। অসমীয়াৰ এই সমস্যাটোৰ অভিজ্ঞতা আৰু শিক্ষা হ'ল ঠেকি। তেওঁলোকে এইটোও শিকিছে যে 'ৰাণ অব দ্য ৰিভাৰ' জলবিদ্যুৎ প্ৰকল্পও আকৰ্ষণীয় নহয়। ইয়াত সদায় হঠাৎ পানী এৰি দিয়াৰ আশংকা থাকে। ভুল তথ্য হ'ল বান্ধসমূহৰ জলভাণ্ডাৰ এবাৰ পূৰ হ'লে অঞ্চলসমূহত পানীৰ অভাৱ নহ'ব। কিন্তু বাস্তৱ সত্যটো হ'ল ই জলাশয়ৰ আকাৰৰ ওপৰত নিৰ্ভৰ কৰে। জলাশয়ৰ আকাৰ বহুত ডাঙৰ হ'লে পূৰ্ণ হ'বলৈ বহু পৰিমাণৰ পানীৰ প্ৰয়োজন হয়।

হিমালয়ৰ বৰফ গলাৰ সময়তে উত্তৰ-পূবত মৌচুমী বায়ুৰ প্ৰভাৱত যথেষ্ট বৃষ্টিপাত হয় ফলত নদীবান্ধৰ জলাশয়বোৰো উপচি পৰে। নদীবান্ধৰ পৰা এৰি দিয়া আকস্মিক বানপানী প্ৰাকৃতিক বানপানীতকৈ অধিক ভয়ঙ্কৰ। দুয়ো বানপানী একেলগে হ'লে মানুহৰ মৃত্যু সম্ভৱপৰ হয়। আনহাতে, খৰালি কালত জলাশয়সমূহ আধাহে পূৰ্ণ হয়, সেয়েহে খুব তাকৰ পৰিমাণৰ পানীহে এৰি দিয়ে। মুঠতে নদীখন ভুলকৈ নিয়ন্ত্ৰিত হয়।

২০১৯ চনৰ আঠ জুলাইত ৰঙা চীনে নদী প্ৰকল্পৰ পানী বাৰিযাৰ দিনত এৰি দিয়াত গাঁওসমূহত বিস্তৰ ক্ষতি হৈছিল।

য়াৰলুং ছাংপোৰ ওপৰত চীনৰ নদীবান্ধ

চীনদেশে ছাংপোৰ ওপৰত নদীবান্ধ কৰা অস্বীকাৰ কৰি আহিছিল যদিও য়াৰলুং ছাংপোৰ ওপৰত পাঁচটা নদীবান্ধ নিৰ্মাণ কৰাটো নিশ্চিত হৈছে। ইয়াৰ এটা য়াৰলুং ছাংপোৰ ওপৰত আৰু বাকী চাৰিটা ছাংপোৰ উপনদীৰ ওপৰত। বৃহৎ অভিযান্তিক প্ৰকল্প চীনৰ সদায় প্ৰিয় আৰু এতিয়া নদীবান্ধ নিৰ্মাণ চীনদেশৰ একপ্ৰকাৰ মেনিয়া হৈ পৰিছে। ২০১৯ চনৰ ৬ জানুৱাৰীত হিন্দুস্তান টাইমছ কাকতে প্ৰকাশ কৰা মতে, চীনে য়াৰলুং ছাংপোৰ উপনদী জীয়াবুকুত নদীত ছিগাতছেত লালহৌ জলবিদ্যুৎ প্ৰকল্পৰ অংশ হিচাবে এটা প্ৰকল্পৰ সিদ্ধান্ত লৈছে। ছিগাতছে ভুটান আৰু ছিকিমৰ জংচনৰ পৰা ড্ৰাইভিং দূৰত্বত। ইয়াৰ পৰা চীনৰ নেপাললৈ ৰে'লপথ কৰাৰ পৰিকল্পনা। এই ঠাইত যাযাবৰী লোকে পশুৰ সৈতে ঘূৰিছিল, গ্ৰীষ্মত ওখলৈ যায় আৰু শীতত নামি আহে। জিয়েস্কু, জাংমৌ আৰু

জিয়াছা ২৫ কিলোমিটাৰৰ ভিতৰত আৰু ভাৰতৰ সীমাৰ ৫৫০ কিলোমিটাৰত। মহাভাঁজৰ যথেষ্ট আগলৈ।

অথচ চীন আৰু ভাৰতৰ ভিতৰত কোনো পানীৰ চুক্তি নাই। যদিও ২০১৩ চনৰ কেদাৰনাথ দুৰ্ঘটনাই হিমালয়ৰ নদীবোৰক যে নিমাত কৰা বা পোহ মনোৱাৰ চেষ্টা নিৰৰ্থক তাক প্ৰমাণ কৰিছে।

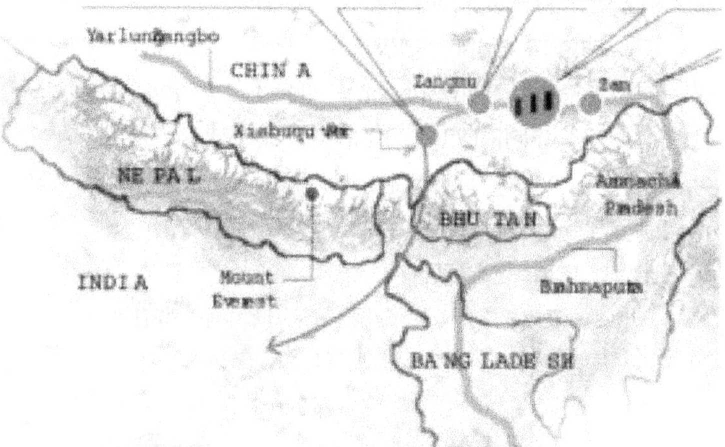

মানচিত্ৰ ঃ (১৫) ছাংপোৰ উপনদী জিয়াবুকুৰ আৰু বাকী চাৰিটা বান্ধৰ অৱস্থান

অন্তৰ্জাতিক নদী সন্থাই লাছাত বিদ্যুৎ নাটনিৰ বাবে ভাৰত-ভূটান সীমান্তৰ পৰা কিছু দূৰত্বত ৫১০ মেগাৱাটৰ জাংমুত নদীবান্ধ নিৰ্মাণ কৰাৰ কথা সুনিশ্চিত কৰে। চীনে অৱশ্যে আগৰ দৰেই চুক্তি কৰাৰ পিচতো ব্ৰহ্মপুত্ৰৰ ওপৰত বান্ধ কৰাৰ কথা প্ৰথমাৱস্থাত অস্বীকাৰ কৰে। পুৰণি খবৰটো, চীনে চীনৰ উত্তৰ-পূবলৈ সুৰঙ্গ কৰাৰ, অসত্য বুলি কয়। সন্থাই টাকলামাকানলৈ সুৰঙ্গৰ খবৰত মন্তব্য আগবঢ়োৱা নাই। অনুসন্ধানৰ বাবেই বিলম্ব বুলি আমি আশা কৰিছোঁ আৰু অন্তৰ্জাতিক নদী সন্থাৰ মন্তব্যলৈ আগ্ৰহেৰে বাট চালোঁ।

বিভিন্নতাৰ ভৰপূৰ য়ুন্নানৰ মাজেৰে ম্যানমাৰ পাৰ হৈ উত্তৰ থাইলেণ্ড পাইছেগৈ। বাৰ্মাত নদীবান্ধ নোহোৱাকৈ থকা এইখন একমাত্ৰ নদী। কিন্তু কেতিয়ালৈকে? আমি চুবুৰীয়া ৰাজ্য চলউইনৰ হকে নদী প্ৰকল্পৰ ক্ষেত্ৰত চোকা নজৰ ৰখাৰ প্ৰয়োজন।

সৰ্বাধিক নদীবান্ধ থকা দেশসমূহ

১) চীন ২২,০০০
২) মাৰ্কিন যুক্তৰাষ্ট্ৰ ৬,৫৭৫
৩) ভাৰত ৪,২৯১
৪) জাপান ২,৬৭৫
৫) স্পেইন ১,১৯৬
৬) কানাডা ৭৯৩
৭) দক্ষিণ কোৰিয়া ৭৬৫
৮) তুৰস্ক ৬২৫
৯) ব্ৰাজিল ৫৯৪
১০) ফ্ৰান্স ৫৬৯
১১) দক্ষিণ আফ্ৰিকা ৫৩৯
১২) মেক্সিকো ৫৩৭
১৩) ইটালী ৫২৪
১৪) ব্ৰিটেইন ৫১৭
১৫) অষ্ট্ৰেলিয়া ৪৮৬
১৬) নৰবে ৩৩৫
১৭) জাৰ্মানী ৩১১
১৮) আলবেনিয়া ৩০৬
১৯) ৰোমানিয়া ২৪৬
২০) জিম্বাব'বে ২১৩

উৎস ঃ WCD, Dams, and Development, Earthscan, London 2000, (from the book 'Silenced Rivers')

০০০

।। সপ্তম অধ্যায় ।।

তিব্বত, তৃতীয় মেৰু আৰু কিছু কথা

পৃথিৱীৰ সৰ্বোচ্চ মালভূমি তিব্বত মালভূমি যদিও পৰ্বতেৰে ভৰা, সমভূমি নহয়। হিমালয় ইয়াৰ দক্ষিণে আছে, কাৰাকোৰম পৰ্বতমালা পশ্চিমৰ আৰু কুনলুন পৰ্বতমালা উত্তৰ-পূবে। এই দেশৰ পৰা বাহিৰলৈ ওলাবলৈ কেইটামানহে বিশেষ গিৰিপথ আছে। কম অক্সিজেনত অভ্যস্ত হৈ জীয়াই থাকিব পৰা লোকসকলহে এই পাহাৰীয়া অঞ্চলত থাকিব পাৰিছিল আৰু ছিল্ক ৰোডে ইয়াৰ উত্তৰহে চুইছিল বাবে এই দেশ একাষৰীয়া আছিল যিটো ১৯৪৯ চনৰ কমিউনিষ্ট চীনৰ আক্ৰমণত সলনি হৈ যায়। তিব্বতৰ বুৰঞ্জী লৈ দ্বিতীয় খণ্ডত আলোকপাত কৰা হ'ব। পশ্চিমৰ গড়ে চাৰে তিনিমাইল উচ্চতাৰ পৰা তিব্বত অৰুণাচলৰ দিশে ডেৰ মাইলমান নামি আহিছে। এই নামি অহা অঞ্চলত পৃথিৱীৰ ডাঙৰ গড়খাৱৈ আছে আৰু এই অঞ্চল বিভিন্ন উদ্ভিদ আৰু জীৱ-জন্তুৰে সমৃদ্ধ। ছাংপো নদীৰ ঠিয় ঢালেৰে নামি অহা আধা ঘূৰণীয়া ঠাইখিনিক BB (The Big Bend or Great Bend) বুলি চিহ্নিত কৰা হৈছে।

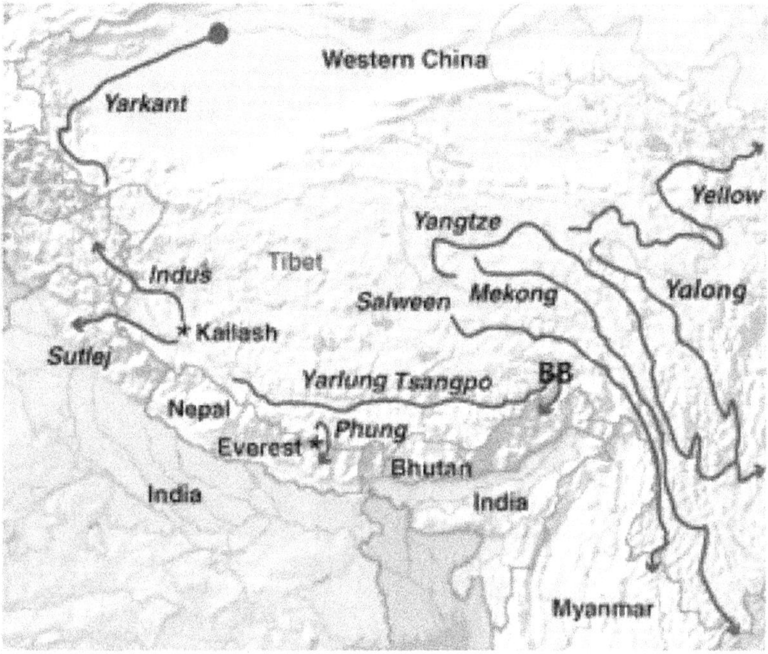

মানচিত্ৰ ঃ (১৭) এছিয়াৰ তৃতীয় মেৰু আৰু জলস্তম্ভ

উচ্চ হিমালয় তিব্বতৰ দক্ষিণে হোৱা বাবদ ই বৰ্ষাছায়াৰ অন্তৰ্গত। হিমালয় পৰ্বতমালাৰ দৈৰ্ঘ্য ১০০০ মাইল আৰু বহল ডেৰশ মাইল। নেপালত অৱস্থিত মাউন্ট এভাৰেষ্ট শীৰ্ষ প্ৰায় চাৰে পাঁচ মাইল উচ্চতাৰ। চতুৰ্থ অধ্যায়ত সেইবাবেই ব্যঙ্গ কৰা হৈছিল যে চীনে পৰ্বতৰ মাজেৰে সুৰঙ্গ কৰিব তাত বৰযুণ দিয়াবলৈ। এনে উচ্চতাৰ বাবে হিমালয়ে মৌচুমী বায়ুক ইয়াৰ মাজেৰে পাৰ হৈ যাবলৈ নিদিয়ে, ফলত তিব্বত উপ তুন্দ্ৰা অঞ্চল হ'ল। আনহাতে, উত্তৰ-পূব ভাৰত আৰু দক্ষিণ-পূব এছিয়াৰ বাবে তিব্বত মৌচুমী বায়ুৰ পৰা বৰ্ষা সৃষ্টিকাৰক, পানীৰ উৎস আৰু জলবায়ু নিয়ন্ত্ৰক এই তিনিওটা। তিব্বতক তৃতীয় মেৰু বুলি কোৱা হয় কাৰণ ই এছিয়াৰ হিমবাহৰ স্থান আৰু দক্ষিণ-পূব এছিয়াৰ প্ৰধান নদীবোৰৰ উৎস।

ওপৰৰ চিত্ৰত সোঁফালে ওপৰৰ নদীখন হ'ল য়েল্লৌ (হালধীয়া) ৰিভাৰ বা হোৱাংহো। বহু পৰিমাণৰ হালধীয়া গেদীয় পলস (loess) উটুৱাই আনে বাবে

ইয়াৰ পানীৰ ৰঙ হালধীয়া। হোৱাংহো চীনা সভ্যতাৰ জন্মস্থান। এই নদীৰ উপত্যকাৰ পৰা কেবাটাও পথ ছিল্ক পথলৈ গৈছে।

হেংডুৱান পৰ্বতমালা চীনৰ উত্তৰা-দক্ষিণা পৰ্বতমালা। পঞ্চম অধ্যায়ত হিমালয়ৰ নামচা বাৰৱা দেখুওৱা হৈছে। গায়লা পেৰী ইয়াৰ ওচৰৰ শিখৰ দুয়োটাকে একেলগে যমজ (twin peak) শিখৰ বোলা হয়। নামচা বাৰৱাৰ পিচতে হিমালয়ে দক্ষিণা-পশ্চিমা হয়। এই পৰ্বতক কেংগৰী গাৰপো বোলা হয়। মিচিমি পাহাৰ কেংগৰী গাৰপোৰ অংশ। হেংডুৱান আৰু হিমালয় লগ হোৱা টেকটনিক প্লেটৰ মাজত এইখিনিতে বৰ চাপ আছে। ১৯৫০ চনৰ ভূমিকম্পৰ এয়াই অভিকেন্দ্ৰ আছিল। তেতিয়া পৰশুকুণ্ডৰ কাষখিনি অলপ সলনি হয়। এই অঞ্চল হ'ল ওখ পৰ্বত আৰু গভীৰ উপত্যকাৰ।

মানচিত্ৰ ঃ (১৮) হেংডুৱান অঞ্চল

য়াংচী, মেকং, চলউইন তিনিওখন নদী তিব্বতৰ পৰা ওলাই আহি হেংডুৱানৰ মাজেদি সমান্তৰালভাৱে বৈ গৈছে। য়াংচী এছিয়াৰ দীৰ্ঘতম নদী আৰু পৃথিবীৰ তৃতীয় দীৰ্ঘতম নদী, এই নদী চাংহাইত শেষ হৈছে। চীনৰ জনসংখ্যাৰ এক চতুৰ্থাংশই এই নদীৰ কাষত বাস কৰে। চীনাসকলে য়াংচী নদীৰ ওপৰৰ অংশক জিন্‌চা বুলি কয়। পৃথিৱীৰ তিনিটা পাহাৰৰ মাজৰ ঠেক অংশত বনোৱা সৰ্ববৃহৎ নদীবান্ধ (Three Gorges Dam) এই নদীতেই আছে। মেকং নদী ম্যানমাৰ আৰু লাওচৰ সীমান্তৰ কিছু অংশৰে প্ৰবাহিত হৈ লাওচ, কম্বোডিয়াত, ভিয়েটনামৰ মাজেদি গৈ হো-চি-মিন চহৰৰ (চাইগন) দক্ষিণৰ দক্ষিণ চীনা সাগৰত পৰিছেগৈ। তিনি নদীৰ উৎস অঞ্চলত মেকং নদীক লানকাং বা লাটচাং বুলি জনা যায়। মেকং নামটো লাও ভাষাৰ— মে নাম খং-ৰ পৰা সংক্ষিপ্ত কৰা হৈছে। নুজিয়াং বা নু বা চলউইন তিব্বতৰ টাংকুলা পৰ্বতৰ পৰা উৎপত্তি হৈ য়ুন্নান আৰু ম্যানমাৰেৰে বৈ গৈ আন্দামান সাগৰত পৰিছে। তীব্ৰ সোঁতৰ এই নদীখনক এনে লাগে যেন এটা সুন্দৰ শক্তিৱান তেজী ঘোঁৰাই ভয়ঙ্কৰ থিয় গৰাইদি চেঁকুৰিছে।

এই তিনিওখন নদী অলপ দূৰৰ বাবে অতি ঠেক অঞ্চলৰ মাজেদি গৈছে, যিখিনিত সমান্তৰাল হৈ আছে তাত তিনি সমান্তৰাল নদীৰ ঐতিহাসিক স্থানৰ প্ৰতিষ্ঠা কৰা হৈছে। এই স্থান অৰুণাচল পূৰ্বতম সীমান্তৰ পৰা বেছি দূৰত নহয়। অসমত অৱস্থিত শদিয়াৰ পূব দিশে লক্ষ্য কৰিলে আচলতে পাঁচখন সমান্তৰাল নদী হয়, যদি আমি লোহিত আৰু ইৰাৱতীক যুক্ত কৰো। অৰ্থাৎ, লোহিত, ইৰাৱতী, নু-চলউইন, মেকং, য়াচিং। ইৰাৱতী, বাৰ্মিজ আয়াৰৱাডী, ম্যানমাৰৰ এখন প্ৰধান নদী। দুশ মাইলজুৰি এই তিনি নদী বোৱাটো এটা বিৰল আৰু অলৌকিক ঘটনা। মেকং আৰ য়াচিঙৰ সকলোতকৈ কম দূৰত্ব ৪১ মাইল আৰু মেকং আৰু চলউইনৰ মাজত ১২ মাইল।

চলউইন ইয়াৰ ৭২টা ভাঁজৰ সৈতে এখন যাদুকৰী, মায়াৱতী, আৰু মোহনীয়া নদী। এইখন নদীত মই জনাত এতিয়ালৈকে বান্ধ হোৱা নাই, অন্তত ম্যানমাৰৰ অংশখিনিত। মহাচীনৰ নদীবোৰক চুপ কৰি দিয়া আৰু 'developments at all costs', জলবিদ্যুতৰ ক্ষুধা আৰু হাবিয়াস বেমাৰৰ দৰে হৈছে। চীনে স্থানীয় মানুহৰ প্ৰতিবাদত বৰ্তমান বান্ধ কৰা স্থগিত ৰাখিছে, কিন্তু কিমান দিনলৈ? মই ক'ৰবাত শুনা মতে, আমেৰিকাৰ শীৰ্ষ কূটনীতিজ্ঞ এজনে ম্যানমাৰত থকা কালতে

খটি বৌদ্ধ ভীক্ষু হয়। তেওঁ শীৰ্ষস্থানীয় সন্মানিত ভীক্ষু এজনক ম্যানমাৰৰ উচ্চতম চৰকাৰী বিষয়াজনৰ ওচৰলৈ আনি উচ্চতম চৰকাৰী বিষয়াজনক জামিনত ৰাখিলে যেতিয়ালৈকে তেওঁ বান্ধৰ অনিষ্টকৰাৰ বিষয়ে পতিয়ন নাযায়। উচ্চতম চৰকাৰী বিষয়াজনে চীনক বান্ধ কৰিবলৈ নিদিবলৈ শপত দিবলগা হ'ল। অৱশ্যে চীনক আকৌ প্ৰজ্জ্বলিত হ'বলৈ কিমানদিন লাগিছে, মাত্ৰ সময়-সুযোগলৈ ৰৈ আছে। ম্যানমাৰৰ বান্ধৰ অনিষ্টকাৰৰ লগত যুঁজ কৰিবলৈ আৰু সজাগ হ'বলৈ উত্তৰ-পূবৰ শিক্ষামূলক দায়িত্ব।

মেকং-চলউইন ভাগ বা Mekong Salween Divide-এ হিমালয় আৰু হেংডুৱানক জীৱ-জন্তু আৰু উদ্ভিদৰ ফালৰ পৰা অতি বিচিত্ৰভাৱে ভাগ কৰিছে। হেংডুৱান বৈচিত্ৰ্য ক্ষেত্ৰৰ অন্যতম কেন্দ্ৰবিন্দু।

চিত্ৰ ঃ (১৬) চেলউইনক ইয়াত পাহাৰীয়া অঞ্চলত নিৰ্মিত ঘাইপথৰ দৰে দেখা গৈছে।

চাৰে তিনি মাইল ওখ বাবে তিব্বত মালভূমিত অক্সিজেনৰ পৰিমাণ কম। এই বিষয়ে আগেয়েও উল্লেখ কৰা হৈছে। শ্বিলং পাহাৰৰ শিখৰ প্ৰায় তিনি মাইল, অৰ্থাৎ তিব্বতত থকা মানে শ্বিলঙত নহয় শ্বিলং পাহাৰৰ শীৰ্যত থকা। যদি পেৰুতেই কাৰোবাৰ শ্বাস-প্ৰশ্বাসত ভোগে তীব্ৰত তেওঁৰ বাবে নহয়। তিব্বতৰ স্থায়ী আৰু মূল মানুহখিনিয়ে কম অক্সিজেনৰ আৰু তিব্বতৰ প্ৰাকৃতিক পৰিৱেশত

থাকিবলৈ অভ্যস্ত। হিমালয় আৰু তিব্বতত যথেষ্ট হিমবাহ আছে আৰু হিমালয় মানেই হিমবাহৰ নিবাস। তিব্বতীয় মূলৰ লোকসকল অতি পৰিৱেশ সচেতন। তেওঁলোকে অতি দুৰ্গম ঠাইত বাস কৰে। এনেয়ে ওখ, তাতে পাহাৰ। মালভূমি অংশত গৰখীয়া (ভেৰাৰখীয়া, আচলতে য়াক ৰখীয়া) যাযাবৰী লোকে গৰমৰ দিনত ওপৰলৈ যায়, ঠাণ্ডাৰ দিনত কিছু তললৈ নামি আহে। য়াক নামৰ গৰুৰ নিচিনা জন্তু তাত পায় আৰু য়াকৰ গাখীৰ খায়, য়াকৰ মঙহো খায়। পাহাৰৰ মাজে মাজে মঠ বা বৌদ্ধ বিহাৰবোৰ আছে। সাধাৰণতে, তাৰ কাষতে গাঁও থাকে। শীতৰ অনুকূল হোৱা ঠাইত তেওঁলোকে তাত ঘেঁহু বা গম আৰু বাৰ্লিৰ খেতি কৰে।

কৈলাস এটা অসাধাৰণ পাহাৰ। হিন্দু, তিব্বতীয়, জৈন সকলোৰে বাবে পৱিত্ৰ আৰু পুণ্যৰ পাহাৰ বাবে চীনে বিশ্বক ভয় কৰি ইয়ালৈ যাবলৈ দি আছে কিন্তু তেওঁলোকৰ খেলৰ বিধি মতে। কৈলাসত চৌম্বকীয় কম্পাছে কাম নকৰে, দিশ মতে নুঘূৰে আৰু তাত সময় দৌৰে বুলি কয়। মানুহৰ নখ এসপ্তাহতে বহু দীঘল হয়। ইয়াত কিবা যে শক্তি আছে সি সঁচা। কৈলাস পাহাৰটো চাৰি চুকৰ বৰ্গক্ষেত্ৰৰ ওপৰত থকা পিৰামিড এটাৰ নিচিনা। ইয়াৰ এটা দিশ দিশত গৌৰী কুণ্ড আৰু নন্দী-ভৃঙ্গি কুণ্ড আছে। ইয়ালৈ যোৱা এটা বাট ভাৰত-নেপাল সীমান্তৰ নেপালগঞ্জৰ পৰা নেপালৰ ছিমিক'টলৈ, ছিমিক'টৰ পৰা খোজকাঢ়ি দুসপ্তাহত কৈলাস ঘূৰিব পাৰি। তীব্বত, উত্তৰাখণ্ড আৰু নেপালৰ ট্ৰাই জংচনত থকা লিপুলেখ গিৰিপথেৰে আগতে কৈলাসলৈ যোৱা হৈছিল। লিপুলেখৰ পৰা কৈলাসলৈ পাঁচ কিলোমিটাৰমান। ভাৰতে এতিয়া লিপুলেখৰ ওচৰলৈকে ৰাস্তা কৰা বাবেই চীনা মহাৰাজৰ খং। ২০২০ৰ চীনা-ভাৰত সংঘৰ্ষ পাঙ্গন চ'ক লৈ। (চ' তিব্বতীয় শব্দ, অৰ্থ হ্ৰদ) পাঙ্গন চ' আগতে কৈ অহা য়ামড্ৰক চ'ৰ দৰে এটা হ্ৰদ যাৰ পৰা পানী বাহিৰলৈ নোলায়। পাঙ্গন চ'ৰ পানী কিন্তু কিছু লুণীয়া।

চীনৰ গোবি মৰুভূমিও তিব্বতৰ পাৰ্বত্য অঞ্চলৰ বৰ্ষাছায়াৰ ফলাফল। গোবি মৰুভূমিৰ অংশ বিশেষ মঙ্গোলিয়াত আৰু কিছু অংশ চীনত পৰে। অজানিত কাৰণত চীনৰ আতংক বঢ়াই গোবি মৰুভূমিৰ বিস্তৃতি বাঢ়িহে গৈছে। যদিও চীন আকাৰত পৃথিৱীৰ চতুৰ্থ ইয়াৰ এক-তৃতীয়াংশতকৈ বেছি মাটি মৰুভূমিৰে ভৰা।

তলত মধ্য স্থানৰ এই বৰফ আবৃত শৃংগটো হৈছে কৈলাস পৰ্বত। মানস

সৰোবৰ হ্ৰদ কোনোমতে দৃশ্যমান। ইয়াত দেখা পোৱা নদীখন হৈছে য়াৰলুং ছাংপো।

চিত্ৰ ঃ (১৭) কৈলাস পাহাৰৰ প্ৰতিসাম্য দিশৰ ছবি, সমুখত ব্ৰহ্মপুত্ৰই গঢ় লৈছে।

ছাংপোৰ মহাভাঁজ (বিগ বেণ্ড বা গ্ৰেট বেণ্ড)

(এই অধ্যায়ৰ প্ৰথমখন চিত্ৰত ইয়াক 'BB' হিচাবে দেখুওৱা হৈছে)

য়াৰলুং ছাংপোৰ বাহিৰে ভাৰতলৈ তিব্বতৰ পৰা অহা আনখন শক্তিশালী নদী হ'ল সিন্ধু। য়াৰলুং ছাংপোৰ গভীৰ খাদ মাৰ্কিন যুক্তৰাষ্ট্ৰৰ গভীৰ খাদতকৈ বেছি দীঘল আৰু ই পৃথিৱীৰ ভিতৰতেই আটাইতকৈ গভীৰ খাদ। ইয়াৰ গভীৰতা ৩১৪ মাইল বা ৫০৪.৬ কিলোমিটাৰ। ভাঁজ অংশত য়াৰলুং ছাংপো অতি সংকীৰ্ণ পথেৰে আগুৱাই আহিছে। ছাংপো নদীৰ উৎপত্তি কৈলাস পৰ্বতৰ গাতে লগা আংছি গ্লেছিয়াৰ যদিও কৈলাস পৰ্বতৰ মুখতে থকা মানস সৰোবৰকে ইয়াৰ উৎপত্তিস্থল বুলি ধৰিব পাৰি। তিব্বতৰ মাজেদি বৈ যাওঁতে স্বীগাতছে, তিব্বতৰ

দ্বিতীয় ডাঙৰ নগৰ আৰু লাছাৰ ওচৰেদি গৈছে। লাছা তিব্বতৰ ৰাজধানী আৰু ছাংপোৰ দক্ষিণত। নদীখন অৰুণাচলৰ উত্তৰত নামছা বাৰৱা নামৰ ওখ পৰ্বত য'ত পাইছে সেইখিনক পেই (Pei) অঞ্চল বোলে। এই গাঁওখনেই য়াৰলুং ছাংপোৰ দ খাৰৈৰ প্ৰৱেশদ্বাৰত স্থিত। ইয়াৰ পৰা নদীখন নামচা বাৰৱাৰ শিখৰৰ চাৰিওফালে ঘূৰি পিছত দক্ষিণলৈ আহিছে। পাহাৰৰ মাজৰ সংকীৰ্ণ ঠাইত ঘূৰোঁতে ই ২,৯০০ মিটাৰ ওখৰ পৰা আৰম্ভ কৰি ১,৫০০ মিটাৰ উচ্চতালৈ নামি আহিছে। ইয়াতেই আন এখন উপনদা প' ছাংপো লগ হৈছে। গড়ে ৬৬০ মিটাৰ উচ্চতাত এই নদীয়ে ভাৰতৰ অৰুণাচলত প্ৰৱেশ কৰিছে, আৰু ভাৰতবৰ্ষত ব্ৰহ্মপুত্ৰ নামেৰে জনাজাত হৈছে। এতিয়ালৈকে তিব্বতৰ মানস সৰোবৰ হ্ৰদৰহে উল্লেখ হৈছে, আচলতে তিব্বতত পৃথিৱীৰ ভিতৰতে আটাইতকৈ সৰহ আলপাইন হ্ৰদ আছে। পৱিত্ৰ মানস সৰোবৰৰ পানী স্ফটিকৰ দৰে স্বচ্ছ। সংস্কৃত ভাষাৰ কবি আৰু নাট্যকাৰ বিখ্যাত কালিদাসে কৈছিল— মানস সৰোবৰৰ পানী 'মুকুতাৰ নিচিনা'। তিব্বতত দহটা পৱিত্ৰ হ্ৰদ আছে। য়ামড্ৰক চ' (মনত ৰাখিব, তিব্বতীয় ভাষাত Tso মানে হ্ৰদ যেনে পাঙ্গন চ', লা মানে পাচ যেনে Se la অৰ্থাৎ চে পাচ, মই তিব্বতীয় ভাষাৰ চ' আৰু লা লিখাটো পচন্দ কৰো) য়ামড্ৰক চ'ৰ পৰা পানী ক'লৈকো নোলায় আৰু কোনো নদী ইয়াত পৰা নাই। ইয়াৰ পানীৰ উৎস ওচৰৰ বৰফাবৃত পৰ্বতৰ শিখৰবোৰ। বৰফ গলা আৰু পানী বাষ্প হোৱাৰ এটা অনুকুল সামঞ্জস্য আছে, কিন্তু এই হ্ৰদৰ পানী শুকাই আহিছে, এটা জলবিদ্যুৎ প্ৰকল্পৰ বাবে। এই প্ৰকল্পই লাছাই বিজুলী যোগায়। এইবোৰ হ্ৰদে পৃথিৱীৰ পৰিবেশতন্ত্ৰলৈ অদান আগবঢ়ায়। চীনে সেউজ বুলি গৰ্ব কৰে, অকল বিজুলীৰ বাবেহে, বিজুলীৰ দ্বাৰা চলিত বাছ চলায়, কিন্তু বিজুলী আহে নদীক চুপ কৰি, তিব্বতৰ ক্ষেত্ৰত তীব্বতৰ পৃথিৱীৰ ওপৰত কি প্ৰভাৱ তাক নাভাবে। য়ামড্ৰক চ' লাছাৰ পৰা মাত্ৰ দুই-তিনি ঘণ্টাৰ বাট। এই পথ সম্পূৰ্ণ বছৰেই সুগম হৈ থাকে। এই হ্ৰদক মিঠা পানীৰ হ্ৰদ বোলা হয়। হ্ৰদটো শীতকালত আংশিকভাৱে গোট মাৰে। আগতেই কৈছোঁ, এই হ্ৰদে প্ৰাকৃতিক পৰিৱেশ ব্যৱস্থাৰ লগত সুৰ মিলায়। তিব্বতত য়ামড্ৰক চ'ৰ নিচিনা বহুতো হ্ৰদ আছে, য'ত কোনো নদী পৰা নাই আৰু য'ৰ পৰা কোনো নদী ওলোৱা নাই। এই হ্ৰদবোৰ পুখুৰীৰ দৰে, ইয়াত পানী নোসোমাইও আৰু পানী ওলাইও নাযায়। এইবোৰ নষ্ট কৰিলে প্ৰাকৃতিক বহু বিনষ্ট হ'ব।

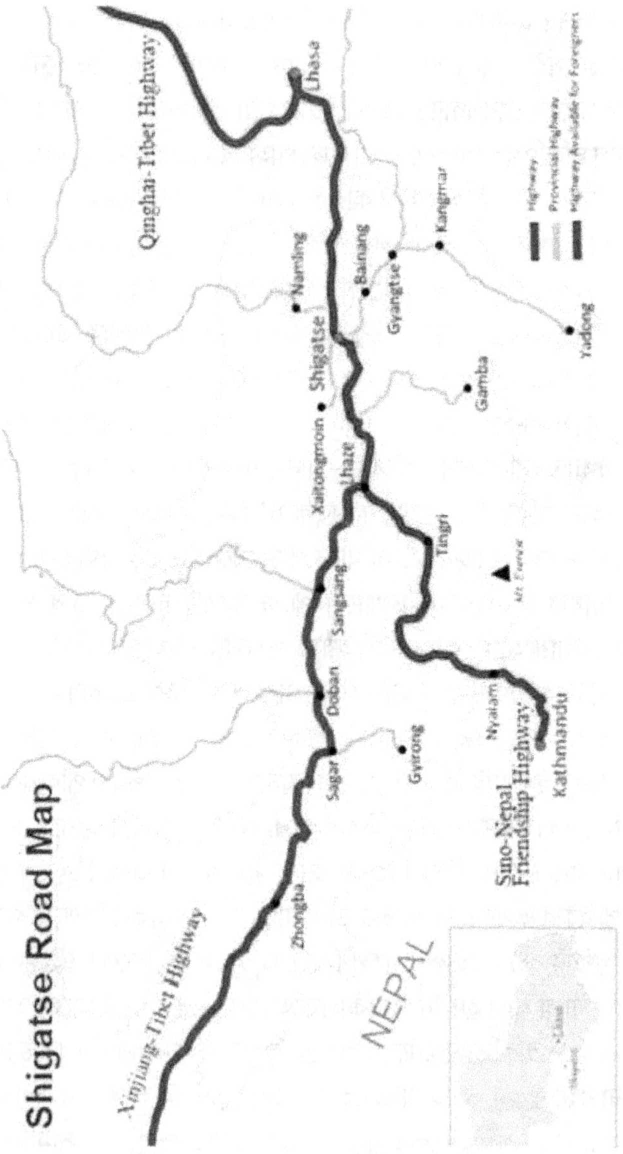

মানচিত্ৰ ঃ (১৬) নতুন ৰাস্তাবোৰ

চীনৰ মালভূমি টাকলা মাকান চীনৰ উত্তৰ-পশ্চিমৰ জিং জিয়াঙত। কথিত মতে, ইয়ালৈকে চীনে য়াৰলুং ছাংপোৰ পানী সুৰঙ্গৰে গতি কৰোৱাৰ আশা ৰাখিছে। ছাংপোৰ পৰা আগতেও পানী উত্তৰ চীনলৈ নিবৰ চেষ্টা চলিছিল কিন্তু উচ্চতাৰ পাৰ্থক্য আৰু আন প্ৰাকৃতিক ভুগোলৰ সুবিধা, উচ্চতা মতে নিমিলিল। টাকলা মাকানলৈ সুৰংগ কৰি পানী বোৱাই নিয়া কাৰণবোৰ জানিবলৈ আমি এই অঞ্চলৰ পানীৰ অৱস্থা জানিব লাগিব আৰু সমস্যাবোৰৰ পৰা শিক্ষা আহৰণ কৰিব লাগিব। চীনৰ এই শুকান অংশটো বৃহত্তম কঁপাহ উৎপাদন কৰা অঞ্চল আছিল। স্থানীয় লোকসকল অৰ্থাৎ তাৰিম নদীৰ পাৰৰ এই স্থানীয় জনগোষ্ঠীৰ কঁপাহ খেতি জীৱিকাৰ প্ৰধান উপায়। এই ঠাই সাগৰৰ লেভেলতকৈ ওখৰ বাবে ইয়াৰ ওচৰৰ বৰফ গলা পানীয়ে এসময়ত তাৰিম নদীৰ পানী উপচাইছিল। শেহতীয়াভাৱে, এই নদীখন ঋতুকালীন নদীত পৰিণত হৈছিল। টাকলা মাকানৰ পাহাৰৰ হিমবাহসমূহ হ্ৰাস হৈ গৈ আছে, যদিও এইখিনিত পৃথিৱীৰ বহুত ওখ শৃংগ আছে। চীনৰ দুই দশকজোৰা তাৰিম নদী নৱজীৱন প্ৰকল্প ব্যৰ্থ হৈছে। মধ্য এছিয়া চীনৰ পশ্চিমৰ অঞ্চল। মধ্য এছিয়াৰ হিমবাহ দ্ৰুত গতিত হ্ৰাস পোৱাত চীনা মহাৰজাই তীব্ৰতলৈ চকু দিছে। চীন বিশ্বৰ এক পঞ্চমাংশ হিমবাহৰ অধিকাৰী। কিন্তু বৰ্তমান যি গতিত হিমবাহ বিলুপ্ত হৈছে, চীনে ভৱিষ্যতৰ বাবে অকল নিজৰ কথা ভাবিছে। মধ্য এছিয়াৰ উত্তৰলৈ ৰাছিয়া আৰু দক্ষিণলৈ কাস্পিয়ান সাগৰ (বা হ্ৰদ)। ইয়াৰ দেশবোৰৰ নামৰ শেষত stan বা 'land of' লগোৱা আছে। উদাহৰণ হ'ল উজবেকিস্তান, তুৰ্কমেনিস্তান, কাজাকাস্তান, তাজিকিস্তান, কিৰ্গিস্তান। এই পামিৰ অঞ্চলক মই তিব্বতীয় মালভূমিৰ পৰিৱেশ অঞ্চল হিচাবে বিবেচনা কৰো। মধ্য এছিয়াত পামিৰ পৰ্বতমালা বেলেগ বেলেগ দিশলৈ বিস্তৃত, পুব পামিৰ, পশ্চিম পামিৰ আৰু পামিৰ-আলাই বুলি জনাজাত। সেইফালৰ পৰা চালে হিমালয়, কাৰাকোৰাম আৰু কুনলুন পুবলৈ আহিছে। আগতে পামিৰকে পৃথিৱীৰ মুধচ বোলা হৈছিল, এতিয়া অৱশ্যে তিব্বতকহে মুধচ বোলা যায়।

আগৰ অধ্যায়ত আৰল সাগৰ শুকোৱা আৰু সংকুচিত হোৱাৰ কথা উল্লেখ কৰা হৈছে। এইটো পৃথিৱীৰ কাৰণে এটা ডাঙৰ মানৱসৃষ্ট প্ৰাকৃতিক দুৰ্যোগ। তলত আৰল সাগৰৰ আৰু চিৰ দৰিয়া, আম্পু আদিৰ মানচিত্ৰ অন্তৰ্ভুক্ত কৰা হৈছে। দুৰ্ভাগ্যবশতঃ মধ্য এছিয়াৰ হিমবাহৰ দুৰ্দশা হিমালয়ৰ দিশে আহিছে।

সমস্যাৰ বিষয়ে নজনা আৰু সমাধানৰ বাবে নভবাটো আমাৰ বাবে এটা ডাঙৰ ভুল হ'ব। শীঘ্ৰেই ইয়াৰ প্ৰতিৰোধৰ বাবে সজাগ হোৱাটো অতি প্ৰয়োজনীয় হৈ পৰিছে।

মানচিত্ৰ ঃ (২০) চিৰ দৰিয়া, আমু দৰিয়া, পামিৰ আৰু তাৰম বেচিন

।। অষ্টম অধ্যায় ।।

পানীৰ চলনা, সাগৰৰ পানী বৃদ্ধি

২১০০ চনত হিমালয় আৰু হিন্দুকোষৰ হিমবাহসমূহ গলি যাব বুলি পৰ্যবেক্ষণ আৰু যুক্তিভিত্তিত ভৱিষ্যদ্বাণী কৰা হৈছে। এই বিষয়ে অস্বীকাৰ ক'তো পোৱা নাযাব। জনপ্ৰিয় প্ৰশ্নটো হ'ল, কেতিয়া অতি বেয়া অৱস্থাটো পাবগৈ? এই কিতাপখনত মই কেৱল উত্তৰ-পূবৰ ৰাজ্যসমূহত গুৰুত্ব দিছোঁ আৰু কেন্দ্ৰীভূত কৰিছোঁ। ব্ৰহ্মপুত্ৰৰ পাৰৰ জনসাধাৰণৰ কাৰণে এটা প্ৰতাৰণামূলক বাস্তৱ ৰৈ আছে। হিমবাহবোৰ গলি যোৱাৰ লগেলগে ব্ৰহ্মপুত্ৰত পানী বাঢ়িব (চীনে ওপৰত একো নকৰে বুলি ধৰি লৈ)। গতিকে যেন ব্ৰহ্মপুত্ৰত যথেষ্ট পানী আছে বুলি ভুল ধাৰণা হ'ব পাৰে। ইয়াকে মই প্ৰতাৰণা পানীৰ চলনা বুলিছোঁ।

অৱশ্যে, যদি হিমপ্ৰৱাহ লাহে লাহে যায় তেতিয়াহে এইটো সত্য হ'ব। যদিহে টুকুৰা টুকুৰ হৈ বৰফ ভাঙি পৰে, এভালান্‌ছ বা হিমস্খলন হয়, বিনাশ বা ক্ষয় চকুত পৰিব। মুঠতে হিমবাহৰ যদি নিৰীক্ষণ বা পৰ্যবেক্ষণ নহয় তলৰ পৰা আচল কাৰণটো গম পোৱা নাযাব। আনহাতে, কাৰাকোৰাম বা হিন্দুকোষৰ নামনি অঞ্চলত বানপানী দেখা যাব পাৰে। কাশ্মীৰৰ হিমালয়ত থকা অৱন্তিপুৰৰ নিচিনা ঠাইত সৰু-সুৰা দলং উটুৱাই নিব পাৰে। যদিহে হিমপ্ৰৱাহৰ পৰ্যবেক্ষণ নিশ্চিত নহয় তেতিয়া জনসাধাৰণক বিপথে পৰিচালিত কৰাৰ সম্ভাৱনা আছে। জলবায়ু পৰিৱৰ্তনৰ কিছু লক্ষণ অসমত পোৱা গৈছে। বজ্ৰপাতৰ ফলত অধিক লোকৰ মৃত্যু হৈছে অৰ্থাৎ ওপৰৰ বায়ুত স্থিতশীল বিজুলী বাঢ়িছে। ইতিমধ্যে, ২০১৯ চনৰ এপ্ৰিল মাহৰ সৰ্বোচ্চ তাপমাত্ৰা ৰেকৰ্ড হৈছে। ২০১৪ চনৰ সময়ছোৱাত অসমত সৰ্বাধিক ভূমিকম্পৰ অভিজ্ঞতা হৈছে। মিজোৰামত ২০২০ চনৰ জুনত এমাহত দহটা ভূমিকম্প হৈছে। মনত ৰাখিব হিমবাহসমূহক গলাৰ পৰা বাধা দিবৰ বাবে গোলকীয় উষ্ণতা দুই ডিগ্ৰী নহ'লেও অন্ততঃ ১.৫ ডিগ্ৰী চেলচিয়াছৰ তলত ৰাখিব লাগিব। ভাৰতবৰ্ষই পোনপটীয়াভাৱে চীনৰ পৰা হিমবাহ সলনিৰ

তথ্য বিচাৰি অনুৰোধ জনাব লাগিব। উত্তৰ-পূব বিশেষকৈ ছাংপোত চীনৰ পাঁচটা নদীবান্ধ হোৱাত যাতে খৰালিও ব্ৰহ্মপুত্ৰই সঠিকভাৱে পানী পায় সেইটোলৈ চকু ৰাখিব লাগিব। সেউজ গৃহ গেছ আৰু কাৰ্বন-ডাই-অক্সাইডৰ পৰিমাণ সৰ্বনিম্নলৈ নিব পাৰিব লাগিব।

বিবিচি নিউজত (নবীন সিং খাদকাৰ, ২৯ মাৰ্চ, ২০১৯) মাউণ্ট এভাৰেষ্টৰ গ্লেছিয়াৰ গলাৰ বাবে বহুত সংখ্যক পৰ্বতাৰোহীৰ মৃতদেহ উদ্ভাসিত হোৱাৰ খবৰ দিছে। মাৰ্কিন যুক্তৰাষ্ট্ৰৰ উপকূলসমূহত সমুদ্ৰ পৃষ্ঠৰ উত্থানে মানুহক আন ঠাইলৈ স্থানচ্যুতি কৰোৱা হৈছে। মেইন, ৰ'ড আইলেণ্ড, লুইজিয়ানা, ফ্লৰিডা, নিউয়ৰ্ক আৰু কেলিফৰ্ণিয়াৰ উপকূলৰ সমুদ্ৰপৃষ্ঠৰ পানী উঠি অহাৰ বাবদ উপকূলীয় সম্প্ৰদায়ৰ সংঘৰ্ষৰ কথা 'Rising, Dispatches from the American Shore' বোলা গ্ৰন্থখনত এলিজাবেথ ৰাছে বৰ্ণনা কৰিছে। আমেৰিকা এখন বিশাল দেশ বাবে ইয়াত অতি বেয়া অৱস্থা অহা নাই। অন্যান্য উপকূলীয় অঞ্চলৰ ভিতৰত চাংহাইৰ কিছু অংশ ডুব যোৱা খবৰ সদৰী হৈছে। বাংলাদেশে সমুদ্ৰস্তৰৰ বৃদ্ধিৰ বিৰুদ্ধে যুঁজ আৰম্ভ কৰিছে। মই এতিয়া এলিজাবেথ ৰাছৰ কিতাপখনৰ কিছু কথালৈ আহিছোঁ।

কিন্তু তাৰ আগতে অলপ ভাৰত-বাংলাদেশৰ সীমান্তৰ বিৱৰণ দিছোঁ। সাধাৰণতে বিভিন্ন দেশৰ মাজত দেৱাল বা কপিবেৰা দিয়া নহয়। বিশেষকৈ বেৰাৰ তলেৰে সুৰঙ্গ খান্দিবলৈ বা আন বুদ্ধি কৰিবলৈ বিশেষ টান নহয়। বাংলাদেশৰ সীমান্ত ভাৰতৰ কে'বাখনো প্ৰদেশৰ মাজেৰে গৈছে। প্ৰদেশবোৰ হ'ল— অসম, মেঘালয়, ত্ৰিপুৰা, মিজোৰাম আৰু পশ্চিমবংগ। সীমান্তৰ গোটেইখিনি নদী তীৰৰ সমভূমি, জংঘল বা সৰু পাহাৰ। কোনো প্ৰাকৃতিক অন্তৰায় বা দুৰ্গম বাধা নাই। জলবহুল আৰু বেছিভাগতে সীমান্তৰ শেষলৈকে খেতিপথাৰ। সমস্যাৰ ভিতৰত অবৈধ গৰুৰ বেপাৰ এটা সমস্যা যিটো বোধকৰো সমাধান কৰিব পৰা যায়। তথাপিও দুশ গাঁৱৰ অৱস্থিতি দুয়োপিনে, বহুত ছিটমহল, সকলো সমস্যা বেৰাই সমাধান কৰিব পৰা নাই। আগেয়ে ৰজাই পাশাখেলত হেৰুৱাই ভূমি স্থানান্তৰ কৰিছিল। এতিয়া এইবোৰ এটা সৰু সৰু অংশ যিটো ইখন ৰাষ্ট্ৰৰ ভিতৰত পৰে। অৰ্থাৎ এখন ভাৰতীয় সৰু গাঁও বাংলাদেশৰ ভিতৰত, কিছু বাংলাদেশী গাঁও ভাৰতত।

বাংলাদেশ আৰু ভাৰতবৰ্ষৰ সীমান্তত কৰা পৃথিৱীৰ আটাইতকৈ দীৰ্ঘতম কাটাতাঁৰৰ ওপৰত ৰিপ'ৰ্ট এটা লিখাৰ এছাইনমেণ্টত এলিজাবেথ ৰাছ আহিছিল বাংলাদেশলৈ। তেতিয়াই এলিজাবেথ ৰাছে বুজি পালে যে কাটাতাঁৰৰ বেৰা কেৱল এটা প্ৰযুক্তিগত কথা, প্ৰকৃত সমস্যাটো হ'ল পানী। তেতিয়াৰ পৰা ৰাছ সমুদ্ৰৰ জলপৃষ্ঠৰ ওপৰলৈ অহাৰ কথাৰ বাবে সচেতন হয়। ফাহাৰুল নামৰ ল'ৰা এটাই তেওঁক ধূলিময় চৰত কৰা সৰিয়হ খেতি দেখুৱাইছিল। সেই ঠাইখিনি এসময়ত খেতিৰ বাবে উপযুক্ত অৰ্থাৎ সাৰুৱা আছিল। ৰাছে লিখিছে, “ফাহাৰুলে নিজৰ শিপা উভালি তাৰ পৰিয়ালৰ পৈতৃক ভূমি এৰি যাবলগাৰ সম্ভাৱনাৰ কথা কৈছিল। তাৰ সম্বন্ধীয় ভায়েকে ইতিমধ্যেই সেই ঠাই এৰি ভাৰতবৰ্ষলৈ গুচি গৈছে।” অৰ্থাৎ সেইখিনি ঠাই অলপতে ডুবিব।

এলিজাবেথ ৰাছে তাৰ পিচত আমেৰিকান উপকূলৰ বেলেগ বেলেগ ঠাইবোৰত সমুদ্ৰ পৃষ্ঠৰ পানী কিমান উঠি আহিছে, সেই বিষয়ে অধ্যয়ন কৰে আৰু তেওঁৰ ‘নেটিভ ইণ্ডিয়ান’ (জন্মগত দেশী মানুহ, আমেৰিকান ইণ্ডিয়ান বুলিও কোৱা হয়) উপকূলৰ অঞ্চল কিছুমানে (নিজৰ আৰু আন) ভ্ৰমণ কৰে। প্ৰথমে, তেওঁ মেইন, গল্‌ফ ক'ষ্ট আদি পানীৰ কাষৰ ঠাইবোৰলৈ যায়। ৰ'ড আইলেণ্ডৰ জেকব প্লেচত তেওঁ প্ৰথমে মৃত ‘টুপোলো’ গছ দেখিবলৈ পায়। মেইন, লুইজিয়ান আৰু দক্ষিণৰ গল্‌ফ ক'ষ্টৰ ওচৰত এই আকৰ্ষণীয় গছজোপা পোৱা যায়। শীতত ইয়াৰ পাতবোৰ ৰঙা হৈ যায়, গৰমত বেৰী ফল উৎপাদন কৰে। যথেষ্ট ওখ হয়, চাইপ্ৰাছ আৰু টুপোলো এইবোৰ ঠাইত একেলগে হোৱা দেখা যায়। লুইজিয়ানাৰ ‘আইল দ্য জিন চাৰ্লছ’ যিখিনি ‘বিলাস্কী-ছিটিমাছা-ছ'কট’ ৰাষ্ট্ৰ স্বীকৃত জনজাতীয় ভূমি তেওঁ ৰেমপাইক, অধিকাংশ মৰা চাইপ্ৰাছ গছ দেখিবলৈ পায়। ৰেমপাইক মানে ঠিয় হৈ থকা, পাত নাইকিয়া, ছাল নাইকিয়া মৃত গছ, সাধাৰণতে জুইত পোৰা গছৰ নিচিনা। এই টুপোলো বা চাইপ্ৰাইছ গছবোৰে সমুদ্ৰৰ লুণীয়া পানী পালে লাহে লাহে মৰিবলৈ আৰম্ভ কৰে। প্ৰথমে পাতবোৰ সৰি যায় তাৰপিছত ইয়াৰ ছালবোৰ এৰাই যায়। অৰ্থাৎ ই লুণীয়া পানীৰ প্ৰৱেশৰ প্ৰথম সংকেত। তেওঁ সম্প্ৰদায়সকলে নিজৰ পিতৃভূমি বা য'ত নিজা মাছধৰা, টুপোলোৰ পৰা মৌ কৰা আদি ত্যাগ কৰি আন এটা স্থানত মাত্ৰ মাটি আৰু ঘৰ এটা পোৱাটো কিমান দুখৰ তাক বৰ্ণনা কৰিছে।

ব্ৰহ্মপুত্ৰৰ নিচিনা ডাঙৰ নদী এখন অসমৰ মাজেৰে প্ৰৱাহিত হোৱাৰ বাবদ আৰু এতিয়াও বাৰিষাত বৰষুণ, কম-বেছি পৰিমাণে হ'লেও, জলবায়ু পৰিৱৰ্তনৰ আহিবলগীয়া কদৰ্য ৰূপটোৰ কথা স্থানীয় লোকে ভবা নাই। আচৰিত যে, কৰোনা ৰোগত লকডাউন হোৱাতহে মানুহে কিমান দূষিত বায়ুত আছিল মন কৰিছে। আমেৰিকাৰ গাড়ীৰ কাৰ্বন-ডাই-অক্সাইডক এসময়ত বিলাসিতা এমিছন বুলি কোৱা চীনেই এতিয়া ধনী আৰু শক্তিশালী হৈ দহগুণ চাৰিলেন হাইৱে' কৰি গাড়ীৰ সংখ্যা এশ গুণ বঢ়াই দূষিত বায়ু কিমান বঢ়ালে উত্তৰ-পূবে তাৰ হিচাপে ৰখা নাই। কিন্তু, এইটো সময় আত্মানুসন্ধান আৰু বিশ্লেষণৰ সময়। সম্ভাব্য সমস্যাবোৰৰ ভিতৰত কি হ'ব যদিহে মৌচুমী বায়ুৰ পেটাৰ্নটো পঞ্চাশ মাইল পূব আৰু পশ্চিমফালে স্থানান্তৰিত হয়। যদি পৰ্যবেক্ষণৰ মানসতা নাথাকে 'বইলিং ফ্ৰগ' লক্ষণ হ'ব। আপুনি যদি ভেকুলী এটা উতলা পানীত দিয়ে সি ততালিকে জাঁপ মাৰে। আনহাতে যদি ঠাণ্ডা পানীত থৈ পানীখিনি লাহে লাহে গৰম কৰে সি অতি গৰম নোহোৱালৈকে নজঁপিয়ায়। কিন্তু তেতিয়ালৈকে সমস্যা দূৰ পাবগৈ। এতিয়ালৈকে বায়ুৰ সকলো ধৰণৰ কম্পিউটাৰ মডেলিং হোৱা নাই, আগলৈ হ'ব পাৰে। কিন্তু তেতিয়ালৈকে বৈ থাকিব নোৱাৰি। এতিয়া চোৱা যাওক বৰষুণৰ উপকাৰিতা কিমান। বৰষুণে বায়ুৰ অপকাৰী সৰু সৰু কণাবোৰ ঘণীভূত কৰে আৰু জলবায়ু পৰিষ্কাৰ কৰে। সেইবোৰত উত্তৰ-পূব দিল্লীৰ দৰে 'লু' বা গৰম ধূলিৰ বতাহ নব'লে। আনহাতে, শীতকালত বহুত ঠাই ধূলিময় হৈ পৰে, সেউজীয়া বৰণ অদৃশ্য হৈ পৰে। ধূলিয়ে ৰোগ বিয়পায়। উত্তৰ-পূবত যিহেতু এটা ঋতুতহে বৰষুণ হয়, এই অঞ্চলে বৰষুণৰ পানী সংগ্ৰহ কৰি ৰাখিব লাগে। শীতত গছ, বটপথ আদিত ঢালিবলৈ যথেষ্ট পানী ৰাখিব লাগে। তদুপৰি, বায়ুৰ অপকাৰী সৰু সৰু কণাবোৰ কেমিকেল হ'লে এচিড বৰষুণ হয়।

ছিয়াং নদীৰ কাহিনীটোলৈ ঘূৰি আহিছোঁ। নদীৰ ওপৰত শেহতীয়া খবৰ এইটো— '২০১৮ চনৰ আগষ্ট মাহত ছিয়াং নদীত সাগৰৰ তৰংগৰ দৰে বিশাল ঢৌ দেখা পোৱা গৈছে'। এই ঢৌ এসপ্তাহ ধৰি আছিল। তাৰ কাৰণ এতিয়ালৈকে জনা হোৱা নাই। ছিয়াঙৰ পানী লেতেৰা হোৱাৰ কাৰণ পলিমাৰৰ ৰেজিন আঠা বুলি অনানুষ্ঠানিকভাৱে জনা গ'ল, ডাঙৰ নিৰ্মাণৰ ধূলি গুচাবলৈ এই আঠা ব্যৱহাৰ কৰা হয়, পানীৰ লগত জড়িত থকা প্ৰকল্পত নহয়। কিন্তু কোনে কি প্ৰকল্প কৰিছে,

সুৰঙ্গৰ বাবেই নে আদি খবৰ ক'তো পোৱা নগ'ল। এই কাহিনীৰ শেষ এতিয়ালৈকে নাই।

Siyang River at Pasighat. A huge current in the river
was observed while visiting Pasighat on 19th Aug.'18.
The level and current is still increasing to a danger
level after China released its three big dams recently
bringing threat to the areas downstream of it.

চিত্ৰ ঃ (১৮) ছিয়াং নদীত সাগৰৰ নিচিনা অশান্ত ঢৌ, আগষ্ট, ২০১৮

ফটো ঃ ডাক্তৰ সনত দত্ত

○○○

।। নৱম অধ্যায় ।।

বৰ্ষা অঞ্চলত পানী সংৰক্ষণ

উত্তৰ-পূবৰ দুটা ডাঙৰ প্ৰত্যাহ্বান, প্ৰথম হিমালয়ৰ নিচিনা চালুকীয়া পৰ্বতৰ ঠিয় গৰাত, গেদ, পলসৰ আশীৰ্বাদ আৰু তৰাং হোৱা নদীৰ কাযত সহবাস কৰা আৰু পৰিবেশতন্ত্ৰ যথাযথভাৱে সংৰক্ষণ কৰা। দ্বিতীয়, বৰ্ষা সময়ৰ পানী অকল বৈ যাবলৈ নিদি শীতলৈ সংৰক্ষণ কৰা।

জলবায়ু সলনি, ফ্লাড প্লেইন, গেদ, স্পঞ্জ চিটি আদি স্থানীয় লোকৰ বাবে সাধাৰণ জ্ঞানৰ কথা, সকলোৰেই একোজন মোলাই (যাদৱ পায়েং) নিজা নিজা অৱদানত। বাঁহৰ পাইপেৰে আৰু সৰু নলাৰে বৰষুণৰ পানী যিমান পাৰে ৰাখক। প্ৰচণ্ডভাৱে অহা পানীক (surge) বলাই ধৰি ৰাখিবলৈ মথাউৰি বা ওখ আলিৰ উপৰি এলানি নলাৰে সংযুক্ত পুখুৰী হ'লেও হ'ব। ৰকেট বিজ্ঞানী নালাগে, দিল্লীৱালা ব্ৰেইনো নালাগে (ৰাজধানীৰ ব্ৰেইন), থলুৱা মাথাৰেই হ'ব, ৰাইজৰ ইচ্ছাহে আৱশ্যক, চৰকাৰক কেৱল যথাযথ মাটিখিনি খোজক। তলত বহলাই লিখিছোঁ। অসম এনেয়েই ন-সম নহয়, উত্তৰ-পূব দিল্লী হ'ব নালাগে। উত্তৰ-

পূবে ভাৰতক অতিকৈ আৱশ্যকীয় অক্সিজেনখিনি দিব দূষিত বায়ু আৰু কাৰ্বন কমাব। হাইলেণ্ড আৰু ল'লেণ্ড দুয়োৱে পানী ক'ত বন্ধ হয়, ক'ত বিপদ ঘটাব পাৰে তাৰ উমৈহতীয়া জ্ঞান থাকিব লাগিব। পাহাৰৰ পাদদেশৰ মাটি পানী শোষণ কৰিব নোৱাৰাকৈ তিতি গ'লে পাহাৰ আৰু ভৈয়াম দুয়োলৈকে বেয়া। পাহাৰৰ ভূমিস্খলন হ'ব।

এখন সুস্থ নদীয়ে বানপানী কৰে, কিন্তু ওপৰত চুপ কৰি দিয়া নদী এখন সুস্থনে? কেনেকুৱা নদীয়ে গেদ বেছি আনে? তৰাং বানপানীৰ আশীৰ্বাদ অসমৰ বাহিৰে কোনে জানে? নদীবান্ধৰ এৰা পানী, বৰফ গলা পানী, মৌচুমী বায়ুৰ বৰ্ষা ক'ত একেলগ কৰাৰ প্ৰাকৃতিক আৰু অভিসন্ধিক প্ৰক্ৰিয়াৰ কথা ৰাইজে তৰ্কিব নোৱাৰে? মই অসমৰ তৰাং পানী, বানপানী তথা তৰাং পানীৰ বহু গভীৰ আলোচনা আৰু ডকুমেণ্ট কৰিছোঁ, সেয়া বেলেগে দিবৰ প্ৰচেষ্টা আছে। ইয়াত ধেমাজি আৰু ৰঙিয়াৰ পানীৰ ভঁৰালৰ আৱশ্যকতা তলত বহলাইছোঁ।

ৰঙিয়া অকল পুঠিমাৰী/বৰলীয়া আৰু পাগলাদিয়াৰ বেছিন বুলি ক'লেই নহয়, ৰঙিয়া, বাক্সা জিলা, ভূটানৰ পাদদেশ। সেইধৰণে, ধেমাজিত জিয়াধল, গাইনদী, কুমতিয়া আদিয়ে পাহাৰৰ প্ৰায় পানী আনিছে। পাাহাৰ আৰু উপত্যকা মিলিত হোৱা ঠাইত পানী সংৰক্ষণ কৰিব লাগে বিভিন্ন উপায়েৰে সংযুক্ত কৰা পুখুৰী, ডাঙৰ চৌবাচ্চা আদিত। পুখুৰী আৰু ডাঙৰ পানীৰ টেঙ্কৰ পাৰ্থক্য হৈছে, পুখুৰীৰ ক্ষেত্ৰত পানী মাটিৰ তললৈও যাব (sponge বা পানী সোহা দৃষ্টিভঙ্গী), পানীৰ টেঙ্কৰ ক্ষেত্ৰত পানী বাচনৰ ভিতৰতে থাকিব। পানীৰ টেঙ্ক বা পুখুৰীবোৰ নলা বা পাইপ আৰু পাম্পেৰে সংযুক্ত হ'ব। প্ৰথম জলাশয় পানীৰে পূৰ্ণ হ'লে, পিচৰটোলৈ পাম্প কৰিব লাগিব। পাম্প নহ'লেও জলাশয়বোৰ তলেৰে সংযুক্ত হ'লে লাহে পানী সকলোলৈকে যাব। পাম্প আজিকালি সিমান খৰচী নহয়, থাকিলে শীতকালত পানীৰ গতিপথ ওলোটা দিশে ঘূৰাব পাৰি। সংৰক্ষিত পানীখিনিক আমি প্ৰাকৃতিকভাৱে পৰিশ্ৰাবন (filter) কৰিব পাৰো, বালি আৰু শিলৰ মাজেৰে যাবলৈ দি খোৱাপানীৰ বাবদ। পুখুৰী কৰিলে তল আৰু কাষত সৰু শিল (গ্ৰেভেল) দিব পাৰিলে ভাল। পুখুৰীৰ তলখিনি সমতল নকৰি কিছু ঢাল দিব লাগিব যাতে পানী কমি গ'লে মাছে কিছুদিন জীয়াব পাৰে। ৰাইজে লগলাগি পুখুৰী সিঁচিবও পাৰিব।

মিছিং জনগোষ্ঠীয়ে ওখ খুঁটাৰ ওপৰত ঘৰ কৰি বানপানীৰ লগত সুৰ মিলাই আছিল। তেওঁলোকে জুহাল কেনেকৈ বাঁহৰ মজিয়াত কৰিছিল পাহৰিলোঁ, অৰুণাচলৰ পাহাৰৰ ওপৰৰ মানুহে চিমনিৰ নিচিনা চুলা কৰা দেখিছোঁ। এতিয়া বহুতে বোখাৰী বোলা চুলা ব্যৱহাৰ কৰে। নৈৰ কাষৰীয়া কিছু ঠাইত এটা কম খুঁটিৰ ওপৰত কৰিব পৰা যায়নে?

শীতৰ দিনত উত্তৰ-পূবত গছ-গছনি ধূলিৰে ঢাক খাই পৰে। এই ধূলিয়ে বেমাৰ বৃদ্ধি কৰে। শীতত সপ্তাহত এদিনকৈ পানী মৰাৰ ব্যৱস্থা হ'ব লাগে।

পকী ঘৰবোৰত (RCC, Reinforced Cement Concrete), অকল চালৰ অলপ ঢালেই যথেষ্ট নহয়। তলৰ ছবিত দিয়াৰ দৰে নেওৰা আৰু পানী সংৰক্ষণৰ ব্যৱস্থা বাধ্যতামূলক হ'ব লাগিব। প্লাষ্টিকৰ নেওৰা (gutter) আৰু পানীৰ সংৰক্ষণৰ বাচন স্থানীয়ভাৱে বনাব লাগে।

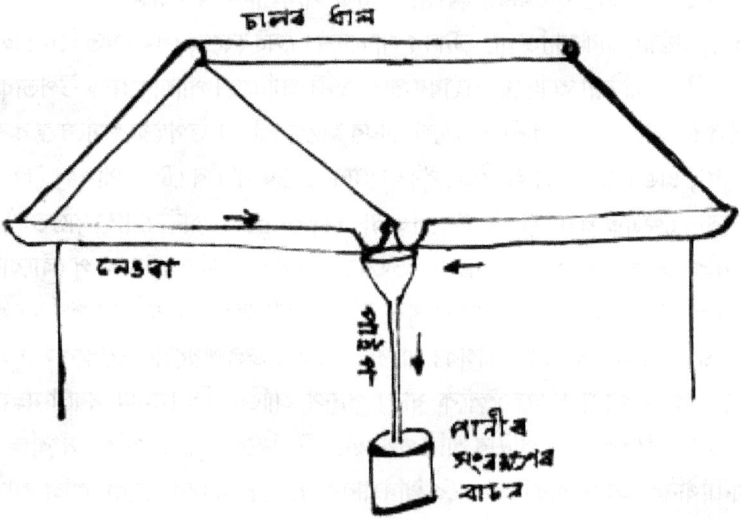

চিত্ৰ ঃ (১৯)

।। দশম অধ্যায় ।।

সংযোগিত বিশ্ব

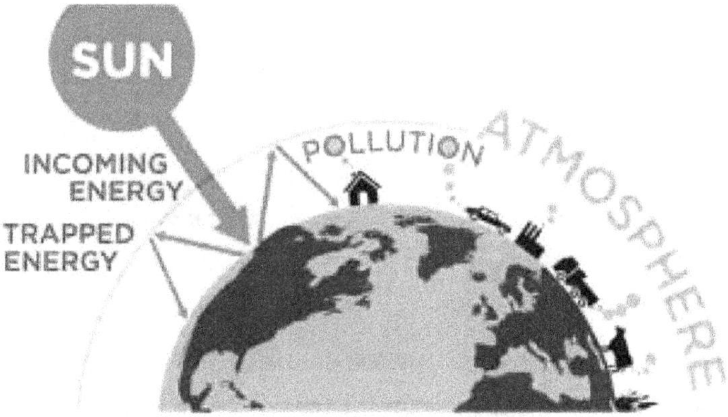

চিত্ৰ ঃ (২১)

মহাকাশৰ পৰা পৃথিৱীলৈ চালে ইয়াক নীলা আৰু বগা সৰু অসহায় বল এটা যেন লাগিব। ইয়াৰ বায়ুৰ পৰিৱৰ্তনে ইয়াক বসতিযুক্ত কৰে সূৰ্যৰ শক্তিশালী অতিবেঙুনীয়া ৰশ্মিৰ পৰা ৰক্ষা কৰি। সাগৰ আৰু মহাসাগৰৰ পানী বাষ্প হৈ মেঘ কৰে, বৰষুণ দিয়ে। বৰষুণৰ পানী নামি বৈ যায় বা মাটিৰ দ্বাৰা শোষিত হয়, মাটিৰ তলৰ জলাশয় হয়। মহাসাগৰেই বতৰ নিৰ্ণয় কৰে। আমাজন হাবিয়ে আগতে পৃথিৱীক ২০ শতাংশ অক্সিজেন দিছিল, বনজুইৰ গছৰ সংখ্যাটো

নাজানো। তিব্বতেও বায়ু নিয়ন্ত্ৰণ কৰে যদিও কম্পিউটাৰ মডেল হোৱা নাই। এতিয়া অক্সিজেন আৰু কাৰ্বন-ডাই-অক্সাইডৰ তুলনামূলক সমানুপাত বেয়া হৈছে, কাৰ্বনৰ অনুপাত বাঢ়িছে। গতিকে গোলকীয় উষ্ণতা বাঢ়িছে, কিছুমান ঠাইত হিমবাহ গলিছেই আৰু বাকীবোৰো গলাৰ ওচৰ পাইছে। ফলত সাগৰ পৃষ্ঠ ওপৰলৈ উঠিছে, মুম্বাইত কিছু দেখা গৈছে, পশ্চিমবঙ্গৰ সুন্দৰবন অঞ্চলত বহুত পৰিবৰ্তন দেখা গৈছে।

জলবায়ু পৰিবৰ্তনে সীমা নামানে। জলবায়ু পৰিবৰ্তনৰ ক্ষেত্ৰত পৃথিৱী একগোট হ'বলৈ ৰাষ্ট্ৰসংঘই শক্তিশালী আৰু শুদ্ধ অৰিহণা দিব লাগিব। মনত ৰাখিব যে দূষিত বায়ুবোৰ পৃথিৱীৰ বায়ুমণ্ডলৰ পৰা প্ৰতিফলন হয়। ২০৪০ত পৃথিৱীৰ অৱস্থা বহুত বেয়া হ'ব। তাৰমানে এইটো নহয় যে আৰু বিছ বছৰ সময় আছে। এতিয়াই সচেতন আৰু সক্ৰিয় নহ'লে ফল বেয়ালৈ গৈ থাকিব। কিছুমান ঠাই অতি ঠাণ্ডা হ'ব, কিছুমান বৰ গৰম হ'ব। গ্ৰেটা আৰু মোৰ টোপনি নাই। অসমত ২০২০ৰ ১১-১৩ আগষ্টত ৩৮ ডিগ্ৰী চেলচিয়াছ হৈছে, এইটো ৰেকৰ্ড ৰক্ষাৰ বুৰঞ্জীত আটাইতকৈ উচ্চ উষ্ণতা।

পৃথিৱীৰ বায়ুমণ্ডলো সংযোগিত, ১৯৮০ৰ মে' মাহত চিয়াটোলৰ ওচৰৰ মাউণ্ট ছেইণ্ট হেলেনছ আগ্নেয়গিৰি উদ্গীৰণ হৈছিল, ইয়াৰ ছাই তিনিবাৰ গোলাৰ্ধ ঘূৰিছিল। চাহাৰা মৰুভূমিৰ ধূলিয়ে আটলাণ্টিক পাৰ হৈ ৫,০০০ মাইল ঘূৰি আমেৰিকাৰ গাল্ফ ক'ষ্ট পাইহি। চাহাৰাৰ ঘন ধূলি কৃত্ৰিম উপগ্ৰহৰ পৰাও দেখা যায়।

সংযোগিত বিশ্বৰ আন এটা সৰু তাণ্ডৱণ হ'ল চালুকীয়া হিমালয়, আনহাতে পূব হিমালয় গোটেই হিমালয়ৰ আন এটা ক্ষুদ্ৰ তাণ্ডৱণ। পূব হিমালয় বাচক নামটো তলৰ অংশখিনিৰ বাবে অনা হৈছে,

মধ্য, দক্ষিণ, আৰু পূব নেপাল,
দাৰ্জিলিং উপ-হিমালয়,
ছিকিম ভাৰতীয় হিমালয়,
অসম উপ-হিমালয়,
ভুটান হিমালয়,
অৰুণাচল হিমালয়।

প্ৰযুক্তিবিদ্যাৰ দিনত তিনিখন উন্নয়নশীল দেশে, ভাৰত, নেপাল, ভুটান, কেনেকৈ এই গোটটো ৰক্ষা কৰিব পাৰে ই এটা চিন্তনীয় বিষয়। পূব হিমালয়ে হেংডুৱান, পেমাকো আৰু ওপৰত দিয়া অঞ্চলৰ বহুত লাগতিয়াল ভূতাত্ত্বিক সাদৃশ্য আনে। হিমবাহে কৰা উপত্যকা বা মৰেইন বা মৰানিক উপত্যকাত ঠায়ে ঠায়ে মসৃণ ঢাপৰ ভূভাগ আছে য'ত terrace খেতি কৰা হৈছে, নিশ্চয়কৈ খেতিয়েই সকলো প্ৰয়োজনীতা পূৰাব নোৱাৰে। মাছ, ঔষধি শাক আৰু চিকাৰে অলপ সহায় কৰে। অৱশ্যেই চিকাৰ অতি বিপদসঙ্কুল, জোখতকৈ বেছি কৰিলেই জন্তুবোৰ লোপ পাব। ভুল প্ৰযুক্তিয়ে পূব হিমালয়ৰ প্ৰাকৃতিক ভাৰসাম্যত বেয়াকৈ প্ৰভাৱ পেলাব পাৰে।

ডাৱৰ বিস্ফোৰণ এটা ঘটনা যাৰ ভাল অধ্যয়ন হোৱা নাই। অসমৰ সমীত্তৱৰ্তী অৰুণাচলত আৰু লাডাখত কিছুমান 'ডাৱৰ বিস্ফোৰণ' বোলা বেয়া ঘটনা ঘটিছে। ২০১৯ চনৰ জুলাই মাহত অৰুণাচলৰ নাগ মন্দিৰৰ ওচৰত বৃষ্টিপাত বিজুলী-ঢেৰেকণি-বজ্ৰপাত পৰাৰ পৰিস্থিতি আহিছিল যাৰ ফলত বৃহৎ ভূমিস্খলন হৈছিল। মই ডাৱৰ বিস্ফোৰণৰ উদাহৰণ পৃথিৱীৰ আন ঠাইত দেখা নাই। কিন্তু জাতিংগাৰ পক্ষী মৰাৰ ঘটনাটোৰ কাৰণ পৰিষ্কাৰ হ'ল। অমাৱস্যাৰ দিনত এটা নিৰ্দিষ্ট দিশত বতাহ থাকিলে পক্ষীবোৰ কুঁৱলীত যাওঁতে যদি জুই দেখে তেন্তে জুইৰ প্ৰতি আকৰ্ষিত হয়। সিহঁতে উৰিবলৈ পাহৰে অৰ্থাৎ দিশহাৰা হয়। গতিকে জাতিংগাৰ ওচৰৰ জনসাধাৰণ আজিকালি বহুত সজাগ। বিগত শতাব্দীত মৌতাম নামৰ এটি ঘটনাই মিজোৰামক বিপদত পেলাইছিল। ৪৭ বছৰীয়া ক্ৰমশঃ এটাত বাঁহ ফুল ফুলি এন্দুৰৰ বৃদ্ধি কৰিছিল। এন্দুৰৰ বৃদ্ধিয়ে খেতি-বাতি সকলো নষ্ট কৰি খাদ্যৰ আকাল ঘটাইছিল। আজিকালি মৌতাম বুৰঞ্জী হ'ল।

০০০

।। দ্বিতীয় পৰ্ব ।।

সূচনা

চীনৰ ১৯৬২ চনৰ ভাৰতৰ পুবৰ বাম্-লা আৰু পশ্চিমৰ ৰেজাং-লা আক্ৰমণ

টোকা ঃ তিব্বতীয় ভাষাত 'লা' মানে গিৰিপথ, ছ' (Pso) মানে হ্ৰদ আ 'ছু' (Chu) মানে সৰু নদী।

ইতিহাসত প্ৰথমবাৰ যেতিয়া চীনে ভাৰতবৰ্ষ আক্ৰমণ কৰিছিল মই তেতিয়া বাৰ বছৰীয়া আছিলোঁ। তেতিয়াৰ পৰাই মোৰ মনলৈ ভাব আহিছিল দুয়োখন দেশে কোনো সমস্যা নোহোৱাকৈয়ে শতাব্দী ধৰি সহাৱস্থান কৰিব পৰাৰ পিছতো চীনে কিয় ভাৰত আক্ৰমণ কৰিলে বিছ শতিকাত। চীনে সভ্যতা পোৱাৰে পৰা চীনৰ উত্তৰে থকা চুবুৰীয়া দেশৰ অৰ্ধ-যাযাবৰ লোকসকলৰ লগত যুদ্ধ কৰিব লগাত পৰিছিল। এই অৰ্ধ-যাযাবৰ লোকসকল আলপাইন তৃণভূমিৰ পৰা আহিছিল, য'ত ডাঙৰ গছ-গছনি নহয়, খেতিৰ বাবে প্ৰাকৃতিক সুবিধাজনক পৰিবেশ নাই। চিকাৰ কৰা মানুহেও জানে যে জোখতকৈ বেছি চিকাৰ কৰিলে জন্তু পাবলৈ নাইকিয়া হয়, গতিকে তেওঁলোকৰ কঁপাহ খেতিৰ বাদে গত্যন্তৰ নাছিল, কঁপাহো

অকল তাৰিম নদীৰ অৱবাহিকাত হৈছিল। চীনত খেতি হয়, গতিকে অৰ্ধ-যাযাবৰ লোকসকলে য'তে হাত দিব পাৰে সেই বস্তুকে চীনলৈ আহি লুণ্ঠন কৰি লৈ যায়— বিনষ্ট, ধ্বংস যি হয় হ'ব ভাবি নোচোৱাকৈ। চীনাসকলৰ বাবে তেওঁলোক দক্ষ চালক, যাযাবৰ গোষ্ঠী জন্মগত যোদ্ধা আছিল যি যিহকে পায় তাকেই নিবলৈ কুণ্ঠিত ন হৈছিল। সেইকাৰণেই চীনে হাজাৰ মাইল দৈৰ্ঘ্যৰ বিখ্যাত 'চীনৰ মহা দেৱাল'খন সাজি উলিয়াব লগা হৈছিল। এই সমস্যায়ে চীনক ব্যস্ত কৰি ৰাখিছিল, ভাৰত-তিব্বতৰ পূবৰ দুৰ্গম প্ৰাচীৰ পাৰ হৈ ভাৰত আক্ৰমণ কৰাৰ কথা চীনৰ পৰিকল্পনাত নাছিল। তাৰপিছত ত্ৰয়োদশ শতিকাত জেংগিছ খানৰ নাতি কুবলাই খানে চীন আক্ৰমণ কৰিছিল আৰু ইউয়ান ৰাজবংশৰ প্ৰতিষ্ঠা কৰিছিল। দেশৰ প্ৰতিৰক্ষা সন্দৰ্ভত বহুতো লাগতিয়াল ঠাই আৰু চুবুৰীয়া দেশৰ জানিবলগা কথাবোৰ ভুৰুকাত ভৰাই তলৰ মেপখন যুগুত কৰা হৈছে।

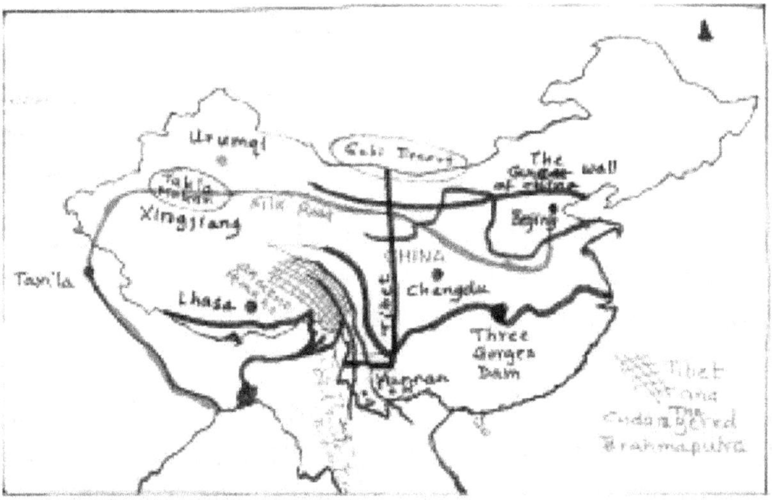

মানচিত্ৰ ঃ (২১)

মানচিত্ৰত চীনদেশ ভাৰতৰ সীমান্তত যদিও পূব ভাৰত আৰু চীনৰ মাজত দুৰ্গম প্ৰাকৃতিক প্ৰাচীৰ আছে। এটা সময়ত চীনৰ পৰা ভাৰতলৈ উত্তৰেদি ঘূৰি আহিছিল। ভাৰতবৰ্ষ, বিশেষকৈ অসম তিব্বতৰ লগতহে যুগ যুগ ধৰি সংযুক্ত পাহাৰৰ গিৰিপথবোৰৰ যোগেদি। এতিয়া তিব্বতৰ অবিহনে ব্ৰহ্মপুত্ৰ অসীম আৰু

ভয়ানক বিপদত, কাৰণ তিব্বতীয়সকলে প্ৰকৃতিক সদায় মৰ্যাদা দি আহিছিল।

উৰাজাহাজৰ সহায়ত চীনদেশে যেনেকৈ পূব ভাৰতৰ মূল্য বুজিলে, কেন্দ্ৰীয় ভাৰত আৰু ভাৰতৰ লোকে সেই সময়ত সিমানে উত্তৰ-পূব ভাৰতৰ মূল্য বুজিবলৈ এৰিলে। আধুনিকতাৰ নামত ঘৰ, ৰাস্তা, কংক্ৰীট, সন্দেহযুক্ত প্ৰযুক্তিয়ে প্ৰাধান্য পালে, যিটো দকৈ ভাবি চোৱাটো আমাৰ কৰ্তব্য। মানুহে ঘৰৰ পানীৰ ভঁৰালটো চুবুৰীয়াক নেবেচে।

দুৰ্গম প্ৰাকৃতিক প্ৰাচীৰ ভাৰতৰ পৰা চীনলৈ, সেয়েহে উত্তৰৰ চীনলৈ যাবলৈ চেংডুলৈকে যোৱা হয় আৰু তাৰপিছত তললৈ যাব লাগে। ওপৰৰ মেপত 'tibet and endangered Brahmaputra' অৰ্থাৎ ৰঙা অথালি-পথালি ৰেখাৰ অংশকে দুৰ্গম প্ৰাকৃতিক প্ৰাচীৰ বুলি ধৰি ল'ব। আচলতে চীনাসকলে ছিল্ক ৰোডেদি তক্ষশিলা পাই দিল্লী, প্ৰয়াগ (এলাহাবাদ)ৰ, পাটনা হৈ পশ্চিমবঙ্গ, বিহাৰলৈ ঘূৰি আহিছিল। অসমৰ পৰা চীনলৈ ম্যানমাৰ হৈ যোৱা বাটটো পাঞ্চু পাচেৰে দক্ষিণলৈ গৈ য়াচিং নদীৰ বাঘৰ জঁপিওৱা ঘাটি পাই ওপৰলৈ যাব লাগিব। নগা পাহাৰৰ প্ৰদেশৰ অন্তৰ্গত পাটকাই পৰ্বতৰ মাজেৰে অন্য এটা পথ আছে য'ত চিমফৌ নগাসকল সীমান্তৰ ম্যানমাৰ সীমান্তৰ উভয় প্ৰান্তত বাস কৰে, যিফালেৰে বহু যুগ ধৰি হাতীৰ দলে অহা-যোৱা কৰি আছে। চীনলৈ যোৱাৰ অন্য পথসমূহ, উদাহৰণস্বৰূপে, মণিপুৰ বা মিজোৰাম হৈ যোৱাপথসমূহ অধিক দক্ষিণ দিশলৈ।

পূৰ্বোত্তৰৰ পাহাৰসমূহ আৰু অসম যুগ যুগ ধৰি তিব্বত আৰু তীব্বতীয় সংস্কৃতিৰ লগত সংযুক্ত হৈ আছে। পৌৰাণিক হিন্দু সাহিত্যত পূৰ্বোত্তৰৰ পাহাৰীয়া লোকসকলক 'কিৰাত' বুলি কোৱা হৈছিল। পাহাৰ-পৰ্বতত, বিশেষকৈ হিমালয় আৰু উত্তৰ-পূবৰ পাহাৰত বাস কৰা লোকসকলৰ সাধাৰণ ভাষাত যিয়ে নিজক চীনা-তিব্বতীয় মূলৰ মানুহ বুলি বিশ্বাস কৰে, আচলতে অকল তিব্বতীয় মূলৰ বুলিলে বেছি সঁচা হয়। তিব্বতীয় মূলৰ মানুহ বাবে সাধাৰণ সংস্কৃত ভাষাত ব্যৱহাৰ কৰা শব্দ হ'ল 'কিৰাত'।

অৰুণাচল প্ৰদেশৰ পৰা তিব্বতলৈ যোৱা পথ হ'ল দফলা, আবৰ আৰু মিচিমি পাহাৰ, নহ'লে টাৱাং হৈ যাব লাগিব। পাহাৰীয়া লোকসকল সকলো পথ আৰু পানীৰ বাটসমূহ সম্পৰ্কে জ্ঞাত আৰু সদায় পথসমূহ আবেগসহ ৰক্ষা কৰি আহিছে। সোৱণশিৰিৰ দাঁতিকাষৰীয়া অঞ্চলত তিব্বতীয় লামাসকলে পৰ্বতৰ পৰা তললৈ

আহিবলৈ ৰছীৰ ব্যৱহাৰ কৰিছিল আৰু স্থানীয় মানুহে তেওঁলোকৰ বাবে নিৰ্দিষ্ট স্থানত চাউল থৈ দিছিল। তিব্বতলৈ অন্য পথসমূহ নিশ্চিতভাৱেই ভূটান আৰু ছিকিম হৈ আছে।

চীনৰ ফালৰ পৰা পেমাকো আৰু মেডগ কাউণ্টিলৈ আহিব নোৱাৰি, মিছিমি পাহাৰ আৰু উজনিৰ ছিয়াং মহকুমাৰ য়িংকিয়ং আদি ঠাই ৰণকৌশলৰ বাবে অতি গুৰুত্বপূৰ্ণ। স্বাধীনতাৰ সময়ত হৈ যোৱা দুই-এটা ভুলৰ শুধৰণিৰ এতিয়াও সময় আছে। মেকমোহন লাইন কেতিয়াবা কাগজৰ লাইন এডাল, উদ্ভিদবিজ্ঞানী কিংডন ৱাৰ্ডে হেংডুৱান আৰু কামডোহে দেখিলে, উটচাং দেখা নাছিল। চীন, মঙ্গোলিয়াৰ লগত মধ্য ৰাষ্ট্ৰ হৈ তিব্বতে ভাৰতৰ হৈ যি কাৰ্য কৰিছিল সেই কাৰ্য দায়িত্বত ভেকুৱামৰ সৃষ্টি হৈছে। পঞ্চশীল অৱজ্ঞা কৰাৰ পিচত নেহেৰু দুবছৰতেই গুচি গ'ল। এইবোৰ সৰু কথা নহয়।

○○○

।। প্ৰথম অধ্যায় ।।

চীনে অৰুণাচল প্ৰদেশ আৱিষ্কাৰ কৰিলে দ্বিতীয় বিশ্বযুদ্ধত

মই এইটো ব্যঙ্গ কৰা নাই, দ্বিতীয় বিশ্বযুদ্ধই চীনৰ বাবে হেংডুৱান আৰু পূৰ্বোত্তৰীয় তিব্বত যথাযথভাৱে উন্মোচিত কৰে। চীনে দ্বিতীয় বিশ্বযুদ্ধত বিশ্বৰ পৰা যথেষ্ট মনোযোগ আকৰ্ষণ কৰিছিল জাপান ম্যানমাৰ পোৱাহি বাবে। চাবুৱা আৰু কলিকতাৰ পৰা চীনলৈ যোৱা 'অ'ভাৰ দ্য হাম্প' (Over the hump) নামৰ বিমানসমূহে চীনলৈ বস্তু-সামগ্ৰী কঢ়িয়াই নিব লাগিছিল। প্ৰকৃততে 'লে'ক অব ন' ৰিটাৰ্ণ' (Lake of No Return) হৈ উঠিছিল 'ভাৰতৰ বাৰ্মুদাট্ৰায়েংগল'। আমি এই বিষয়ে বিস্তাৰিতভাৱে আলোচনা কৰিম। চীনে অৰুণাচল প্ৰদেশ আৱিষ্কাৰ কৰিলে দ্বিতীয় বিশ্বযুদ্ধত, আনহাতে ভাৰতে তিব্বতক পাহৰিলে সেই একে সময়তে।

এই গ্ৰন্থৰ প্ৰথম খণ্ড লিখি থকাৰ সময়ত মই মোৰ প্ৰশ্ন, চীনে কিয় ভাৰত আক্ৰমণ কৰিলে বিছ শতিকাত, তাৰ উত্তৰ পাইছিলোঁ। মই মোৰ উত্তৰ প্ৰকাশ কৰাৰ আগতে প্ৰমাণ আৰু ভৌগোলিক তথ্য উপস্থাপন কৰিবলৈ বিচাৰিছোঁ। আনকি, ভাৰতবৰ্ষৰ পূৰ্বতম অঞ্চল অৰুণাচল প্ৰদেশৰ কাষৰীয়া অঞ্চলতে চীন আৰু ভাৰতবৰ্ষৰ সীমা আছে আৰু ইয়াক উচ্চ পৰ্বত আৰু গভীৰ উপত্যকাই পৃথক কৰিছে। হিমালয়ে অৰুণাচলক পূবৰ পৰা দক্ষিণ দিশলৈকে চাৰিওফালৰ পৰা আৱৰি ৰাখিছে আৰু তাৰপিছত দুৰ্দান্ত এক সীমা নিৰ্মাণৰ বাবে পূব-দক্ষিণ হেংডুৱান পৰ্বতমালাৰ সৈতে যোগ দিয়ে। প্ৰত্যেকেই পৰ্বতৰ সিপাৰে কি আছে চাবলৈ বিচাৰে। কিন্তু অৰুণাচলৰ মিচিমি পাহাৰৰ ইটো পাৰে উলম্ব উপশমৰ

সৈতে উচ্চতম পৰ্বতমালা বাবে কাউৰী উৰি যোৱাৰ দৰে সীমান্ত পাৰ কৰাৰ সম্ভাৱনাও নাই। এই ঠাইৰ ওখ পৰ্বত আৰু দ উপত্যকাত এনে কিছুমান ঠাই আছে য'ত মানুহৰ ভৰি কেতিয়াও পৰা নাই। যদি পৰিছে সেয়া পাহাৰ পূজা কৰা তিব্বতীয়সকলৰ যিসকলে ভু-মাতৃৰ ওপৰত আলফুলে ভৰি দিয়ে। এই ঠাইত এনে জলবায়ু বৈশিষ্ট্য আছে যে আপুনি গ্লেচিয়াৰ পোৱাৰ কিছু দূৰতে তাল গছ পাব। গেৰী মাৰকিউজৰ চিনেমাখনে মোক নিশ্চিত কৰিলে যে পূব সীমান্তৰ দুয়ো প্ৰান্তে একে জনজাতিয়েই আছে আৰু তেওঁলোক তিব্বতীয় মূলৰ। য়ুন্নানৰ ডালি আৰু কুনমিংহে চীনৰ ফালৰ পৰা প্ৰৱেশ কৰা ঠাই। বাকীবোৰ, মানে দুৰ্গম পূবৰ য়ুন্নান তিব্বতীয় মূলৰ। চীনৰ উত্তৰ-পূবৰ পাহাৰ, হিমালয়ৰ ওচৰৰ সকলো ঠাই চীনৰ মেপৰ পৰা নাইকিয়া কৰা কথাই মোৰ উদ্বেগ বঢ়ালে আৰু কৌতুহলী আৰু সন্ধানী কৰিলে। বিশেষকৈ মই কাগজে-পত্ৰই কৃত্ৰিম গ্ৰহৰ পৰা পৰীক্ষণ কৰিবলৈ দিহা-পৰামৰ্শ দিয়া আৰম্ভ কৰিলোঁ।

চাবুৱা আৰু কলিকতাৰ পৰা কুন্‌মিনলৈ উৰাজাহাজেৰ হাম্প ৰুট, 'উচ্চ হাম্প' আৰু 'নিম্ন হাম্প'ৰ উৰাজাহাজৰ বাটৰ আৰম্ভ, চীনৰ এই অঞ্চলৰ ওপৰত চকু, নিহিত সম্ভাৱনাৰ সপোন মুকলি ঃ

এইখিনিতেই আহিব সকলোতকৈ আকৰ্ষণীয় অংশটো, যেতিয়া দ্বিতীয় বিশ্বযুদ্ধত কুন্‌মিংলৈ নিয়মিত উৰাজাহাজ ব্যৱহাৰ আৰম্ভ হ'ল, হয় চাবুৱাৰ পৰা নহয় কলিকতাৰ পৰা। হাম্প মানে কুঁজ, এই কুঁজ পাৰ হ'বলৈ কিমান উঠি আকৌ কিমান নামিব লাগিব তাৰ গূঢ়াৰ্থ অনা হৈছে। ইয়াত হাম্প মানে পাহাৰৰ কিমান ওপৰ হ'ব লাগিব পাহাৰ শিখৰত খুন্দা নোখোৱাকৈ, আৰু তাৰ পিচত কিমান নামিব লাগিব বুজোৱা হৈছে। চাবুৱাৰ পৰা কুনমিঙলৈ সকলোতকৈ দূৰত্ব কম, কিন্তু ই 'high hump' বাট, পৰিৱৰ্তে কলিকতাৰ পৰা কুন্‌মিঙলৈ দূৰত্ব বেছি কিন্তু 'Low hump'। চাবুৱাৰ পৰা সকলোতকৈ ভয়ংকৰ পথটো আছিল আৰু সময়ত পৰ্বত শৃংখলা আৰু মানুহৰ বাবে ইয়াৰ দুৰ্গমতা সম্পৰ্কে বৰ্ণনা কৰা হ'ব। মনত ৰাখিব যদি এখন এজনীয়া মানুহৰ যুঁজাৰু বিমান হয়, ওপৰলৈ উঠি তললৈ নমাই তাৰ কাম, এইক্ষেত্ৰত মানুহ, গেলামাল, পেট্ৰ'লৰ টেঙ্ক সকলো নিব লাগিব, তাকো তাহানিৰ দিনত। পথ দুটা বুজিবলৈ অনুগ্ৰহ কৰি তলৰ

মানচিত্ৰখন চাওক। ১৯৪২ চনৰ মে' মাহৰ পৰা হাম্প (পৰ্বতৰ কুঁজৰ ওপৰেৰে) নিয়মিত C-47s-ৰে ক্ৰিয়াকলাপ আৰম্ভ হৈছিল। C-47 বেছিভাগ ড'গ্লাছ DC-3 মডেলৰ জাহাজ কিছু সাল-সলনি কৰি C-47 উৰাজাহাজ কৰা হৈছিল। য'ত শক্তিশালী মজিয়া আৰু ডাঙৰ দুৱাৰ আছিল।

মানচিত্ৰ ঃ (২২) উচ্চ 'হাম্প' আৰু 'নিম্ন হাম্প'

'এলুমিনিয়াম সিঁচৰতি হোৱা বাটৰ পম খেদি'

প্ৰকৃততে এইটো এটা ভয়ানক উৰণ আছিল, বৰফৰ সমস্যাটো ১২,০০০ ফুট ওপৰত আছিল আৰু সমস্যাটোৱে সহজেই এখন উৰাজাহাজৰ পিছত খুন্দা দিব পাৰিলেহেঁতেন য'ত উৰাজাহাজৰ পাখি কেইখনো বিকৃত হৈ গ'লহেঁতেন। যদিও উৰাজাহাজবোৰ 'হাম্প'ৰ ওপৰেৰে যাব পৰাকৈ সক্ষম নহয়, তথাপি C-47-এ সেই নিৰ্দিষ্ট ঠাই নিয়মিতভাৱেই অতিক্ৰম কৰিছিল। সেইকাৰণে তাত দুৰ্ঘটনাবোৰ হৈছিল আৰু এলুমিনিয়ামৰ অংশবোৰ (Aluminium trail) অৰণ্যতেই পৰি ৰৈছিল। এই অভিযানৰ সময়ত ৫০৯খন বিমান হেৰাই গৈছিল, হাজাৰ

হাজাৰ বিমানৰ চালক আৰু পৰিচালকৰ দল নিহত হৈছিল, ৩৪৫ জন লোক নিখোঁজ হৈছিল। আৰু কিছু সংখ্যক উৰাজাহাজ 'লে'ক অব ন' ৰিটাৰ্ণ' (Lake of no return)ৰ ওপৰতে নোহোৱা হৈছে। বিমানচালকসকলে যান্ত্ৰিক বিজুতিৰ পিছত সহজ অৱতৰণৰ বাবে হয় এই হ্ৰদটো ব্যৱহাৰ কৰিছিল নহ'লে উৰি ফুৰোতে কুঁৱলীত বেছি দূৰ নেদেখি হেৰাই গৈছিল।

'লে'ক অফ্ ন' ৰিটাৰ্ণ' হ্ৰদটো ম্যানমাৰত অৱস্থিত, পাংছাও গাঁৱৰ দক্ষিণ ভাৰত-ম্যানমাৰ সীমান্তত পাংছাও গিৰিপথৰ (৩৭২৭) অঞ্চলত ই আছে।

চিয়াং কাই-ছেকে পাৰ কৰিবৰ বাবে ১০,০০০ টন বিচাৰিছিল প্ৰতিমাহে। ৬৫০,০০০ পেট্ৰ'ল সৰবৰাহ আৰু মানুহ চীনলৈ লৈ যোৱা হৈছিল। এইখিনিতে এটা কথাৰ উল্লেখ কৰো, বৰ্তমানৰ অসমৰ মুখ্যমন্ত্ৰী সৰ্বানন্দ সোণোৱালৰ পিতৃয়ে হেনো সৰুতে চাবুৱাত দিনটোত কেইখন প্লেন উঠিছে আৰু নামিছে তাৰ হিচাব কৰি ৰেকৰ্ড কৰা কামটো কৰিছিল, কেতিয়াবা প্ৰমাণ কৰিবলৈ আশা ৰাখিছোঁ।

এই 'হাম্প'ৰ কথাটোৱে বহুত প্ৰসঙ্গ উত্থাপন কৰে। তীব্ৰতীয়সকলে যুগ যুগ ধৰি ডকুমেণ্ট কৰা আৰু আলফুলকৈ ৰক্ষা কৰা বহু ভৌগোলিক কথা হঠাতে পৃথিৱীৰ অৱগত হ'ল। ভূমিপুত্ৰৰ নিজৰ দেশলৈ মৰম, চীন দেশৰ চকু মাথোঁ সম্পদৰ ওপৰত। ক'ত কি খনি পাব, পাহাৰীয়া নদীৰ মানে চীনদেশৰ চকুত কেৱল নদীবান্ধ। তীব্ৰতীয়সকলে আনকি সোণো খনন কৰা নাছিল। তীব্ৰতৰ বাবে হোৱা অন্যায় বিশ্বই যদি শুধৰণি নকৰে এই গোলকীয় উষ্ণতা বৃদ্ধিৰ সময়ত গোটেই বিশ্বই জীয়াতু ভুগিব। হিমালয় অকল ভাৰতৰ উত্তৰতে নহয়, উত্তৰ-পূবত হিমালয় নাটকীয়, ওখ আৰু বিস্ময়কৰ।

অলপ এয়াৰ'প্লেনৰ কথা যাওক। এখন ফাইটাৰ জেটে এই হাম্পৰ ওপৰ-তল সহজে কৰিব পাৰে। এজনীয়া প্লেন সেইবাবেই বনোৱা হয়। আনহাতে মানুহ কঢ়িওৱা প্লেনে আধা মানুহ নিয়ে, আধা মালবস্তু নিয়ে। ই ফাইটাৰ প্লেনৰ বাবে দ্ৰুতগামী, চট্ফটিয়া হ'ব নোৱাৰে। DC-3 ৰ মানুহ কঢ়িওৱা প্লেনখনক এই কুঁজৰ ওপৰেৰে নিয়া হৈছিল। পাহাৰৰ অকণমানত খুন্দা খালেই পাখিবোৰ বিকৃত হৈছিল বা কিছু ভাগিছিল। ডাঙৰ প্লেনবোৰে বহু ওখত উৰিহে ভাল পায়।

০০০

।। দ্বিতীয় অধ্যায় ।।

তিব্বত ঃ কি, ক'ত, কিয় বিখ্যাত

ইয়াত মই মোৰ কথাখিনি বৰ্ণনা কৰিবলৈ অংকিত চিত্ৰ, মানচিত্ৰ আৰু ফটোৰ সহায় ল'ম (প্ৰথম পৰ্বৰ তিব্বত আকৌ পঢ়ক)। তিব্বত হ'ল এক সংস্কৃতি, এক মালভূমি। তিব্বতৰ বৰ্ণনা কৰিবৰ সময়ত যুগ যুগৰ ইতিহাসত এতিয়ালৈকে বিদ্বানসকলে কেৱল এটি সৰু সৰু অংশহে স্পৰ্শ কৰে। ই অতীতত কেৱল ঘোঁৰা, খচ্চৰ, গাধ বা য়াকৰ পিঠিত উঠিহে যাব পৰা অপ্ৰৱেশযোগ্য ভূখণ্ড আছিল, কিন্তু তিব্বতীয়সকলে এই ভূখণ্ডৰ প্ৰাকৃতিক দুৰ্যোগৰ লগতো সুৰ মিলাই আছিল। বৰফৰ মাজত জীৱন-যাপন কৰিবলৈ চেষ্টা কৰিছিল আৰু তাৰ গিৰিপথ-বাটসমূহৰ কঠিন বিৱৰণ সংৰক্ষণ কৰিছিল, যদিও পাহাৰ আৰু অঞ্চলসমূহ বিচাৰি উলিওৱা সহজ নাছিল। চীনা লোকসকলৰ বাবে পশ্চিম চীন কেৱল পৰ্বত আছিল। তেওঁলোক পূবত বেইজিঙৰ ওচৰৰ উপত্যকাত কেন্দ্ৰীভূত আছিল। হোৱাংহো উপত্যকাটো ইউৰোপৰ পৰা পোন পথেৰে পৰিছিল আৰু চীনা সভ্যতাত উৎপত্তিস্থল আছিল। তিব্বত আৰু চীন খামডো আৰু আমডোতহে ওচৰ আছিল। আন এটা গুৰুত্বপূৰ্ণ তথ্য হ'ল যে তিব্বতীয়সকল বহু পুৰণি কালৰ পৰা হিমালয়ত আছে আৰু তেওঁলোকে বহুতো মহাপ্ৰলয়, সলনি হোৱা ভূগোল, ভূমিকম্প

আদি প্ৰত্যক্ষ কৰিছে।

তলত তিব্বতৰ এখন সম্পূৰ্ণ মানচিত্ৰ দিয়া হৈছে, উচাং আৰু খাম আৰু আগৰ অসমৰ লগত ওতঃপ্ৰোতভাৱে জড়িত। পুৰণা পেমাকো আৰু অৰুণাচলৰ পেমাকো ব্ৰহ্মপুত্ৰৰ সাললনিৰ প্ৰমাণ স্থান। তিব্বতীয়সকল চাচুকীয়া হিমালয়ক বুজা মানুহ।

মানচিত্ৰ : (২৩) তিব্বত হৈছে পৃথিৱীৰ মুকুট আৰু এছিয়াৰ জলস্তম্ভ। প্ৰায় চাৰে তিনি মাইল ওখত ই হিমালয়ৰ উত্তৰে তিব্বতে ভাৰতক আৰু পূবে মংগোলিয়া আৰু চীনৰ পৰা ভাৰতক পৃথক কৰি ৰাখিছে, অকল সীমান্ত হিচাবেই নহয় ইয়াৰ উচ্চতাৰ বাবেও।

আমি এই মেপখন তলৰ মেপত প্ৰক্ষেপণ কৰিলে তিব্বতৰ উচ্চতা কেনেকৈ অৰুণাচলৰ পুৱলৈ কমিছে বুজিব পাৰো। এতিয়া আমি নিম্ন উল্লিখিত ছবিখনত এই ভূখণ্ডক স্থাপন কৰিবলৈ চেষ্টা কৰিম। সৰ্বপ্ৰথমতে এই মানচিত্ৰত তিব্বতৰ খণ্ড খণ্ডটো চিহ্নিত কৰো। যি ইয়াৰ উচ্চতা বুজায়। য়ুন্নান প্ৰান্তৰ ওপৰত তিব্বতৰ সীমা সম্পূৰ্ণ এক প্ৰাকৃতিক বাধা। লক্ষ্য ৰাখিব, চীনে যাক বৰ্তমান তিব্বত স্বায়ত্ত ক্ষেত্ৰ বুলি উল্লেখ কৰে, সেয়া প্ৰকৃত তিব্বতৰ কিছু বেলেগ। অৰুণাচলত চীনৰ বাবে প্ৰৱেশ সুলভ নাছিল আৰু তাৰবাবে যত্নও কৰা নাছিল। তিব্বতৰ লাছা চীনৰ বাবে বেছি প্ৰৱেশ সুলভ আছিল আৰু ভাৰতবৰ্ষলৈ আফগানিস্তান হৈ ঘূৰি আহিছিল। এতিয়া প্ৰথম পৰ্বৰ সপ্তম অধ্যায় আকৌ পঢ়ক।

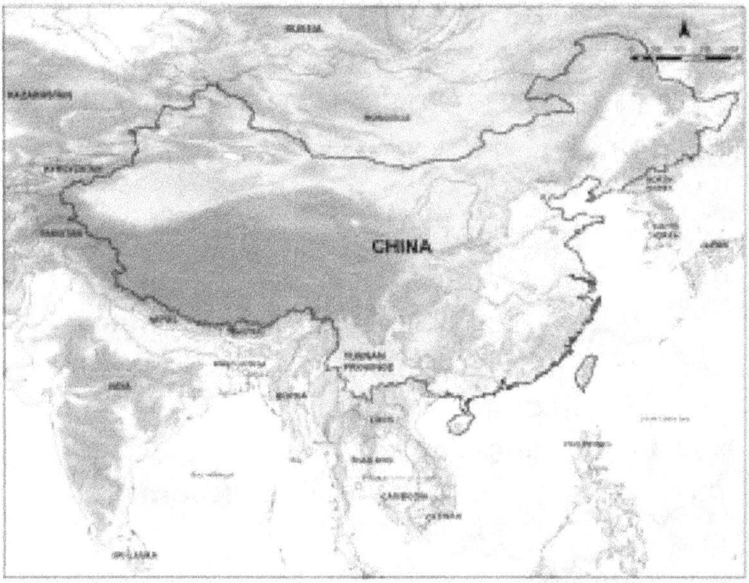

মানচিত্ৰ ঃ (২৪)

অসমত 'ভোৰতাল' নামেৰে প্ৰচলিত তাল বা বৰতাল তিব্বত আৰু উত্তৰ-পূবত ব্যৱহাৰ হোৱা উমৈহতীয়া বাদ্য। হাস্যকৰ বিষয়টো হ'ল যে চীনে অৰুণাচল প্ৰদেশ বিচৰা আৰম্ভ কৰিছিল দালাই লামা অহা বাটটোৰ উৱাদিহ পোৱাৰ পিচত। চীনৰ অৰুণাচলৰ লগতো বিশেষ সংস্পৰ্শ নাছিল, তিব্বতৰহে আছিল।

স্থানীয় জ্ঞান

স্থানীয় জ্ঞান যথেষ্ট শক্তিশালী আৰু উত্তৰ-পূবৰ তিব্বতৰ লগত বহুত গিৰিপথ আছে। বেছি সংখ্যক মানুহৰ বাবে ছিল্ক ৰোডৰ ওচৰৰ তিব্বতৰ উত্তৰ অংশটোৱেই তিব্বত আছিল বুলি জানিছিল। বাকীসকলৰ বাবে, দক্ষিণ-পূবৰ অংশটো 'খাম' লোকসকলৰ বাসস্থান খামড' অলপ জনা ঠাই আছিল। এতিয়ালৈকে কোনেও সমগ্ৰ তিব্বতৰ বিষয়ে বৰ্ণনা দিব পৰা নাই। যিখিনি কেৱল তিব্বতীয়সকলেহে জানে। তিব্বতীয়সকল একমাত্ৰ পৰ্বতীয়া লোক আছিল, যিয়ে দুৰ্গম পৰ্বত, চৰম ভূ-জলবায়ু পৰিস্থিতিৰ লগত মোকাবিলা কৰিব পাৰে আৰু প্ৰকৃতিৰ সৈতে

সহাৱস্থান কৰিব পাৰে। তেওঁলোকে এইটো বোজা বুলি নল'লে বৰঞ্চ প্ৰকৃতিক মৰ্যাদা দিবলৈ শিকিলে।

অলপ সময়ৰ বাবে ভুটানলৈ আহিছোঁ, ভুটানৰ চাকেতাং বন্যপ্ৰাণী অভয়াৰণ্য এখন সুন্দৰ ৰাষ্ট্ৰীয় উদ্যান, ভাৰতবৰ্ষৰ অৰুণাচল প্ৰদেশৰ সীমাৰ লগত অৱস্থিত। ভুটানৰ কিছুসংখ্যক দুৰ্লভ জীৱৰ বাবে ই ঘৰ সদৃশ, উদাহৰণস্বৰূপে ৰঙা পাণ্ডা আৰু হিমালয়ান 'মোনাল' ৰঙীন পক্ষী বিশেষ ইত্যাদি। ২০২০ চনৰ ৩০ জুন তাৰিখে এটা আকৰ্ষণীয় ঘটনা ঘটিছিল। চীনে চাকতেং বন্যপ্ৰাণী অভয়াৰণ্য দাবী কৰিছিল আৰু ইয়াক 'বিতৰ্কিত' অঞ্চল হিচাপে অভিহিত কৰিছিল। এইটো অতি অদ্ভুত কথা আছিল। যদিও ভাগ্যক্ৰমে ৰাষ্ট্ৰসংঘত কোনেও এই কথা গুৰুত্ব সহকাৰে নল'লে। অৰুণাচলৰ ক্ষেত্ৰতো সেয়ে স্পষ্ট হ'ব। হিমালয় তুলনামূলকভাৱে তৰুণ পৰ্বত হোৱাৰ বাবে এই অংশটো বস্তুবোৰ পৰিৱৰ্তনৰ মাজেৰে পাৰ হৈ গৈছে যিবিলাক মোৰ কিতাপৰ প্ৰথম অংশৰ মূল বিষয়। ভৌগোলিক পৰিৱৰ্তন বুজিবলৈ বিশ্বক তিব্বতীয় যুগ যুগৰ জ্ঞান আমাক লাগে।

স্পেৰ' জিহাদ, মাও-চে-তুং

যেতিয়া মই 'ৰেকিং দ্য গ্ৰীণ টাইগাৰ' (২০১১) চলচ্চিত্ৰখন চাইছিলোঁ, নিৰ্দেশক গেৰী মাৰ্কিউজে মোক কেৱল কীট-পতংগ, চৰাই-প্ৰাণী, যেনে, ঘনচিৰিকা, ম'হ, এন্দুৰ মৰাৰ কথা, সৰু সৰু ঘৰুৱা ভাতিবোৰত ষ্টীল তৈয়াৰ কৰাৰ কথা মনত পেলোৱাতকৈ বৰঞ্চ মাওৰ প্ৰকৃতি বিবেচনাসমূহৰ কথাবোৰ মনত পেলাই দিলে। যেতিয়া জলবায়ু পৰিৱৰ্তন বাস্তৱ আৰু গোলকীয় উষ্ণতা বৃদ্ধি পাইছে, এইটো এটা গুৰুত্বপূৰ্ণ সময় তিব্বতীয়সকলৰ অৰিহণাক সন্মান দিয়া। সকলোবোৰ শীৰ্ষত ৰাখিবলৈ ২০২০ চনটোত মহামাৰীয়ে পৃথিৱীক পৰীক্ষা কৰি আছে। ঘনচিৰিকাবোৰ মাৰি পেলোৱা কাৰ্যই পাৰিৱেশিক সন্তুলন অশান্ত কৰাৰ বাবে প্ৰাকৃতিক কীটনাশকবোৰ নোহোৱাৰ সুযোগত কীট-পতংগই খেতিসমূহ নষ্ট কৰিছিল। মই মাওৰ প্ৰকৃতি অপ্ৰিয় প্ৰভাৱ চীনৰ পৰা সম্পূৰ্ণ লোপ পোৱা বুলি জীয়াই থাকিবলৈ কিমান ধন-সম্পত্তি লাগে, কিমান প্ৰকৃতিক লাগে এইবোৰ এটা জীৱনত সলনি হয় ভাবিবলৈ টান পাইছোঁ। জলবায়ু পৰিৱৰ্তন বাস্তৱ আৰু গোলকীয় উষ্ণতা যে বৃদ্ধি পাইছে সেইটো সঁচা, এইটো এটা গুৰুত্বপূৰ্ণ

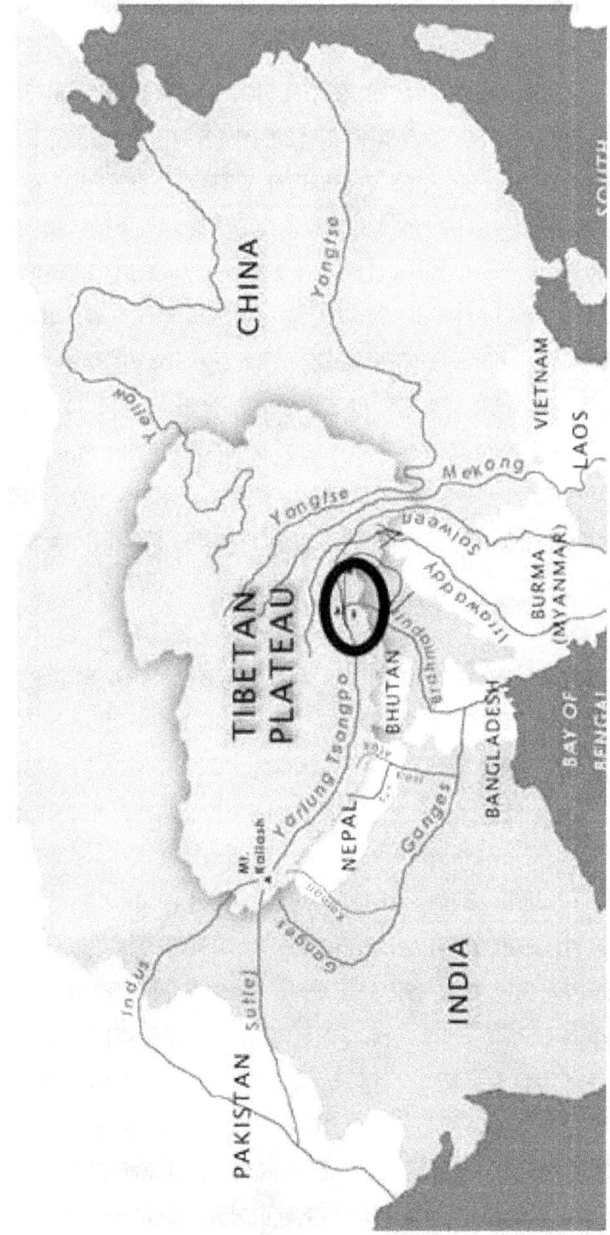
CHINA
Yangtse
Yellow
TIBETAN
PLATEAU
Yarlung Tsangpo
Mt. Kailash
Indus
Sutlej
Ganges
NEPAL
BHUTAN
Brahmaputra
Irrawaddy
Salween
Mekong
VIETNAM
LAOS
BURMA
(MYANMAR)
BANGLADESH
BAY OF
BENGAL
INDIA
PAKISTAN
SOUTH

মানচিত্ৰ ঃ (২৫)

সময়। মাওৰ, নদীৰ গতিপথ ৰুদ্ধ কৰিবলৈ বাধ্য বুলি কোৱা বিচলিতকাৰী মন্তব্য বিশ্বই পাহৰা নাই। কোনো নেতাই বিশাল পৰ্বত আৰু শক্তিশালী নদীসমূহক এনেদৰে তুচ্ছ কৰি পেলোৱা নাই।

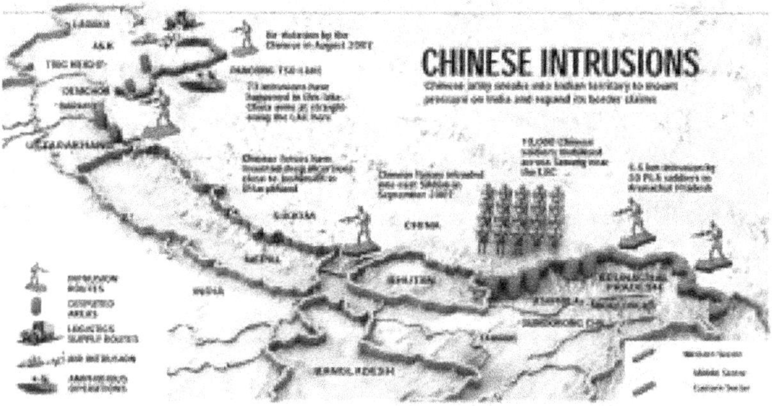

মানচিত্ৰ ঃ (২৬) চীনে তিব্বত অধিকাৰ কৰাৰ পিচত এতিয়ালৈকে ক'ত আক্ৰমণ কৰিছে

চীনে ভাৰতবৰ্ষৰ ভূখণ্ড দাবী কৰা কাৰ্য বৰ পুৰণি নহয়। অৰুণাচলৰ কিছু অঞ্চল বা গোটেইখিনিক সুমুৱাই ল'ব খোজে। সেইবাবে এই কথাৰ ইয়াত স্পষ্টীকৰণ দিয়া হ'ল। চীনদেশৰ অৰুণাচলৰ ওপৰত মনোযোগ অতি নতুন কথা। এইবিলাক মোৰ জীৱন কালতেই ঘটিছে। যেতিয়া ভাৰতবৰ্ষই পুৰণি তিব্বতৰ সীমা ঠিক কৰিছিল তেতিয়া তাত কোনো সীমা চিহ্নৰ প্ৰয়োজনীয়তা নাছিল। গোট মাৰি থকা নদীসমূহৰ ঋতুকালিন পথ, অৰ্থাৎ বতৰৰ ওপৰত নিৰ্ভৰ কৰিহে কিছু গিৰিপথো বা নদীপথ মুকলি আছিল। দুয়োখন দেশেই বন্ধুসুলভ আৰু শান্তিপূৰ্ণ আছিল। আগতেই কৈছোঁ, চীনে তিব্বতৰ বিষয়ে বহুবোৰ কথাই নাজানিছিল, একমাত্ৰ খামড', লাছা আৰু উত্তৰ তিব্বতে ছিল্ক ৰোডক চুই যোৱা অংশৰ বাহিৰে। চীনে তিব্বতক এখন উচ্চ দেশ হিচাপে বিচাৰি পালে আৰু চীনে তিব্বতক আক্ৰমণ কৰি অন্যায়ভাবে দখল কৰিলে কাৰণ তিব্বতৰ ওচৰত কোনো ডাঙৰ সেনাবাহিনী নাছিল। দীঘলীয়া বুৰঞ্জীত আৰু তাৰ আগতো চীনে তিব্বতক গুৰুত্ব দিয়া নাছিল। চীনাসকল ভাৰতলৈ পাকিস্তানৰ ফালৰপৰা অহা কথাই

ইয়াক প্ৰমাণ কৰে। ইয়াৰ পাহাৰৰ মাজৰ চুক বাবেই ইয়াৰ মূল্য নাছিল, প্ৰযুক্তিৰ যুগত সেয়া সলনি হৈ গ'ল, মোৰ জীৱনৰ সময়ৰ ভিতৰতে। অৰুণাচলৰ স্থানীয় গিৰিপথসমূহ সম্পৰ্কে চীনৰ জানিবলৈ কোনো সুযোগ নাছিল, যিফালেৰে তৰুণ দালাই লামা চেলা হৈ ভাৰতবৰ্ষলৈ পলাই গৈছিল সেই টাৱাঙৰ পথটোৰ বিষয়ে চীনৰ কোনো ধাৰণাই নাছিল। ভাৰতবৰ্ষত দালাই লামাই শৰণ লোৱা কথাটোত খং দেখুৱাবলৈ চীনে সেই পথটোত আক্ৰমণ কৰিব বুলি কৈছিল। প্ৰথমে চীনে অক্সাই চীন অধিকাৰ কৰে আৰু তাৰপিছত অনুভৱ কৰে যে তেওঁলোকক তাৰ উত্তপ্ত জুৰিবোৰক নালাগে, তেওঁলোকে মিলিটেৰী লাভালাভ বিচাৰে। তেতিয়াৰ পৰাই সকলোবোৰ গিৰিপথ বিচাৰি আছে। তাৰ পিছত ১৯৬২ত দালাই লামা অহা বাটেৰে আগ্ৰাসন আৰম্ভ কৰে।

১৯৬২ ঃ বাম-লা আৰু ৰেজাং-লা

১৯৬৭ ঃ লাখু-লা আৰু ছ'-লা

১৯৮৭ ঃ চুমদ্ৰং ছু। সেই বছৰেই প্ৰধানমন্ত্ৰী লালবাহাদুৰ শাস্ত্ৰীক হেৰুৱাইছিলোঁ।

২০১৭ ঃ ড'ক্লাম

২০২০ ঃ পূব লাডাখ, পাংগং ছ'

১৯৬২ চনত চীনে অসম সীমান্তক অপ্ৰস্তুত অৱস্থাত পাইছিল। বৰফত অনুশীলনৰ অভাৱ, অস্ত্ৰ আৰু গোলাবাৰুদৰ নাটনি, গৰম কাপোৰ আৰু সঠিক আহাৰৰ অভাৱ আছিল। তেতিয়াৰ পৰাই চীনে ভাৰতবৰ্ষক অপ্ৰস্তুত ৰূপত পাবলৈ আশা কৰি আছে। কিন্তু, ভাৰতীয় সেনাৰ দেশপ্ৰেম অতুলনীয় বুলি প্ৰমাণ হৈছে। ড্ৰেগন ভক্ষণৰ বাবে ড্ৰেগনে প্ৰতিবাৰে ভাৰতবৰ্ষক পৰীক্ষা কৰি আছে। এই কথা প্ৰমাণিত যে চীনে তিব্বতীয় লোক বা তিব্বতীয় ভূ-খণ্ডৰ লগত কোনো সংবেদনশীল যোগাযোগ ৰখা নাই। চীনৰ তেওঁলোকৰ মিছাইলসমূহ ভাৰতলৈ নিম্নমুখী কৰি টোঁৱাই ৰাখিবলৈ এইখনেই একমাত্ৰ উচ্চ স্থান। তদুপৰি, দক্ষিণ-পশ্চিম দেশৰ লগত পানীখিনি ভাগ কৰাতকৈ তৰ্জন-গৰ্জনৰ ভাওনা এখনৰ লোভ সামৰিব নোৱাৰে। চাকেতাঙৰ শেহতীয়া দাবীটোৱে বুজাই যে চীনৰ নতুন অঞ্চল দাবীবোৰ কি ধৰণেৰে হাস্যকৰ হৈ পৰিছে আৰু কিদৰে নেপাল আৰু পাকিস্তানক উচটাইছে। অৰুণাচল প্ৰদেশ তিব্বতৰ প্ৰৱেশদ্বাৰ হোৱাৰ বাবে চীনে

অৰুণাচলখন বিচাৰিছে, কাৰণ অৰুণাচল অবিহনে বহুবোৰ ঠাইলৈ চীনৰ ফালৰপৰা যোৱাটো অসম্ভৱ। এই উচ্চ সকাহুপূৰ্ণ পৰ্বতসমূহত খোঁৰা চলোৱাও বিপদজনক।

এইটোৱেই উপযুক্ত সময় তিব্বতৰ লগত হোৱা অন্যায়সমূহৰ শুধৰণি কৰাৰ। পটালা প্ৰাসাদ চীনে আক্ৰমণ কৰাৰ সময়ত আধৰুৱা থাকি যোৱা কামবোৰ এতিয়া সম্পূৰ্ণ কৰাৰ সময়। এয়াই তিব্বতক স্বীকৃতি দিয়াৰ আৰু সমগ্ৰ বিশ্বৰ সমৰ্থন লাভ কৰাৰ প্ৰকৃত সময়। জলবায়ু পৰিৱৰ্তনৰ দিশৰপৰা চাবলৈ গ'লে তিব্বতৰ মূল লোকসকলক তিব্বতলৈ ঘূৰাই অনাটো অতি প্ৰয়োজনীয় কথা। প্ৰকৃতিৰ সৈতে সহবাস কৰাটো প্ৰত্যেক তিব্বতীয়সকলৰ জিনতে আছে। আনহাতে, তাত যদি এতিয়া আধুনিকীকৰণৰ নামত কংক্ৰিটৰ ঘৰ সাজি ঘৰত মানুহক মাস্কৰ যোগেদি অক্সিজেন দি ঘৰ গৰম কৰি ৰখা হয় পৰিৱেশতন্ত্ৰৰ হত্যা কৰা হ'ব। হিমালয় তুলনামূলকভাৱে নতুন পৰ্বতমালা। তিব্বতীয়সকলৰ পৰা ভূমিকম্প আৰু অন্যান্য মহাপ্ৰলয়সমূহ সম্পৰ্কে তথ্যৰ আমাৰ অতি প্ৰয়োজন। তেওঁলোকে এই তথ্যসমূহ বৰ সুন্দৰকৈ সংৰক্ষণ কৰিছিল। পৰিৱেশ বৰ্তমান সময়ৰ এটা অতি গুৰুত্বপূৰ্ণ বিষয়ঙ্গ চীন মাও-চে-তুঙৰ প্ৰকৃতি বিদ্বেষী ক্ৰিয়া-কলাপসমূহৰ পৰা এতিয়াও মুক্ত হোৱা নাই বুলি আগতে কৈছোঁ। অসমৰ গঁড়সমূহ একমাত্ৰ তাৰ খৰ্গৰ বাবে হত্যা কৰা হয়। এই ব্যৱসায়টো যোৱা শতিকাৰ পৰা চোৰাং চিকাৰীবোৰক মোটা অংকৰ ধন দি একাধিক চোৰাং ব্যৱসায়ীয়ে কেৱল ব্যৱসায়িক উদ্দেশ্যত কৰি আহিছে। কেৱল খৰ্গৰ বাবে গঁড় হত্যা কৰাটো অসভ্যতা। চীনে তেওঁলোকৰ পণ্য বজাৰখনৰ বিষয়ে উত্থাপন কৰা সকলোবোৰ প্ৰশ্নৰ উত্তৰ দিয়া নাই। চীনে এতিয়াও ছাৰ্কৰ ফানৰ চুৰুহা খায়। এটা ডাঙৰ ছাৰ্ক হত্যা কৰা হয় একমাত্ৰ তাৰ ফানৰ বাবে। ই মোটা অংকৰ ধন দিয়ে আৰু এতিয়াও ভাৰত মহাসাগৰত এই কাৰ্য চলি আছে। এইবোৰ বিষয়ত চিনৰ দায়বদ্ধতা ক'ত?

কেৱল তিব্বতেই নহয়, বৰঞ্চ যদি আমি ডিএনএ পৰীক্ষা কৰো উত্তৰ-পূবৰ ৯০ শতাংশ লোকৰ গাত তিব্বতীয় ডিএনএ পোৱা যাব। চীনে সেই সত্যটোৰ লগত সংঘাত কৰিব নোৱাৰে। উত্তৰ-পূব চীন আৰু ভাৰতৰ মধ্যাৱস্থাৰ দেশ।

যি কি নহওক, ভাৰতীয়সকলৰ বাবে এটা বাৰ্তা, মই অসমৰ। মোক তিব্বতীয় মূলৰ বুলি ক'ব।

০০০

|| তৃতীয় অধ্যায় ||

এটা মনোৰঞ্জক অংশ

চীনে উচ্চ হিমালয়ত সুৰংগ নিৰ্মাণ কৰিছে

চিত্ৰ ঃ(২১) মোৰ সৃষ্টিত হিমালয়ৰ মাজেৰ সুৰংগ

চীনৰ এক তৃতীয়াংশ ওখ পৰ্বতেৰে ভৰা হোৱাৰ বাবদ আৰু 'পৃথিৱীৰ টিং' তিনি মাইল উচ্চতত থকা তিব্বতো ইয়াতে থকা বাবে কিছু ঠাইত বৰষুণ নহয়। হিমালয় পাহাৰৰ গাত ঠেকা খাই মৌচুমী বতাহে ডাৱৰ আৰু বৰষুণৰ সৃষ্টি কৰে, আনহাতে পাহাৰৰ পিচফালে বৰ্ষাছায়া অঞ্চলৰ সৃষ্টি হয়। সেয়েহে ওখ ওখ পাহাৰৰ মাজেৰে যদি মৌচুমী বতাহ পাৰ হ'বলৈ সুৰঙ্গ কৰিব পাৰে ফলপ্ৰসূ হোৱা যাব। সকলো গভীৰ আলোচনাৰ পৰা আঁতৰি এইটো এটা আমোদজনক বিৰতি। এইটো মোৰ ব্লগ 'ব্ৰহ্মপুত্ৰ, য়াৰলুং ছাংপো, ছিয়াং, দিহিং, লুইত'ৰ পৰা লোৱা হৈছে।

২০১৭ৰ খ্ৰীষ্টমাছৰ দিনা ভাৰতৰ তদানীন্তন বিদেশ মন্ত্ৰী সুস্মা স্বৰাজে ভাৰতত থকা চীনৰ ৰাষ্ট্ৰদূত লু যাওহুইক ছাংগ্ৰী কাউণ্ট্ৰিত কৰিব খোজা ছাংপোৰ সুৰঙ্গৰ বাতৰিৰ বাবে অভিযোগ কৰিবলৈ দেখা কৰে। তাৰে এক অৱলোকণ আগবঢ়োৱা হ'ল।

লু ঃ কি সুৰঙ্গ মহোদয়া ? চীনে ছাংপো নদীৰ তলেৰে কি সুৰঙ্গ বনাব ? জানেনে এইটো য়াৰলুং চাংপোৰ খীচন মানে দুটা বেলেগ বেলেগ ভূভাগৰ মাজৰ চিলাই।

সু ঃ ঠিকেই আছে, ময়ো আচৰিত হৈছিলোঁ। দুটা বিবৰ্তনিক ভূখণ্ড তাতেই মিলিত হৈছে। সেয়ে এই সংযুক্ত অংশ এটা শিথিল সংযোজন। তাত যদি সুৰঙ্গ নিৰ্মাণ কৰা যায় ই চিৰস্থায়ী নহ'ব।

লু ঃ আমি সেই সম্পৰ্কে অতি সচেতন মহোদয়া, হিমালয় উদিত হৈছে, নামচা বাৰৱা ডুবি গৈছে। সুৰঙ্গ নিৰ্মাণ কৰাটো বিপৰ্যয়কৰ হ'ব।

সু ঃ এনে সুৰংগ সেই ভংগুৰ পৰ্বত শাৰীৰ মাজৰ ফাঁকেৰে সকলো দিশৰ পৰা ডুবি পৰিব পাৰে।

লু ঃ আমি সেই সম্পৰ্কেও অতি সচেতন, তদুপৰি মাউণ্ট এভাৰেষ্ট তিব্বতৰ মধ্যভাগত, বৃহত্তৰ অংশত বৰ্ষাছায়াৰ সৃষ্টি কৰে। তিব্বত ৩.৫ মাইল উচ্চতাৰ, সেয়েহে ইয়াত অক্সিজেনৰ পৰিমাণ যথেষ্ট কম। কাজেই কোনো প্ৰকাৰৰ আৰামদায়ক ঠাই নহয়।

সু ঃ শুনিছোঁ যে তিব্বতীয় লোকসকলক বেইজিঙলৈ স্থানান্তৰিত কৰাৰ পাচত তেওঁলোকৰ ভাল সময়েই পাৰ হৈছে। কিন্তু তেওঁলোকৰ স্থান ল'বলৈ চীনৰ আন ঠাইৰ পৰা মানুহ আহিবলৈ ৰাজী নহয়।

লু ঃ সেইটো সঁচা, নিশ্চিত থাকক, এই কাৰণতে আমি তাত সুৰংগ বনাব নোৱাৰো।

সু ঃ কিন্তু তাকলামাকানলৈ যে পানীৰ সুৰঙ্গ কৰাৰ খবৰবোৰ পাওঁ সেই বিষয়ে আপুনি কি কয়?

লু ঃ আমি তালৈ পানীৰ ব্যৱস্থা কৰিলেও লছ্‌ভেগাছ বা কেলিফৰ্ণিয়াৰ দৰে শক্তিশালী কৰিব নোৱাৰিম। বহু ঠাইত বৰ্ষাছায়া থাকিবই।

সু ঃ ধন্যবাদ।

লু ঃ আমি যদি সুৰঙ্গ নিৰ্মাণ কৰোৰেই তেতিয়া একেবাৰে পাহাৰৰ মাজেৰেই কৰিম যাতে মৌচুমী বতাহ পাৰ হৈ যাব পাৰে। তদুপৰি, ই প্ৰকৃতিৰ প্ৰতি অনুকূল ইংগিত হ'ব। পৃথিৱীৰ এনেকুৱা বহুত পক্ষী আছে যিয়ে এই ওখ পৰ্বতবোৰ পাৰ হ'ব নোৱাৰে আৰু একা-বেঁকা কঠিন পথ ল'ব লগাত পৰে। এই সুৰঙ্গটো হ'লে এই পক্ষীবোৰ সহজে পাৰ হৈ যাব পাৰিব।

সু ঃ যেতিয়ালৈকে আপোনালোকে ভাৰতবৰ্ষ, নেপাল আদি দেশৰ পৰা শুল্ক আদায় নকৰে তেতিয়ালৈকে আমি একো অভিযোগ নকৰো।

লু ঃ আমাৰ বেংকত বহু টকা আছেঙ্গ

(সমাপ্ত)

এই তীব্ৰ ব্যঙ্গতাৰ ব্যাখ্যা কিতাপৰ মাজে মাজে পাই যাব। এটা সময়ত চীনে টাকলা মাকানত ভেগাছৰ নিচিনা চহৰ কৰাৰ খবৰ ওলাইছিল। তাৰ বাবে পানী লাগিব। মহাৰজা চীনৰ বৃহৎ অভিযান্ত্ৰিক প্ৰকল্প বৰ প্ৰিয়। যেহেতু হিমালয়ৰ বৰ্ষাছায়াৰ বাবে তাত বৰষুণ নহয়, মহাৰজা চীনে এভাৰেষ্টৰ শৃঙ্গ ফুটা কৰি মৌচুমী বায়ু বলাই নিব বুলি ব্যঙ্গ কৰা হৈছে। অৱশ্যে এভাৰেষ্ট শৃঙ্গ নেপালত অৱস্থিত, কিন্তু নেপালৰ স্কুলত যদি মেন্দাৰিণ শিকাব পাৰে, পৰ্বতৰ শিখৰ ফুটা কৰানো কি কথা? মাত্ৰ চাৰি মাইল ওখ ক্ৰেইন এখন লাগে। চীনা মহাৰজাই তিনি/চাৰি মাইলৰ 'জেভিচি' এখন কৰে, মোৰ পৰা বাহ্-বাহ্ নাপায়।

স্পষ্টীকৰণ ঃ ওপৰৰ খণ্ডটো কাল্পনিক কথা-বতৰাৰ অংশহে মাথোন। যদি কোনো জীৱিত ব্যক্তিৰ সৈতে ইয়াৰ সাদৃশ্য পোৱা যায, তাৰ বাবে লেখক দায়ী নহয়।

০০০

।। চতুৰ্থ অধ্যায় ।।

মহাদেৱৰ মহাজঁটা

পৃথিৱীৰ সকলো পৰ্বতেই এসময়ত চালুকীয়া আছিল, মসৃণ হ'বলৈ বিলিয়ন বছৰ লাগিছিল। এইটো সময়ত পৃথিৱীৰ চালুকীয়া বা তৰুণ পৰ্বতমালা হ'ল আমাৰ ভাৰতৰ হিমালয়। মই তৰুণতকৈ চালুকীয়া শব্দটো ভালপাওঁ, কাৰণ ই বাঢ়ি অহাৰ ব্যথা (growing pains)ৰ কথাও মনলৈ আনে। মোৰ এটা যুক্তিসঙ্গত আৰু অনুমানসিদ্ধ ধাৰণা, চালুকীয়া পাহাৰৰ খহনীয়া, ভূমিস্খলন, নদীৰ গতি সলনি আদি সকলো ভালকৈ প্ৰকাশ পাইছে ব্ৰহ্মপুত্ৰ কৰিডৰত। ব্ৰহ্মপুত্ৰৰ ক্ষেত্ৰত গ্লেচিয়েল উপত্যকা পদ্ধতি হোৱাৰ আশা কৰা নাযায়, আনহাতে হিমবাহ গলিলে পশ্চিমৰ হিন্দুকোষ আদি পাহাৰৰো সলনি আহিব। ব্ৰহ্মপুত্ৰক এখন মাজ দ নদী (U shape) বুলি ভুলতো ভাবিব নাপায়, অথচ সেইটোকে কৰা হৈছে। মাজে মাজে গভীৰতা অৱশ্যেই আছে, কিন্তু ওপৰৰ কথাশাৰী গড় হিচাবত কোৱা হৈছে। এই নদীৰ খহনীয়াই পূৰা ৰূপ পালে। বুৰঞ্জী হিচাবত তথ্য এটাৰ পম খেদা আৰু ভূতাত্বিক পদ্ধতিৰে কৰা সম্পূৰ্ণ বেলেগ। বালি কোন পাৰৰ পৰা আন পাৰলৈ কেনেকৈ, কেতিয়া গ'ল সেই তথ্যৰো মূল্য আছে। কিন্তু ভূতাত্বিকসকলে বিভিন্ন পদ্ধতিৰে, যেনে মাটিৰ স্তৰ, শিলৰ প্ৰব্ৰজন, শিলৰ বয়স আদিৰ দ্বাৰা, মিলিয়ন বছৰৰ কথা ক' ব পাৰে। ব্ৰহ্মপুত্ৰৰ লগত সুৰ মিলাই সহবাস কৰিবলৈ আমি লক্ষ্যসহ অধ্যয়ন কৰিব লাগে। সেইক্ষেত্ৰত মই মোৰ পৰামৰ্শ আগবঢ়ালোঁ।

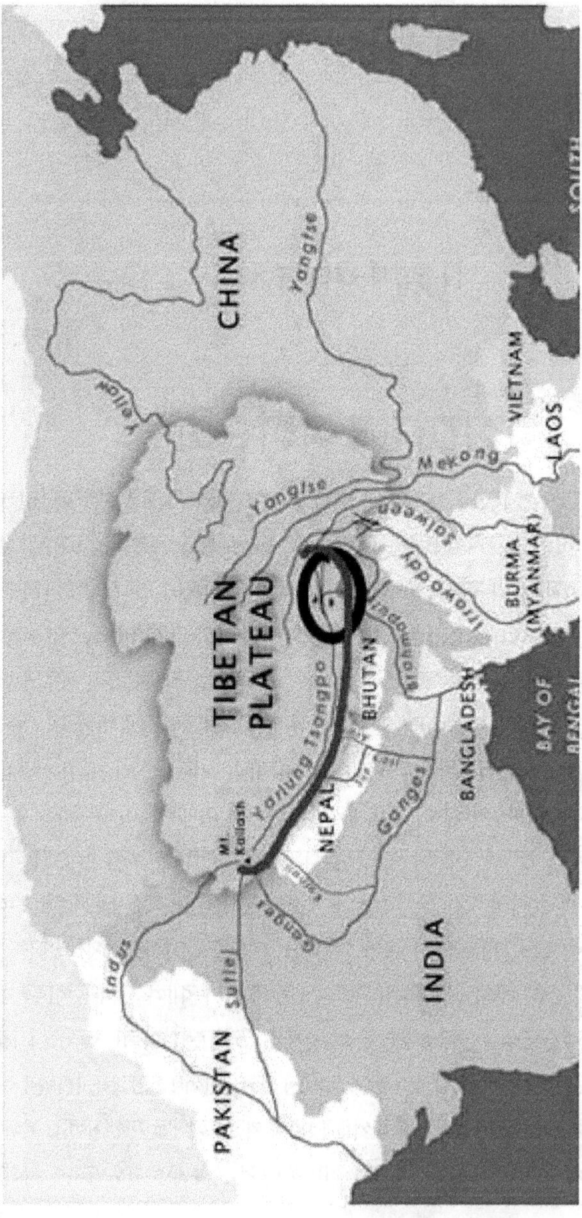

মানচিত্ৰ ঃ (২৭) মহাদেৱৰ মহাজিঙ্গী মডেল

ভূতাত্ত্বিকসকলক সজাগ কৰিবলৈ মই মহাদেৱৰ মহাজঁটা মডেলটো আগবঢ়াইছোঁ। মাউণ্ট কৈলাসৰ পৰা নীলা ৰঙেৰে আঁকা এই বক্ৰ ৰেখাই ছাংপোৰ কাযেদি কান্‌গৰী গাৰপোৰ কান্‌গৰী প' নদীৰ বাৰিগা আদি গ্লেচিয়াৰলৈকে গৈছে। এই অংশটোকে মই মহাদেৱৰ মহাজঁটা বুলিছোঁ। ই অৰুণাচলৰ উত্তৰৰ পেমাকো, চিত্ৰত ক'লা বৃত্তটো য'ত ক'লা ফুট দুটাৰে নামচা বাৰৱা আৰু গায়লা পেৰীৰ শৃঙ্গ দুটা দেখুওৱা হৈছে, সম্পূৰ্ণকৈ অন্তভুক্ত কৰা হৈছে। কান্‌গৰী প' নদীক অসমত তথা ভাৰতত লোহিত বোলা হয়। আগতে গোটেই মহাদেৱৰ মহাজঁটা তিব্বতত পৰিছিল। উল্লেখ কৰিবলগীয়া যে শিৱৰ মহাজঁটা মাত্ৰ বিছ শতিকাত ভুলতে চীনাই লৈছে। ইয়াৰ পেমাকো অংশলৈ উত্তৰ ছিয়াঙৰ য়ংকিঙৰ পৰা যাব পাৰি, বাৰিগা আদিলৈ মিছিমি পাহাৰেদি যাব পাৰি। বহুত অংশ চীনৰ পৰা এতিয়াও প্ৰৱেশ কৰিব নোৱাৰি। মোৰ ধাৰণা মহাজঁটা নদীও নহয়, হ্ৰদো নহয়, ই মহা খুন্দাৰ বাবদ চেপা খাই হোৱা টেথিছ সাগৰৰ কুণ্ড যেন শিৱই পানীখিনি তেওঁৰ শিৰৰ জঁটাত ধৰি থৈছে। মোৰ হতাশা আৰু প্ৰত্যাশাৰ প্ৰতীক হৈছে, মহাদেৱৰ মহাজঁটা। মই প্ৰত্যাহ্বান জনাইছোঁ জিঅ'ফিজিষ্ট, ভূতত্ত্ববিদ আৰু সাধাৰণ জ্ঞানৰ বিজ্ঞানী আৰু অভিযন্তাসকললৈ, মহাদেৱৰ মহাজঁটাৰ সম্পূৰ্ণ চ্যুতি, গঠন, মানে কোনখিনি ছ্ফ্‌ট পাহাৰ কোনখিনি বাথলিট ৰাইজে বুজিব পৰা স্তৰলৈ আনক। ক'ত নিৰ্মাণকাৰ্য কৰিব নাপায় আৰু কৰিলেও মাটি কেনেকৈ শক্তিশালী কৰি ল'ব ডকুমেণ্ট কৰক। নামচা বাৰৱা, গাইলা পেৰী আৰু কাঙ্গৰী গাৰ্পো যে উচ্চ হিমালয় আৰু কাষতে অৰুণাচলৰ শিৱালিক আৰু হেংডুৱানৰ মাজৰ সকলোবোৰ ভূতাত্ত্বিক জটিলতা হাইস্কুলৰ ল'ৰা-ছোৱালীয়ে বুজিব পৰাকৈ লেখক। হেংডুৱানৰ আগৰ তিব্বতত পৰাখিনি ভালকৈ দেখুৱাওক। তাৰ কাষৰ হিমবাহবোৰৰ বিশিষ্টতা ৰাইজক ভালকৈ জানিবলৈ দিয়ক। ৰাইজে তিব্বত আৰু চীনৰ অৱস্থিতি আৰু অতীতৰ বন্ধুত্ব নজনা বাবে এতিয়া এই সংকটত পৰিছে। তিব্বতীয় লিখা পাহাৰৰ ফলকত দেখিলে অসমীয়াৰ নিচিনাই লাগিব, সংস্কৃত ভিত্তিক। চীনা লিপি সম্পূৰ্ণ বেলেগ। দেখা গৈছে যে হিন্দীভাষী বা দিক্ষণ ভাৰতৰ কিছু ৰাইজে আজিকালি চীন-তিব্বতৰ পাৰ্থক্য পাহৰিছে। উত্তৰ-পূবে সেই দোষ কৰাটো মাৰ্জনীয় নহয়। তিব্বতীয়সকলে বুৰঞ্জীত ভৈয়ামক আক্ৰমণ কৰা নাই বাবেই মনত নৰখাৰ ভুলটোৰ বাবে সজাগ হ'ব লাগে। তেওঁলোক ভাৰতৰ চীন মঙ্গোলীয়া, ৰাছিয়াৰ লগত

বিভাজক, মধ্যৱৰ্তী ৰাষ্ট্ৰ। আনহাতে, প্ৰাকৃতিকভাৱে যিখিনি ঠায়ে আগতে একত্ব কৰিছিল, যুঁজাৰু বিমান, উৰাজাহাজ, হেলিকপ্টাৰৰ যুগত সেইবোৰৰ মূল্য বেলেগ হৈ গ'ল, ৰাইজেহে সজাগ আৰু সচেতন হ'বলৈ এৰিছে। কিন্তু স্থানীয় জ্ঞান, আগতেও উল্লেখ কৰিছোঁ, যাব ক'লৈ?

শদিযাত জন্ম হোৱা ভুপেনদাই কালজয়ী গানত কৈ গৈছে,

হেনো হিমালয় ভাৰতৰ প্ৰহৰী,
তাহানি শুনিছিলোঁ কাহিনী,
আজি শতেক জোৱানসৰে চিএগুৰিছে,
লাগে চিৰ জাগ্ৰত এটি বাহিনী...

উত্তৰ-পূবৰ ল'ৰা-ছোৱালীয়ে পেমাকো আৰু মহাদেৱৰ মহাজঁটাক এটা ভৌগোলিক অৱস্থিতি হিচাবে, চালুকীয়া হিমালয়ক চালুকীয়াভাৱে ভালপাবলৈ আৰু অসম কিয় ন-সম সকলোভাৱে, জনা উচিত বুলি মই ভাবোঁ।

অহৌবলিয়া চীনৰ যুক্তি, অৰুণাচলক দাবী কৰা, যিক্ষেত্ৰত ভাৰতে গোটেই পেমাকো দাবী কৰা উচিত, ৰাইজৰ মাত নুশুনো কিয়? আজি চীনে, কালি নেপালে, পৰহি পাকিস্তানে নতুন মেপ উলিয়াইছে। এই বলিয়ালিৰ শীঘ্ৰে শেষ হ'ব লাগে।

ভূতাত্ত্বিকে মহাদেৱৰ মহাজঁটা

ভালকৈ অধ্যয়ন কৰিব লাগে তলৰ তথ্যলৈ লক্ষ্য ৰাখি।

১) ওপৰৰ চিত্ৰতে সৰু ক'লা বক্ৰ ৰেখাৰে দেখুওৱা হৈছে, ছাংপো প্ৰথম ইৰাৱতীৰ লগত সংলংগ্ন, তাৰ পিচত ঘড়ীৰ কাঁটাৰ দিশত ঘূৰি লোহিতক পকৰাই লোৱা, আকৌ ঘড়ীৰ কাঁটাৰ দিশত ঘূৰি নামচা বাৰৱাৰ পাহাৰ কাটি ছিয়াঙক সংলগ্ন কৰা। ব্ৰহ্মপুত্ৰৰ এই ঘড়ীৰ কাঁটাৰ দিশত ঘূৰা স্পৃহা এতিয়াও আছে নেকি?

২) চীনাই জীয়াবুকুৰ বান্ধ, ডাগু, জিয়েচু, জাংমো আৰু জিয়াছা বান্ধ কৰি প্ৰকৃতি আৰু পানীৰ ভাৰসাম্য নস্যাৎ কৰিছে। ছাংপোৱে পাহাৰ কাটি ছিগাতছে আৰু লাছাৰ মাজৰ কোনো ঠাইদি চুম্বি উপত্যকাৰ পৰা তললৈ নামি অহাৰ সম্ভাৱনা কিমান?

৩) মই নিশ্চিতভাৱে কৈছোঁ যে ছাংপো নদী ব্যৱস্থা অসাধাৰণীয়, কৈলাসৰ

পৰা চাৰিখন নদী চাৰিওফালে ওলাইছে, সিন্ধু, ছাংপো, কৰ্ণালী, চটলেজ্ব। ছাংপো, ব্ৰহ্মপুত্ৰ, পদ্মা, কৰ্ণালীয়ে এটা চক্ৰ পথৰ সৃষ্টি কৰিছে। সেইবাবে মই মানস-তিস্তা-সোণকোষ নদী সংলগ্ন অৰ্থহীন বুলিছিলোঁ। চীনৰ বান্ধবোৰে এই চক্ৰ পথৰ নদীবোৰৰ প্ৰাকৃতিক ভাৰসাম্যতালৈ আসন্ন বিপদ আনিছে।

ভূতাত্ত্বিকে হাজাৰ বছৰ আগৰ কথাহে অধ্যয়ন কৰিব, সেই যুগ গ'ল। এতিয়া

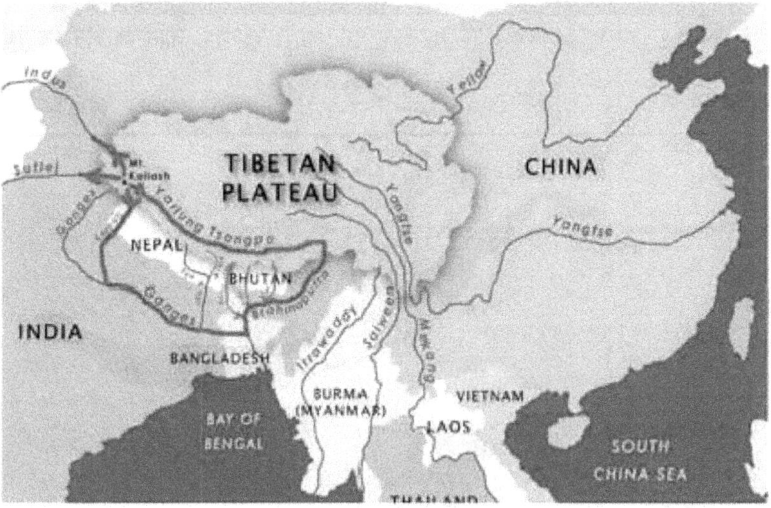

মানচিত্ৰ ঃ (২৮)

ভূতাত্ত্বিক পৰীক্ষাৰে মাটিৰ তলত কি ধৰণৰ শিল আছে ক'ব পাৰে, ব্ৰহ্মপুত্ৰৰ গেদৰ কি শতাংশ নামচা বাৰৱা কাটি অহাৰ বাবদ কিমানখিনি অৰুণাচলৰ কোন অঞ্চলৰ, পাহাৰ আৰু ভৈয়ামৰ ক'ত যৌথ নীৰ্ভৰশীলতা বিশ্লেষণ নীৰিক্ষণ পৰীক্ষণ কৰিব পাৰে।

তলৰ চিত্ৰৰ পৰা এই অঞ্চল কিমানলৈ আহিল, অন্তত গেদ পলসৰ ক্ষেত্ৰত, সকলো ৰাইজে বিদিত আৰু সতৰ্ক হ'ব লাগে। এইখিনিতে 'বাথলিট' মানে মই কি বুজোঁ কৈছোঁ। 'বাথলিট' হৈছে পৃথিৱীৰ পৰা ওলাই অহা মেগমা (গলিত শিল) যি ঠাণ্ডা হৈ ডাঙৰ অঞ্চলত শিল কৰে। আগ্নেয়গিৰিৰ শিল, লাভা, মেগমা বাহিৰলৈ ওলাই বিস্ফোৰণ কৰে, কিন্তু বাথলিটৰ ক্ষেত্ৰত ই পৃথিৱীৰ বহিঃপৃষ্ঠতে

ৰৈ যায়। বাথলিট অৰুণাচলৰ দুই-একঅঞ্চলত আছে। পাহাৰৰ মাটিৰকম্পজিছনৰ বিষয়ে বহুত অধ্যয়ন হ'ব লাগে। মোৰ মতে, পেমাকোৰ লুকাই থকা হ্ৰদটোৰ কাষত এটা 'মৰেইন' আছে। 'মৰেইন' মানে হিমবাহে থৈ যোৱা ডাঙৰ আকাৰৰ শিল। আনহাতে, ব্ৰহ্মপুত্ৰৰ দিহিং চৈখোৱাৰ ব্ৰেইডেড পেটাৰ্ণ আৰু গেদৰ ঢালৰ পৰা ব্ৰহ্মপুত্ৰই কোনপিনে মোৰ ল'ব খুজিছে, কি অঞ্চল ওখ কৰিব খুজিছে বাইজে পতিয়ন যোৱাকৈ ডকুমেণ্ট হ'ব লাগিব।

শিল নোহোৱা পলস মাটিয়ে অতিশয় পানী শোষণ কৰিলে গৰাখহনীয়া

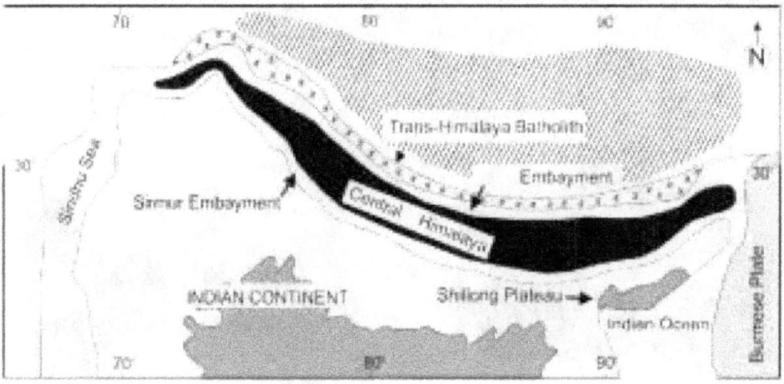

মানচিত্ৰ ঃ (২৯)

হ'বই। এমাইল দুমাইল তিতা মাটি হ'লে ইটা, চিমেণ্ট, শিল দি শক্তিশালী কৰিব পাৰি, দুশ মাইল হ'লে কৰিবলৈ কিমান খৰচ পৰিব? নেহেমীয়া হোৱা ব্ৰহ্মপুত্ৰ তেজপুৰৰ ওচৰত, গুৱাহাটীৰ ওচৰৰ পাহাৰৰ মাজৰ সংকীৰ্ণতাৰ মাজেদি আহোঁতে কিমান গেদ টানিব পাৰে? এই সাধাৰণ জ্ঞানৰ উত্তৰখিনি ৰাইজৰ হাতত পৰিব লাগে।

স্কুলৰ ল'ৰা-ছোৱালীৰ বাবে গেদ নোহোৱা নদী দেখুৱাবলৈ নগা পাহাৰ, মিজো আৰু মেঘালয়লৈ ক্ষেত্ৰ অধ্যয়নৰ বাবে নিব লাগে। উত্তৰ-পূবত স্কুলবোৰত বিদ্যাৰ্থী একচেঞ্জ প্ৰ'গ্ৰাম হ'ব লাগে। পাহাৰ-ভৈয়ামৰ তুলনা আৰু পাৰ্থক্য স্বচক্ষুৰে দেখিবলৈ পাব লাগে। গোলাঘাটত আগতে বানপানী ন'হৈছিল, ধনশিৰি নগা

পৰ্বতৰ পৰা অহা। পাৰ্ক, বানপানী, ভূমিকম্প আদি কামৰ বাবে হাতে-কামে শিকিব পৰা লোক লাগে।

ৰাজনৈতিক আৰু প্ৰাকৃতিক সীমা একে নহয়, গোদ-পলস, চালুকীয়া হিমালয়ৰ বৈশিষ্ট্য, ভূমিকম্প, ভূমিস্খলন তথা গৰাখহনীয়া, চ্যুতি, ছুচাৰ আদি প্ৰাকৃতিক অধ্যয়ন উত্তৰ-পূবে একেলগে কৰিব লাগিব।

কৈলাসৰ পৰা কাংগৰী প' নদীলৈ (কাংগৰী প' লোহিতৰ উজনিৰ নদী অংশ) এই পানী অংশৰ বিশেষত্ব আছে। আগৰ টেথিচ সাগৰৰ পানীও ইয়াত কুণ্ড হৈ আছে, হিমালয়ৰ গঠনত এই পানী অংশৰ বহুত সা-সলনি হৈছে। মিচিমি পাহাৰৰ ওপৰৰ ব্ৰজ যোগিনীৰ শিৰ অতি শীঘ্ৰে প্ৰতীক হিচাপে তীব্ৰতীয় মূলৰ আৰু বহুত স্থানীয় লোকৰ হৈ মহাৰাজ চীনে নতুনকৈ বুৰঞ্জী লিখাৰ আগতে ৰক্ষা কৰক।

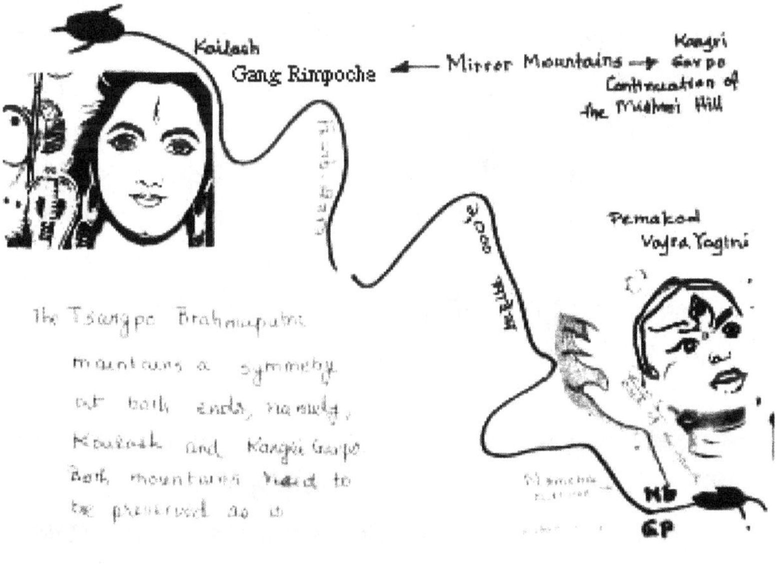

শিৱ-ব্ৰজ যোগিনী

চিত্ৰ : (২২) কৈলাস আৰু মিচিমি পাহাৰৰ ওপৰৰ

কংম্পং কাউণ্ট্ৰি। ছাংপো-ব্ৰহ্মপুত্ৰ সাধাৰণ নৈ নহয়, ইয়াৰ বহুত অধ্যয়নৰ আৱশ্যক

০০০

পৰিশিষ্ট (APPENDIX)

মোৰ ব্লগ ২০১৭ৰ নৱেম্বৰত ছিয়াং নদীৰ প্ৰদূষণ আৰু চীনাই ছাংপোৰ পৰা কৰা সুৰঙ্গৰ খবৰৰ ওপৰত, সেই সময়ৰ এটা চুটি আলোকচিত্ৰ।

'দ্য ব্ৰহ্মপুত্ৰ, য়াৰলুং ছাংপো, জাংবো, ছিয়াং, দিহিং, লোহিত', (The Brahmaputra, youlong Tsangpo, Zangbo, Siang, Dihing, Lohit)

মোৰ দ্বাৰা সংগৃহীত ২০১৭ চনৰ সংক্ষিপ্ত বাতৰি

১) ভাৰত চৰকাৰৰ বাতৰিৰ টাইমলাইনৰ পৰা লোৱা (বেছি সংখ্যকেই সংসদত উত্থাপন কৰা প্ৰশ্ন), ডিচেম্বৰ ২৮, ২০১৭; কেন্দ্ৰই আজি কৈছে যে ছিয়াং নদীৰ পানী অস্বচ্ছতাৰ পৰিৱৰ্তনৰ কাৰণ এতিয়াও জানিব পৰা হোৱা নাই। লোকসভাৰ জলসম্পদ মন্ত্ৰী অৰ্জুন ৰাম মেঘৱালে এই প্ৰশ্নৰ উত্তৰত কৈছিল, ১১ ডিচেম্বৰত চীনৰ বিদেশ মন্ত্ৰীৰ সাম্প্ৰতিক ভাৰত যাত্ৰাৰ সময়ত ছিয়াং নদীৰ পানীৰ গুণগতভাৱে অস্বাভাৱিক পৰিৱৰ্তন সম্পৰ্কে সাম্প্ৰতিক প্ৰতিবেদনসহ আন্তঃসীমান্ত নদী সম্পৰ্কীয় বিষয়সমূহ চীন পক্ষৰ আগত উত্থাপন কৰা হৈছিল।

২) নৱেম্বৰ ১০, ২০১৭; মেঘৱালে কৈছিল যে, ১০ নৱেম্বৰত ছিয়াং নদীৰ পানীৰ ৰঙৰ পৰিৱৰ্তন অৰুণাচল প্ৰদেশৰ কেন্দ্ৰীয় জল আয়োগ দ্বাৰা (CWC) টিউটিং হাইড্ৰল'জিকেল পৰ্যবেক্ষণ (HO) এলেকাত দেখা গৈছে।

৩) ইয়াৰোপৰি, পাচিঘাটৰ পানীৰ নমুনাসমূহৰ পৰা আৰুণাচল প্ৰদেশ চৰকাৰৰ জলস্বাস্থ্য অভিযান্ত্ৰিক আৰু জল সৰবৰাহ বিভাগৰ দ্বাৰা পৰিচালিত পানীৰ গুণগত পৰীক্ষাৰ ফলাফলসমূহত অনুমোদিত সীমাৰ উপৰঞ্চি গেদ আৰু লৌহ পোৱা গৈছে। ইয়াৰ উপৰি নেৰিৱাল্‌ম (NERIWALM)ৰ সঞ্চালনাত পাচিঘাট আৰু জোনাইত ছিয়াঙৰ পৰা লোৱা পানীৰ নমুনাৰ ভৌতিক ৰাসায়নিক

বিশ্লেষণত সেৱন কৰিবৰ উপযোগী আৰু অনুমেয় সীমাৰ ওপত এলুমিনিয়াম আৰু আইৰন পোৱা বুলি মন্ত্ৰীজনে কয়। টিউটিঙত পানীৰ স্তৰৰ পৰিৱৰ্তনো কেন্দ্ৰীয় জল আয়োগ (CWC)ৰ দ্বাৰা পৰ্যবেক্ষণ কৰা হয়।

৪) ভাৰতবৰ্ষৰ দুজন বিজ্ঞানী, চিন্তন শেঠ আৰু অনিৰ্বান দত্ত ৰয়ে এটা প্ৰবন্ধত লিখিছিল ঃ তিব্বতৰ ভূমিকম্পৰ ফলত হোৱা বৃহৎ ভূমিস্খলৰ বাবে ব্ৰহ্মপুত্ৰৰ পানী লেতেৰা বুলি এজন সাংসদে লোকসভাত প্ৰকাশ কৰিছিল। জমা হোৱা লেতেৰা বস্তুবোৰে তিনি ঠাইত আংশিকভাৱে বাধাৰ সৃষ্টি কৰিছে আৰু যাৰ বাবে চীনৰ ৬ কিঃমিঃ সীমাৰ প্ৰাকৃতিক নদীবান্ধ ১২ কিঃমিঃ দৈৰ্ঘ্যজুৰি সৃষ্টি হৈছে। আৰু পোৱা গৈছে যে নৱেম্বৰ '১৮-১৯ত টিউটিভত পানীৰ প্ৰৱাহ হ্ৰাস পাইছিল (প্ৰায় ১.৯৬ মিটাৰ, হয়টো স্তৰ আৰু আনুমানিক ৫০ শতাংশ পানীৰ প্ৰৱাহ হ্ৰাস পায়)।

৫) তাৰ মাজত, ব্ৰহ্মপুত্ৰৰ পানী অন্য পথেৰে লৈ যাবলৈ চীনে নিৰ্মাণ কৰা ১,০০০ কিঃমিঃ দৈৰ্ঘ্যৰ সুৰঙ্গৰ প্ৰসংগত কৰা প্ৰশ্নৰ উত্তৰ দিবলৈ গৈ ৰাজ্যিক বৈদেশিক পৰিক্ৰমা মন্ত্ৰীয়ে ক'লে, ব্ৰহ্মপুত্ৰৰ পানীৰ গতিপথ সলনি কৰা কাৰ্য আলোচনাত অন্তৰ্ভুক্ত নাই। মন্ত্ৰীজনে লগতে ক'লে যে, "আমি অন্তঃসীমান্তৰ্বৰ্তী নদীসমূহৰ বিষয়টোত ব্যস্ত থাকিব খোজোঁ আমাৰ স্বাৰ্থ ৰক্ষা কৰিবৰ বাবে।"

৬) ভূমিকম্পৰ কিছু তথ্য আৰু পূৰ্বাভাস আইআইটি, ৰুড়কীৰ পৰা আহিছিল। এই স্থানীয় অংশগ্ৰহণ গুৰুত্বপূৰ্ণ। এইটোও লক্ষণীয় যে ব্ৰহ্মপুত্ৰ নদীখন এতিয়াও ডিব্ৰু-চৈখোৱাৰ ওচৰৰ অঞ্চলৰ বৰ্যাৰণ্যত আৰু নৱেম্বৰ '১৮-১৯ত স্বমীৰ টিউটিভত পানী প্ৰৱাহ হ্ৰাস পাইছিল (প্ৰায় ১.৯৬ মিটাৰ হয়গৈ স্তৰ আৰু আনুমানিক ৫০ শতাংশ পানীৰ প্ৰৱাহ হ্ৰাস পায়)। তাৰ মাজতে, ব্ৰহ্মপুত্ৰৰ পানী অন্য পথেৰে লৈ যাবলৈ চীনে নিৰ্মাণ কৰা ১,০০০ কিঃমিঃ দৈৰ্ঘ্যৰ সুৰঙ্গৰ প্ৰসংগত কৰা প্ৰশ্নৰ উত্তৰ দিবলৈ গৈ ৰাজ্যিক বৈদেশিক পৰিক্ৰমা মন্ত্ৰী (অৱসৰপ্ৰাপ্ত) ভি কে সিঙক কৈছিল যে চীনা পক্ষই কেইবাবাৰো আমাক অৱগত কৰিছিল যে তেওঁলোকে কেৱল নদী জলবিদ্যুৎ প্ৰকল্প চলাই আছে, য'ত ব্ৰহ্মপুত্ৰৰ পানীৰ গতি সলনি কৰা কাৰ্য অন্তৰ্ভুক্ত নাই।

গাঁও আৰু অন্য ঠাইত ২০০০ চনৰ এনে মহাপ্লাৱন হোৱাৰ তথ্য পোৱা যায়।

(সংক্ষিপ্ত খবৰৰ সমাপ্তি)

মোৰ ব্লগ

তাৎপৰ্যপূৰ্ণভাৱে, ১৭ নৱেম্বৰ, ২০১৭ৰ ৬.৪ প্ৰাবল্যৰ ভূমিকম্পত ভূমিস্খলনৰ সৃষ্টি হোৱা বুলি কোৱা হয়; ভাৰত বতৰ বজ্ঞান বিভাগৰ ৱেবছাইট য'ত ভাৰতক প্ৰভাৱিত কৰা ভূমিকম্পৰ পৰ্যবেক্ষণ কৰা হয়, তাত সেই ভূমিকম্প আৰু তাৰ পিছৰ সংঘৰ্ষ সম্পৰ্কে কোনো উল্লেখ নাই। এইটো লিপিবদ্ধ কৰি ৰাখক যে কেৱল চীনে সেই ভূমিকম্পৰ বিষয়ে প্ৰতিবেদন আগবঢ়াইছিল, কিন্তু কিয়?

দুৰ্যোগ ব্যৱস্থাপনা

অত্যন্ত উদ্বেগজনক বিষয়টো হ'ল, কাকতসমূহে ভূমিস্খলন বা সুৰংগৰ কাহিনী প্ৰকাশৰ ক্ষেত্ৰত দুয়োটাৰ ভিতৰত এটাহে প্ৰকাশ কৰিছে। চীনাই নামছা বাৰবাৰ ভূমিস্খলন তিনিটা প্ৰাকৃতিক বান্ধে কৰিছে বুলি কৈছে। গছ-গছনি আৰু ভূমিস্খলনে মাটি আৰু আন জাবৰ গোট খুৱাই এই পৰিস্থিতি কৰিছে। মই এই বিশ্লেষণ বুজিবলৈ পৰা নাই। তাৰমানে এতিয়া ভাৰবৰ্ষৰ কাৰণে প্ৰধান উত্তেজনাৰ আৰু উদ্বেগৰ বিষয় হ'ল যে এই তিনিটা প্ৰাকৃতিক বান্ধে, অতি সোনকালেই মহাপ্লাৱন প্ৰৱাহিত কৰিব। ছিয়াং সীমান্তৰ ওচৰৰ এই বান্ধ (বাধা)সমূহ পৰিষ্কাৰ কৰা আৰু পানীৰ বাবে তাত সৰু সৰু পথ তৈয়াৰ কৰা আৰু পানীৰ প্ৰৱাহটো লাহে লাহে বাহিৰৰ ফালে যাবলৈ দিয়াত কি ইমান জটিলতা আছে? বৰ্তমান খনন কাৰ্য চলোৱা সহজ। টিপাৰ আৰু সকলো ধৰণৰ ট্ৰেক্টৰসমূহ আৰু গধুৰ যন্ত্ৰাংশ চীনে ভাৰত বা অৰুণাচললৈ ৰুটিনমতে আনে। কিয় এনে ভূমিস্খলন সৃষ্টিৰ সাধাৰণ ছবি প্ৰকাশ কৰা নাই? তিব্বতত ব্ৰহ্মপুত্ৰৰ উত্থানৰ বাবে বাংলাদেশে কিয় কোনো আগ্ৰহ বা পৰামৰ্শ প্ৰদান কৰা নাই?

এইটো সঁচা যে বাংলাদেশে এতিয়াও ফাৰাক্কা বান্ধৰ বিষয়টোতে লাগি আছে। যি কি নহওক, এতিয়া গাংগা গোমুখী হিমবাহ শুকাই যোৱাৰ পিছত ই সকলোৰে বিষয়ে সমস্যা। বাংলাদেশে কেৱল ভুটানক তাৰ উজনিৰ মানস-সন্তোষ-তিস্তামুখী উচ্চ ভূমি হিচাপেহে গণ্য কৰে। যদি দুখন দেশে একেলগে কাম নকৰে, এক প্ৰবল মহাপ্লাৱন যিকোনো সময়তেই হ'ব পাৰে। প্ৰত্যেক ব্যক্তিয়ে সদায় ঘটনাৰ

ৰাজনীতিকৰণৰ ওপৰত কাম কৰিব নালাগে, তাৰ ঠাইত বাস্তৱতাক প্ৰকাশ কৰিব লাগে আৰু তৎকালীন সমাধানৰ বাবে সচেতন হ'ব লাগে।

২০১৮ৰ ব্লগ 'দ্য ব্ৰহ্মপুত্ৰ, য়াৰলুং ছাংপো, জাংবো, ছিয়াং, দিহিং, লোহিত', (The Brahmaputra, Yarlung Tsangpo, Zangbo, Siang, Dihing, Lohit)

সকলোতকৈ ভয়ঙ্কৰ খবৰটো আহিল 'ডি প্ৰিণ্ট' ৱেবছাইটটোৰ পৰা। "শেহতীয়াভাবে কৃত্ৰিম উপগ্ৰহৰ পৰা সংগ্ৰহ কৰা চিত্ৰত দেখা গৈছে যে ব্ৰহ্মপুত্ৰ, য়াৰলুং ছাংপো নদী চীনৰ চাৰিশ মিটাৰ ভূগৰ্ভস্থ সুৰঙ্গ এটাত বিলীন হৈ গৈছে।" —এই শিৰোনামৰ অৱসৰপ্ৰাপ্ত কৰ্ণেল বিনায়ক ভাটে লিখা খবৰ এটাত। মই 'ডি প্ৰিণ্ট'লৈ ধন্যবাদসহ সসম্ভ্ৰমেৰে তেওঁৰ উক্তিটো তুলি দিছোঁ। ভাটে এইটো অতি ক্ষিপ্ৰতাৰে কৰা নিৰ্মাণ কাৰ্য বুলিছে।

"Satellite images clearly show stone crushers and cement plants at the site. The products of this facility are obviously used inside these tunnels for construction purposes. The material being quarried from inside these tunnels is being piled along the river up to the road level. Most of the stones have been crushed to different sizes and some of it may be pushed into the river along with the water flow. A large number of tippers and other vehicles are seen carrying material to and from this area. We also see an administrative area east of the project with a large number of red-roofed houses and barracks, possibly living quarters for staff and may also contain administrative buildings."

(কৃত্ৰিম উপগ্ৰহৰ পৰা পোৱা চিত্ৰখনত স্পষ্টভাৱে সেই স্থানৰ শিল ভঙা মেচিন তথা কোৰেৰী আৰু চিমেণ্ট প্ৰস্তুত কৰা অংশ দেখা পোৱা গৈছে। ইয়াৰ উৎপাদিক সামগ্ৰী এই সুৰঙ্গ নিৰ্মাণৰ উদ্দেশ্যে ব্যৱহাৰ কৰা হ'ব। ...)

BLACK WATERS

Satellite imagery shows that polymer resin adhesives are being sprayed by China all around this project area as a dust suppressant system. The resin adhesives are commonly used for large construction projects but are never used for projects near water, according to some water projects construction engineers, since these polymer resin adhesives are said to be harmful to humans and animals.

ক'লা পানী

(কৃত্ৰিম উপগ্ৰহৰ পৰা লোৱা চিত্ৰত দেখা গৈছে যে এই প্ৰকল্প ক্ষেত্ৰৰ চাৰিওফালে ধূলিৰ চামনি কমাবলৈ পলিমাৰৰ ৰেজিন আঠা ছটিয়াই দিছে। ৰেজিন আঠা সাধাৰণতে ডাঙৰ প্ৰকল্পত ব্যৱহাৰ কৰা হয়, কিন্তু পানীৰ লগত জড়িত থকা প্ৰকল্পত নহয়, যিহেতুকে এই আঠা জীৱ-জন্তুৰ বাবে অপকাৰী।)

০০০

সূচকাঙ্ক

Bibliography (missing publisher info)

- Elizabeth Rush, "Rising, Dispatch from the New American Shore", Milkweed Editions, 03/12/2019
- Fred Pearce, "When the Rivers Run DryÊ. Water, the Defining Crisis of the Twenty-first Century", Beacon Press, 2006
- Dalai Lama, "My Land, My People".
- Patrick McCully, "Silenced RiversThe Ecology and Politics of Large Dams", Zed Books
- Craig Simmons, "The Devouring Dragon. Ê. How China's Rise Threatens Our Natural World", St. Martin's Publishing Group, 2013
- Maro De Villiers, "Water, The facts of our Most Precious Resource", Houghton Mifflin
- Brahma Chelanney, "Water, Asia's New battleground", Georgetown University Press, 2011
- Laurence C. Smith, "The World in 2050", Penguin Publishing Group, 2010
- A documentary by Gary Marcuse, "Waking the Green Tiger"
- JR Mukherjee, "An Insider's Experience of Insurgency in India's North-East, Anthem Press
- Jorge Daniel Taillant, "Glaciers,The Politics of Ice".Oxford University Press
- Lyman P. Van Slyke, "Yangtze, Nature, History, and the River". Addison Wesley
- GilbertM.Masters,WendellP.Ela,IntroductiontoEnvironmental Engineering and Science,3rd Edition, Pearson New International
- Water ReuseÊ. Issues, Technologies, and Applications by Marlton Books.
- J. Michael Duncan, Stephen G. Wright, and Thomas L. Brandon, Soil Strength and Slope Stability

- JudithShapiro,China'sEnvironmentalChallenges
- Tucker, David A, "Geology Underfoot in Western Washington"
- Miller, Marli Bryant,Roadside Geology of Washington Rothary, David A., "Geology"
- Naresh Chandra Ghose, Nilanjan Chatterjee, Fereeduddin, A., "Petrographic Atlas of OphioliteÊ. An example from the eastern India-Asia Collision Zone".
- Yu-Hsual Liang et.al., "Detrital zircon Evidence from Brahmaputra for Reorganization of the East Himalayan Rivers",
- TY - JOUR,AU - Liang, Y.-H,AU - Chung, Sun-Lin,AU - Liu, Da he,AU - Xu, Ye,AU - Wu, Fu-Yuan,AU - Yang, Jin-Hui,AU - Wang, Yue,AU - Lo, Ching-Hua,PY - 2008/04/01, " Detrital zircon evidence from Burma for reorganization of the eastern Himalayan river system", JO - American Journal of Science , AMER J SCI, American Journal of Science, April 2008.
- Ruth A.J.Robinsona, Cynthia A.Brezinaa, Randall R.Parrishbc, Matt S.A.Horstwoodc, Nay Win Ood, Michael I.Birdae, Myint Theinf, Abigail S.Waltersa, Grahame J.H.Olivera, Khin Zawg, "Large rivers and orogensÊ. The evolution of the Yarlung Tsangpo–Irrawaddy system and the eastern Himalayan syntaxis"
- T.K.Goswami, "Geodynamicsignificanceofleucograniteintrusions in the Lohit Batholith near Walong, Eastern Arunachal Pradesh, India"
- Denise Faye S. Janer of Nationla Institute Of Geological Sciences, University of the Philippines, "Geologies of Iloco Norte, Philippines".
- Golam Mahabub Sarwar/Mamunul H. Khan, "Sea Level Rise. A Threat to the Coast of Bangladesh"

- https://pisaspeak.wordpress.com/tag/sea-level-rise/
- https://www.internationalrivers.org/blogs/435/, "the latest version of the China Global Dams Database"
- https://www.theguardian.com/world/2017/dec/28/chinas-sponge-cities-are-turning-streets-green-to-combat-flooding
- https://www.dailykos.com/stories/2018/10/23/1806681/-NW-Hawaiian-Island-Vanished-Was-Critical-Breeding-Ground-for-Turtles-Monk-Seals-Birds
- https://theprint.in/
- Watitemsu Imchen, S.K. Patil, V. Rao, GlennT. Thong, "Geochemistry, petrography and rock magnetism of the basalts of Phek distict, Nagaland, Research Article.
- B.V. Rao, Chonchibeni Ezung and Ranjit Nayak, "Geology, Genesis and Tectonic Setting of Volcanic Rocks from Naga Ophiolite Belt".
- Sankar Chatterjee, "India's Northward Drift from Gondwana to Asia during the Late Cretaceous-Eocene".
- https://www.reuters.com, "Thaw of Himalayas set to disrupt Asia's rivers, cropsÊ. study / Reuters
- https://www.independent.co.uk, "Climate change will cause a third of ice in Himalayas and Hindukush to thaw this century, scientists warn.
- https://www.wlrn.org/post/south-florida-doomed-sea-level-rise-experts-say-no-fact-theyre-optimistic
- edugeneral.org/.../the-himalayan-range-of-mountains
- Khin Zaw, Win Swe, A.J. Barber, M.J. Crow, Yin Yin New, "Introduction to the Geology of Myanmar", correspondence: khin.zaw@utas.edu.au
- Yu-Hsuan Ling et.al., "Detrital Zircon Evidence from Burma for reorganization of the Eastern Himalayan River Sytem.
- https://en.wikipedia.org/wiki/Cherrapunji
- https://en.wikipedia.org/wiki/Continental_drift

- https://en.wikipedia.org/wiki/Andes
- https//geomaps.wr.usgs.gov/parks/province/appalach.html
- https://en.wikipedia.org, "Four Pests Campaign"
- https://en.wikipedia.org, "Mount Kailash"
- https://en.wikipedia.org , "Tibet"
- https://en.wikipedia.org/wiki/Endorheic_basin
- Climate change: Warming threatens Himalayan glaciers
- By Matt McGrath Environment correspondent BBC
- https://www.ozy.com "230000-died-in-a-dam-collapse-that-china-kept-secret-for-years/91699"
- "YaleEnvironment360" called Melting Glaciers May Worsen Northwest China's Water Woes"
- Science & EnvironmentNepaltimes.com
- By Jen Christensen, CNN, Updated 10.41 PM ET, Mon February 4, Climate change will melt vast parts of the Himalayas, study says
- https://www.weforum.org, "A third of Himalayan ice will be gone by 2100"
- Melting glaciers reveal Everest bodies - bbc.com,www.bbc.com/news/science-environment-47638436
- https://www.tibettravel.org/top-10-lakes/
- Dutta, Arup Kumar; "The Brahmaputra", National Book Trust, India, 2001

OOO

About the Author

Dr. Arati Bora Baruah is a retired Senior Specialist Engineer who worked for Boeing for 35 years and as flight test engineer for the last decade. Born in Guwahati, she came of age being educated in local educational institutions including Cotton College and Gauhati University. She continued her education in the USA at Indiana University, Bloomington, followed by University of Washington, Seattle. She completed her PhD. in Electrical Engineering at the University of Washington. As a "loaned executive" she was sent by Boeing to be professor at a local engineering college for two years. She continued to be adjunct professor for another decade. Most of her career was at Boeing.

For the past ten years she has dedicated her life to the water issues of India and global warming by research and applying her knowledge and experience in science to that end. Her accomplishments, after her retirement from Boeing, include the study of the circular nature of Brahmaputra River by working with models; proving why the rivers Teesta, Santosh and Manas should not be linked; investigating the manmade floods of Guwahati; writing various articles in *Amar Asom* regarding Subansiri Dam and the deadly folly of making mega dams for hydroelectricity in the Eastern Himalayas pointedly due to their soft-soil nature, and explaining flooding in terms of rivers accumulating slit and sedimentation. In communications tech, Dr. Baruah made a valuable contribution by being a early and vocal advocate for the Assamese Unicode standard.

SPEAKING FOR
SUCCESS
EXPANDED 10TH EDITION
IDEA-RICH TECHNIQUES TO
MASTER YOUR MESSAGE
AND POWER UP YOUR
PRESENTATIONS!
Bob 'Idea Man' Hooey
Author of "Why Didn't I THINK of That?"

10th Edition: Revised and expanded
Ingram Spark Print Edition ISBN 978-1-896737-93-5

Foreword by Peter Legge, CSP, CPAE, Hall of Fame

Dedicated to my wife, Irene Gaudet, whose encouragement, editing and dedicated support inspires me to continue **Speaking for Success! around the globe.**

Dedicated as well to those professional speaker colleagues
CAPS, NSA, VSAI, PSA-SPAIN, GSF
whose encouragement and example have helped me hone the skills needed to continue
Speaking for Success!

Dedicated to my generous professional colleagues around the globe, whose wisdom is drawn from in expanding this 10th edition. Their experience and willingness to share keeps me **Speaking for Success!**

Dedicated to my fellow Accredited Speakers, and my amazing Toastmasters friends across the globe who inspire me to keep **Speaking for Success!**

Dedicated to my amazing audiences around the globe whose attention and encouragement inspire me to keep **Speaking for Success!**

Thanks to these guest experts and friends who generously shared their wisdom…

Brian Tracy, Michael Kerr, Eilidh Milnes, Hugh Culver, Ian Gibbs, Claire Boscq-Scott, Paula Morand, David Papp, Steve Lowell, Greg Gazin, Marc Haine, Drs. Joyce Carols, Doug Stevenson, Darci Lang, Shirley Borrelli, Paul ter Wal, Barbara Khozam, David Gouthro, David Saxby, Irene Gaudet, Les Kletke, Amélie Yan-Gouiffes, Peter Legge, Mike Ogilvie, Chris Davidson, Tom Sligting, James Taylor, Julie Lewis, Sheena Walker, Alison Burns, Terry Mayfield, Sebastian Millecamps, Lani Donaldson

Speaking around the globe – a dream in process

As we begin: *32 plus years ago, I had a dream to speak my way around the globe. The challenge then* **was that** *I wasn't a great speaker and had no idea where to start. Then I met Immediate Past International President John Noonan at a business organization. I shared my goal, and he asked if I had heard of Toastmasters and encouraged me to take that first step to start my adventure. I did and it helped launch this amazing journey.*

This success manual is full of ideas, tips, and techniques learned over the past 32 years, as well as Pro-tips from fellow professionals encountered around the globe. ***2023:*** *I have travelled, in person, to 68 countries so far (will surpass 72 by the end of this year) and spoken in person in 29 countries on 6 continents, so far. As well, I have presented virtually in at least 20 since covid hit. This book contains solid foundational steps to help build both your confidence and competence as a more professional speaker. I keep updating it as I learn new skills and encounter lessons along the way.* ***I want you to succeed.*** *You can make your dream a reality, and we can help. Read on my new friends and fellow travelers!*

13 Steps, A Shaky Start

The night was dark, it was raining, and the wind was howling. There were 13 steps, in a darkened outside entrance from the dimly lit parking lot, down into the basement meeting room. How did I know? I counted them as I went down, went back up, and then, *screwed up* my courage and went back down again.

I descended slowly, hesitantly for the second time, reached out and nervously placed my hand on the doorknob. My heart was pumping (fast ☺), my legs were shaky, and my breathing was short and labored. Was I making the right decision? What would I find on the other side of the door? Maybe I should just turn around and go home? How would I react? Whose crazy idea was this anyway? Would they like me, help me, or reject me? *"Ok, Hooey, go for it!"*

I *forced* a smile on my face, turned the knob, and opened the door. I stood there for a minute, took a deep breath, and stepped into Vancouver based ***Toastmasters of Today!*** **I made that first step that has taken me around the world sharing my message of hope and encouragement.**

I still remember my first visit that Tuesday night, mid-March 1991. I was *nervous* and shy. Now, anyone who knows me will find that hard to believe, but it was very true, back then. This was a scary moment for me. I had recently come through a devastating and debilitating divorce. Frankly, I didn't feel very confident in myself or my speaking abilities. If you're a Toastmaster, remember your first visit to your club. Perhaps, like me, you felt a little nervous or intimidated by members who could get up and seemingly speak without notes or nervousness. But perhaps you too pushed past it.

I was there, reviving a dream of being a professional speaker and someday being able to stand on the big stage sharing my ideas, travelling the world, and inspiring and investing in the lives of those in the audience. It worked, well!

What I found at the bottom of those 13 steps was a supportive, friendly group of people who befriended me and became my champions, coaches, and cheerleaders; some of whom still play that encouraging role today.

- Perhaps you have had a similar experience as you began something?
- Perhaps you are feeling a bit shaky about starting down this path to becoming a better speaker? Perhaps you too want to be a more professional speaker?
- Perhaps you have played a similar role in the growth of a Toastmaster member or business friend? Coaching and mentoring work!

That **one step** into the room, following the 13 down made an amazing difference in my life and my career.

In 1998, I had the *distinct* pleasure of walking across a Palm Desert, California stage to be inducted into the Toastmasters International Hall of Fame as the 48th professional level Accredited Speaker in our rich history.

In 2008, I had the *rare* privilege of keynoting the leadership luncheon at the Toastmasters International convention in Calgary, Alberta. As part of my introduction, they played a video of me walking across that Palm Desert stage. My opening words were, ***"I may have walked across that stage by myself... but I did not get there by myself!"*** ☺

- It took those first 13 steps, ***plus*** the loving, supportive investment of thousands of fellow Toastmasters, CAPS, GSF, and NSA colleagues, over many years, to help move me toward that goal.
- It took those first 13 steps to start me on the path to living my dream of travelling the world sharing ideas and challenging people to reach out and build foundations of success under their dreams.

In 2011, I was selected as one of 300 Toastmasters International Brand Ambassadors, around the globe, appointed as influencers to help with the launch of the first re-brand in their history. I served as one of our Learning Masters as we evolved our programs. 2018-2019, I served as Region 4 Advisor. I am glad to serve and give back to this amazing organization.

When I received **The Spirit of CAPS** award (the highest award given in our Canadian speaking industry) at our 2011 Canadian Association of Professional Speakers convention in Toronto, I shared it with those in attendance. I emphasized that all the nice things our President Ravi Tangri, CSP mentioned in his introduction were not accomplished, *"by myself"*. **I simply had an idea, asked for help, a lot, and got it. So, can you!**

Your dream may not be to become a professional speaker. But, if you have invested in this book my guess is you have a desire to become a better, more confident speaker, right?

You can learn to 'Present like a PRO!' We can help!

What follows in these **'Speaking for Success'** pages are tips, creative techniques, ***proven ideas***, and exercises to help you move that dream or desire into a reality. **Ideas, when acted upon, can become forces for good that can change the world.** Evocative, engaging words reinforce those ideas and add power to your presentation inspiring people to act on your ideas.

PS: I have wished I had videos of my early speeches from Toastmasters. I tried so hard to be 'motivational', to encourage. Sadly, what I did was preach. I was stiff, didn't smile, didn't move, and came across as knowing it all. I'll give you a few links to more current videos throughout the book.

PRO-Tip: "Every member of your audience can increase their capacity to learn and go away with meaningful, valuable information providing you deliver it in consumable chunks."
Lani Donaldson, *www.lanidonaldson.com*

What is your next step?

Bob 'Idea Man' Hooey

Distinguished Toastmaster
48th Accredited Speaker worldwide
Past District 21 Governor
Toastmasters Brand Ambassador
Past Region 4 Advisor
Charter member CAPS & GSF
Member NSA-Arizona
2011 Spirit of CAPS recipient
Past CAPS National Director
Past CAPS Foundation Trustee
1998 & 1999 President CAPS BC
2012 President CAPS Edmonton
Past NSA CLC member
Charter member PSA-SPAIN, VSAI
Certified Virtual Presenter

I remember someone saying, "You should smile more." I thought I was, but ***I was so focused on 'being' that I was not allowing myself to 'become'.*** *I never realized I wasn't having fun, I was stressing.*

Later, I started relaxing and allowing my fun side to show. This was when I started connecting with my audiences. I realized that it was not about me, it was about them. When I started focusing on them and allowed myself to be 'real' on stage it all started coming together. They laughed with me, and I started becoming more effective in sharing my ideas. I love hearing them laugh.

Now, I do my homework and prepare my programs. Then I simply go on stage and 'play' along with my audiences around the globe. ***What a great idea – wished I had found out earlier.***

Bob in Athens (November 2022) where he did two presentations on leadership and professional speaking while there.

Bob's demo video: https://youtu.be/-fAFD9mkUPo www.ideaman.net

Foreword by Dr. Peter Legge, *CSP, CPAE, HofF*

So, you want to be a *more* professional speaker?

It has been said that 80 percent of the speakers in this business 10 years ago are no longer in the business. Why, you ask? They forgot it was a business and got carried away with the glamour and excitement of travel to foreign destinations, standing ovations, staying in wonderful hotels and being treated as a star – and yes, that is certainly part of the package, but first and foremost, it is a business and a tough business in which to survive and be profitable.

"Bob 'Idea Man' Hooey is a living example of the pursuit of excellence coupled with a servant spirit. His is a lasting legacy of what it means to be a true professional speaker."

His book **Speaking for Success – 10th edition** is a must-read packed with valuable ideas and "Ah-ha's" for you in your quest to stay in this business longer than 10 years.

What does it take to be a professional speaker?

My very first public engagement was when I was nine years old. We were living in England, and I had been asked to sing at the local cinema in our hometown, Greenford. The Granada Cinema on the high street held a 10 a.m. Saturday kids show way back when it was the only show in town and just about every kid in Greenford would always attend. I performed Mr. Sandman.

Was I a hit? I have no idea, but something inside me turned on to show business and little did I know that some 30 years later, I would be back on the stage as a professional speaker, travelling around the world sharing my philosophy and stories of success, from Vancouver to London to Boston to Hong Kong. I speak to varied audiences, from small groups of 25 to large theatres of some 3,000. I also travel about 100,000 miles every year. I must confess that sometimes the travel gets a bit tiring, always in and out of airports and hotels, encountering strange cab drivers from another planet, poor sound systems and many other spirit-testing problems. However, the excitement of being in front of an audience is so exhilarating and full of adventure that some days I can't believe my good fortune at getting paid handsomely for a craft that I love so much.

I have been speaking professionally for 40 plus years. I learned at the very outset that this was not a profession for wimps, nor was it a profession that was as easy as it looked. In fact, it might have been one of the biggest dreams I ever wrote down: my determination to speak on the international stage.

John Stott is the author of *Basic Christianity* and the director of the London Institute for Contemporary Christianity. He is also one of the world's foremost preachers. In 1982 I was given one of his books titled, *The Art of Preaching in the Twentieth Century – Between Two Worlds*. In it, he tells a story about the importance of preparing sermons. It is also vital to consider his words for the kind of motivational speaking that I do:

"Once upon a time there was an Anglican clergyman who was lazy. He had long ago given up the bother of preparing his sermons. He had considerable native intelligence and fluency of speech, and his congregation were simple people. So, he got by pretty well with his unprepared sermons. Yet in order to live with his conscience he took a vow that he would always preach extemporaneously.

Everything was fine until one day a few minutes before the morning service began, who should walk in to find a place in the pews but the Bishop. The parson was embarrassed. He had managed to bluff the congregation, but he was much less sure that he would hoodwink the Bishop. So, he told the Bishop that he had taken a vow to speak extemporaneously. The Bishop seemed to understand, and the service began. To the preacher's great consternation, halfway through the sermon the Bishop got up from his pew and walked to the back of the church and scribbled a note and left it on the vestry table. The Bishop wrote to the Preacher, 'I absolve you from your vow.'"

I first spoke for free whenever and wherever I could. I believed I had something worthwhile to say and that I needed exposure and self-confidence. **Practice, practice, practice**... some 500 speaking engagements for free to begin to learn the art of speaking. At the beginning I was amazed how difficult it was and to learn that most people would rather die than give a speech – which means at a funeral, you would rather be in the casket than giving the eulogy. I persisted and very slowly someone in my audience would ask me to speak at a company sales rally, perhaps for a fee of $100. I later was convinced to join the National Speakers Association. This worldwide organization is based in Phoenix, Arizona. I was told that my speaking profession would improve faster as a member of this organization.

I have some marvelous role models in the speaking profession who always encourage and motivate me to be the best I can be... **Nido Qubein**, CPAE; **Jim Cathcart**, CPAE; **Bill Bachrach**, CPAE. I then joined CAPS when we formed in 1997, as part of the Global Speakers Federation.

What makes a good keynote speaker?

1. **Passion**. First and foremost, that special something that puts a glow around you. A conviction about the subject that is supported by experience and is quickly obvious by the energy and enthusiasm of the presenter
2. **Exceptional story-telling** ability. An absolute must
3. **Confidence** on the platform
4. Obvious and **believable leadership** in your given field
5. The **ability to speak extemporaneously**. Little reference to notes except as A/V aids
6. **Humour**. A wonderful conduit for connecting with and inspiring the audience
7. **Commitment to keep learning** and passing along client experiences on an ongoing basis. (There's nothing as revealing about a speaker as stale material)
8. **Respect** for the audience. Humility laced with a strong dose of confidence is a powerful blend
9. **Courtesy** – off the stage. As important as platform skills
10. Having the **courage to try new things** with existing and new material and presentation styles. Willingness to be self-revealing
11. **Grace.** This quality, or lack of it, has a lot to do with how long a speaker lasts in the business

Learn from Ideaman Bob Hooey – I do!

Enjoy this wonderful career as a professional speaker and make a difference.

Dr. Peter Legge, OBC, CSP, CPAE, HoF
CEO/Chairman Canada Wide Media Ltd.
www.PeterLegge.com

Editor's note: *Pete and I have been friends and colleagues for many years. I first met him through his dad, Bernie, from New Westminster. I learned first-hand what it takes to be an effective professional speaker while watching Pete in action. He is a brilliant storyteller who knows how to connect with his audiences. He is also a founding member of CAPS and a member of NSA, as am I. Although I lived about 10 minutes from him when I was in BC, we normally saw each other at events and occasionally even spoke at the same ones.*

Table of Contents

Speaking for Success!
Idea-rich techniques to master your message and power up your presentation!

As you begin this journey, perhaps you might wonder, **"Why would I want to invest time to improve my speaking skills?"** The answers to these questions should provide insights into your speaking journey.

- Are you interested in learning thinking and communication skills that will **make a major difference in your long-term career** success?
- Are you interested in acquiring leadership and communication skills that will **develop your abilities** to more successfully work with other people and foster an enhanced sense of team?
- Are you interested in changing or **enhancing** your career?
- Would you like to learn an interviewing technique and enhance your confidence to **give you an *edge* on your competition**?
- Do you want to feel more **comfortable speaking** in any public situation?
- Do you have a **dream** of being a professional speaker, trainer, or facilitator?

Then, read on fellow traveler on this self-paced path of learning!

Why do some people succeed in advancing their careers while others do not? A couple of decades ago, AT&T commissioned California's Stanford University to conduct a survey to see if there were any reliable indicators.

Surprisingly, their results revealed that ***"…the top predictors of success and upward mobility, professionally, were how much you enjoy public speaking and how effective you are at it!"***

Based on my nearly 3 decades of leadership and speaking experience, this was no real surprise. Later, that same year, a report from Canadian Business Magazine mentioned 'their two indicators' were **comfort in speaking and your ability to work with people**. Frankly, the results would be similar if the study was done today.

People who become proficient at something that most of us fear tend to be noticed and often get promoted quicker!

According to the Book of Lists, **the number one fear** for most of us is speaking in public. (It has dropped in number recently.) The old joke, ***"Most people are so afraid of giving a speech they'd rather be in the casket than giving the eulogy!"*** certainly still applies. Many people are still very uncomfortable expressing their thoughts in a public forum. Perhaps you are one of them! **Good news**, you can overcome that fear… we can help!

Those who confront their fear of speaking in public gain self-confidence. Their self-confidence filters through to other areas of their professional lives and actions. This happened time and time again with my students at various colleges. This material, shared here, forms a foundational part of my executive speech coaching sessions as well.

We've had the opportunity to share these powerful ideas with leaders from some of **Canada's 50 Best Managed Companies**. I had the privilege of working with one CEO in writing and coaching his presentations when he received several Entrepreneur of the Year awards across Canada, North America, and later the globe. I've seen it demonstrated even more dramatically in one-to-one coaching sessions or in small group settings. **Mastering this leaders' skill may well be the '*pivotal*' success point in your life and career.**

Our focus is to share some basic ideas and guidelines that will help you improve your presentation skills as well as help position you to succeed in your chosen field of endeavor. It will take disciplined **'work'** on your part; but it is worth the effort! No skill is ever acquired without concentrated and continuous effort on the part of the student. **It can also be fun!** What is shared here has been proven in the lives and improved abilities of thousands of professionals who've applied these ideas, guidelines, and techniques.

In originally creating (1998), updating, and rewriting numerous times; and now (2023) expanding this **10th edition of Speaking for Success**, I drew on my personal experience as a globe-trotting, highly *paid* professional speaker and trainer. I drew, as well, from my work and management background; and my extremely *(how did I ever survive without it!)* helpful experience and learning curve in Toastmasters International as well as NSA, VSAI, GSF, and CAPS.

I un-ashamedly drew on the ideas, wisdom, notes, tips, examples, and techniques gleaned from my association with some of the world's top speaking professionals; members of NSA, CAPS, VSAI and GSF. Their creative examples and gentle support taught and continued to encourage me to work harder, to push further. Thanks, my friends!

I drew from **audience and platform PROVEN** techniques, as demonstrated in front of live audiences around the world that, with practice and application, you can turn into communication and career enhancement tools. I've seen them work when applied! You can achieve this!

Many of you will not have the dream of being a professional speaker, as I did when I started down this path some 32 plus years ago. However, each of you can learn to be more *proficient* from the examples of those who practice these results-oriented skills to earn their livelihood as professional speakers, facilitators, or trainers. I did and continue to do so on a regular basis! "**School is never out for the true professional!"** We keep learning new lessons from our peers and our audiences. That keeps us fresh and relevant in our role.

Best-selling author, management guru, and successful speaker, **Peter Drucker** wisely forecast, ***"As soon as you move one step up from the bottom, your effectiveness depends on your ability to reach others through the spoken or written word."***

Learning and applying these platform techniques and audience-proven tips and ideas will prove invaluable as you pursue your new career or advance your existing position. They have certainly worked for me. They will for you!

Effective communications training is a **'Foundation for success!'** I dedicate a significant portion of my time, study, and energy to learning, applying, adapting, and teaching these SIMPLE but POWERFUL techniques.

Speaking for Success has been a work-in-progress, designed as a stand-alone publication. When I teach a presentation skills course on-site or professionally coach a client, we use videos, coaching, lots of participation, as well as hands-on practice and on-site feedback to augment it.

You can apply and practice these ideas/skills alone or by enlisting supportive friends or family to act as evaluators or a practice audience. Better yet, join a Toastmasters Club in your area. It's a great, cost-effective way to learn and reinforce these newfound skills with great people who are also learning.

For information on how to locate a club in an area near you, visit their website: **www.toastmasters.org** (Be sure to tell them Bob Hooey sent you!) Perhaps you might attend a local NSA, CAPS Chapter, or one of the GSF meetings to observe and learn from some of the industry's top presenters.

Visit **www.NSAspeaker.org, www.CanadianSpeakers.org,** or **www.globalspeakers.net** to find a meeting near you. Tell them **Bob Hooey** sent you: ☺

Your ability to confidently and powerfully speak in front of audiences will improve in **direct** proportion to the amount of effort you invest to prepare and practice your skills. These ideas/skills are not learned *'just'* from a book, but from *'real life'* experience in front of an audience.

When I started down this path in March 1991 and joined my first Toastmasters Club, I realized the only way to improve would be in getting up and speaking. I made a commitment, that, whenever possible, to never turn down an opportunity to speak.

***To date**, other than scheduling conflicts, very few opportunities have been missed. It has helped immensely over the years! (This shot was taken during my keynote at PSASA in Cape Town, SA April 18th, 2015).*

Whether your desire is to simply overcome your fear of standing and delivering a presentation in front of an audience or stepping onto the stage as a *paid* professional speaker, these idea-rich tips and techniques will form the foundation to see that desire fulfilled. Speaking can be fun ***(yes, I said fun!)*** if you've done your homework and keep your focus on the audience. The hard work is done before you walk on stage. Then you relax and play! That's what I do!

The *hardest* part of being a professional speaker is the homework done before walking on stage to deliver your presentation. Once the homework is done, I simply get up and share my ideas, stories, and messages with the audience. It gets easier as I apply my skills and refine my focus by making sure that what is shared is of value for the audiences. You can too!

Thanks again to the tens of thousands of people in various paid audiences, Toastmasters Clubs, GSF conventions, as well as my fellow CAPS, GSF, VSAI & NSA professional speakers for their investment in my life and growth as a speaker. I hope, in passing along the secrets we've shared here, to partially repay their faith and contributions. Enjoy their PRO-tips as well!

"There are always three speeches, for every one you actually gave. The one you practiced, the one you gave, and the one you wish you gave."

Dale Carnegie

I wish you a fun-filled, life-long adventure, in following through on this major step you've undertaken in your personal and career success.

It can be a richly rewarding journey, one that you will pause and reflect upon in years to come. You'll look back and see the significant changes you've made in your life, career, and your personal effectiveness. **Enjoy the journey!**

Bob 'Idea Man' Hooey

PRO-Tip: Performance by Design is Positioning YOU as an Authority

Great Positioning will establish what you are known for in your field. It will establish your Brand Identity. This will attract the right type of client into your speaking business. As Professional Speakers and Business experts we are living in a dynamic economy. This world is dramatically changing and the way you operate needs to change. Can you imagine the future right now? Ask yourself "Am I productizing my knowledge, skills, ideas and experience as a Professional Speaker". Do you want to be that go to expert with the competitive edge? The speaker that leads the field in their industry!

Signature Model. Want to position yourself as an expert? You need to take your knowledge and skills and create your own **Unique Signature Solution.** Presenting an innovative creative framework will give your audience a map of where they are now and how you can take them to where they want to be. Without a Model, a Framework, a System, your audience will find it difficult to follow your advice. Show them a direct route to their success.

Call to Action: Revisit your solution to solve your clients' problems. Research: there are always experts out there. Reverse Engineer – what answers do your clients want. Re-organize all the challenges and what you do that gets results. Think as a futurist and lead the field.

Sheena Walker, *BA CIPD www.sheenawalker.com*

Ideas to Get The Best Use From 'Your' expanded copy of Speaking For Success

Speaking for Success contains a range of tips, techniques, and **proven ideas** to help you improve the way you create and deliver oral presentations. **It was not originally created as a book**, but a course guide for programs delivered by the author in various BC colleges. It evolved to its present ***idea-rich*** form with the inclusion of stories, creative ideas, and first-hand experiences based on copious conversations and observations of fellow professional speakers; as well as my own experiences in speaking across North America and the globe.

This is not just a book for 'casual' reading. It is a self-paced manual to be used, to be dipped into, and to be a resource or reference guide. It contains many ideas you can use. It is your personal resource, so mark it, *highlight* it, and make notes in the margins. Adopt and adapt its ideas as needed!

To get the best from this book, first visit the Table of Contents to identify which chapters and topics meet your needs. Read them carefully and make sure you understand and apply the guidelines and advice given. Some topics may not be of direct interest to you, depending on your needs. You may wish to read some of the other chapters so that you can understand the needs of other speakers or real-life scenarios where *effective* presentations are given.

Speaking for Success *does not* contain ALL the answers. It is a collection of thoughts, tips, techniques, lessons learned, and **ideas** shared from one speaker's viewpoint, *mine.* It is intended as an aid to your reflection, learning, and inspiration – a resource full of ideas that you can draw upon in preparation for your presentations. Its aim is to give you an idea-rich resource that, when applied and practiced in real presentations, will help you develop and build both your confidence and competence as a presenter.

A productive approach for its use would be to take the ideas, tips, and concepts presented here and blend them with your own style, personality, and creativity. Keep in mind your own time constraints and 'comfort zone as a presenter,' to generate unique and personalized ideas on how you can create, give, and improve your presentations.

2023: This idea-rich book was re-designed and expanded to offer you flexibility in terms of how you use it.

1) You can sit down for an hour or two and read it **cover to cover**. This is a great way to start by getting a feel for what is included, especially for newer or beginning speakers who want to gain the full benefit from their investment.

A word of advice:

Speaking for Success *is the result of 32 plus years of determined study and 30 years first-hand experience on the stage, in the classroom, and coaching executive clients. It might seem overwhelming or a bit confusing at first with the range of ideas and information we've included here. Once you have done a quick read of the whole book, I suggest you then identify specific sections, ideas, or tips that interest you and work on more manageable chunks at a time. As you gain confidence, tackle another piece.*

2) You can select one **chapter** or **section** at a time and work to incorporate the ideas you find into your own presentation style.

3) You can look at the **Table of Contents** and jump straight to the tips, ideas, or areas of study that particularly interest you.

We have attempted to incorporate something of benefit for everyone, regardless of your current level or skill in public speaking. You might even find some *seemingly* contradictory advice in different parts of the book! This is because there is no single, universal **'right answer'** – you must find what is right for you, your objective, and your audience's needs. What works for you is what is best! Choose it, try it, and adapt it as needed to serve you in your quest to be a more powerful speaker.

"Effective speaking communicates the message in a way that makes it easier for the listener to relate and react positively to what they (listener) understand. Effective speaking is helped or enhanced by 'charting-a-course' to convey your message with impact."

Bob 'Idea Man' Hooey

We've created a series of Speaking Videos just for our readers. You can find them plus others on my YouTube channel. **www.youtube.com/user/ideamanbob**

Where Do I Stand Now In My Journey As A Speaker?

Think about the last time you gave a presentation or spoke in front of a group (*however small)*. Think back and give yourself some honest feedback on your performance and perceptions as a speaker or presenter. The key to a successful journey or goal is in accurately determining your starting point.

Someone asked me these types of questions at the start of my Toastmasters journey in 1991. I admit, I said "NO" to too many of them at that time. Each, however, points to a skill that can be easily acquired, polished, and applied. **Practice, Practice, Practice!**

Remember these questions are for your information only, so be honest.

DO I PRESENTLY…

	Yes	No
1. Feel comfortable talking to other people?	___	___
2. Have trouble explaining my views or ideas?	___	___
3. Have nervous habits when I speak, such as saying um, uh Ok, you know, and ah, or fumbling with buttons, clothes, glasses, or change in my pocket?	___	___
4. Focus on the audience's needs and interests when I make a presentation? (It's not about me)	___	___
5. Plan my presentations with a clear purpose in mind?	___	___
6. Appear to be natural and sincere when I'm speaking?	___	___
7. Listen carefully and analytically to other speakers?	___	___
8. Feel comfortable receiving feedback from others?	___	___
9. Offer feedback in a constructive, positive way that doesn't cause others pain or embarrassment?	___	___

Your answers to these questions can prove to be the guideposts to the specific areas that you need to learn and the skills you need to apply in your pursuit to become a powerful presenter. It might be a good idea to come back several times as you proceed through this course of self-study and evaluate your progress.

Apply yourself and practice the ideas and techniques in this book and **you'll be amazed with the results!**

"WORK... Nothing worthwhile comes easily. Half effort does not produce half results, it produces no results. Work, continuous work and hard work, it is the only way to accomplish results that last."

Hamilton Holt

You'll see Pro-tips sprinkled throughout this expanded 10th edition. I've invited some of my professional colleagues from around the world to share ideas from their experience and expertise. **Thanks to each friend who generously shared their wisdom and insights!**

Here are a few to whet your appetite: Enjoy!

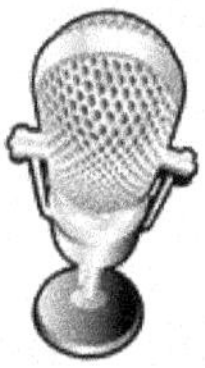

PRO-Tip: Speaker G.L.U.E.

I highly recommend speakers take time to **G.L.U.E – Gather Lots of Unusual Experiences!** Experiences, be they good, bad or downright ugly, give us great stories to share with our audiences. Building a strong emotional connection from the stage is essential to success. Referencing your experiences and sharing the parallels to business & life gives speakers the leading edge. Go out today and gather some unusual experiences!

Bonus tip – when you are travelling overseas to speak at an event get there a day earlier where possible, explore the location and add in a story about what you saw / experienced – it's an audience winner! At the very least learn how to say "hello" and "thank you" in the language of the country you are speaking in.

Julie Lewis, *www.julie-lewis.com*

PRO-Tip: "Speak with enthusiasm:

Perhaps it's self-evident, however. it is also elementary that to be a good speaker you need to speak with enthusiasm; project a confident stance, maintain a positive posture. You are your number one visual, and you need to make your first impression count.

You also want your material to be memorable and beneficial to your audience. I suggest that you drop your DNA into your talk. By that I mean **D**eliver with style, know your **Ni**che, and be your **A**uthentic self.

D = delivery
N = niche
A = authenticity

Drama is everything! So is fun! When you arrive on the platform, stand for a few moments; let the audience anticipate your presentation or say something funny to relax them, if you can manage both that's fantastic. Let your humor shine. Boring speakers are a dozen dime. **Be different. Create a mental and visual sorbet!**

I love to use props, 'Humor Enhancers' or 'Memory Activators'. I'm known for 'Positive Pointers'. Clients love them too. What can you do to boost the enjoyment of your audiences? Something that will linger in their memories; help them to reframe your message and embed your key action points?

Take time to have fun, as Bob Hooey does. Audiences will love the difference! They will remember you and your quality content. And who knows where that will lead?"

Eildh Milnes, FPSA Past President PSA-UKI (deceased)

PRO-Tip:

"As a professional speaker, I find myself in front of audiences who hire me to speak and inspire day after day. However, it is when I find myself in front of one person**, a coach** that I hire, that I can receive the feedback I need to improve and be better for my clients."

Sébastien Millecamps
Professional speaker, coach, trainer, author of French Flair
www.sebastienmillecamps.com

Ideas on Entertaining and Special Occasion Presentations

You may never dream of becoming a professional speaker, but if you are reading this you most likely want to be more comfortable when you are called on to speak or make a presentation. You may encounter some of these opportunities to give specialized presentations. You can speak like a PRO! The basic ideas and use-immediately techniques covered in **Speaking for Success** will certainly apply to each of these examples.

You need to be aware of these different types of speeches and realize **their objectives determine and influence their format**. Knowing that helps you craft and deliver more effective presentations.

- **Introductions:** You might be called on to introduce a speaker, facilitator, official, or trainer brought in to do a presentation.
- **Welcome presentations:** You might also be called on to say a few words if a group visits your workplace.
- **Acceptance speeches:** Imagine you've just been honored or given an award.

Nov. 28th, 2011: *I was surprised with the highest honor given within the Canadian Association of Professional Speakers –* ***The Spirit of CAPS award****. As I headed up to the stage, I worked to calm myself and collect my thoughts. While we were taking pictures, my mind was grasping for the words to express how I felt at that moment.*

Visit: **www.ideaman.net/SoC.htm** to view the award presentation and my impromptu acceptance speech.

- **Inauguration speech:** You've just been elected to a leadership role in a volunteer group and are called on to say a few words following the election.
- **Eulogies:** This can be an emotionally challenging role, if you were close to the person who has recently passed away and are called to say a few words about their life.

I remember choking back my own tears as I said goodbye to my dad while watching my mom silently crying in the audience. I spoke from the heart about my dad as a man, as a father, as a compassionate caring person, and as a role model.

- **Toastmaster/MC:** Perhaps you are called on to Emcee (MC) or are the toastmaster at a wedding or an award ceremony.

I had the privilege of doing this for two of our friends in 2011 and was able to work in some special 'fun' pieces just for them. I've also been hired as a professional MC too.

- **New employee orientations:** Perhaps your employer will ask you to help orient new hires.

When I was part of the opening management team for the 1st two BC, Home Depots, we used to take turns doing this for new hires to outline what we expected and help them settle into our culture.

- **The farewell speech:** Stepping down from a leadership role and leaving a long-term position in a company or group – you might want to say a few words of thanks and reflect on the time you spent and the people who enriched your life.

I remember saying my 'official' goodbyes when I stepped off the CAPS Foundation board at the end of year 5 of my 3-year term. ☺ It was hard to say goodbye, but it was time to allow someone else to step in and take over. ***Update 2023:*** *They have done an amazing job.*

Each of these unique presentation scenarios has a different focus and purpose and would then be structured and delivered appropriately. If presented with an opportunity of doing one of these:

- Take a minute to decide what you want to accomplish.
- Give some thought on how to structure it to best reach that goal or objective.
- **Treat each as an opportunity to practice and polish your skills.**
- Treat each as an opportunity to expand your toolbox of experience in front of an audience.
- You will grow, only by stretching and expanding past your comfort zones.

Speak to inspire!

"What is our aim? I answer in one word. Victory – victory at all costs, victory in spite of all terror, victory, however long and hard the road may be; for without victory, there is no survival."

Winston Churchill

Qualities of An EFFECTIVE Leader, Speaker, or Coach

Becoming an effective leader, facilitator, speaker, trainer, or coach means learning to draw on your abilities and skills to train those who need your help. Since I moved into the realm of professional speaking and training, I've learned first-hand the importance of these traits. **EFFECTIVE impactful, communication is a critical skill in each of these roles.**

I have worked diligently to enhance them in my own efforts as a leader and trainer, as well as a presenter and traveler around the globe. (67 countries, so far) In addition to my speaking, training, or facilitation roles, they work very well in management situations, on the job, and in the co-ordination, motivation, and management of volunteers and direct reports as well.

Many of these traits are demonstrated by the top leaders across North America, which is why 'leader' is in this list. As a speaker, trainer, coach, or facilitator part of what we are doing is *leading and guiding* our audiences. As a leader, your ability to communicate is critical. Here are some of the **traits of successful and *effective* leaders, speakers, trainers, and coaches.**

Good Communications Skills

- Use clear and concise language to instruct, direct, and coach
- Use *active* listening skills to draw them out and fully understand them
- Maintain eye contact

Solid understanding of the subject

- Comprehensive understanding of the subject or skills
- Willingness to draw from your background as a bridge or foundation to teach and connect
- Willingness to grow and update your professional development

Experience

- It helps if you have done the job personally (*and well would be good, too*)
- Previous experience in speaking, facilitation, or training

Patience

- New people often make mistakes while they learn

- It often takes a few tries to get it right (*keep up encouragement*)
- Remember how it was for you when you started out?

Interest in being a trainer, speaker, facilitator, etc.

- You need to *seriously* enjoy helping people
- Seeing people grow and learn makes you feel good
- Seeing others' success gives you a sense of pride and satisfaction

Genuine respect for other people

- People view you as being knowledgeable *(you model it)*
- People view you as being trustful and trustworthy *(you've earned it)*

Well-developed sense of humor

- You see the humor in the situation (*you express it*)
- You don't take yourself or life too seriously (*you lighten it*)
- It helps you deal with some of the *'challenges'* of training and working with people. ☺

Having these traits and skills won't *guarantee* your success as a leader, facilitator, speaker, trainer, or coach. However, they will give you a better chance to do the job effectively enroute to greater success.

If you are committed to building your career and/or want to move into speaking or training or are already a speaker or trainer; then these traits need to be a solid part of how you live your life in that role.

The more you demonstrate these traits, the more your audiences and teams will respond to your leadership, and the more productive they will become. If your role is already that of a leader, these skills will enhance it dramatically.

PRO-tip:

"My advice on starting any new (speaking) venture is not to expect miracles to happen overnight. Work on your message, polish your delivery, grow your network, cultivate your social media, improve your website, build bridges little-by-little. If you do a little something every day, then after a year people will start to take you seriously."

Ian Gibbs, *founder PSA Spain, www.iangibbs.es*

"I hear and I forget.

I see and I remember.

I do and I understand!"

Confucius

These *wise words* were written thousands of years ago and yet, they ring just as true in our 21st century lives and evolving business endeavors. We *best equip* those we lead with *use-it-now information*, practical tools, and applicable actions; *when we facilitate* them to get their hands *dirty* or get up using what we provide.

For example: *In our in-person, presentation skills training or executive speech coaching programs the quicker we get our students or clients up speaking, the better they learn and accelerate their learning curve. Consider the thousands of Toastmasters around the world, each year, who nervously start speaking and find that their confidence and competence increases in direct relation to how often they are in front of an audience and in how well they apply the helpful feedback received.* **www.Toastmasters.org**

Becoming an effective presenter is **not** learned *exclusively* from a book or by observing others in action. It is essentially a **learn-as-you-do** project. Kind of like life! **My challenge for you** is to revisit what you are doing for your own learning curve, as well as those you work with. See where you can adapt it to add more *hands-on* experience. How can you make it more experiential to anchor the learning and enhance the skill?

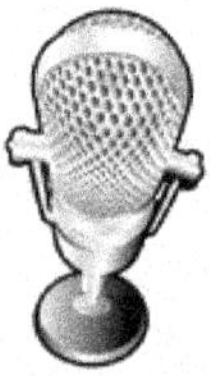

PRO-tip:

"I am full of energy, yes, I am a ball of energy! Before going on stage, I will anchor even more energy. Using the chakra system originated in India, I take 10 minutes in a quiet place and concentrate on my solar plexus chakra, which relate to **'Radiating your power in the world.'** The energy of the third chakra is characterized by the expression of will, personal power, and mental abilities. It is a yellow colour. I imagine having a ball of sun in my solar plexus area. The more I focus on that radiant ball the more that ball grows, glows and shines energy first within me; then it becomes so extended that it goes out to everyone around me. A fantastic way to be ready to share your energy with your audience and keeping your energy flowing too."

Claire Boscq-Scott, CVP, *www.claireboscqscott.com*

Three Key Ideas To 'Successful' Speeches

The cardinal rule to being effective in public speaking is **"NEVER BE BORING!"** But how do we do this when we are nervous and under *pressure to perform?*

I've been teaching my clients and various in-person classes that the **"three key ideas to speaking success"** are based on acquiring the knowledge you need to successfully capture their attention, to connect with your audience, and to achieve your shared objectives.

Those three key ideas to speaking success are:

KNOW your subject or topic
KNOW your audience
KNOW yourself

If you **know your subject** and are thoroughly prepared, you will be much more relaxed and effective than if you are just 'winging' it.

Taking time to organize and delve into your topic will give you a sense of the depth you bring to the platform. It will also give you much more information than you will be able to deliver, which gives you back-up information for additional presentations and questions. This confidence, based on acquired knowledge, works wonders in helping to keep the "butterflies flying in formation," as we used to say in Toastmasters.

If you **know your audience**, you will be better prepared to effectively analyze their needs and select from the body of knowledge you've acquired on your topic to serve or solve those needs; to *actually* present something that is relevant and helpful to them.

The better you know or *understand* their backgrounds, history, connections, education, gender, and their ages; the better you will be able to construct and deliver your presentation in a way that is interesting, relevant, and informative to them.

If you **know yourself**, you can draw on your own experiences and build on your own strengths in developing your own 'unique' speaking style.

You can share your own ideas and 'unique' stories in a way that allows you to be most effective. Self-knowledge is a tool of effective and successful communication.

Continually ask yourself, ***"If I was in the audience, why would I be interested in this point or topic?"*** Then simply make sure you have a good answer for that question. Your audiences are people, just like you. The better you know yourself, the better equipped you are to effectively reach them.

By skillfully combining your knowledge of self, your subject, and your audience, you will effectively increase your impact. You will also expand your impact as a presenter, interviewee, or speaker.

A final note here:
Be sure to apply the **3 Ps of public speaking –**
PREPARATION, PRACTICE, and PERFORMANCE!

There is no substitute for being prepared, by practicing until you are certain that you are ready to present your material in a confident manner. Anyone who says they just get up and *fake it* is leading you down the wrong path. Prepare, practice, and polish and then, confidently walk on stage and *play* with the audience. That is what I've learned, and it works well for me.

The masters *only* make it look easy. They have put in the time, (*lots of it*) far from the public eye, long before they are introduced… and it shows!

Share your dreams, take some risks!

"Twenty years from now you will be more disappointed by the things you didn't do than by the ones you did do. Explore. Dream. Discover." **Mark Twain**

PRO-tip: "Know that your story matters.
Don't try and contrive something that doesn't align with who you are but rather use your life experiences, knowledge, and passion to share through speaking.

Love the Journey. Celebrate your accomplishments and understand that the business of speaking is 'built upon'. You never just get there, but rather journey there through speaking over and over again with different groups and trying different things. You will keep refining your skill set and identifying the best types of audiences for you." **Paula Morand**, *CSP www.paulamorand.com*

Introducing A Speaker

Introducing a speaker is a *specialized* form of presentation. Your role as the MC or introducer is tremendously important to the success of the speaker and the audience. *I coach my introducers so they will understand the importance they play in my delivering the best performance possible.*

- As the MC you have the awesome responsibility of helping the speaker **begin with a kick-start!**
- You set the tone, establish their credibility, build a bond (create a bridge) between the audience and speaker, and answer these important questions for the audience.

Often, they are thinking about them, so why not answer these questions during the speaker's introduction? I learned this early in my Toastmasters journey.

- **Why this *specific* speaker?**
- **Why this *specific* topic?**
- **Why this *specific* audience?**
- **Why now?**

Exercise: To learn and to begin speaking and to understand the importance of a good introduction.

Recruit a partner and spend a few minutes interviewing along the following lines. Then change off and be the interviewee. When you are done, take turns introducing each other to an audience of your peers.

- **Name?**
- **Favorite color, food, or hobby?**
- **Why are they interested in becoming a better speaker?**
- **Secret – i.e., something we don't know about them?**
- **Best thing learned so far in life?**

You can change the questions to be more relevant to your situation. Perhaps getting information about their hobbies, career, company, or community involvement would work.

"It's the little things that make the big things possible. Only close attention to the fine details of any operation makes the operation first class."

J. Willard Marriott

W. Clement Stone, who built a billion-dollar *sales* organization out of the depths of the great depression (*early 1900s*), shared a ***key*** quote that has been close to my own growth and success. He worked with **Napoleon Hill**, who authored, ***Think and Grow Rich***, published ***Success Magazine***, and mentored his employee, **Og Mandino**, who authored motivational classic, ***The Greatest Salesman in the World.***

Stone wrote: ***"Little hinges swing big doors."*** Successful, entrepreneurial leaders and great speakers constantly search and are open to finding the next '*slight edge*', the next profitable idea, or '*little hinge*'. I do too!

Travelling North America and more recently the globe, I share a few basic ideas or messages with my audiences. One of them is, ***"Once people fully understand the 'Why?' (purpose) the 'How's?' (processes or procedures) tend to take care of themselves."*** Simple little idea, isn't it?

However, these *little* things seem to slip the grasp of many of our global and North American leaders. We tend to complicate things. What little hinges have you applied in your life to open big doors or opportunities? What hinges have you used to leverage your speaking and leadership skills and expertise to better your career, company, or community?

PRO-tip: "Tech Tips - Be prepared!

If using a laptop, ensure all updates are applied before you begin and reboot more than once to be sure. Avoid the embarrassment of a forced lengthy update occurring when you try to begin. Show up early and test your connections at the venue. Always have a backup plan as Murphy strikes when you least expect it. This can include spare batteries, different adapters to connect to older projectors and audio splitters, longer extension cables, a speaker, a copy of your slide deck on a USB stick or when all tech fails, a printout of your slides."

David Papp, *www.davidpapp.com*

Prepare Yourself To WIN!

"I hated every minute of training, but I said, "Don't quit. Suffer now and live the rest of your life as a champion." **Muhammad Ali**

Building a successful leadership, sales career, or business takes hard work and applied energy. Becoming a competent, confident speaker does too. Success as a speaker follows a similar path. If it was that easy, everyone would be doing it. Sometimes you will reach the end of your strength or run head-on into a roadblock or wall – stay the course and continue.

You can live the rest of your life as a champion.

- A champion of your **creativity**.
- A champion of your **courage**.
- A champion of your **causes** and concerns.
- A champion of your sales team and your **clients**.
- A champion of living and sharing your **message**.
- A champion of your successful **career** path.
- A champion of your **dreams** (turning them into reality).

This is something experienced first-hand. I worked to overcome serious challenges and difficulties to prepare for the first-level audition while working towards the Accredited Speaker designation. There were times I thought about throwing in the towel. When I spoke in San Diego (1995) and was not successful, I pulled myself up and worked harder for my opportunity to speak the following year in Saint Louis (1996).

When I again fell short, I was tempted to quit. I was frustrated, disappointed in my performance, and inclined to move on; to forget my dream of becoming a professional speaker. Something would not let me quit! My success team would not let me quit either. They believed in me even when my belief wavered.

I took a break the next year as I was serving as District Governor for D21's 4500 Toastmasters.

In August 1998, when I *finally* walked across a Palm Desert, California stage to become the 48th person in the world to earn this coveted professional level Toastmasters International designation; I felt like a champion who had gone 10 rounds and emerged bloodied, but unbeaten.

The applause and cheers of 2200 plus fellow Toastmasters still echo in my ears. It was a pinnacle point in my life as a professional speaker; the first of many. If you would like to see it, **follow this link:**

https://youtu.be/5hyX_3wG468

Was it the three speeches I prepared and presented on the TM world stage that earned this professional designation? Partially! Looking back, I believe it was the hundreds of prepared presentations given in various Toastmaster clubs and in community events across the country; as well as for paying clients that built the foundations for this eventual success on the world stage.

You can succeed in whatever field you enter if you are willing to prepare. You can become a top performing professional; be the champion you were meant to be. If I can do it, so can you!

The **Indiana University Hoosiers** basketball team were proven winners. They remained undefeated throughout their 1976 season and captured the NCAA National Championship under coach **Bobby Knight**. The '60 Minutes' commentator asked him about this amazing feat and why they were so successful. He asked, "*Was it their will to succeed?*"

"*The will to succeed is important,*" replied Knight, "*but I'll tell you what is more important –* ***it's the will to prepare.*** *It's the will to go out there every day, training and building those muscles and sharpening those skills.*"

- Want to be a champion salesperson? – **Prepare**
- Want to be an effective leader? – **Prepare**
- Want to create a profitable and winning business? – **Prepare**
- Want to be a powerful presenter or speaker? – **Prepare**
- Want to live an effective and meaningful life? – **Prepare**

Bill Bradley (scholar, basketball star, and former US Senator) reminds us, ***"When you are not practicing, remember someone somewhere is practicing; and when you meet him or her, they will win."***

Prepare, practice, and act decisively when the time is right! Prepare and make this your time to win!

Benchmark Project - "So Tell Me About Yourself?"

For many years I had the pleasure of teaching presentation skills at several lower mainland BC colleges. I taught a wide range of students who were there to learn how to confront their fears, construct their thoughts, and speak without mumbling and fumbling. They wanted to be able to speak more powerfully and successfully. I would give them in-class-exercises so they would have the opportunity first-hand of speaking in public. Over the years literally hundreds started speaking with nervousness and left with increased confidence and competence in their presentation skills. Bravo!

This is one of those exercises. They would have 5-10 minutes of class time to prepare and then we would have each member of the class present. Now some of you are saying to yourselves, ***"Bob, 5 to 10 Minutes... that is not enough!"*** Truth be told, that is just about right for this simple exercise. The objective is not to *over think* it or dig in too deep; but to organize your thoughts and speak on a subject you know well (YOU) for about 2 minutes.

Objectives of this exercise:

- Introduce yourself to a small group or class.
- Establish a beginning point to *benchmark* your speaking skills and development to date. This will give you a reference point to chart your progress and growth as you continue to hone your **Speaking for Success** skills.
- Start speaking before an audience.
- Begin working on channeling or controlling your nervousness.

Suggested time: TWO minutes maximum

Using this project to set a base line can be very helpful for you as well as to anyone who is sharing this material. This project gives you an opportunity to get up and try your skills and evaluate them for future growth and polishing. The guiding rule is, **"...whatever you do is ok!"** This is simply a starting point for your development into a more confident and articulate presenter.

The topic is one subject on which you are the expert – YOU!

Obviously, in only two short minutes, you can't paint too broad a picture but you can share enough with your audience so they will get a sense of 'you' as a person. You might consider taking a historical base for your talk, i.e., birthplace, education, or family involvement.

You might share how you came to be interested in the profession you're pursuing or your job experience or share some of your ambitions or dreams. If you'd like to avoid using an autobiographical style, you might want to talk about your hobbies, sports, or anything that specifically relates to who you are as an individual. **You might even want to take this as a practice time for interview skills** and create a verbal answer or crafted self-promotion to the typical question, **"So, tell me about yourself?"**

Take 5-10 minutes to prepare your talk. Keep it simple and don't try to memorize it or over prepare. The concept behind starting with **'YOU'** is to allow you to talk about a topic on which you are *truly* the expert. Choose something you know very well!

A few tips: Select your points wisely for their impact. Keep in mind the concept of using an **opening, body development, and conclusion**. Try to capture your audience's attention with your opening statement. Remember that this talk is in front of friends, family, or people who are learning alongside you; people who will be supportive of your efforts. Share something of common interest to help minimize your nervousness.

Remember to breathe! Relax and enjoy this; smile and have fun!

If you are using notes, try not to hold them. Place them down so you can refer to them *when* necessary. Since you are talking about yourself, relax and try not to use notes. You might just surprise yourself and your audience.

PS: This is a great exercise to get ready for an interview. Often your interviewer will ask you to tell them about yourself. This is a great opportunity to smoothly transition into a 2-minute ***info-mercial*** on why they should hire or select you for the position. **Enjoy the journey!**

PRO-tip: "The difference between the good speakers and the really awesome speakers is usually not in the speaking itself, it's in their ability to reach their audience at a level that improves something about their lives so that they, in some way, become more than they were when they first sat down."

Steve Lowell, *CSP, Past GSF President, www.stevelowell.com*

Ideas To 'Handle' Your Nervousness

Here are a few easily applied ideas and techniques on how to handle and overcome your nervousness:

1. **Don't fight it!** Realize that being a *little* nervous is normal. I accept that and allow that nervous energy to propel me to a more impactful presentation. Remember, **"Nervous is Normal!"**
2. Being **mentally prepared** is a good part of winning and Speaking for Success. Being physically prepared is another aspect of the journey.
3. Do something **physical** to work out nervous energy.
    - Take a brisk walk.
    - Don't sit with your legs or arms crossed.
    - Let your arms dangle at your sides while you're sitting waiting to speak.
    - While your arms are dangling, twirl your wrists so your fingers shake loosely.
    - Pretend you're wearing a heavy overcoat or jacket and feel it on your shoulders as you shrug them repeatedly up and down.
    - Waggle your jaw back and forth a few times to loosen it up. This relaxes your face and allows you to speak better and be heard.
    - Deep breathing can help, but don't hyperventilate.
    - Use the power of self-talk, say, 'Let's go!' or use some of the affirmations I share with you later in this Speaking for Success self-paced manual.

Don't be self-conscious about having a warm-up routine. Champion athletes do warm-ups because they know it helps them prepare to do their best. It also reduces the chance of injury. Warming up allows you to be at your best in front of an audience. It also allows you to loosen up and be more relaxed. Find out what works for you and build it into your preparation routine.

Here is a mental tip: I learned early on that nervousness and '*being excited*' are two sides of the same equation. Mentally move into the '*being excited*' about the opportunity you have to share your ideas and to positively influence this audience's lives for the better!

Bob's Foundations for Speaking Success!

When this material is taught in person, one of the areas covered as an overview is what I call my **'Foundations for Speaking Success!'**

Investing time to make sure you have completely thought through and answered these questions is essential to your confidence and success on the platform. These ideas were gleaned and adapted from conversations with fellow professional speakers across the globe. I've added to their wisdom from my own first-hand experience. These *'foundations'* have worked for me, and **they will work for you!** The knowledge gleaned from their *wisdom* is the secret to being able to walk confidently up to the front and deliver a message that means something to your audiences. I include them for your illumination.

The secret to ensuring the audience gets the best presentation possible, with the most value, blended with personal stories and teaching points, **is in the pre-preparation**. This is what you do *well* before you start crafting your presentation and step on stage.

Questions, thoughtful questions like these, can be the keys that unlock the door to success in any venture. This is no less true if your desire is to be a confident, powerful speaker, who connects with their audience, and leaves them wanting more.

- **WHY** are you speaking?
- **WHAT** do you want to accomplish?
- **WHO** is your audience?
- **WHEN** will you be speaking?
- **HOW** long will you be speaking?
- **WHERE** will you be speaking?
- **WHAT** tools will you use?

WHY ARE YOU SPEAKING?

- **Major theme.** What is it and why is it of importance to the audience? What is the central theme you wish to speak about? Why would it be of interest to an audience, especially this one? Is there a theme or major message your client would like you to deliver?

- **What moves YOU?** What motivates you to want to speak about this specific topic? Why is it important to you and the audience?
- **Experience.** Do you have some relevant experience that qualifies you to speak on this topic? What do you bring to the platform? How does your experience prepare you to share this message? How does it prepare you to understand their needs and build a bond with them?
- **Credibility.** Why 'YOU' and not someone else? Do you have some academic, unique, or special job-related qualifications that lend support to you as a speaker? Have you done your homework to make sure you've fully researched and prepared for this presentation and this audience?
- **Background.** How does your background prepare you to speak to this group? Are there shared or common elements in your background that give you a sense of what would be most helpful to those in your audience?

Answering these questions is a key to reinforcing your confidence and presentation skills. It will allow you to speak with greater conviction and passion. **Make sure 'YOU' are the person** who is well qualified and prepared for the presentation. Believe me, it helps!

WHAT DO YOU WANT TO ACCOMPLISH?

In April 1991, when I first joined Toastmasters, our manuals outlined various speaking projects that allowed us to focus on a specific goal in our speaking. Being able to know what end-result to shoot for helped me in preparing more effectively. (I visited mid-March and officially joined in April) Here are some of the speaking goals, as recalled, from the various manuals:

- **Speaking to inform?** Do you have a new policy, procedure, or point of information to pass on to the audience? How do you make sure they understand and apply it?
- **Speaking to persuade?** Do you have a passion for something and want them to change direction or follow you in making a change? Do you want them to buy from you, hire you, or promote you? How do you convince them you are the best person for the job?
- **Speaking to entertain?** Is it your primary purpose to help them have an enjoyable time; to make them laugh and forget their troubles for a bit? This is a very tough way to speak, but if you do it well, you can enhance your career.
- **Speaking to inspire or motivate?** Is your purpose to inspire them, to lift their spirits, to encourage them to try again or a little harder? What specifically would you like them to feel empowered to do when you are finished speaking?

- **Speaking with a call to action?** Do you have a specific goal in mind that you'd like them to help you with? Do you want them to sign up, step up, or join you in taking a stand or an action?
- **Some other objectives?** What specifically is it you want them to get from your presentation?

Be clear about the end-results or goal in mind, while making your presentation is essential. Being able to pull the relevant information together will make your points come alive!

Be clear in what result you desire, what you want the audience to get from your presentation, or what action you want the audience to take.

As someone once said, ***"If you don't know where you're going, any road will get you there!"***

WHO IS YOUR AUDIENCE?

- **Age ranges.** Knowing their age ranges will be helpful in preparing and selecting stories, illustrations, and other supportive material. It will also help you determine how to structure your presentation for maximum effectiveness.
- **Gender Mix.** Are you speaking to a group of men? A group of women? A mixed group? How many of each? Knowing this will help you present your message so it appeals effectively to both genders and ensures it will be understood in relation to their mind-set. It will also help you select examples or stories that are relevant to them.
- **Backgrounds.** What do you know about these people? What do they do for a living? What educational background do they have? What ethnic or family backgrounds do they have? Do you have any common backgrounds, connections, or experiences with them that you can draw or build on?
- **Common bonds.** Do they share any common experiences, bonds, or backgrounds? Are they all parents? Members of a special group? Volunteers? Do you have any connection with this common bond you can draw or build on?
- **Reason they are attending.** Knowing why they are in the audience can be very important in your preparation. It is a foundation to making sure you present your message to maximize your chances of having them take it in.

Are they there because your topic is of interest to them or someone close to them? Are they there because they've been told to show up by a boss or other authority figure? Is attendance a reward or punishment? ***Makes a big difference!***

Knowing your audience is one of the essential keys to presenting a great speech. Knowing them allows you to present the information most helpful to them. Doing your research and getting to know your audience can make a major difference. *Before undertaking any speaking engagement, I make it a point to talk in advance to some of the people who will be in the audience.*

WHEN WILL YOU SPEAK?

- **Time of day.** Make sure you know when on the day you'll be speaking. If you are speaking later in the afternoon or following a heavy meal, you will have a more difficult time with the audience. Early mornings can be difficult, too!
- **On the program.** Are you speaking as a keynote or opening general session? Are you following 2-hour happy hours and a big meal? You're your remarks accordingly.
- **In relation to other speakers.** Are you sandwiched between other speakers? Do you follow another speaker? Who are they? What will they be speaking on? Find out about your fellow speakers and their topics. Be prepared to adapt or change your presentation, stories, or jokes.

*At one engagement, I was to follow Alberta's Lt. Governor **Lois Hole.** The organizer asked that I be ready to adjust my time as Her Honor was known to occasionally go long. I stood at the back of the room as she was piped in and watched in amazement as she stopped to hug people on her way in.*

She was close to her time. I was happy to adjust my remarks following this wonderful lady, who was a credit to the Province of Alberta. I was asked to speak on her behalf years later when she was suffering from chemo as well as the death of her husband. Also, an honor.

- **Date and time.** Make sure you know exactly when and what day you are speaking. Make sure you confirm it closer to the date. Seems a simple thing, but I know more than one professional speaker who missed an engagement when they neglected to confirm and showed up *'late'* due to a change. Don't schedule too close to the event start, either.

Early in my speaking career, pre-cell phones, I remember approaching our landing in Omaha barely 45 minutes before I was scheduled to speak, arriving at the hotel to find a very concerned client. Bad weather and a mechanical breakdown on two of my flights wiped out a 4-hour window and brought me close to missing my presentation. Now, I travel well in advance to make sure I am there; rested and ready to give my best.

Your time and position on the agenda can affect your audience's ability to respond or retain your message. You need to be aware of those factors and make changes to give yourself the best chance of effectively delivering your message and having it heard.

HOW LONG WILL YOU SPEAK?

Consider your audience. Have you ever been sitting on a hard chair, butt aching, eyes hurting, back straining while listening to a speaker drone on and on, oblivious to the time and the audience? Put yourself in the audiences' position and make sure you structure your time wisely for maximum interest and benefit for them. Focus on your audience!

Organize your presentation. Knowing how long you speak will allow you to organize your thoughts to make sure they flow logically. Also, if you have a shorter time, you will need to get to the point quicker and support it with fewer relevant points. If you are speaking longer, you'll need to **consider the following points in constructing your presentation.**

- **5-to-7-minute segments:** consider the attention span of your audiences and try to design your presentation in smaller segments. People traditionally need a change of pace every 5-7 minutes, so schedule or structure your presentation accordingly. Wonder if this was why most of our Toastmasters projects were 5-7 minutes? Hmmm!
- **Group participation exercises.** If you are planning a longer presentation, please incorporate some group work. This will allow you to take mini-breaks and allow your audiences to have a change of pace. You'll all appreciate it!
- **Consider audience involvement.** Regardless of the length of your presentation, having audience participation is a key to making your message work. Ask questions? Get them to volunteer to help you demonstrate something, hand out something. Get them to briefly share with each other. Get them involved and keep them involved. More on this later.

Structure and time your presentation to maximize your impact takes planning and practice. The results are more than worth your effort!

WHERE WILL YOU SPEAK?

- **Location and logistics.** Make sure you know precisely where you will be speaking; location, address, how to get there, and any other logistics that make it work for you to be there ready and prepared to do your best.

One speaker friend found himself checking into his hotel in the wrong town the night before he was to speak. Same name, different state. This made for a long night of travel to be there for the next day. I'll bet that from now on he double checks the location.

Updated: *I remember laughing about his challenge. Years later, I had a client call me about an after-dinner presentation in Portland. I looked at my schedule and saw I was speaking in Boise, Idaho for two days in the early afternoons. My thoughts are getting a flight, fly over, deliver my speech, and fly back later in the evening or early the next morning. Or so, I thought! I told the client this and she laughed. She said,* ***"Bob, I am calling about speaking in Portland, Maine."*** *I had thought she meant Portland, Oregon - oops! With the time change, I would have been late before I even left for the airport. I wasn't able to help her for that date, but she did hire me for the following year.* ☺

- **Room layout.** How is the room laid out for your presentation? Give the organizer specific instructions if you need to set it up in a special way for your presentation. Always get there at least 1-2 hours early in case it isn't set up. Sometimes, you will have to make do. **Don't be a *prima donna*.** You can always make some changes to make it work a bit better for you and your audience. This is your responsibility – use it wisely.
- **Sound system needs and capability.** If you need one, is there one available? I'd suggest if you are speaking to any group larger than 40-50 people, it might be wise to have one. Make sure you arrive early enough to test it and know how to adjust it for comfort levels.
- **Audio-visual needs and location.** What audio-visual tools are available for use? Do you need them? Discuss this in advance with your meeting planner or the organizer and plan accordingly. Always have a backup plan when 'Murphy's Law' strikes and the tool you were planning on using isn't available. **Hooey's corollary: Remember, 'You' are the message – bring it!**
- **Climate control.** Make sure you know where the climate controls are and how to adjust them or get help quickly. It is your responsibility to make sure your audience is comfortable.

You need to be aware of the logistics around where you are speaking. This allows you to prepare with confidence, by minimizing the *'little things'* that can worry you or detract you.

WHAT TOOLS WILL YOU USE?

- **Flip chart or white board.** Is it visible to the audience? Use big letters, not too much on each page, and please use **colors** that your audience can see from anywhere in the room.

Keep in mind, you may have color blind audience members. Flip charts/white boards are great for smaller groups and interactive sessions.

- **Computer and LCD projector.** Using PowerPoint or other presentation slide software can make or enhance your presentation. Make sure it is simple, not crowded, and not too slick. Hint: don't be too dependent on the tools. They are there to reinforce your message and they sometimes go down or don't work. Don't let them distract your audience.
- **TV and VCR.** Do you have video clips? Please cue them in advance and make sure the equipment is set up and ready to go when you need it. Again, make sure you've assigned someone to help. Today most of this is shared with your computer and an LCD projector, but the guidelines still work.

When I co-hosted the Cancun Wealth Creation Summit, we were fortunate to have a professional Canadian crew for our filming. I worked out the film clips and camera cues in advance with one of the crew members. Amazing how much professionalism it added to our overall sessions, and the follow up video series. Make sure your audience can see the big screen easily. ***Hint: If it can't be seen, it shouldn't be used.***

- **Charts and posters.** Keep them simple and make sure they are readable from anywhere in the room. Make sure they are sturdy and positioned for easy access.
- **Slide projector. This is a good tool, although your computer often takes its place today.** Is it positioned correctly so everyone can see the screen? Make sure you've run through your entire presentation to make sure your slides/ppt are in the correct order and right side up.
- **Handouts/learning guides.** Make sure they are relevant to your topic. Give the audience a reason to take them home and use them or refer to them. Decide in advance **when** you will hand them out. If they are not needed during the presentation for reference, handing them out at the end of your presentation would be better. Let your audience know they are coming.
- **Props.** Can be very effective tools in demonstrating a point or principle. Props work to keep your audience involved in your presentation. Make sure they are positioned for easy access and are ready to go when you need them. Can everyone see them?
- **Costumes.** Would dressing to illustrate your topic be a benefit? It might but consider it carefully. Make sure it enhances your message and credibility and doesn't become a distraction.

I've played with costumes as ways to frame my remarks. Please make sure they add to your presentation, and not detract from it, so your audience doesn't get confused.

Selecting the proper tool to assist in making your presentation more powerful, more memorable, and more easily understood is an important element in your success. Always consider the size and layout of the room and the visibility of any tool you select. **If they can't see it, it won't work;** and quite likely will detract from your overall presentation.

Never use a tool unless you've *practiced* with it in advance. Make sure you are proficient in its use. If you fumble on stage, you will lose your credibility and possibly the audience's attention.

Always have a plan 'B': Murphy's Law was designed for speakers. Make sure you have back-ups and know when and how to use them. If something goes wrong, simply move ahead and switch to plan 'B' or 'C' as smoothly as you can. **Be the professional in the room!**

Don't be dependent on your tools!

Your audience is not there to *just* enjoy a multi-media presentation. They are there to hear you speak about something they hope will prove valuable in their lives and/or careers. Choose your tools wisely; but don't be dependent on them. They are there to make you look good, reinforce or support your points, visually demonstrate a point, or simply help keep your audience involved in your message.

Don't forget **'YOU are the message'** and these tools are yours to use to enhance your ability to get that message out effectively. Very much like the frames chosen to enhance a painting, your tools enhance and power up your message. The more *effective* speakers know how to leverage their tools wisely and professionally, so that the tools are not the focal point in their presentation. After all, you want them to walk out of the room talking about you or your topic, not the visuals.

PRO-tip:

"We are well into the 21st Century now and rapidly discovering that it's very different to one we left behind. People expect more involvement in what's going on around them and yet at the same time, it's more difficult to attract their attention. The secret to on-stage success lies in overcoming this challenge - giving people the involvement they want, while allowing them the freedom to roam. For those who make their living performing on stage, this means an even greater adherence to the adage **'it's all about them, not you'**. Hold front and centre the needs of your audience and deliver you message so it fits within their frame of reference." **Chris Davidson**, *www.activepresence.com*

Roles for Trainers, Facilitators, and Keynoters

If we are to be effective in our roles as presenters, it is important to understand the similarities and differences that encompass the three major functions played by our CAPS/NSA/GSF members. (speakers in general.) I realize many of you might not have the focus of becoming a professional; however, each of us can increase our professionalism when we present.

The Canadian Association of Professional Speakers **(CAPS)** defined the three major aspects of what our **'Experts Who Speak!'** do for their respective clients. Helps us make sense of the roles and the expected results.

My speaking journey began *primarily* in classroom **training.** I still do quite a bit of training for professional associations and corporate clients across North America. I've had the privilege of training and coaching senior executives, CEOs, and Presidents from Canada's 50 Best Managed Companies.

Facilitation is another skill that draws on your speaking, listening, and thinking skills. You, as the facilitator, are the catalyst that allows the group to openly discuss and reach decisions.

I've increasingly been working as a **motivational keynote speaker.** This was the original goal and dream when I joined Toastmasters to hone and add to my skills, back in April of 1991.

Here are the three areas with explanations as to how they play out.

TRAINING

Desired result:	acquire, build or enhance 'success' skills
Communication style:	2-way between speaker and audience – interaction carries audience
Energy flow pattern:	between trainer and audience and among audience participants
Learning style:	primarily through activity, discovery, and interaction
Attention focus:	shared focus between audience and the trainer

Critical success factor: new skillset or behaviour learned, plus commitment to apply or use it back home or on the job – **Ideas At Work!**

Presenter brings: expertise in subject matter, skills (adult learning design of training), patience, explanation, demonstration, and feedback abilities

FACILITATION

Desired result: bring group to a point of self-management of its own processes to achieve the results it chooses or desires

Communication style: normally among group members themselves

Energy flow pattern: generated by, and maintained by the group – boosted from time-to-time, by the facilitator

Learning style: occurs through interaction, experimentation, and self-assessment

Attention focus: group themselves – the facilitator is there to assist them!

Critical success factor: group owns/takes responsibility for its solutions and decisions, fresh awareness of its nature, processes, and greater openness and trust

Presenter brings: sensitivity to people and climate; here and now awareness; focus; willingness to intervene, challenge, and teach; flexibility; patience

KEYNOTING

Desired result: motivate or inspire to action, provide context/meaning, set theme

Communication style: 1-way, speaker generally carries the audience

Energy flow pattern: speaker to audience (more energy in short time – pushed)

Learning style: occurs silently, individually, in the audience's head and heart

Attention focus: the speaker, their message, and their delivery

Critical success factor: a few key points – reinforced and driven home!

Presenter brings: high energy and commitment; mastery of the platform; ability to evoke feelings, challenge thoughts and assumptions; and willingness to challenge audience to think, and to act!

As you can see, each of these presentation areas has its own focus, skill set, and critical success factors. Being aware of the differences and expectations for each area will assist you in your preparation and success!

Presentation tip: Why would you want to take the extra time and effort it takes to make an effective presentation? What would it accomplish? What is your motivation for investing your time in researching, creating, or crafting and then practicing and honing it before you deliver it?

An effective presentation:

- Demonstrates that you are thoroughly **prepared** and have done your homework.
- Has its information well **organized** in a complete and concise format.
- Reveals your human side and acts as a **catalyst** to connect with your audience.
- Reveals your **competency** – demonstrates that you do indeed have the skill set and the ability to successfully complete your assignment or project.
- Consistently **keeps your audience** awake and aware of your actions.

PRO-tip: Quality Audio Recording.

"I always try to record every speech I do. Video is ideal, but at least get an audio recording so you can review your presentation and hear what the audience heard. While the quality of internal microphones on modern gadgets has improved, their physical location on your device may not be ideal when presenting live. If you don't have a plug-in lav mic, using an external microphone will not only give you a little more flexibility in terms of positioning. They give you a better-quality recording which you can use for product sales, promotional clips, or for the media. Even if your presentation is being recorded at the event, it's good to have a backup in case it fails."

Greg Gazin, *DTM, www.GadgetGuy.ca*

Ideas on Getting to Know Your Audience

At an NSA Platform Skills Lab training session, fellow speaker **Steve Moroski** from Atlanta, GA shared insights he'd picked up on *getting to know* his audiences. He also shared some enlightening *'trends'* that can impact how we prepare and how we present. I share them from my notes and memory.

Steve encouraged us to **open up a two-way flow** between our audience and ourselves prior to walking on stage.

He suggested a few ideas to increase this flow.

- Kick-off calls to organizer to make sure we know '*who*' is coming.
- Pre-program questionnaire to organizer and audience survey.
- Gap analysis to determine areas where training or additional skills might help.
- Conference call or calls with several people who are attending.
- Email from their leader telling attendees about the upcoming session and inviting them to visit his website.
- Conversations on-site (*prior to your session*).
- Connecting and interaction during the session.

One of the keys to being effective on the platform is in knowing your audience. These are a few ways that I can attest to work well in that regard. *I've added to that with short video greetings to my audiences well in advance of my program. I even do them while travelling. Here is one I did in advance of my keynote for Paris August (2015).* **https://youtu.be/b2EsPXhWe2U**

Here are a few Trends you should be aware of as well.

TREND 1:

Audiences today are very sociable. Schedule more frequent breaks and small group work. Throw out more questions. Allow them to share and dialogue among themselves. Encourage them to Tweet during your presentation. **Hint:** Give them something great to Tweet about! ☺

TREND 2:

Audiences today don't read much. They expect to be entertained. Use props, audience involvement, stories, visuals, and more effective use of lights.

TREND 3:

Audiences today are risk takers. Take some risks yourself. Bring them up on stage. Challenge them in stories, programs, etc. They may not remember what you did, but they will remember how you made them *feel* and what you challenged them to think. Take risks to connect and challenge them to grow!

TREND 4:

Audiences today are more cynical. Use metaphors vs. gimmicks, allow for more laughter (*opens the soul and allows you to share points*). Make your introductions more *relevant* and applicable to them. Make fun of yourself.

TREND 5:

Audiences today are tired of being talked at. Involve them! Use story holes (*e.g., People were (______) 'amazed'*) and let them fill in the blanks. Look for opportunities to interact and to allow them to do so.

TREND 6:

Audiences today are suspicious *of us and our promises.* Watch your clothing choices as well. Dress appropriately for credibility. Verbally come off the platform and the *pedestal.*

Honesty is important.
Tell the story behind the story. Tell the story you're not telling. Tell the struggles, the challenges that led to your eventual outcome or achievement. Being real is being honest and sharing accordingly.

TREND 7:

Audiences today are more highly web-savvy/educated. They will check out websites and do their own on-line research. Show them how to use what you teach. Use everyday stories. Show them where it fits in their lives and careers, and they will respond. Some of them will have researched your topic and might be more informed than you, unless you've done your homework.

What Audiences Know…

What audiences know...

(without being told)

...how you feel that day

...if you don't like or respect them

...when you've memorized your presentation

...when you're lying or bluffing

...when you're giving them a sales pitch

...when you've given up on yourself

Never underestimate the sensitivity of your audience! Be open and let them in!

Principles made personal yield powerful results - Ideas At Work!

"You are as young as your faith, as old as your doubt; as young as your self-confidence, as old as your fear; as young as your hope, as old as your despair."

Samuel Ullman

Mastery of The Message
Using the 3 M's for Speaking Success

I still remember my first experience of being in the 'magic of the moment' – the zone if you will! *We'd truly connected – my audience and me. They were with me fully, completely. I could take them where I wanted. WOW, what an experience! It was amazing, and nearly 30 years later, I can still vividly recall being in the moment (zone) with them and how it felt. Awesome!*

Yes, I have been there since, and work to go there often. The freshness of that experience lives on in my memory. It inspires and drives me to work diligently to prepare each session, to give my best, and to be fully there for my audiences.

That is the true 'mastery of the message' – as shown in the results and reactions of those who receive and act on it!

Mastery is an attainable skill; if you care enough and are willing to pay the price and put in the effort. I have carefully observed my CAPS, NSA, and GSF colleagues and friends. I have watched those who are acknowledged *masters* on the platform and in the training room, to see what they do and what they bring to their mastery. Each has their own unique style and substance. Each has a shared commitment to mastery and serving their audience's highest needs. I have sought to apply what I observed during my own time in front of audiences.

Let's explore the **3 M's for Speaking Success**™ that lead to the mastery of the message and give you entrance into the magic of the shared moment.

MESSAGE

First, make sure you have something to say!

This should be a given, but it isn't for many emerging speakers. All too often, I have seen beginning speakers who simply *parrot* something they've read or heard from another speaker or author. It is not real in their lives or *relevant* for them or for their audiences and sadly, it shows.

Not that sharing a message *gleaned* from a master or a group of masters is a bad thing. **Presenting it as though it is your own is!** It is unprofessional and borders on plagiarism or intellectual property theft. **DON'T DO IT!**

Make sure you've *fully* researched and thought through your material, so you have some depth and are not just another 'book-report' speaker.

To reach your audience you need to *filter your message* through your life and your experiences to make sure it is real and relevant to them. If it is not real or relevant to you, it won't connect, and you'll fail.

- How well do you know your audience? What do you know about them that would guide you in the research and the crafting of your message?
- How much time have they given you to share it?
- What gems of wisdom, what stories, what experiences can you draw on to flesh it out and make your message live, connect, and remain embedded in their hearts?
- What do you want them to learn, understand, or act on from your message?

Dig deep into your message and prepare well.

The masters never shirk their diligence in preparation!

MESSENGER

You as the messenger bear a strong responsibility for the success of your message being received and acted upon by your audiences.

It needs to be fully integrated and involved in your life to become real and relevant to them. It needs to be in line with what you truly believe to be credible and, even more importantly, achievable by action on their part.

They will believe your message and act on it, when they believe you!

What is your motive and motivation for speaking to them? It is important to know why you are speaking and where you are coming from, if you would seek to succeed with them, connect with them, and impact their lives.

Be honest with yourself in what you seek here. Do you seek to simply entertain yourself at their expense or use them for therapy? Or are you seeking to impart and inspire them to gain knowledge, take action, and rally around the flag to a better life or a more effective career or business?

The masters know themselves and share openly and boldly!

Knowing yourself helps you take what you know about them and apply it in crafting your message and in more skillfully delivering it.

METHOD

This is the *easier* part of the presentation equation. ☺ If you've dug deep enough to make sure 'what' you have to say is truly valuable and has relevance to your audience, make sure it is in-line with your own integrity and life; it will be so much easier to communicate effectively with an audience.

Once you've decided what outcome you desire from the communication of your message, it is easier to structure the delivery system. Depending on the message and the desired outcome, (*and of course the time constraints you have to deliver it*), you can blend in stories, audience interaction and exercises, and inspirational bits.

Time is one of the biggest factors that impact the delivery method you choose.

I've grown to love the interaction with audiences. I find when keynoting, that my ability to incorporate active dialogue with them is more challenging than during breakouts and training sessions. That being said, I still work in some areas where they can actively give feedback or respond to the message being shared.

Asking questions, getting them to share something with a neighbor, or simply using rhetorical questions to draw them in; these techniques will work in building a bridge to the hearts and minds of your audiences.

The **effective use of storytelling** is *under-rated* and ignored by speakers in many levels and arenas. Sometimes the most effective way to communicate a message is to wrap it tenderly in a story. How many Sunday school lessons do you still remember; how many nursery rhymes or children's stories can you still recall? My bet, lots of them – and if you can recall the story, you can retain the lesson and the message behind the story.

The masters weave stories to last a lifetime!

A few final ideas…

If you want to achieve the 'mastery of the message' you will need to dig deep to master yourself first and then draw from that in preparing and delivering your message. **Applying the 3 M's will help you succeed.**

You owe it to your audiences to diligently prepare and to bring forth your best. Anything else would be a waste of everyone's time and energy.

Seeking to become a '*master of the message*' is the beginning of attaining the mastery – and the journey is worth it!

Use story starters to warm up your brain. To get you started, I've included some of my own story starters. These story starters give my brain a mental kick and get me thinking about something I might put into an easy format to capture and share an idea. Perhaps they will work for you too?

Ideas on using a 'How to' story starter:

- How I learned the importance of ________________:
- How I got started in the ______________ business.
- My worse Customer Service experience: Why?
- My favorite customer: Why?
- The best lesson I learned last year:
- Something funny happened to me:
- How to overcome _________________________:
- How to initiate ________________________________:
- How to unravel the secret of ______________________:
- My dream company: Why? ______________________:
- The best lesson I've learned here at _________________:

PRO-tip: "Be a Contributor!

Wherever or whenever you speak, there is an event professional sweating all the details. Our job as professional speakers is to make sure we are contributing to the success of the event. We must make sure we understand the needs of the event planner and the needs of the participants. If we look at ourselves as being high-stakes partners in the event, rather than just a contractor, we set ourselves up to do whatever we can to make sure the event (and our presentation) is memorable and has incredible value to all stakeholders. We can no longer afford to be just the Sage on the Stage." **Marc Haine**, *www.marchaine.com*

PRO-tip: Five Ways to Captivate Your Audience

"Memorable presentations have one thing in common – they feature presenters that connect with their audience and capture their attention and often their imaginations. Entertainers understand that the audience wants to be engaged, involved in, or cheering for other members of the crowd or the performer. They also understand the need to earn the audience's love, rather than anticipating that they already have it.

So now it's your turn... you've just been introduced, the crowd is clapping, and you're heading up to center stage. For hours, the audience members have been Power Pointed to death, and now it's nearly lunch (or just after). You've only got a moment to make an impression – how can you captivate this audience and show them your presentation will be a little different or refreshing?

1. **Create an epic experience for your audiences – one filled with emotion, value, action, and relevancy at every choreographed stage!** Grab the audience's attention early by beginning with a powerful story or something that adds shock value. (Not inappropriate shock value, mind you.) Our brains crave the opportunity to be in AWE! When we're sort of infused with this, it changes and alters our perception of things. It changes what we see. It changes what we remember.

2. **Think like an entertainer.** Brain research shows that we don't pay attention to boring things. Surprise your audiences with a hook that immediately grabs their attention. Keep your opening introduction brief and to the point. Use music, lighting, and all the elements of stagecraft to heighten anticipation before you take the stage. This is something that entertainers do well, and speakers sometimes overlook.

3. **Spice up your presentations intentionally and then mind what works.** You may be surprised by what audiences respond to. Sometimes "We just don't know what or why something resonates". What you think is important or funny is a lot less important than what the audience thinks. If you're consistently getting a response, either positive or negative, learn from it and adapt accordingly.

Video/Graphics: Some topics are best introduced without words. Instead of telling the audience how a new product works, show them; humans have excellent imaginations, but sometimes it's easier to do the work for your audience. Graphics that are compelling and that can complement your talk track are especially useful for presenters who may not have a way with words. Let multimedia lend you a hand.

Shock/Surprise: This hook type isn't appropriate for all presentations. Used appropriately, a surprising comment can pique an audience's interest by, frankly, making them uncomfortable. Always consider it but use with caution. The audience is the only true judge of your hook, so make sure you don't overlook how they react.

4. **Mind your Movements**. On the platform, it is an essential part of your message and can help you enhance the words you use to create pictures in the minds of your audience. Avoid making the same movements or gestures repeatedly. Remember, if you lose track of your gestures, it doesn't mean your audience will. Avoid using gestures (or phrases) too often or too broadly. The same applies to facial expressions and movement of your position on the platform. Certain posture positions, fidgeting and self-touching (think playing with your ring, your hair, or touching the back of your neck) can be a sign of anxiety and stress. Learning how to remain calm under pressure is a critical skill to acquire.

5. **Be a Passionate Storyteller and avoid HEALING from the stage**. Think for a moment of a young child you know or your own kids when they were little. When telling a story that they truly want you to 'get', their voice is filled with unexpected sounds and huge shifts in volume and tone; their bodies is alive with animation. The fact is, they are 100% committed. How much or how little animating you do depend on the venue, the audience, your message, and your objectives... a boardroom presentation is vastly different from a keynote address at an arena-sized space, but audiences will never care about your message unless you care first. The only caution – do not tell a story that you are not ready to tell. Your audiences want to love you and come along the journey with you, but they feel awkward when you break down and they suddenly feel like your therapist."

PRO-tip from my amazing friend and fellow leader, **Faith Wood,** *CSP,* *www.faithwood.com or www.imind.ca*

Here is a short clip from my Paris speech in May 2019
https://youtu.be/nsb1jn6lcA4

An Open and Closed Case

The first time I created the **'hand illustration'** was in front of a class of students, some of them who had English as their second language. I told them, creating a speech, without notes, is as simple as… as your hand. (See page 63 for more on this.)

- The opening *(thumb)* is **telling your audience what you're going to tell them** or the central theme or objective of your presentation.
- The three points *(middle fingers)* illustrate, expand, develop, or support that theme. Simply, **telling them.** Cover the first point and then move on to each successive one. Depending on the time allotted, your points can be expanded or contracted, by adding additional stories, examples, or illustrations.
- The conclusion *(little finger)* reminds them of the central theme, summarizes the 3 points and of course **tells them what you've just told them.**

When you are speaking, *extra* attention needs to be given to crafting your openings and conclusions. Often people will only remember your opening statement or something you've said in closing. Accepting this trend in audience behavior as accurate, it makes sense to work a little harder on your opening and conclusions, to ensure they are tight and create pictures in your audience's minds. In fact, if you were to memorize these would be the two areas where it might be appropriate.

At a special NSA Platform Skills Lab in Tempe, AZ, one of our coaches, **John Alston,** CSP *(known for his ability to grab an audience with his openings)* shared a few thoughts on effective openings with us. I took copious notes. ☺
John shared his three rules on creative, impactful openings:

1. **Get their attention and keep it!** *(By any means possible)* This sometimes means getting *outside* of your comfort zone to capture and keep their attention. If your message is worth sharing, it's worth being dramatic to give them a chance to hear it and you. John walked on the stage carrying a briefcase and proceeded to drop it with a loud bang which caught our attention for sure.
2. **Remain current and relevant with your content and context** – know your audience. *(Use surveys and reviews).* If you are to effectively reach your

audience, you need to go where they are – and that requires getting to know them. John shared the differences, for example, of speaking to young people vs. CEO's and how you would structure your opening to target either group.

3. **Find and exploit your common ground** – look for the universals. *(What do we have in common?)* Ask yourself what you have in common with your potential audience. Is there a universal principle that underlies that commonality? If so, can you build on that principle or idea? Often, this commonality is the secret to building a good rapport with your audience or a bridge to allow them to join you on your journey in words.

Good openings make or break your presentation and help establish a connection with your audience. We learned about openings when I joined Toastmasters twenty plus years ago. **Good openings incorporate some of these elements:**

- Tend to be short, punchy, and dramatic or thought provoking.
- Can contain a startling statement, position, intrigue, or a challenging question.
- Can incorporate an appropriate and relevant quotation, story excerpts, paradoxes, good and bad experiences, or a personal story or illustration.
- References a shared or common experience with your audience.
- Drawn from life, based on journalized stories, reading, listening to stories, and conversations with others.
- A general or *universal* statement that ties in or relates to your subject, while acting as an attention getter to draw them into your presentation.
- Visuals, a display, or an appropriate or relevant prop or picture.

As an audience member, you have about 30 seconds to capture my attention and draw me into the subject of your presentation.

Choose your opening words carefully.

- Avoid weak or timid openings with trite questions like; "Do you ever wonder?" "How many of you have…?" *(These have been vastly overdone in my opinion)*
- Avoid a slow moving, lengthy statement or story that doesn't relate to your subject. Start fast and get us involved with your presentation.
- Avoid an apologetic statement or excuse such as *"I wasn't ready, but…"* **Never build a case against yourself or tell me you're not prepared… let me find out for myself!** ☺ Telling me you aren't prepared says, *"I'm not important enough for you to do your homework and prepare in advance to meet my needs."* It insults the audience.

- Don't open with a joke or humorous story unless you have it down cold. It needs to be relevant to the audience and supports your presentation.
- Don't waste the audience's time with *stereotypical* thank-you and general opening remarks. Get into the meat of your presentation and grab my mind and my heart!

Having said that, it is important to acknowledge the person who introduced you and the audience. Most of the time I see this overdone, and it weakens your opening impact. Do it briefly and move on or start your presentation and then acknowledge them. Make sure they know you are planning it this way. Save it for a bit later, after you have the audience members hooked into your presentation! Very much like a movie where they show a part of it and then show the titles before moving ahead to the rest of the film.

Keeping our attention is a challenge itself. People can listen at 400-500 words per minute while we normally talk at 125-175 per minute. This leaves **a listening gap** that needs to be handled in the development of your presentation.

Remember to create vivid word pictures for our minds. If you don't, we tend to think or fantasize about other areas. We think about grocery lists, work undone, or even, I'm told; fantasize about *sexual* things when we are not involved mentally. I tell my students if they smile as they leave, at least I know they've had a good time. ☺ I work to *verbally paint vivid pictures* that challenge them to think about what I'm saying and keep them actively involved in my presentation.

Similarly, **captivating closings** are critical to your success. **Effective closings also incorporate certain key elements:**

- Summarize your major speech points and the conclusion or action drawn from them.
- Bring them back to the main theme or purpose of your presentation.
- A relevant story, illustration, or quotation that re-emphasizes the major point or central theme of your presentation.

In addition to the above, my friend and co-author NSA Past President **Mark Sanborn**, *CSP, CPAE* shared some thoughts on what he called *Grand Slam* closings with us in Tempe. Again, I share what I recall and have applied in my own presentations.

Mark talked about ensuring that our closings were changed in focus from ***Event to Experience***.

He challenged us to not simply close, but to help our audience *experience* the completion of our speeches. He also challenged us to make sure our closings were an *integral* part of our presentation and not just slapped on as we ran out of time. They needed to be part of the flow of our presentation and not just a fancy closing *'tacked on'* for effect.

Mark shared some thoughts on audience retention too. He said, ***"Raw is real,"*** in that we shouldn't sanitize our material or try to make it too perfect. Makes sense to reach an audience by being ourselves. He mentioned that "*less is more*" in that we tend to put too much into our presentations. *I've found myself doing that on occasion. It is an area that I am aware of and am still working on to make sure I allow the real Bob out so my audiences can see and experience what I really believe.*

Mark talked about timing, too. **FEAR – false endings appearing real**. Have you ever been listening to a speaker and thought they were closing, only to find they still had lots to say? How did you feel? Don't do that to your audience. When it's time to close, do so and do it with impact. Don't fool your audiences – go for the close and finish on time.

One of the most effective things Mark did was share what he called the Lincoln insight. Here is the story I recall him sharing it with us.

*"**President Lincoln** had a political adversary who was a 'church going' man. To avoid controversy President Lincoln would often sneak into services after they started and leave just before they finished.*

One Sunday, as President Lincoln was leaving, he was approached by a Presidential aide who asked him if he enjoyed the sermon. His reply was, "It was well crafted and delivered." His aide pursued the matter and asked again, "So you liked the sermon?"

Irritated, Lincoln replied, "No son, I did not!" Confused, the aide stammered, "Buuuut, you said it was well crafted and delivered?" Lincoln went on to explain, "It was well crafted and delivered, but the preacher failed in one thing." "What was that?" the aide asked.

Lincoln replied, ***"He didn't challenge us to do anything GREAT with what he shared - in that he failed."***

Mark's story and its lesson caught my attention! I am committed to making sure I don't make the same mistake when I speak. Mark asked us some questions that are worth asking you to think about as well:

- Are your closings a culmination **or** simply a stopping point?
- What one thing could you do to make your presentation more of an experience? *(Esthetics, escapism, education, entertainment?)*
- What impression are you trying to leave **after** your speech? Why?
- What are the 2-3 most important values that drive your life? Do they show up in your presentations? How? *(This was one of the major shifts for me in my speaking career.)*
- What great thing are you asking listeners to do when you close?

Your thoughts and answers on these questions will give you a better insight into *'who you are'* and what you need to share to be effective as a speaker.

And isn't that what you really want?

Ask yourself, "If I had only sixty seconds on the stage, what would I absolutely have to say to get my message across?" **Jeff Dewar**

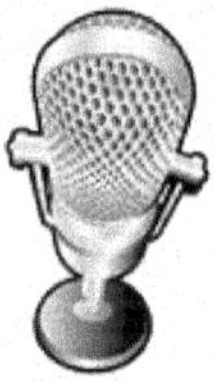

PRO-tip:

"**Understanding your own mind** and the mind and behavior of others, is the beginning of crafting a speech that engages, that moves, and that your audience will remember and even put into action. Most speakers know how to deliver content in a timely, efficient, and from time-to-time engaging matter. This type of speech usually only touches an audience on an intellectual level.

A **world-class speaker** will deliver a speech that moves the audience. Within a split second after you walk onstage, your audience already starts to create an image, expectation, and emotions about you, before you've even spoken a word! In their mind, they subconsciously answer the following two questions Can I trust this person? Can I respect this person? **Psychologists** call these factors warmth and competence, and ideally you want to be perceived as both.

A strong power pose will help your audience see you as the leader you are expected to be on that stage and will give your brain signals to distribute more "strength and power" hormones into your system. End your speech with either a summary or repetition of your opening. This will close the story loop in your listeners' brains and give them room to process what you've said."

Drs. Joyce Carols, *www.joycecarols.com Excerpt, Unleash Your Voice*

Class Notes and Ideas

This section draws from a/v, ppt slides and ideas used in my various on-site or live classes. I expound and expand on elements from each one, based on my own experience and application. On-site, I spend time, sharing my own stories and on-stage lessons to help my students grasp and built on these ideas. This made this course a favorite at several colleges in the Vancouver area for the 6 or so years where I taught before moving to Alberta.

One college voted me the **'most marketable instructor'** and gave me a nice plaque. Their sales staff often used my series of presentation skills classes as a selling or closing point when enrolling new students. Being they were on commission, I found this very interesting. ☺

I've drawn these idea-rich **'class notes'** from many sources: books I've studied, notes taken, in depth conversations, observations, and Q&A sessions with fellow professionals, my Toastmasters experience, and my own experiences on the professional platform over 30 plus years across the globe.

Make a point of personalizing or internalizing them to your own specific situation and needs. Use the ones that apply to the type of presentation and style you've chosen.

TOUCHING ON THE BASICS

Speaker **Dorothy Leeds**, best-selling author of **'POWER SPEAK'** built a very successful career working with people by helping them be more effective as presenters. Dorothy discovered the majority of her clients and struggling speakers had a pattern of flaws leading to ineffective speaking.

These **six major faults** in speaking often separate the successful speaker from the mediocre speaker. In our live classes this section is prefaced with a story of growing up in California and living close to a fault line; a fault line that made the ground less stable and more susceptible to earthquakes. And sleeping through my first one. When you craft your presentation make sure you build on solid foundations.

Give some thought to each of the six speaking faults. Have you seen it in your own presentations? Have you seen it in the efforts of others? How would you avoid each fault or minimize it in your own speaking?

- **An unclear purpose** *(direction)*
- **Lack of clear organization and leadership** *(structure)*
- **Too much information or data** *(content)*
- **Not enough '*support*' for your ideas, concepts, or information**
- **Monotonous voice or sloppy speech habits** *(speaking style)*
- **Not meeting the real needs of the audience** *(research)*

Keep in mind, challenging each of these speaking 'faults' face-on is an opportunity for you to grow as a speaker. There is not one fault listed here that cannot be overcome or minimized in your striving to be a better speaker.

'Miracles' happen when students apply their efforts and focus to replacing these faults with strong foundations and practicing until those foundations are strong enough to support them effectively. **You can too!**

Platform professional **Ira M. Hayes** shared several focus points he considered necessary for successful presentations. I adapted his ideas and frequently share these with my students as the **'SEVEN BE-ATTITUDES' of Effective Speaking.**

BE - informative
BE - valuable
BE - interesting
BE - memorable
BE - believable
Strive to **BE** - inspirational
BE - enjoyable!

Give some thought on how to best incorporate these **BE-attitudes** into your presentations. When you apply some new attitudes, you often get some new responses from your audiences.

Speaking professional, **Ty Boyd,** *CSP, CPAE*, from Charlotte, NC had **ten points or building blocks for success** he felt you needed to be effective as a communicator. Based on his long and successful run as a professional speaker, I took note! His lessons live on in those of us who apply them in our careers. When he spoke at NSA in Orlando, at 80 years old, he still had it! He still brought it! I was inspired… Thanks Ty!

1. **FIRE** in your belly
2. Have **FOCUS**
3. Good speakers **PERFORM**
4. Use **COLOR** in your voice, your body, and your energy

5. Use your face – **SMILE!**
6. Use the rest of your **BODY** too (be aware of body language)
7. Learn to effectively use your **EYES**
8. Maintain physical **BALANCE**
9. **INVOLVE** your audience
10. **PRACTICE, practice, practice!**

One of the biggest *misconceptions* of public speaking I've encountered over the years is people's persistence in separating platform style presentations from one-to-one meeting or smaller group presentations.

Often this is simply a matter of perception, **"Oh my, I have to give a presentation!"** People in business – powerful people – have learned to harness the power of speaking whenever and wherever they are communicating verbally. Leaders leverage the power of their spoken word. You can too, using some of the tips and techniques outlined in this book.

One question I frequently get from my clients and students is **"How do you give your presentations without notes?"** A good question! Sometimes I do use notes. I don't have a problem with having someone using them, as long as they are unobtrusive and don't take audience focus away from your delivery and presentation. There are several famous speakers who effectively use notes in their presentations.

Using notes as a back-up to give you a sense of confidence is okay. So is using notes as reference or to for a fact or quotation. Keep them simple and don't get in the habit of depending on them or obviously referring to them during your presentation.

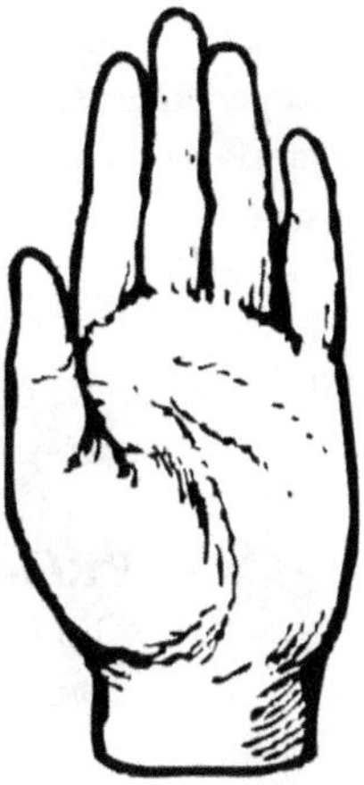

One exercise shared with my students was to ask them to hold up and look at their hand. **"What do you see?"** They usually say, **"A thumb and four fingers,"** which is of course, the obvious answer.

My answer to that same question is **"A presentation, without notes, up to 20 minutes."** I see an opening, three points and a conclusion.

I can remember 5 points or 5 things! Can't you? When we keep it simple and focus on the main points it makes it easier to remember.

USING GESTURES

Here are a few ideas on using gestures to add movement and energy to your presentation. Effective use of gestures enhances your audience connections.

Use gestures to channel your nervous muscle tension by carefully selecting or choreographing body movements that emphasize specific speech points. Nervous energy can effectively be used to lend welcome animation to your movements and presentation.

Using **gestures** effectively is a whole area of its own, but a few points must be made here. Audiences will believe what they see in your face, manners, and body movement long BEFORE they believe what you say.

Gestures can amplify your speech by including facial expressions and body language to illustrate pain, pleasure, sarcasm, sincerity, enthusiasm, or disinterest, as well as other emotions.

Here are a few more story starter ideas for you.

Use them to kick start your brain or perhaps as the basis for a story to include in one of your speeches.

Ideas for your use as a foundation for a story:

The number 1 principle for success __________:
2 ways of approaching ____________________:
3 questions to ask when __________________________:
4 cornerstones of ______________________________:
5 key elements of ____________________:
6 steps to creating a ______________________________:
7 ways to __________________________:
8 secrets of ____________________________:
9 lies or myths in the __________________________:
10 tips when using _______________________:

PRO-tip:
"To take a more ethical view of your speaking business you have to first step back, then step into the shoes of others. Flipping your perspective is a great way of assessing how your actions will impact the world."

Alison Burns, *www.alisonburns.com*

Ten Commandments of Informative Presentations

Here are a few comments on tips gleaned from ideas shared by my friend **Marjorie Brody**, *CSP, CPAE* on how to be more effective when presenting.

- **Less is more:** Avoid the mistake of the amateur speaker and resist the urge to give them *everything you've researched* about your topic. Share only the relevant points and information needed to get your message across and call them to action.
- **It's a *'jungle'* to the audience:** They don't always see the whole or BIG picture. Part of your role as the informative speaker is to be their *guide* and direct their path; to cut a *clear* path that they can follow.
- **Assume they don't understand:** This is where many amateur speakers fail by assuming their audiences understand the words and the concepts they share. Start with the lowest denominator and build or expand on their current understanding. Then skillfully move them along the path to where you are.
- **Keep relating back** to what they already know: This allows people to assimilate and start mentally comparing what you are saying to what they know. This allows them to see where it might apply to them and acts as a springboard to getting them to accept and act on the information you share. Metaphors work well in this respect.
- **Use visuals and simplify:** Many people *get it* better when they can *see it!* Using visuals allows you to augment your words and helps keep it simple. Share only enough information to give them the sense and the direction you want.
- **Keep lingo and jargon to a minimum: Please!!!!** Stay away from shoptalk and business or industry buzzwords. There will be people in your audience who will not know them and will be mentally left at the starting gate. Our role as presenters is to bridge the gap and share knowledge, not erect barriers.
- **Insist on their interaction:** When people are involved and interact, it facilitates growth and allows them to take in the information. It helps in the retention and follow-up action after you finish.
- **Demonstrate:** *'Show'* them is always better than *'tell'* them! What they see and experience they more successfully retain.
- **Do the unexpected:** This is where your *creative* side is called into play. What do you need to do to get their attention, keep it, and motivate them to do something with what you are outlining?

- **Sell:** Even though you are sharing information, you still have to sell it. What are they going to do with it, when, and why? If you don't sell it, they will not apply it.

In addition to being a delightful person, Marjorie Brody is a commiserate professional on the platform and one of the most successful entrepreneurs in this field I have ever met. She has been so helpful to me in my own growth.

Give some thought to the points she taught me as you structure and prepare your sessions. **These tips work – very well!**

Another set of story starters - ideas for your use.
These take a different approach in sharing warnings or cautions that might be of interest to your prospective audiences.

Ideas using warning or cautions as a basis for stories:

- The single biggest fallacy of ____________________:
- 2 dangers of ____:
- 3 wrong turns made by ________________________:
- 4 common mistakes of ______________________________:
- The 5 myths of ____________________________:
- 6 major obstacles in ___________________________:
- 7 deadly sins in _______________________________:
- 8 roadblocks to __________________:
- 9 detours in _______________________________:
- 10 ways to waste __________________________________:

PRO-tip: Story Telling.
"The secret to telling great stories is that they have a crisis, obstacle, or challenge that is overcome. The obstacle doesn't need to be profound, only that the lesson learned is practical and meaningful to your audience.

1. Focus each story on one and only one point. Keep it simple.
2. Brand your lesson with a call to action: e.g., Phrase That Pays. Make your move. Get back on the bike. Look forward, not back.
3. Feel the emotion of the moment. Don't describe emotions, show them."

Doug Stevenson, *CSP, www.storytelling-in-business.com*

Ten Success Guides

Ideas for effective business presentations

These ideas work just as well on stage as they do in the boardroom or in front of a client. Presentations are more successful when prepared and presented with a clear focus. We teach these same points when working with salespeople who depend on their ability to present and persuade them to make a living. In our speaking and training, we often help salespeople become sales leaders – and applying these points is one of the ways they succeed. Use them to be more effective when you are presenting your ideas.

- **Keep it short:** Time is precious and more so as you move up the leadership chain. Value their time and keep it simple, short, and to the point. Focus and deliver solid value in the time allotted.
- **Know your audience:** Do your homework in advance so you can tailor or customize your presentation (sales, informative, interview, etc.) to your audience and get and keep their interest.
- **Use visuals to add interest:** Pictures, props, and visuals help your audience get the point or reinforce your message in a shorter period.
- **Get them involved:** Audience involvement and interaction is essential in this very competitive arena. If you have figures to be worked out, ask them to do so with you. Remember, if it is their data, they trust it and give it more credibility.
- **Start and end on time!** I can't emphasize this one enough. If you ask for 15 minutes of someone's time, you'd better be closing your mouth and your briefcase on or before the 15-minute mark. If you are given 45 minutes to make a presentation, make sure you are done at or before the 45-minute mark. This is what separates the *professionals* from the mediocre performers.

I have never had a client complain that I finished a minute or so ahead of schedule. I have seen many speakers lose credibility when they went over their time and made the meeting run late. **Good lesson – always strive to finish on time!**

- **Dress appropriately:** Dress for Success – not excess! Make a point of understanding the dress code for the group or situation. One suggestion would be to always be **slightly** better dressed than the best dressed person in attendance.
- **Use short sentences, simple phrases:** Make it easy for the audience to gain acceptance and understanding of your concepts. Don't assume that they are fully literate – keep in mind most of the morning newspapers *(read by many executives)* are written to grade 6 to 8 reading levels.
- **Avoid humor unless appropriate:** Effective use of humor can be a great bridge. However, you can blow yourself out of the running by using something that offends someone in the audience. They may not even tell you, but they won't buy from you or deal with you. I've learned that the hard way once or twice along the way. Often, by mistake.
- **Distribute handouts at the end of your presentation:** This idea applies to any use of handouts. Unless you need to have them, refer to them, use them as a tool, or write something in them during your presentation – leave them for the end. People tend to read what you've given them instead of listening to you.
- **Don't bluff. If you don't know, find out!** Your credibility is a fragile thing in the business arena. Do your homework so you have the basics at your fingertips. Don't try to wing it or fake it when asked a question outside that parameter. Make sure you understand the question and make a specific commitment to find out and get back to them. Then do so!

If your career or success depends on your ability to persuade an audience or buyer, these tips will help you understand how to structure your presentation for maximum effect.

Business leaders are *busy* (their time is valuable) and you need to be clear and concise to win and keep their attention. Unless you know them, start strong, present value, and conclude with impact.

Your career, and your success in your business and your community has a direct relationship to your effectiveness in working with people – your superiors, your staff, your suppliers, your co-workers, and most especially your clients. Doesn't it make sense to invest the effort to ensure you have the best opportunity to succeed?

View a video I did for Alberta-based Business Link on productivity a few years back. **https://youtu.be/EcySZ1AD8UY**

A 12-Step Process for Building A Good Presentation

This is almost self-explanatory as a guideline in preparing for a presentation. The secret is in being systematic and building toward your worthy goal of constructing a successful presentation. Use this format or the other examples as methods to help gather your thoughts, organize them in a relevant and orderly manner, and then deliver them with passion to persuade your audience to accept and act on them.

- **Select the Topic**
- **Limit the Topic to One Central Theme** (what is the most important goal you want to achieve?)
- **Gather the Information**
- **Choose a Method of Organization** (see examples pages 90-91)
- **Outline Your Main Points**
- **Collect Supporting Data**
- **Check for Accuracy**
- **Design the Introduction**
- **Write a Strong Conclusion**
- **Put Together a Final Draft**
- **Practice Your Presentation**
- **Practice, Practice, Practice**
- **Confidently deliver it with passion and power!**

Following this simple 12-step process will help you take the journey from idea to implementation in front of an audience. It works because it is systematic and helps you create a logical flow for your presentation.

PRO-tip:

"My presentation is **'Focus on the 90%'** and rather than build my topic for one audience I built it for all audiences. Focus on the 90% became very much the "Chicken Soup for Soul" idea: the same book but for nurses, dog owners, teachers etc. Focus on the 90%: for leaders, for teachers, for nurses etc. Not only could I customize the presentation for each group I spoke to, but I also created, 'Focus on the 90%', 'Living the 90%', 'Embrace the 90%' and 'Lead the 90%'. So have a look at your presentation. Could you make it your 'Chicken Soup for the Soul'?"

Darci Lang, *HofF, www.darcilang.com*

Five Steps to Persuasion

...ideas to create successful presentations

Every presentation aims to persuade an audience. We seek to persuade them to listen and perhaps agree with what we present. Carefully crafting our thoughts and ideas keeping this in mind is what proves our professionalism.

- **Get their attention:** If you don't capture my attention, you'll never gain my acceptance or my action on your behalf. What does it take to do that? Do it!
- **Demonstrate their need to know:** This is where you help me see the relevance of what you are about to share. If I don't see a need in my life, career, or company I will not respond favorably to your call to action, and you are wasting time for us both.
- **Satisfy that need:** This is where you outline the solutions in ways that I can apply and benefit.
- **Visualize the results:** Help me see the *finished* results, the changes as outlined in your solution. Give me a *mental* picture of my need being met and my satisfaction attained, and I will be more receptive to act or buy.
- **Request their action:** This is where many mediocre salespeople blow it. **Ask for the order**. Call me to action! Challenge me to do something great! Same objective if you are selling ideas in a presentation!

This is a brief summary of the steps behind persuasion. Keep them in mind as you structure your presentation. Keep in mind what the audience reaction will be to each area. Selling your ideas as a presenter is very similar to what profession salespeople do with their clients and the process follows a similar path.

PRO-tip: Dress for Success! "Your personal appearance and grooming have a profound effect on the visual delivery of your speech. Your audience will need to believe in you before they consume your message. Therefore, present yourself appropriately for the culture of your audience. This will show you respect them, and it will build your credibility. They will now be able to hear what you have to say because your appearance is not a distraction to your message. Most countries now accept Western World business styles as appropriate."

Shirley Borrelli, *B.Ed. Image Consultant www.ShirleyBorrelli.com*

Using Humor… A Few Safety Tips

In the professional speakers' world there is a saying in response to the question, **"Do you have to be funny? Only, if you want to be paid!"**

While that is not entirely true, humor, when properly used, does make your presentation more interesting and helps build bridges with your audience. I have learned to leverage humor as a way to build bridges with my audiences and enjoy sharing a laugh with them. But I don't deliberately try for the laugh.

A few tips to remember if you plan on including *relevant* humor:

- Punch lines? Remember them!!!! Practice until you can nail it if awoken from a dead sleep.
- Ensure the anecdote is appropriate and relates to your presentation – not just inserted for the laughs. Too many amateurs undermine their efforts when they insert something funny that doesn't relate to their audiences.
- Timing is everything – practice it! A lot!!!
- **BE KIND!** Don't pick on any group or person. Hint: Pick on yourself! Make fun of YOU! This also helps build bridges with your audience by showing you are a real, authentic person.
- Vulgarity and sexist remarks are NOT allowed. They always work against you.
- Humor doesn't travel well. Make sure it works in different locations. Humor doesn't always translate to other cultures.

Bob signing books in Tehran, Iran

While speaking in Tehran, Iran (2009) I shared a story that always got a laugh in North America. Nothing! No laughter, no chuckles, nothing. I asked the translator about it, and he said, "I didn't get it!" Once I explained it to him, he laughed and said, "That's funny!"

Later that week we used it again in Kish to 300 university students, and we got laughs, lots of laughs. He was funny and he helped me bridge the cultural laughter gap.

PRO-tip: Tips on using humour

"The biggest mistake I see speakers make when it comes to humour is **trying too hard to be funny**. Don't try to be funny, instead focus on having fun and just being yourself. And give yourself license to mess up! It's okay to be messy! When you screw up on stage it just shows that you're human and it reassures the audience that you are truly in the moment and not just delivering a slick, 'canned' presentation. And, as an added bonus, it's a fabulous source for spontaneous humour!

Don't think of humour and serious content as an either/or choice. Humour is simply another vehicle for delivering your content and, when done right, one of the most effective ways to make a point. So always start by being crystal clear on the content and messages you want to deliver, then look for creative ways to deliver that content in a fun, humorous manner."

Michael Kerr, CSP, HoF, Past CAPS President, *www.mikekerr.com*

Note: To touch back on the previous list of tips: Humor doesn't travel well. Make sure it works in different locations. Humor doesn't always translate to other cultures.

As I shared in my story from Iran, I have learned to ask for advice from fellow speakers and organizers in places away from home. At times, I even share a story or two with them to see if it works or is appropriate. Humor, well suited and delivered can make you a superstar, but it can hurt you as well. Be cautious in where and when you use it and make sure you nail it.

PRO-tip: Creative Humor

"Adding humor is not a simple coincidence; it is a technique. You play a game with the brains of your audience. When you tell a story, and you go three times to 'the right,' everybody expects the next line will also go the right. If that is not the case, there will be a short *happy tension* in their brain. When people laugh, they get rid of that tension. So, that's the reason why we laugh. *Laughter* stimulates the release of feel-good substances, like dopamine. That is why it is healthy to laugh. So next time you tell a story, you add up facts, as clearly as possible. You make them think in one direction. Then suddenly, you say something that is the opposite of what people are thinking (or bigger, higher, thinner, etc.) Now, their brain does not understand that bit, you create positive tension, and they will laugh!"

Tom Sligting, *www.tomsligting.nl*

Using Visual Aids Effectively

In the past few years, there has been a bit of a backlash to visuals like PowerPoint, primarily because they have been overdone and detract from the presentation. Too many speakers stumble through presentations using visuals as visual crutches and not catch points to reinforce their message.

Many speakers are staying away from using them or use them sparingly. *I recall a meeting planner saying, "Thank you," when told I wasn't going to use PowerPoint with her group.* ***Death by PowerPoint*** *is a sign of poor expertise in action.*

If you are going to use visuals, *sparingly* use them to support and reinforce the message you intend to share with your audience. Here are a few ideas on their effective use.

- **Test for clarity:** Can they be clearly understood by the audience?
- **Make them relevant to the presentation:** Use only the ones that will reinforce or make your presentation stronger and more memorable. If they don't relate to the audience or the topic – dump them!
- **Use sparingly:** Professionals use only enough to get the job done or to visually illustrate a point. Remember they aren't there to see a slide show, but to listen to what you have to say.
- **Keep them simple:** Don't overdo it… and please don't use every aid in the book or all the bells and whistles *(PowerPoint has been overdone to death!)*
- **Keep them short:** Rule of thumb, 6 words per line and a maximum of 6 lines on any slide. Less is more in this case. Remember they are there as a guide or reinforcement not a stand-alone learning piece.
- **DON'T read your slides:** If all your information is on your slides and you are merely reading them, why do you need to be there?
- **Pictures:** Often the best slides are those which are more visual to help the audience see or experience something. Adding a few words may help to clarify what they are seeing. Keep it short.
- **Don't show prematurely:** Practice with them so they come up only as needed and are taken off just as quickly.
- **Show only when referring to them:** They are there to **reinforce** or illustrate your presentation. They should only be there when you are referring to them. Don't be afraid to build in blanks or know how to go to blank screen (CTRL B) or white screen (CTRL W) when needed.

- **Make direct reference to them:** This is one time where it is occasionally good to turn and look at a visual for a moment. This helps draw the audience's eyes accordingly.
- **Don't talk to visual aids – talk to us:** Having said that, don't talk while your back is turned to the audience. Look, turn back, and talk to your audience!
- **Maintain them in good order:** Just like shining your shoes and pressing your clothes, keep your visuals in good working order. If they get frayed, worn, overused, or outdated, replace them.

If you are planning to use visuals, plan to execute them well. Understand they are there to reinforce what you have to say and keep them clear, concise, and relevant to your presentation. If you are using them, make sure they are a value-added accessory – not a distraction.

Answering audience questions

There are times when taking questions from your audience can enhance your chances of getting your message across as well as help your audience learn by being more interactive. **Here are a few tips to help in that regard:**

- **Announce the Q&A session period in advance:** If you are going to incorporate this into your presentation, let your audience know early. Then make sure you structure your presentation to allow enough time for Q&A.
- **Don't evaluate questions:** You aren't there to judge or evaluate – but to share answers and help them clarify or amplify what you've just said.
- **Answer pleasantly and politely:** If you get ruffled or take questions as a personal challenge it will show. This will undermine your credibility faster than anything I have seen. So be cool **or** don't open yourself up to be challenged.
- **Use paralanguage *(voice and body)* to respond to questions:** '*Let me see if I understand you correctly?*" Clarify and respond to show them you listened and value their input. This is also where you can state or restate the question to ensure the rest of the audience or the audience on tape hears it prior to the answer being given.
- **Look directly at the audience when you answer:** This is one time when looking directly at the person who asked you the question is a good thing. Respect them and answer them directly.

- **Admit to not knowing ALL the answers:** We don't have to be the expert on everything. Make sure you understand what they are asking and make a commitment to get back to them with the answer. Then do it!
- **Ask for audience help *(when necessary)*:** This can be a good model even when you know the answer. Let other people be the heroes and share the stage. It works wonders in making the session a shared and memorable one.

Question periods can be a **wonderful way to involve your audience** and add additional points not already covered in your presentation. Additionally, they allow you to develop and share additional material from your wealth of knowledge. Have a few questions to prime the pump if necessary. *"One of the more frequent questions I get is…"* or *"The other day someone asked me…."* It works!

One final tip: **Never end in a Q&A session**. Always have a few closing comments or a story to finish and allow the audience to experience the end of your presentation on a high point. Nothing is lamer than asking and not getting any questions and following that embarrassing silence, closing on that experience.

"A theme is a memory aid; it helps you through the presentation just as it also provides the thread of continuity for your audience."

Dave Carey

PRO-tip:

"To become a professional speaker, you need to be an expert of a certain topic. And you need to have stage presence and stage crafts as well. All clear. And connecting with your audience is very important.

That's where my pro tip is going to: you need to know and live your core-values or better non-negotiables. You need to know what drives you, what your purpose is. Knowing your core values will help you to find your passion, your niche, your talents, and it will help you to really connect with YOUR audience. Who do you want to speak to?

But also, it will help you to see from your core values what the opportunities and options are and make the right choices in your life and career. This is the real foundation for a successful life and speaker career."

Paul ter Wal, LL.M CSP FPSA, Past President of the Global Speakers Federation *www.paulterwal.com*

Moving Upward

Moving upward

"the top predictor of success and upward mobility, professionally, is how much you enjoy public speaking and how effective you are at it!"

Stanford University Survey for AT&T

"As soon as you move one step up from the bottom, your effectiveness depends on your ability to reach others through the spoken or written word."

Peter Drucker - Author

"Effective speaking skills are an essential foundation for success in any endeavor. Professionally or personally, it is one of the most important skills you'll ever acquire! And it is easily acquired!"

Bob 'idea Man' Hooey
Accredited Speaker
Presentations Skills Success Coach

PRO-tip:
"For me, the day I became a successful speaker was the day I became vulnerable and let my true personality shine. At the suggestion of another speaker, I let go of how I was 'supposed' to act and spoke the way that was natural for me. According to the participants in the audience, they felt a connection to me and my message which had rarely happened before. AND it was easier for me to be authentically me than a fake someone else. What a relief and a huge step forward."

Barbara Khozam, Accredited Speaker *www.barbarakhozam.com*

Ideas on Getting Your Competitive Edge

When I joined Toastmasters, my mentor, **Gary Harper** told me about the value of competition. He said, "*Hooey, if you want to get good, get into competition.*"

There are valid reasons why competition can be a success tool in honing your skills and moving them to another level. One, of course, would be that competition itself will pull something *extra* out of you. The stretch of being competitive can be a benefit itself.

The other benefit is the potential of winning and getting the opportunity to hone a *single* speech through up to 5 levels of competition in Toastmasters (Club, Area, Division, District, and World-semis). Each time your presentation gets tighter, more focused, and perhaps even funnier.

I had the privilege coaching Calgarian, **Rowena Romero** to the 2005 Toastmasters International World Championships held in Toronto, Ontario. She was diligent in working and fine-tuning her speech. We went through countless re-writes, phone calls, and two trips to Calgary to see and coach on-site before she was satisfied and ready to take it to Toronto. I was so impressed by her commitment to giving her best and to allowing me to creatively work with her. She was a joy to coach.

Rowena's kind words to me: "*YOU were part of that performance for me. Working with you last year provided a good training ground for me to fully utilize facial, hand, and body gestures. I always used these aspects before, but not to the level that I am now. Many people commented on how I "commanded the stage" or that I "owned the stage" – that I didn't just deliver a speech, I brought the scene to life. The audience felt like they were in the car with me looking at Naked Guy or that they were Officer Kowalchuk. (Characters in Rowena's speech.)*

I gained the confidence of 'striking a pose' and not having to say a word. Before, I would have wanted to continue talking through every motion. (Show it - don't tell it!) However, this truly became 'actions speak louder than words' – everything from posing like Naked Guy, to the head going side-to-side for the windshield wipers, to the blinking hands for the hazard lights. I felt confident enough to just let the 'physical' do the 'talking' for me. Thank you for the training!"

I was humbled by her words!

That brings me to my touch point. When competing, it is important to maintain your focus on *giving* the audience something of value. Your *primary* job as a speaker is to deliver your best possible presentation (that day).

Hint: Each time you present, ***you are competing with your 'last' performance***. This applies in non-competitive presentations as well. In business as well as sales you are competing with other people to earn the respect and business of your clients. You are also competing with your last sales conversation.

A presentation should be structured and directed to *giving* definite benefits to those in the audience. The judge's job is to listen to each speaker and pick the top three presentations. Competitors lose when they attempt to do the judges' job.

As I reminded Rowena *(and remind myself each time I speak)*, trust the process, do your homework, and know there is someone in the audience who really needs to hear what you have to say. **Speak to that person**, even though you may never know who they are, or how you helped them. That is the win and that is what continues to motivate me to push through in my delivery.

Our *real* competition is *within* ourselves. Are you better today than you were the last time you spoke? Did the value you bring to the stage increase? The *competitive edge* is in pushing yourself to be better than you've ever been before.

Enjoy the competitions in your life and in speaking. But remember, the real prize is winning over the hearts and minds of your audience.

When Speaking for Success – **speak to win… their hearts and minds.**

PRO-tip: "Every speaker should have two speaking mentors. One older or more experienced, whose job is to tell you the best path to take based upon where you are in your journey. They will share the common mistakes and pitfalls that can befall many new or aspiring speakers. Also, have a mentor younger than you - important, if you've been speaking professionally. A younger mentor will bring the benefits of a beginner's mind and will ensure you stay relevant, help you see new opportunities, and keep you hungry for success. Both older and younger mentors will prove invaluable as you develop mastery in your craft, build your speaking business, and reach your potential as a speaker. Between them they will help you in finding your own way to a happy, healthy and prosperous speaking career."

James Taylor, *MBA FRSA, www.jamestaylor.me*

Effective Communication Is Really A Part of The 'Sales' And Management Process

People buy, agree, or say, *'yes'* to something, for emotional reasons in relation to benefits 'perceived' and sometimes received. They often use facts to back up or justify their purchase or decision.

- This also applies in leading teams and generating buy-in for programs, policies, or goals.
- It definitely applies to being a successful, profitable salesperson.
- **It applies, as well, to being successful in making a presentation.**

In your communication, it would be wise to keep in mind that people will react *'emotionally'* to what you say or write. **You are '*selling*' your ideas**, your position, your services, your products, and most importantly *yourself* whenever you communicate.

Perhaps it would be beneficial to take a moment and discuss the basic reasons we've found that people buy into or say 'yes' to something. These emotional needs underlie the reason they buy into your programs, buy your products, or buy you as a person to work with, follow, or deal with; why they can be persuaded to say 'yes' to something. They also provide guidance as you craft a impactful presentation.

Psychologist **Abraham Maslow** did exhaustive research and concluded that all people had a hierarchy of needs. He ranked them from the most basic to the loftiest: **physiological (sheer survival), security, social, self-esteem, and self-actualization.**

Remember, when you communicate effectively, people want to be involved in your life, your projects, and helping you succeed. Effective leadership is focused on pulling diverse talents, skills, needs, and drives of your team into common goals and to focusing their energies to succeed.

These insights or ideas on emotional needs can help you design and deliver powerful presentations.

Emotional needs:

25 TOP

1. To make money
2. To save money
3. To save time
4. To avoid effort
5. To gain comfort
6. To improve health
7. To escape pain
8. To be popular
9. To attract the opposite sex
10. To gain praise
11. To conserve our possessions
12. To increase our enjoyment
13. To satisfy curiosity
14. To protect our family
15. To be in style
16. To satisfy an appetite
17. To emulate others
18. To have beautiful things
19. To avoid criticism
20. To avoid trouble
21. To take advantage of opportunities
22. To be individual and unique
23. To protect our reputation
24. To gain control over aspects of our lives
25. To be safe

Whether you are talking one-on-one, presenting to a group of people, or communicating in writing, your audience, team, or readers will be evaluating and reacting to your words and *'filtering'* them through one or more of the above emotional needs.

Tough sell, isn't it? But if you have done your homework and researched the needs, background, and thought processes of those you want to reach, it will be much easier. You can enhance your chances of success by carefully crafting your communication to touch or draw on the emotional needs of your audience, team, or readership. Be cautious in its use.

Some would ask, isn't this like manipulation? My gut reaction would be to say no! On the surface it might appear that way, but only you know your *'true'* motives.

If your *'true'* motive is to communicate more clearly, more effectively; and your desire is to serve them by giving them all the relevant information they need in a way that makes it easier for them to relate to it – then I say go for it! Having an honest desire to help people is what builds a foundation for success under your career or business and helps ensure both longevity and success. That is one of the key secrets to Speaking for Success.

This applies to working with family and friends, as well as clients, co-workers, management, and staff. So, remember, communication, especially effective communication, is really a process of selling – selling your ideas, your desires, your dreams, and your future. How effective will you be in persuading people to buy in? How successful will you be in inspiring them to help you?

The Gettysburg Address by President Abraham Lincoln was short and historically impactful to help bring the nation back together. It was powerful in its simplicity and its structure. Take a moment to read this, perhaps out loud, and enjoy its power. Then use its inspiration as you work to craft your own.

"Fourscore and seven years ago our fathers brought forth on this continent a new nation, conceived in liberty and dedicated to the proposition that all men are created equal.

Now we are engaged in a great civil war, testing whether that nation or any nation so conceived and so dedicated can long endure. We are met on a great battlefield of that war.

We have come to dedicate a portion of that field as a final resting-place for those who here gave their lives that that nation might live. It is altogether fitting and proper that we should do this.

But in a larger sense, we cannot dedicate, we cannot consecrate, we cannot hallow this ground. The brave men, living and dead who struggled here have consecrated it far above our poor power to add or detract.

The world will little note nor long remember what we say here, but it can never forget what they did here. It is for us the living rather to be dedicated here to the unfinished work which they who fought here have thus far so nobly advanced.

It is rather for us to be here dedicated to the great task remaining before us - that from these honoured dead we take increased devotion to that cause for which they gave the last full measure of devotion - that we here highly resolve that these dead shall not have died in vain, that this nation under God shall have a new birth freedom, and ***that government of the people, by the people, for the people shall not perish from the earth."***

Interestingly enough, the papers of the time simply said, "…and the President also spoke!" hmmm

Descriptive Stories Sell on More Than One Level

If you know anything about business or sales, perhaps you've heard taught that communicating **Features, Advantages,** and **Benefits (FAB)** is a more effective approach than just feature dumping on our prospective customers.

It is!

- But how effectively do we incorporate that in our sales conversations?
- How effectively do we incorporate it in our oral presentations or communication? **Remember, you are selling your ideas when you speak! Leverage these tips to more effectively connect with them.**

Let me share a simple experience where a young shoe salesman (Joseph) did this very well as he presented his product. We all need shoes and, hopefully, since we are on our feet a lot, we select some that are comfortable, yet stylish to wear when we are at work. *At least that is my story.* ☺

Feature	/ **Advantage** (which means)	/ **Benefit** (to customer)
Calfskin leather	/ molds to your foot	/ custom made feel
Full leather lining	/ finished feel	/ instant comfort
Traditional loafer	/ will stay in style	/ wear for years

One winter, I was sailing in Puerto Vallarta, Mexico. One afternoon I was enjoying a quiet break doing some window shopping. A very stylish, yet simple, pair of two-tone loafers caught my eye in a little shoe store off the quaint cobblestone street. Thinking I was *only* looking, I stepped into the store to check them out. I picked them up and quickly put them down. My initial reaction was, *"Wow... these are not cheap, even for here!"*

My young and *very wise* shoe expert approached and engaged me in conversation about my visit to his store, to Puerto Vallarta, and what I did for a living.

I made the mistake of telling him I was a professional speaker and sales success trainer who traveled sharing ideas on how others could be more successful in their lives, careers, sales, etc. (Guess he figured I could really afford them.☺)

Picking up the shoes and holding them with care, he said, *"You know, when you wear these traditional loafers, you're going to have a big smile on your face because* ***'one of the great things'*** *about these shoes is they're soft calfskin leather with a full leather lining. And as you wear them, they will mold to the shape of your feet, giving you a custom-made feel."*

He continued, *"It would be fun to walk around in custom-made shoes, don't you think?"* I hesitantly agreed, "*…it would be great.*" He could have just said, "*These shoes are all leather, which is flexible, making them very comfortable.*" On the surface that sounds good, doesn't it? What he said engaged me and was much more effective in getting me to seriously consider investing in a pair for myself, don't you think?

He talked about how the shoes were made. He mentioned they were bench-crafted, which meant **one** person was completely responsible for making **this specific pair** of shoes.

Joseph then went in for the kill, *"Since they are bench-crafted, they have the artisan's name on them. When they're finished, these shoes have no nicks, no scratches, and all the components fit perfectly. Unlike shoes made on an assembly line, these shoes are* ***one of a kind.***" Then he asked me a simple closing question, "*What size do you wear?*" He then proceeded to have me try on a pair in my size; just to see how they felt. ☺

Long story, made short:

He was right, they are delightful to wear. When I walked out of his store, both of us had big smiles on our faces. I could hardly wait for the snow to leave so I could take them out for a walk back home in Northern Alberta.

Simple story of how one young salesman took his craft to the next level by engaging his client (audience) and telling a story that allowed me to see myself in those shoes. I still remember him when I slip them on. ☺

- Do you do that with your clients when they come into your store?
- Or when you visit them in their place of business?
- Do you do this when you speak to your audience?

PRO-tip: "Using Multimedia (PowerPoint, Keynote): Your slides are not meant to be the 'star of the show'. People came to hear you and be moved or informed by you and your message."
David Saxby, *www.sparkcommunications.com*

For example:

Do you know enough about your ideas and products that you can craft engaging stories to help your customers (audience) see themselves sitting in front of that big screen Plasma TV, on that leather sofa with matching love seat and chair, end tables, coordinated lamps and accents to enjoy that quiet evening together?

- Can they see themselves enjoying their well-funded retirement?
- Can they see themselves driving that navy blue, sporty new Mustang convertible or metallic navy Mazda CX5 (like we just bought ☺) ?

You get the point!

Are you willing to engage your clients (audience) to help them see it in their mind's eye before they see it in their house, office, or life? Do you know enough about the benefits your services provide that you can create captivating stories that help your prospective clients see themselves enjoying the benefit of wisely selecting you to help enhance their lives, businesses, and careers?

- Do you think this might help you build and expand your business or enhance your career?
- Do you think you can craft your presentation successfully to help your audience accept and act on your message?

Get walking and talking on your journey to **Speaking for Success** and in selling your message.

"I learned this, at least, by my experiment: that if one advances confidently in the direction of his dreams, and endeavors to live the life which he had imagined, he will meet with a success unexpected in common hours."
Henry David Thoreau, *Walden, or Life in the Woods*

PRO-tip: Speak your passion!
"How many times have you listened to someone speaking and felt like saying "Throw away your notes and speak from your heart!" Find a topic you are passionate about. Know your subject matter well. Then, just **speak your passion!** You won't have to rely on your notes except as pointers and your passion and enthusiasm will come through when you speak." **Irene Gaudet**, *www.VitrakCreative.com*

Crafting Your Message – The 'IT' Method

People often ask how I create and develop my topics and presentations. They want to know how I am able to skillfully infuse creativity into each one. Being Canada's 'Idea Man' helps. ☺

One of those methods is the **'IT' Method** which is a creativity exercise to help you **develop, organize, and dynamically deliver the content** of your presentation. In computer jargon 'I.T.' *usually* indicates information technology. In that same sense, when you are speaking, you are *essentially* imparting or transmitting specific knowledge, expertise, experience, or information.

Let's use that same acronym to help build the components of your successful presentation.

The Stick IT! Method, as envisioned, has five basic components or sequences to follow.

- **Thunder Think™ IT!** (Creative thinking by Bob 'Idea Man' Hooey)
- **Re-group IT!**
- **Fine-Tune IT!**
- **Spice IT up!**
- **Do IT!**

Thunder Think IT!

This is your chance to brainstorm: capture idea-rich concepts and related information. Brainstorming is a method for developing creative solutions to problems. Your goal here is to think freely, putting everything that you may want to say down on paper or on your screen. You can *brainstorm* or *thunder-think* on your own, but often a small group brainstorming together can really augment this creative process.

Over the years I found the **power of *leveraged* brainpower** to be an effective tool in problem solving; business planning and development; and in creating customized, effective presentations for my various audiences. I use a brainstorming method to create and design my presentations. Even when I have presented the topic numerous times, following this path allows me to remain fresh and create something specifically designed for each client.

Yellow sticky-notes, such as Post-its™, can give the creative process great fertility and flexibility. You can brainstorm more freely when not hampered by a linear outline or a sequentially generated form or structure. You can do this in a mind mapping format, but this works well from a visual and has a built-in flexibility factor.

With your primary topic or presentation theme identified, and the yellow sticky-notes in hand, capture any and all:

- **Ideas**
- **Facts**
- **Related stories**
- **Examples**
- **Jokes or funny connections**
- **Personal experiences**
- **Miscellaneous**

Yellow-sticky note everything and anything that relates to your subject, perhaps *flavored* by the particular audience. Don't be concerned about relating all your ideas or whether you even plan to use all the generated ideas. Just capture ideas – one per yellow sticky note! Collect the ideas and stick ALL of them on a flipchart or a nearby blank wall or picture window.

Try to keep your left-brain (*your internal editor*) out of this brainstorming process. This activity is strictly a right-brain function – pure free association, idea generation. **HAVE FUN!**

TIP: Brainstorming works best when a time limit is established.

Re-group IT!

Now step back mentally from this sea of yellow sticky notes and do what you might naturally do – put the notes in groups or clusters!

Group your ideas on the notes according to the natural associations you observe in the evolving material. Do not try to *force* every idea into a category; some will be left over. If you've ever done Mind Mapping, this is a very similar process. What parts *(notes)* relate to each other and form natural groups or clusters?

I use this method when I am assembling publications like this one where I was drawing on two or more books to create this expanded 10th version just for you.

TIP: If you find that a category has more than 10 notes, consider whether it should really be more than one category! Split it for better impact!

After you group the sticky notes, give each group a *working* name or title. Next, ask yourself the question: "Given this *particular* audience, which of these groups do I want them to hear about first, in the body of the presentation, second, third," and so on. Try to keep the number of groups relatively small.

Many people believe that three to five is the ideal number of points around which to organize your presentation. This is not absolute! Just try to keep it simple.

Save the unused groups. They may provide input for other parts of the presentation. These groups also can provide a source for the question-and-answer period of the presentation and may be used in future presentations on the same subject to other audiences. They can form the foundation for additional presentations or articles.

Look at all the sticky notes generated from the brainstorming and see what categories or groups you can come up with. Write these in large circles on the flipchart.

Fine-Tune IT!

Applying sound *simplicity* principles, trim the ideas within each group and put them into a logical order or sequence. Remember, even though many experts believe three is the ideal number, you are not bound to it.

Go back to your presentation strategy and review your position, desired actions, and listener benefits. Make sure you define these items in your presentation. Usually, the desired actions and listener benefits should be stated and restated in the introduction and in the conclusion.

Spice IT up!

You are now ready to add some 'spice' to your presentation framework! The purpose of spice is to add *memor-ability*, en-liven, aid retention, and otherwise provide interesting relief and reinforcement of your program or message. Use it wisely – but use it!

Spice it all! Don't forget to spice up the beginning and the ending or conclusion. Remember the opening and the closing thoughts or statements are the most important items in the presentation. These items are the most likely to be 'remembered' by your audiences. Identify where the *peaks* and *valleys* of the presentation are and what type of spice could be added to the *new* or *improved* presentation.

Here are some ideas to make your speech a bit more appealing to your audiences. These ingredients are the contents of your own **'Spice Cupboard':**

- **Stories** – that convey emotion and grab their attention and encapsulate the lessons. Make sure to use your own stories. If you share something from another source, credit it!
- **Quotes** – that reinforce or remind them of your message can be sprinkled throughout your speech.
- **Facts** – that substantiate or reinforce your credibility on the platform are always a welcome addition.
- **Props** – that help visually illustrate or command attention.
- **Costumes** – if they enhance your presentation and illustrate your point. Choose wisely! ☺ I remember, and so did my audience, walking on stage at our CAPS convention in Vancouver. I did so, at 7AM in my PJs to illustrate a point. Even though this occurred 20 some years ago, I still get comments. Hmmm!
- **Handouts** – that give solid value and follow up information or resources or are an interactive part of the session. Most professionals call them learning guides or resource guides which help us reinforce their value.
- **Audio** – sound bites and background music to assist in the lesson or setting moods.
- **Video** – illustrate a point; introduce another concept or expert into the mix. YouTube has provided some invaluable visuals for presentations. Use selectively and make sure they are relevant to your program or presentation.
- **Slides** – overheads, Keynote™ or PowerPoint™ that are used as a tool to reinforce, remind, or help the audience visualize something you as the speaker are saying.

Anything you use from your 'Spice Cupboard' is *only* there to support and make what you say more impactful, easier to understand, or more memorable.

If it overshadows you as the speaker – reduce its use or eliminate it entirely. The audience wants to hear and see 'YOU', not a *slick, canned* slide show. Along the lines of an ostentatious frame for a painting.

Do IT!

Now that all the planning work has been done, the presenter must create, write, and edit, edit, edit, edit before developing the visuals or other aids to accompany the presentation.

Building the foundation and organization or structure using the IT method is the start. To bring your presentation to fruition and effectively present IT takes additional thought and polishing as you flesh IT out and prepare IT in its final form. **Good luck in your quest.**

On the following pages, I have included two examples of speech outlines for your information.

1) **The first is a linear outline, similar to what we were taught in school to help us in writing our compositions.**

I've blocked it out so you can write in your answers in the appropriate places. Then, as you fine tune your presentation, you can add, subtract or edit your thoughts. This can be an effective tool in helping you think through the flow of ideas and structure in your speech.

2) **The second is a sample of a modified, stylized creative mind map styled speech organization tool.**

This is more along the method I use and dovetails nicely with the ideas expressed in Crafting the 'IT' way. It allows you to let your mind flow and generate ideas.

Capture the ideas and then group them into clusters or natural connections. I simply restructure the clusters into a natural flow which becomes my speech outline and path. Feel free to copy them ***for your personal use*** in preparing your own speeches.

Visit: **www.successpublications.ca/PIVOT.html** to download a complimentary copy of **PIVOT to Present** (written after Covid-19 hit)

Speech Formats and Construction – Traditional Linear Style

Speech Crafting

Main Message
Opening
1st Point
2nd Point
3rd Point
Close

Simple and to the point! Make notes in the appropriate boxes and then fine tune your thoughts and ideas as you move on to create your presentation.

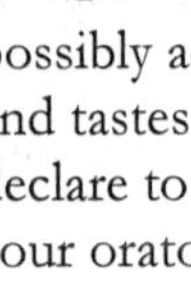

PRO-Tip: "Self-Love for confident and convincing speaking. Will people like me? It's normal to search for love and validation when we get on stage. This expectation is the main cause of our nerves and stress. We know from experience it is impossible to force someone to like or love us. How could we possibly achieve this from a stage, with hundreds of different backgrounds and tastes in the room? Before you deliver your talk: Look in the mirror and declare to yourself this love you are craving. Repeat mentally and affirm all your oratory strengths. Reconnect with your core message and the objective of speaking: sharing a message and speaking your legacy. Dare to shine from a place of love and you shall be loved."

Amélie Yan-Gouiffes, *www.ameliespeaks.com*

Speech Formats and Construction – Creative Style

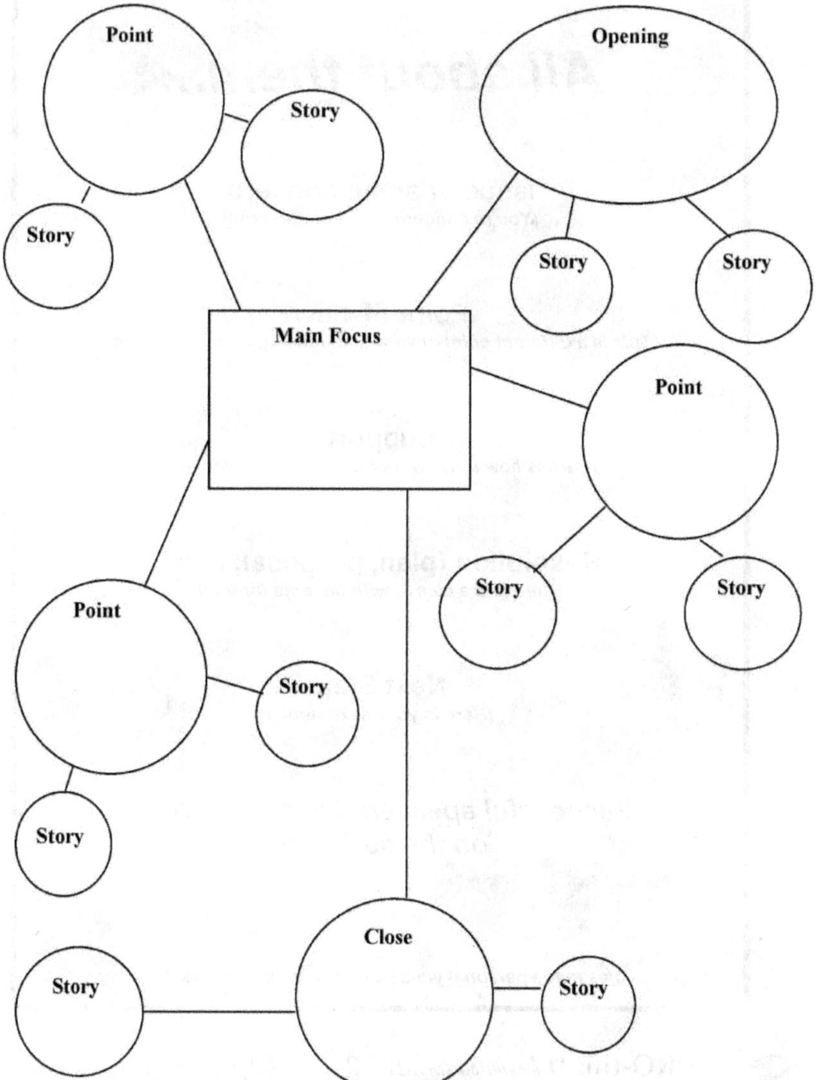

Sample Speech Outline

This style is a bit more creative and more like how most of us think. Gather your points and then organize them as you move ahead to create your presentation.

All About Them…

All about them...

Issue of some concern
(You're concerned ... I understand)

Point of view
(This is a different point of view ... of looking at your problem)

Support
(Here is how it will work for you ... the evidence)

Resolution (plan, proposal, idea)
(Here is the idea ... with benefits for you)

Next Step
(Here is your next step...)

Successful speakers keep their focus on the audience

Principles made personal yield powerful results - Ideas At Work!

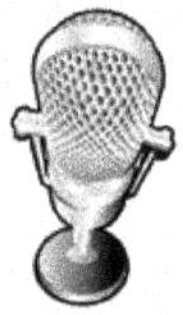

PRO-tip: *"I keynoted the AFCP (French Speakers Assn) August 2015. Their theme was* ***Words Matter: Influence, Inspire, Impact.*** *I worked to construct my remarks, ideas, and weave stories to focus on the power of words in our lives and in the lives of our audiences. Choose your words wisely, for they have the power to move millions.*

In 2019, *I spoke for them again and challenged them to hone their skills and mastery using the backdrop of European artists and architects to make my point."*

Bob 'Idea Man' Hooey, *Accredited Speaker, www.BobHooey.training*

Interpersonal Communication

"It's important to talk to people in their own language. If you do it well, they'll say, 'He said exactly what I was thinking.' And when they begin to respect you; they'll follow you to the death." **Lee Iacocca**

Words are powerful, so choose them with great care. Keep in mind, the 500 *commonly used* business words in the English language have over 14,000 definitions based on their usage and context.

Choose them *wisely* to best communicate the message you want to convey. Say it in their language, not yours. It works! Communication comes from the Latin root word *'commune,'* which loosely translated means *'held in common.'*

I worked with an interpreter (not a translator) when speaking in Vladivostok, Far Eastern Russia. She was a marvelous lady who taught at one of the universities. I noticed she would often take longer to share my thoughts in Russian than I did in English. I asked her why. She told me she wanted to make sure the audience understood my references, so she added some informative bits to make it work better for all of us. And, she was funny, so the audience laughed in most of the right places. This was one of my highlights for 2010.

To effectively communicate, we need to go the extra mile to ensure those we are talking with understand what we are saying, as well as we do. It is not just sending a message – it is creating a shared meaning and mutual understanding – quickly, clearly, and concisely. We must also be an *active* listener to ensure we draw out and understand what they are attempting to communicate to us.

This is a foundation for building a workable, lasting relationship – in work or in your personal life. When you establish such a relationship, **I'd suggest focusing on these areas:**

- **Be open**
- **Recognize**
- **Accept**
- **Appreciate other viewpoints**

This is the secret to effective communication – being open and flexible. How we listen and respond will dramatically impact our ability to understand and communicate.

Phrases that fire them up:
I like that; I'm glad you brought that up; that is great! We can do that; I agree; Yes, I think you might be onto something; Great work! We can do something with that idea; Tell me more; That is interesting, could you explain?

Phrases that dampen them:
Be practical; You haven't considered; The problem with that is…; I don't see how that can work; No way, that will work; If I had been doing it…; We don't have the time or money; Let me tell you…; I'm not interested, now get back to work.

"The real art of conversation is not only to say the right thing in the right place, but to leave unsaid the wrong thing at the tempting moment."
Dorothy Nevill

To minimize the chance of being misunderstood, especially with so many definitions, take a moment and **paraphrase what is being said to you.**

- It helps you get on track – the same track – with the speaker.
- It helps you focus.
- It helps identify areas that need clearing up.
- It lets the other person know they are 'actually' being heard.
- It can help identify goals and common objectives – *'commune'*

Here are some examples of paraphrasing:
- Are you saying?
- If I hear you correctly?
- Do I understand that you?
- Let me see if I understood you correctly?

Effective communication, as an active listener, is based on:
- Looking at the person
- Being an active, involved listener
- Asking questions
- Searching for common ground
- Being in the present – being present! *(Two words – two meanings!)*
- Not being stuck in the past or in history
- Focusing on ideas, concepts – not just the words
- Willing to deal with the issues, not the personalities
- Being positive and remaining open and flexible in your thinking.

"Communication does not begin with being understood, but with understanding others." **W. Steven Brown**

Did you know? I've been told…

- At age one, the average child has a vocabulary of three words
- At fifteen months – nineteen words
- At two years of age – a working knowledge of 272 words
- Age three – big jump to 896 words
- Age four – 1,540 words
- Age five – 2072 words
- Age six – communication with 2,562 words

Ever wonder how many words we have each added to our list since we entered grade one? Have you consciously added to your vocabulary as tools to allow you to create more vivid word pictures?

Words are tools that help paint a mental picture. How many colors have you created in your palate to be able to paint word pictures more creatively?

"Give yourself an even greater challenge than the one you are trying to master, and you will develop the powers necessary to overcome the original difficulty."
William J. Bennett - *The Book of Virtues*

PRO-tip:

"A long time ago a wise man told me "if you write about things, it will become dated, if you understand and write about people, it will stand the test of time." **Clay Gilson's** words were true then and are still true now. After a few decades in the business, I would add that if you write and speak with emotion, your words will stand through time.

We have become too 'politically correct', and the result is too much is created that says nothing to anyone. When you write or speak, take a position, share your views and be ready to defend them; that is the mark of a true wordsmith who wants to say something to this and future generations. Understand the 'people' in the audience and your material will never be dated."

Les Kletke, *www.globalghostwriter.com*

Good Stories = Better Speeches

Some of the world's greatest speakers are also great story tellers. Interesting observation, isn't it?

- My long-time friend and mentor, **Peter Legge** has gained international respect from his peers for his ability to weave a powerful, engaging story on the platform. Peter is amazing to experience, on and off stage.

- My friend and birthday-twin ☺, **Patricia Fripp** has the unique ability to add drama and a touch of Hollywood to make her stories memorable. She is in high demand as a speaker and more recently as a highly-paid speech coach primarily for this expertise.

There are too many more to mention here. I would worry I would forget some of the amazingly talented people I've grown to love and respect. If you would become a great speaker, you need to deal effectively with storytelling.

First, decide why you want to include or feature relevant stories in your presentation.

- Would they *actually* help you?
- What do you want to accomplish and *will stories add* to that objective?
- Which stories *reinforce* what you are trying to convey in your message?

Why do stories work?

- People like stories
- People pay attention
- People remember them
- Stories can stimulate *both sides* of the brain
- They can add humor
- Stories can be used as a motivational tool

If a picture is worth a 1000-words, at times a properly placed and performed story is worth 10,000 words in the minds of your audience.

Keep in mind the three basic STORY components:

- **The Premise**
- **The Problem**
- **The Payoff**

Each story has its own special use, placement, and characteristics. Learn to apply them where they are best suited to reinforce your message and help your audiences understand and retain your points.

One of the most impactful techniques I've acquired from several coaches and professional speakers is:

"Experience the story — don't just tell the story!"

It is important to help the audience *receive* your story on all three levels: visually, audibly, and, at times in a kinesthetic manner. Being ***in-the-moment*** helps form realistic mental images and anchor them in the minds of your audience.

There are eight essential steps in a typical story development:

1. **Set the scene**
2. **Introduce the story's characters**
3. **Begin the journey**
4. **Encounter the obstacle, opportunity, or challenge**
5. **Overcome the obstacle, challenge, or engage the opportunity**
6. **Resolve the story**
7. **Make your point**
8. **Ask the question**

Understanding and applying the proper sequence in building a story will help you successfully re-create it in the minds of your audiences.

Two other techniques:

- Foreshadowing
- Flash backs

You might be familiar with these two as they are used in many applications: songs, movies, and books to mention a few.

Foreshadowing sets the audience up for something that will appear or be brought to the forefront later in the speech.

Flashbacks are a great way to take your audience back to an earlier time in the history or development of your story.

Using your own stories is a recipe for success on the platform.

- **Learning how to structure.**
- **Selecting the right story for the right moment or audience.**
- **Strategically placing stories for maximum impact.**
- **Adding a bit of drama or Hollywood pizzazz to help your audiences see the scene you are experiencing.**

Using stories effectively will do wonders for your success on the platform, on the sales floor, and in the boardroom.

The key ingredient to an effective speech is to have a unifying theme throughout.

These **topic starter ideas** can help you structure or form interesting speeches that will keep the audience's attention.

1. **The importance of setting goals – dream big**
2. **Taking responsibility for your actions – personal leadership**
3. **Using mistakes to build a bright future – leveraged lessons**
4. **Finding inspiration in the world around you – observe**
5. **Never giving up on a dream – persevere and win**
6. **Creating a personal 'Code' to live by – integrity**
7. **The golden rule (Do unto others) – lead by example**
8. **Never forgetting your roots – keeping it real**
9. **Focusing on the important things in life – path to success**
10. **Setting high expectations – strive to grow**

Visit: **www.successpublications.ca/PIVOT.html** to download a complimentary copy of **PIVOT to Present** (written after Covid-19 hit)

Learning From The Masters – A Life-Long Lesson

I've been inspired by some great speakers over the years and share a few recollections and lessons from that inspiration. In 1972, I watched veteran performer **Art Linkletter** entertain his audience while I waited backstage for **Dr. Vincent Peale** to go on at the Jubilee Auditorium in Calgary, Alberta.

Off stage Dr. Peale sounded and acted like a typical grandpa. Visualize a 65 plus year old man, walking *slowly* on stage to thunderous applause, after being introduced by MC, **Don Hudson**, CSP. I wondered how he would do.

He was inspirational! For nearly an hour he *captivated* that audience with the power of his *'enthusiasm'* and the power of that gravelly, vibrant voice. Story after story about what we could do with our lives if we *believed;* really *believed.*

I was inspired… and a strange thought entered my mind… *"I would love to be able to do what he was doing!"* Well, some 20 years later, I started following him down this speaking path!

Show your passion – it moves people!

In 1992, I sat down for the *first time* with my now, long-time friend **Dr. Peter Legge, CSP, CPAE, HoF.** Peter was then only known to me as *the successful son* of my friend **Bernie Legge**. I am honored that Peter penned the foreword for Speaking for Success.

I'd seen Peter speak and asked him for help with my Toastmasters Clubs when I was a newly elected Area Governor. I felt if they could see a *great* speaker, they might *'sense'* what they could gain from applying their skills. It might get them inspired. He spoke and boy did they get inspired.

I asked Peter, *"What is the secret to being a great speaker?"* Peter told me the secret was *"…in telling your own stories"*. He shared that when he started, he didn't think that anyone wanted to hear his stories but found when he started sharing them his audience connection and his career vastly improved. I would say so!

Tell your own stories!

I shared my dream of becoming a professional speaker with **Peter J. Daniels**, who I'd met when he spoke in Vancouver, BC along with best-selling author **Og Mandino**. He had invited me to call, if I was ever in his neck of the world. Several months later, sitting in a fish and chips shop in Adelaide, Australia I listened as Peter challenged me to **dream big – that my dreams were too small**. He told me I needed to challenge myself to set and reach larger goals in my speaking career. He said, *"I would need bigger dreams to keep me focused and engaged to endure the risks, detours, and challenges I would encounter along the path I had chosen."* He was so right!

Take risks if you want results.

While sitting next to **Patricia Fripp, CSP, CPAE** during a National Speakers Association (NSA) Platform Skills lab, I watched her madly writing notes as each presenter shared their ideas. I was amazed at how smart she was in writing down some of the same things I was. ☺ I learned that one of the reasons the great ones are great – they never stop learning, experimenting, or sharing. **Thanks, Fripp!** ☺ Fripp challenged me to start sharing my *"Typhoon en route to Japan"* story, as even though to me it was old, it would be fresh and exciting to my audiences. Was she ever right!

Use powerful words to explode the mental images of your stories.

Jim and **Naomi Rhode, CSP's, CPAE's** made a special trip to visit to our Vancouver, BC CAPS Chapter when I was President. Naomi skillfully wove stories from personal experience and observation into her session. I watched as my colleagues fell under her spell. Later, Jim talked about the importance of taking care of the business of speaking. I remember the first time I met Naomi. She came over to me after I'd spoken at CAMP-NSA, leaned into my ear and told me she loved what I said, and that *'I was a great speaker.'* I was both humbled and inspired by her *gracious* words.

Connect from the heart and share the little things. They matter!

There are so many more speakers to whom I owe my inspiration, encouragement, and thanks. I've been inspired by many speakers within Toastmasters as well as the professional arena around the globe. If you want to become a great speaker – hang out with great people and ask questions. You'll be amazed at what they are willing to teach you. Every month CAPS, NSA, GSF, and Toastmasters have meetings around the world. You have that opportunity. **Don't miss it!**

Presenting With 'Passion' And Power

This is another in-class exercise used with my students and executives. This one is geared to encourage them to speak with conviction about a subject they are passionate about. Again, the purpose is not to over think, but to speak and allow your passion to help your presentation.

Objectives of this exercise:

- To continue working on any nervousness you still have in speaking in front of an audience.
- To share with your audience your honest conviction, sincerity, and earnestness on a subject that is of great importance or concern to you.
- To project and apply your passion in being able to be a more powerful speaker.

Suggested presentation time: 2 to 3 minutes

For this exercise I'd suggest picking a topic that really concerns you, one on which you are passionate about, its defense, demise, or cause.

Be natural, yet forceful! Your major purpose is to convey your true and honest feelings to an audience. A combination of strong feeling and thought should allow you to give a true expression of your personality. Your goal is to share your focus with your audience and make them understand; and possibly join you in support of this enthusiastic point of view you express.

This project focus was chosen for a specific reason and was designed to help you succeed. **If something is important to you, it will reflect in your speech.** It will be easier for you to speak about something you deeply care about than to deliver a scripted or lackluster speech on a less important or assigned topic. You will gain confidence and confidence only when you are doing this in front of other people.

Awaken your audience with your introduction. Capture their attention. Make them sit up and want to listen to you. Interest them in your choice of subjects. Demonstrate your chosen topic's relevance and timeliness to them.

Identify the source of your concern and show how the problem or challenge can be solved during the body of your presentation. Bring your audiences' understanding and sympathy to your side, hopefully in support of you and your convictions.

A few general ideas and tips:

- **Be enthusiastic and positive** in your approach. This is a more effective way, even when dealing with a tough challenge or hostile audience.
- **Try it without notes.** You are telling your listeners what you really believe, rather than reading a script. Remember the 'hand' illustration. Since this is something, you are passionate about it would lend itself to being delivered without notes.
- If you need notes, use cards where each point is illustrated by a simple phrase.
- If you're *really* ambitious, use large cards, graphs, charts, or power point slides to illustrate each main idea. Refer to these visual aids only as necessary.
- **Focus your 'nervous' energy** on the communication of your conviction, sincerity, and belief in the subject that you are presenting.
- Wrap up with a **strong note of appeal or call to action** for your audience. Challenge them to do something 'GREAT' with what you've just told them. Remember the lesson from the Abraham Lincoln story.
- Assume you've won over your audience and challenge them to act on your message, to put it into practice.

Take time to thoroughly rehearse this presentation. Try several different approaches and refine it as you go through each rehearsal. Enjoy the adventure!

Becoming effective and comfortable in front of an audience is attainable and cumulative – it takes time, practice, more practice, and persistence.

PRO-tip: "**Grab the audience's attention immediately**. No waffle. 'Go for their throats' immediately with an opening story that will intrigue, will amuse, but most importantly that will want to keep them listening to the rest of your speech."

Mike Ogilvie, *FPSA, Past President PSA UKI www.mikeogilvie.com*

Applying The 3 R's in Building A Relationship With Your Audience

Remember the very old adage about the basics of learning, as it applied to schoolin' – the 3 R's, which were: **R**eading, w-**R**iting and a-**R**ithmetic! I would like to draw on a different set of 3 Rs in my desire to assist you in successfully building a solid, impactful relationship with your audiences.

- A relationship that will allow you to deliver your message more effectively with impact and staying power.
- A relationship that will extend the trust you earn with them and continue to earn, as you deliver your message, set forth your case, and challenge them to act on what you've given them.

Let's explore 3 R's that can help you achieve this worthy goal.

REAL

Is the message you seek to deliver real? Is it based on truth, grounded in reality, and filtered through the reality of your life and your experience? If so, you have a solid foundation on which to successfully build your relationship and to move your audience to actively respond to your challenge.

- Real does not mean you can't use creative license to make your stories live, to make them more vivid and memorable – but they must be based on truth to strike a chord in the lives of your audiences. **If they don't believe them – they won't believe you!**
- Real is how you convey your message, how you present yourself and how you connect. Who are you? Is your audience seeing the 'real' you? Faking it is a prelude to failure!

Hint: You don't always have to be the hero of your own stories. It is ok to share stories where you didn't win or had to learn a serious lesson.

Some of the most effective audience relationships were built on honest discussion of the lessons I'd learned from messing up. Given time to reflect and age a bit, our 'mess' can become a 'mess-age' of hope, encouragement, and empowerment. Isn't that what we want to accomplish as speakers? The best part of this business has been the people I have met and befriended around the world. I love them!

Have the courage to be yourself and share you with your audiences – it will move them! **Real people learn and leverage from their lessons in life!**

RELEVANT

Is what you seek to share relevant to the audience's needs, experiences, relationships, or desires? How do you know? Have you invested the time to find out? This is where doing your homework works.

The more you know about your audience, the better chance you have of choosing the stories, word pictures, experiences, thoughts, and ideas that will relate to them. Building relevance takes time and diligence on our part – but if we truly desire to reach our audiences, it is our responsibility.

People relate to you when you share points that are relevant and real in their lives and experience. We seek a connection that will allow us to move them to action, not simply file away our words as more 'information'.

I repeat: This is where your homework or audience research pays off. Knowing them, what is it you can share from your experience, expertise, or research that would be the most beneficial? Then, work to weave that into your presentation.

Our goal is to 'build a bridge' to shared learning and this bridge is anchored by ensuring what we share is relevant on both ends.

Relevance builds relationships.

RELIGION (REACHING OUT)

Now here I bet some of you are saying, *"OK, where did he get this from?"* Or *"I don't get it – religion?"* But I do have a purpose here – stay with me. When I was attempting to sleep and was pondering this section, searching for a 3rd R, 'religion' came to mind. I immediately thought, *"No way – how does that apply?"*

I took a closer look to find the verse that had come to mind from a distant sermon, heard, filed, and seemingly forgotten. In the book of James, he writes, *'**Religion** that God our father accepts as pure and faultless is this: **to look after orphans and widows in their distress**…'* James 1:27 NIV

He was taking about being a 'doer' of the word and not just a 'hearer' of the word – that 'real religion' was hands on, impacting, and helping people in their daily lives and struggles, not just words. Didn't Jesus model that?

The next morning, I suddenly saw the gem in the message he was conveying and understood how we can apply it in our desire to serve and challenge our audiences. I'm not talking about a spiritual connection, but a more person-to-person one.

To be effective, our message must be 'grounded' in a call to action for our audiences and built on our true desire to serve; to visit them in their affliction, confusion, or pain and to help them do something about it. I seek to be an encourager to those in my audiences as I travel the globe.

To that extent, when we put ourselves on the line and reach out to our audiences, we will see them respond and react to what we say. If we want to reach them, teach them, and move them to act on what we share, we need to visit them where they are (figuratively or metaphorically at least). They will respond to our efforts and give what we share more relevance when we do.

Religion in its purer sense is 'reaching out' in helping people and building a relationship to that end. I can do that, bet you can too!

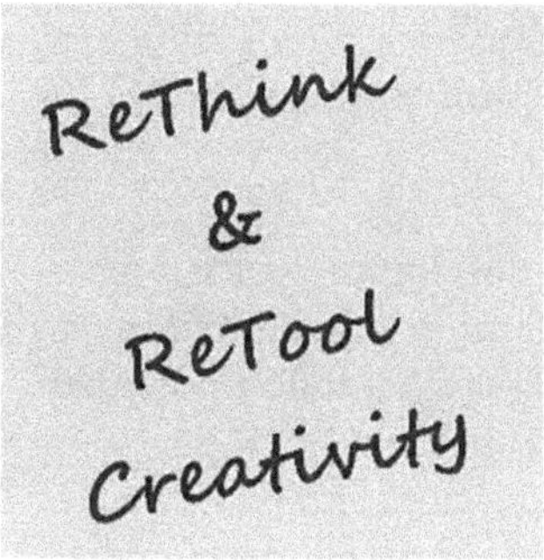

I remember saying to someone early on in this last recession, ***"When things are tough, people need help, and they need hope. That is just what I bring!"***

As speakers, we are at our best when this is where we are coming from when we deliver our message. When we seek to reach out to our audiences, we can lift their sights and their spirits. People need that more than ever!

I tell emerging speakers, consider there is at least one person in your audience who desperately needs to hear what you have to say today. Our effectiveness as speakers is built on establishing relationships with those in our audiences.

Being real, working to establish 'relevance' and reaching out will go a long way to build solid foundation for your success on the platform, on the sales floor, and even in the boardroom!

"Make sure that you have finished speaking* before *your audience has finished listening! "
Dorothy Sarnoff

Your Voice as a Powerful Communication Tool!

Your voice can be the most powerful tool in your communications by conveying information, meaning, emotion, and enthusiasm for your subject. **It can also work against you, to make it hard for your audience to grasp what you are trying to say.**

Early in my speaking journey I was taught that there are **five basic characteristics of a good speaking voice.**

1. A **pleasant tone**, which can convey a sense of warmth and friendliness.
2. A **vitality**, which lends the impression of force, strength, and conviction.
3. A **natural sound** that reflects and echoes your sincerity and true personality.
4. Portrays various **shades of meaning** to minimize monotony or lack of emotion.
5. **Easily heard** learn and apply proper volume, projection, and **ar-tic-u-lation.**

Over the years I have sought coaching to help me develop my voice range and my projection. I am learning how to better use my voice as a tool or instrument and in that to be more effective in using it to its fullest potential.

The objective of a good speaking voice is to find, develop, and maintain a balance between the extremes of volume, pitch, and rate, while seeking to find and deliver a pleasing sound quality. It sounds hard, but it simply requires awareness and application of some basic principles. Perhaps a little coaching wouldn't hurt either. ☺

- **Volume**: can be varied to add emphasis or dramatic impact. Make sure everyone can hear you. Don't overpower your audience.

Early in my speaking career I encountered a situation where my soft-spoken style worked against me. I was speaking in San Diego to an overflow group of about 350 people in a long three-section room. The air conditioning unit in the center portion was very loud, which meant that when I went low to emphasize a point, that group couldn't hear me. This caused them to miss a good part of the message I was trying to convey.

Now, I know better to be aware and equipped to project, to ensure everyone can hear me. At the time I was a bit green and thought they could hear me with a sound system.

I asked one of my coaches ***John Howard,*** *DTM, PID (now deceased), in Salt Lake City about it as he coached me. He even had me singing to work on it. Also, he referred me to one of his associates. She picked me up and we drove out into the desert foothills. We stopped and climbed this little hill in the 108-degree sun. About 1000 yards up the hill; she stopped and motioned me to go on for another 100 yards. Once I was up the mountain, she proceeded to have me give my speech so she could hear it. I learned a valuable lesson concerning projection without having to yell. Thanks* ***Billy Jones****, DTM, I owe you one.*

- **Pitch.** Can be varied to convey emotion and conviction. Avoid a too high pitch. This can suggest immaturity and excitability or reveal your nervousness. All of these take away from your strength and credibility as a presenter. Make a conscious effort to be *conversational* in your speaking. Focus on making it easy for your audience to hear and listen to you.
- **Rate.** Maintain a rate of 125-160 words per minute, which seems to be the most effective speaking rate. Vary your rate during your presentation to create emphasis and reflect mood changes. Slow down when you want the audience to listen carefully or emphasize an important point. Speed up to convey urgency or excitement in the moment.
- **Quality.** Relax your throat while you speak for increased vocal quality. Do a warm-up before you begin to speak to allow your throat and muscles to prepare to deliver their best for you. *(I sometimes do it in the washroom before I am scheduled to speak.)* Think in terms of friendliness, confidence, and a desire to communicate clearly with your audience.
- **Tone.** Work to mold your tone; friendly and pleasant, not harsh and monotonous. Your audience will appreciate it and stay tuned to hear what you are saying.
- **Vitality.** Work on making your voice forceful and expressive when appropriate in your presentation and consistent with what you really feel. My fellow CAPS member **Betty Cooper** (sadly gone now) taught me to work on this area to add more *vim to my vigor* and make my stories sing with excitement.
- **Ar-tic-u-lation.** If they don't hear you clearly, your message will be lost. Work to be clear and distinct. Don't drop hard letters like ***'g'*** at the end of words. Learn and apply the proper pronunciations for words.

Don't let your message be misunderstood just because your words are misunderstood or mispronounced.

In business, we have about 500 commonly used English words with close to 5000 connotations. The wide range of connotations depends on how they are used and pronounced. Be clear, let us hear and understand you!

A few more ideas…

- Practice using **warm-up exercises** to give your voice its optimum range and to give your audience the best message possible.
- Make sure you **drink lots of water** – room temperature water with *no ice* before you speak. Don't be afraid to have water close at hand or to stop and take a sip from time to time while speaking. It's also a nice way to take a break and collect your thoughts. ☺
- A slice of lemon can be added to the water. Drinking ice water can be tough on your throat, as it tends to shrink or cause your muscles to contract. Remember the last time you had a sprain and had an ice pack. Don't do that to your throat, especially at a time when it is already under stress.
- Take a moment to **breathe and ground yourself** prior to speaking, especially if you've had a bit of a walk or gone up steps to a platform. This will give your voice a chance to adjust and be normal in a 'nervous' situation.
- Breathing is the most important point I can stress in being a good speaker. **Breathe from your diaphragm,** deeply and fully. Vocal sounds are made when air passes across your larynx. If you aren't breathing properly, your ability to project naturally is diminished.
- **Check out the room and sound system** before you speak. Try speaking in the spot where you'll be presenting to allow yourself to become acclimatized to the environment and to reduce your nervousness. Have the soundman adjust for your range from soft to the highest volume so you'll be comfortable and still be heard.
    - **Don't smoke or drink coffee** or caffeine-based products before you speak. Caffeine can act as a diuretic, putting pressure on your bladder when you really don't need it. Smoking will add hoarseness to your voice and minimize the fluid in your mouth. This can minimize your ability to fully speak and project warmth and friendliness.

Remember your voice box is a muscle. It works better when warmed up and taken care of prior to speaking.

Cowboys and Communication

A cowboy gets up every day and knows he has a job to do… to get a herd of independently thinking cows across the prairies to a siding, where they will be shipped to market. He gains satisfaction from doing his job well and will continue to do so today and tomorrow and the day after that… because he is, a cowboy! Along the way he will battle unforgiving elements, sickness, boredom, balking cows, demanding terrain, and loneliness.

In our search as professional speakers, or to become effective communicators, we too will encounter numerous challenges… challenges that when overcome, will become the very foundations for our continuing success!

A cowboy doesn't think anything special about his skills and talents in roping, cutting, riding, or throwing… he just uses them as part of his daily tools in doing his job. Similarly, with our communication skills, we need to take them into our daily lives and workplace to become truly proficient and effective in their use. Our audiences deserve our best! This is the essence of true professionalism! This is the secret behind Toastmasters International, NSA, CAPS, and the GSF in helping us to reach our goals and our audiences.

A cowboy doesn't whine when he comes to a detour or problem. He doesn't cry when his horse throws him. He gingerly picks himself up, dusts himself off, and gets back on again. When he comes to a dry hole, he simply mounts his horse and rides on in search of a well to water himself and his livestock.

Neither should we whine when we go through a dry spell… a relationship that doesn't work, a business that doesn't perform, or a speech that doesn't quite come off as well as we'd planned. We can, like the cowboy, simply pick ourselves up, refocus our energies, and move on in search of our future success!

A cowboy is the quintessential role model of the entrepreneurial communicator, in choosing his words carefully, planning and executing his actions wisely, and persistently focusing his energies on the job at hand. He listens slowly to hear the hidden meaning and then acts with confidence. We can learn well from this role model and can apply these same traits and dedications to our own success as speakers and communicators. Our audiences deserve our best!

Bob 'Idea Man' Hooey, CKDE, DTM, PRA, Accredited Speaker
This was used as a part of a unique keynote presentation given in Trail, BC to honor a special fund-raising cattle drive.

Affirmations and Visualization -
The POWER of positive self-talk

Medal winning Olympic athletes, award winning actors, writers, creative people, and, yes, even successful public and professional speakers have learned **the power of self-talk through affirmations** and the applied use of visualization techniques. These tools help them to **see** themselves performing at their best or presenting in a positive manner and enjoy the sense of accomplishment in advance.

Visualization is simple. ***Take a moment and imagine yourself*** *walking confidently to the front of the room, enjoying thunderous applause as you are introduced. Imagine walking up the stairs to the stage and shaking hands with your MC. Then imagine turning, taking a moment to make eye contact with the audience, as you ground yourself and take a few deep breaths. You smile and the audience smiles back at you! You feel accepted and confident! You visibly see and feel their support and encouragement. You begin your presentation with a strong clear voice and sense the excitement flowing through the crowd as your opening captivates their attention. (or, cruising through the Mediterranean from Athens 2022)*

As you continue to speak, you experience them laughing with you. Your heart soars with excitement. You skillfully lead them through the points you outlined and see them ***'getting your message!'*** *You lead up to a powerful conclusion and end with a call to action that brings them to their feet clapping and cheering. You bask in the warmth of their appreciation and smile at them. As you return to your seat,* ***you realize you never even had to look at your notes. You did great!***

Visualization allows your mind to experience the event before you perform it. The amazing thing is it can be so vivid, that when you present you are more relaxed, because you've already done it.

It works very well*, as I found out when I was preparing for each of my three performances in the accredited speaker program. I did this prior to leaving for the Toastmasters International conferences in San Diego, St. Louis, and finally Palm Desert. I also checked out the room where I would be presenting and did a quick run through of my presentation in the room. Finally, when I had a chance, I practiced walking across the main stage to receive my plaque as a professional level Accredited Speaker (way back in 1995).*

In August 1998, on an extremely hot sunny day, I walked across that stage in Palm Desert, CA to receive my professional level Accredited Speaker designation following the World Championships. I wondrously experienced, for real, the emotions I had earlier imagined, to the thunderous roar of applause, whistles, and cheers of over 2200 Toastmasters from around the world. ***I had been there before – in my imagination FOUR years earlier.***

Visualization is the secret to seeing and achieving your goals as a successful speaker. How do you keep yourself positive as you journey toward your goal? **Positive self-talk and affirmations** will work wonders to keep you focused and on track to your success.

Affirmations work by **'speaking the truth, as you would see it'** to your mind and your heart. To be effective, affirmations must possess these three criteria:

- They must be **positive**!
- They must be in the **present tense** (today).
- And they must be **personal**.

Here are some ideas I've used over the years. Create your own, make them yours, and use them, as needed, **daily**, for best results. I've used them individually or as groups. Create what works for you.

Having some instrumental music playing in the background helps me relax and enhances the experience. Try this for yourself when things are quiet, and you won't be disturbed. Let these ideas germinate in your mind.

- My breathing is relaxed and effortless
- My heartbeat is slow and regular
- My muscles are relaxed and warm
- I feel at peace… I am at peace
- I am aware that I am a unique and special person
- Now is the best time to be alive… I am glad I am alive!
- I give the best of myself in everything I undertake!

- I keep the commitments I make
- I earn the respect of others
- I have a sense of adventure
- I have a sense of excitement!
- I am enjoying my work and the success I've earned
- I see new opportunities each day
- I am gentle… I demonstrate my caring for others
- I take time to play like a child… I enjoy my life
- I am strong… I am a winner!!!
- Today is the best day of my life… so far
- I thank GOD for His many gifts to me
- I encourage and support others in achieving their goals
- I am confident in my abilities and skills!
- I inspire confidence from my audiences!
- I grow friendships… I am a true friend
- I look for new ways to give value to my audiences
- I grow relationships with people I like, to spend time with and learn from
- I offer a service that improves the quality of other's lives, to increase their wealth, well-being, and happiness
- I remember my presentation without pause or need of notes
- I know my subject and have selected that which is most valuable to share
- I am prepared, practiced, and polished for my presentation today!!!
- I will give each presentation as though it were my last
- I am excited about the opportunity to share my Ideas At Work!
- I will live my life today as though it was my last
- I will laugh and share my love with each person I meet

Try the above on for size; change them or add to this list as you discover what is truly important for you. **Positive self-talk works.**

Listen to your heart!
Then share your words with passion and power!

"Always give a speech that you would like to hear."
Andrii Sedniev

On The Road… Again!

Time-after-time I hear the amazement and sometimes envy in people's voices when they comment on what I do for a living – travel the world sharing my **Ideas At Work!** and encouraging people to live life as an adventure. I love what I do, but it is, at times, tough mentally and physically. Being what they call a 'road warrior' takes its toll. Ask anyone who travels regularly for work, and they'll agree on the costs.

Newer speakers and audience members say things like, ***"Must be nice to fly all over the world!"*** Or ***"You get to stay in nice hotels!"*** Or ***"You get to eat out in nice restaurants too!"*** In part, these comments are true. In the interest of full disclosure, some of this does wear thin at times. The *novelty* wore off about twenty years ago. **I still very much love what I do. I am more aware of the cost of being on the road,** a cost to my health, my comfort, and sometimes to relationships. This is one of the reasons I savor opportunities to speak closer to home.

The author pictured here (above left) heading out, again; packed, prepared, and full of potential.

In any role there are trade-offs. I accept that and advise newer speakers that it is not **all** fun and games. It can, at times, be arduous!

Sitting in airports waiting for a delayed or cancelled flight due to mechanical or weather challenges is tiring, even fatiguing. Sitting in a seat for 8 to 18 hours flight time can beat you down. Fast food eaten on the fly, if you have time, doesn't help your digestion. Running through airports to catch a flight, because your last one came in late, is not real exercise.

Eating alone, in a strange new place is never fun. Sleeping in a strange bed without the woman you love is boring at best. Sleeping in a strange bed itself is a challenge for me. It often takes me a day or two to acclimatize. Sadly, I may not be there more than one night. (**Covid note**: Now I also work from home sharing my ideas around the globe in virtual environments.)

On the positive side, meeting new people, enjoying new adventures and seeing parts of the globe only seen on TV are amazing. Being well paid to do so and having your expenses covered is very nice. I explore different cultures and see first-hand the similarities we share. I share my ideas and exchange lessons with my new friends. I have new friends around the world and have been able to travel to 68 countries on 6 continents, so far (2023). I expect to visit many more in the years to come. Irene's retirement allows her to go on more of the adventures.

This picture (above right) was taken along the banks of the Seine in Paris where Irene met me on my way back from speaking in Mumbai, India. Occasionally, she gets to come along or meet me enroute. I look forward to having her join me on many new adventures in the future. And she does! ☺

If I was totally honest, I would say this role I have chosen has its own unique drawbacks and its challenges. It is hard on me physically more so than mentally. It challenges me to see beyond the current discomfort to the future satisfaction. **Being a travelling professional speaker is the hardest career you'll ever love.**

Enjoy the journey.

Pictured above: After speaking in Paris, Irene and I enjoy a reflective moment in front of one of the most famous smiles in the world. We smiled in response. We visit Mona each time we go to Paris.

"What lies behind us and what lies before us are tiny matters compared to what lies within us."
Oliver Wendell Holmes

Clip of my Paris presentation in 2022: https://youtu.be/fcXQO9b79M0

The Spirit of CAPS Award

Have you ever been totally surprised at something? Surprised that you had done something that people noticed? So, surprised you were almost speechless? Me too! ☺

The trip to Toronto, Ontario for our 2011 CAPS convention started with a hectic rush to make airline connections to arrive just in time to help my friend **Wayne Lee** with our CAPS Foundation fundraising event we'd worked on for about 6 months. It was a gratifying success, raising **$35,083** over the evening. This was a great highlight of the year for me, for my fellow CAPS Foundation Trustees, and for the work everyone put into this evening.

Then, at the end of the awards banquet the next evening, **2011 CAPS President Ravi Tangri** came on stage to present **The Spirit of CAPS,** which is the highest award we present within the Canadian Association of Professional Speakers. We had given it previously to only 10 speakers in our 15-year history

"The Spirit of CAPS may be awarded to one CAPS member each year who demonstrates the spirit of sharing, leading, and inspiring other professional speakers, trainers, and facilitators within the mission, vision, and values of CAPS. This member will have demonstrated the qualities of generosity, spirit, and professionalism over many years and reflected outstanding credit, respect, honor, and admiration in the Association."

When Ravi was introducing the 2011recipient, he mentioned this person was the **1st Canadian to attend CAMP NSA.** I realized he was talking about me. I couldn't believe what I was hearing. I was both shocked and deeply touched at the same time. I handed my camera to a colleague and asked him to take a few pictures to capture the moment.

As I wiped the tears from my eyes on the way to the stage to accept this amazing award, I wondered what I would say. From what people said, I simply shared this award with the hundreds of people who said 'yes' when I asked for help. Also, even though I was singled out for this honor, I did not achieve it alone. I had help – a lot of help!

Visit: **www.ideaman.net/SoC.htm** for more information on this award, my acceptance speech, and my fellow recipients.

We don't work for honor and recognition, but it sure is nice to find out someone noticed and appreciated our efforts. That, in itself, spurs us on to find other ways to serve. It does me! Writing and again rewriting this book (2023) is a way to continue that service to helping others find their voice and hone their message.

Bob 'Idea Man' Hooey, CVP, Accredited Speaker, CKD-Emeritus
2011 Spirit of CAPS Recipient
Past CAPS National Board Member
Charter member CAPS & GSF
Member NSA-Arizona
Charter member PSA SPAIN
Past Chapter President (Vancouver, BC and Edmonton, AB)
Past CAPS Foundation Trustee
Charter member – Virtual Speakers Association International
Past Region Advisor – Toastmasters International
Certified Virtual Presenter

"The greater danger for most of us lies not in setting our aim too high and falling short; but in setting our aim too low and achieving our mark."

Michelangelo

Toastmasters - Accredited Speaker Program

Over the past 25 years, many people have inquired about my Accredited Speaker Designation (Toastmasters International) and how it came to be. As it played a critical part in my desire to become a professional speaker, I include this brief story of my professional journey for your information.

In November of 1993, 32 Toastmasters from around the world sent in audition tapes and applications for judging in the first level of the Toastmasters International prestigious professional level Accredited Speaker Program.

In February of 1994, *five* were notified of acceptance and invited to speak at the Toastmasters International convention for second level judging. Of those five, three were Canadians. All three were from BC, from the same Toastmasters Club – ASK, the Advanced Speaker Klub. They were DTMs, **Margaret Hope, Judy Johnson, and me.**

How did this unique result happen?

It started back in 1992, when seven BC Toastmasters met to investigate the Toastmasters International Accredited Speaker program and continued to meet monthly for the next year and a bit. Each month we would meet, present, and evaluate our results. We worked as a team in all respects including creating a non-Toastmasters event where we each presented and recorded our presentations. We did that twice so we could choose the better of the two recordings. In November of 1993, Margaret Hope, Judy Johnson, and I felt ready to apply and sent in our audition tapes.

Margaret received her Accredited Speaker designation in San Diego in 1995, becoming the 41st speaker inducted into Toastmasters Hall of Fame for this award. Judy and I were not successful in our first attempt in San Diego. I spoke again the following year in St. Louis and was again not successful. I took 1997 off as I had taken on the District Governor role for BC's 4500 Toastmasters. But I kept working on it to hone my skills. I moved into the realm of professional speaking taking my presentations to a new level. I helped launch CAPS Vancouver in April of 1997 as a part of founding CAPS National across Canada.

The dream became a reality when I walked across a stage to the cheers of 2200-plus, fellow Toastmasters from around the world to be inducted into the Toastmasters Hall of Fame and received mine in Palm Desert in 1998; becoming the 48 professional level Accredited Speaker in our history, and only the 5th Canadian to earn this designation.

Update (2023), there are only ninety people world-wide, who have made this walk of fame. Only twelve are Canadians.

Toastmasters initiated their professional level, Accredited Speakers program in 1981, some 42 years ago. **Follow this link to learn more: www.toastmasters.org/membership/accredited-speaker** Visit for more information on the professional level program and its Hall of Fame recipients.

I focused on this program early in my TM life, as my dream was to become a professional speaker. I remember when I got my Able Toastmaster (ATM); it came with a flyer for the Accredited Speaker Program which said in big letters**, "Are you good enough to be a PRO?"** I wrote on it, **"Not yet, but I will be!"** For two years it challenged me, inspired me, pushed me forward!

The real win in this program, wasn't the designation itself or the worldwide recognition, although that was very satisfying. **The *real win* for me was in the progression of my skills and entry into the world of professional speaking;** in being able to have people see, firsthand, the value in what I brought to the training room or the platform and pay me accordingly.

The real win was in being better at sharing my messages for the benefit of my audiences around the world. Being a global speaker was a win for me!

If you have a dream to become a professional trainer, facilitator, or keynoter, then perhaps you should investigate this program. For me the journey was well worth the effort. It still was as I learned to **Pivot to Present** virtually during the covid crisis.

Thanks for investing in Speaking for Success

Each time I prepare to step on the stage; each time I sit down to write or in this case to re-write for this expanded 10th edition, I am challenged to ensure I deliver something that will be of use-it-now value to my reader.

- I ask myself, **"If I was reading this, what would I be looking for?"**
- As well as **"Why is this relevant to me, today?"**

These two questions help to keep me focused and help me to remain clear on my objectives. They help to remind me to dig into my experiences, stories, examples, and research to provide solid information that will be of benefit and help my readers, when they apply it, succeed. That can be an exciting challenge! Perhaps they should be ones you ask yourself?

I trust we have done that for you in this updated primer on more effective communication and presentation skills. **Speaking for Success** is my attempt to capture some of the lessons learned first-hand on stage and share the stage with many speaking masters and to share them with you.

I'd love to hear from you and read your success stories. If you would be so kind, please drop me a quick email at: **bhooey@mcsnet.ca** or

Bob 'Idea Man' Hooey
2011 Spirit of CAPS recipient
www.ideaman.net
www.HaveMouthWillTravel.com
Bob in Mumbai, India (left)

Connect with me on:

- **Facebook:** www.facebook.com/bob.hooey
- **LinkedIn:** www.linkedin.com/in/canadianideamanbobhooey
- **YouTube:** www.youtube.com/ideamanbob
- **Smashwords:** www.smashwords.com/profile/view/Hooey
- **Amazon:** www.amazon.com/Bob-Idea-Man-Hooey/e/B00FACOHNY

About the Author

Bob 'Idea Man' Hooey is a charismatic, confident leader, corporate trainer, inspiring facilitator, Emcee, prolific author, and motivational keynote speaker on creativity, inspirational leadership, sales success, business innovation, and enhancing team performance.

Using personal stories drawn from idea-rich experience, he challenges his audiences to engage his **Ideas At Work! – to act on what they hear,** with clear, innovative building-blocks and field-proven success techniques to increase their effectiveness. Bob challenges them to hone specific 'success skills' critical to their personal and professional advancement.

Bob outlines real-life, results-based, innovative ideas personally drawn from 29 plus years of rich leadership experience in retail, sales, construction, small business, entrepreneurship, manufacturing, association, consulting, community service, and commercial management.

Bob's conversational, often humorous, professional, and sometimes-provocative style continues to inspire and challenge his audiences across the globe. Bob's motivational, innovative, challenging, and practical **Ideas At Work!** have been successfully applied by thousands of sales leaders and professionals, just like you.

Bob is a frequent contributor to North American consumer, corporate, association, trade, and on-line publications on leadership, sales success, employee motivation and training; as well as creativity and innovative problem solving, priority and time management, and effective customer service. He is the inspirational author of 30-plus publications including print (several reaching the Amazon best-seller lists), e-books, and Pocket Wisdom series. Visit: **www.SuccessPublications.ca** for more information.

Retired, award winning kitchen designer, Bob Hooey, CKD-Emeritus was one of only 75 Canadian designers to earn this prestigious certification by the National Kitchen and Bath Association.

In December 2000, Bob was given a special CAPS National Presidential award **"…for his energetic contribution to the advancement of CAPS and his living example of the power of one"** in addition to being elected to the CAPS National Board. He has been recognized by the National Speakers Association for his leadership contributions.

Bob is a co-founder and past President of the CAPS Vancouver, BC Chapter and served as 2012 President of the CAPS Edmonton, AB Chapter. He is a member of the NSA-Arizona Chapter and active in the National Speakers Association, a charter member of the Canadian Association of Professional Speakers, a charter member of PSA-SPAIN, VSAI, and, of course, the Global Speakers Federation. He has spoken at 8 of the 17 GSF member association' conventions, so far.

In 1998, Toastmasters International recognized Bob **"…for his professionalism and outstanding achievements in public speaking".** That August in Palm Desert, California Bob became the 48th speaker in the world to be awarded this prestigious professional level honor as an Accredited Speaker. He has been inducted into their Hall of Fame on several other occasions for his leadership contributions.

Bob has been honored by the United Nations Association of BC (1993) and received the CANADA 125 award (1992) for his ongoing contributions to the community.

In 1998, Bob joined 3 other men to sail a 65-foot gaff rigged schooner from Honolulu, Hawaii to Kobe, Japan, barely surviving a 'baby' typhoon enroute.

In November 2011, Bob was awarded The Spirit of CAPS *(the highest award given in the Canadian speaking industry)* at their annual convention, becoming the 11th speaker to earn this prestigious national award.

Bob loves to travel, and his speaking and writing have allowed him to visit 68 countries on 6 continents, so far. Perhaps your organization would like to bring Bob in to share a few ideas with your team.

Bob is a **Certified Virtual Presenter** and can zoom in to work with you.

Visit: **www.HaveMouthWillTravel.com** for more information.

Bob's B.E.S.T. Publications

Bob is a *prolific* author who has been capturing and sharing his wisdom and experience in print and electronic formats for the past fifteen plus years.

In addition to the following publications, several of them bestsellers, he has written for consumer, corporate, professional associations, trade, and on-line publications across the globe. His articles have frequently been featured on association and trade sites.

Bob has been engaged to write and assist on publications by other best-selling writers and successful companies. His publications are listed to give you an idea of the scope and topics he writes about.

Bob's **B**usiness **E**nhancement **S**uccess **T**ools.

Leadership, business, and career development series

- **Running TOO Fast** (8th edition 2019)
- **Legacy of Leadership** (3rd edition 2022)
- **Make ME Feel Special!** (6th edition 2022)
- **Why Didn't I 'THINK' of That?** (6th edition 2022)
- **Speaking for Success!** (10th edition 2023)
- **THINK Beyond the First Sale** (3rd edition 2022)
- **Prepare Yourself to Win!** (3rd edition 2017)
- **The early years… 1998-2009 – A Tip of the Hat collection** (2020)
- **The saga continues… 2010-2019 – A Tip of the Hat collection** (2020)
- **Sales Success Secrets -2 volume set** (2022)

Bob's Mini-book success series

- **The Courage to Lead!** (4th edition 2017)
- **Creative Conflict** (3rd edition 2017)
- **Get to YES!** (3rd edition 2017)
- **THINK Before You Ink!** (3rd edition 2017)
- **Running to Win!** (2nd edition 2017)

- **How to Generate More Sales** (4th edition 2017)
- **Unleash your Business Potential** (3rd edition 2017)
- **Maximize Meetings** (2019)
- **Learn to Listen** (2nd edition 2017)
- **Creativity Counts!** (2016)
- **Create Your Future!** (3rd edition 2017)

Bob's Pocket Wisdom series – *print and epub formats*

- **Pocket Wisdom for Speakers** (updated 2019)
- **Pocket Wisdom for Leaders – Power of One!** (updated 2019)

Kindle Shorts (2017-2020) series - *more to come in 2023*

- **SPEAK!**
- **LEAD!**
- **SERVE!**
- **CREATE!**
- **CONFLICT!**
- **TIME!**
- **SUCCEED!**
- **WRITE ON!**

Co-authored books created by Bob

- **In The Company of Leaders** (95th anniversary Edition 2019)
- **Foundational Success** (2nd Edition 2013)
- **PIVOT to Present** (2020) to assist in speaking virtually

Visit: www.SuccessPublications.ca for more information on Bob's publications and other success resources.

"Speaking is simple when you focus on the audience and do your homework, before you open your mouth and heart. Writing follows a similar path: Capture the thoughts, make the connection – the rest is editing." Bob 'Idea Man' Hooey, Author, Certified Virtual Presenter

Visit: **www.successpublications.ca/PIVOT.html** to download a complimentary copy of **PIVOT to Present** (written after Covid-19 hit)

Contacts for Your Reference

Feel free to investigate these organizations. Each has their specific focus and has at their core a dedication to help people be more effective as presenters.

TI - Toastmasters International: *www.Toastmasters.org*
This is where I got my start and built most of the foundations for my entrance into the speaking business. I remain active in my local advanced club as I continue to learn and hone my skills as I continue to serve in various leadership roles. **I also speak for various Districts, schedule permitting.**

NSA - National Speakers Association: *www.NSAspeaker.org*
Before we started CAPS (1997), four of us travelled from Vancouver to Seattle every month to attend the NSA chapter to learn more about this new business we had become a part of. It was a long drive but worth the trip. I am still a member of NSA-Arizona.

Canadian Association of Professional Speakers: *www.CanadianSpeakers.org*
CAPS became a national organization in 1997 alongside the creation of what has become the Global Speakers Federation. I had the privilege of helping start the CAPS Vancouver Chapter which helped to create our CAPS National organization. I am pleased to be a charter member.

Global Speakers Federation: *www.globalspeakers.net*
This is the umbrella organization of 17 national speaking organizations with more being added each year. I am pleased to be a charter member.

Alberta Speakers: *www.AlbertaSpeakers.com*
This is a simple joint venture project we started 15 plus years ago with professional speakers from Alberta. We each contribute to support the website and buy print advertisements that promote the website.

Accredited Speakers: *www.toastmasters.org/membership/accredited-speaker* Visit this site for information and resources to our Toastmasters around the globe.

Excerpts from Pivot to Present (©2020)

PIVOT
To Present
Idea-rich strategies to deliver your virtual message with impact
Bob 'Idea Man' Hooey
Author of Speaking for Success!

Bob Hooey & friends share helpful tips and techniques

"You're muted!" or "Un-mute Yourself!"
2020-2022's most used catch phrases

Visit: **www.successpublications.ca/PIVOT.html** to download a complimentary copy of **PIVOT to Present** (written after Covid-19 hit)

As we dig into our 'virtual' pivot

Pivot (noun) *A fixed point supporting something which turns or balances or a thing on which something else depends…* (American Dictionary)

Pivot (verb): *to change your opinions, statements, decisions, etc., so that they are different to what they were before:* (Cambridge Dictionary)

This word, pivot, was around long before COVID-19 hit; but it certainly found more wide-spread acceptance and its use expanded once we were locked down. We are not certain of when it became a world pandemic, and frankly that doesn't matter. It is and it has impacted us tremendously.

As I wrote and edited contributions for this little book, we were in a world-wide **COVID-19 pandemic**. Cities, states, and countries were in lockdown around the globe. Businesses were closed and workers were sitting at home, worried and waiting for it to work its way out (we hope!). Second and third waves have now hit us, and variants continue to emerge.

Governments are still playing catch up, most having been caught totally unprepared, flat-footed, to lead and to cope with this global emergency. By the time it has worked its way out, millions more will die. Not a fun scene, by any means.

Also important in this crisis are the long-range economic impacts of that series of shutdowns. No travel, little manufacturing, only essential businesses remained open (like groceries, pharmacies, hardware stores, etc.) This was a serious challenge for those of us in business if **we want to survive and stay in business over the long-haul.** And, we now have the time to work on it!

Disruption has changed our lives, both personal and corporate, as we knew them! Overnight, businesses shuttered their doors, laid off their staff, and turned off their lights. Overnight, businesses had to pivot to survive. Overnight, many workers and leaders have been thrust into the digital, virtually interconnected world. Working from home, in physical isolation, became our new norm. **How would we adapt and continue to deal with this new global challenge?** The results are still being written and evaluated. But it is an exciting time too, if we embrace it.

Quite simply, we don't know yet. We are still making it up as we go along, feeling our way, one day at a time in totally unchartered territories. Some had already started down this virtual path of digital connection, collaboration, and creation. For others, thrust into this digitally changing world, the results remain to be seen. More than ever, we need to work together to find our way in this confusing new hybrid world.

Update 2023: The world is continuing to open up as vaccinations are taking effect. However, we are not out of the woods yet with variants and outbreaks around the globe causing us to remain vigilant, mask, and play it safe.

Suddenly being able to communicate, connect, and even conduct business in a virtual environment has become exceedingly important, even critical. We had to **mentally pivot to explore new ways to do all these important actions**.

Bob in Paris, France (2022)

I admit, I was a bit depressed when international engagements keep being postponed, canceled, or moved on-line. I had to get my mindset in adjustment that '**even though I was not able to travel, my ideas could'**, and they have.

Like many of my speaking and training colleagues, I explored different ways to continue to deliver solid value to my clients – **digital ways to connect, educate, and engage**. My commitment to help my clients was as strong as ever, stronger, just the delivery methods had changed.

This was a very real challenge for our business owners, sales professionals, and many who were sent home, or are now working from home face every day. Many were looking at making a pivot to a new job or career as their previous one evaporated and will most likely not return, even when COVID-19 was under control.

"In challenging times people need HELP and they need HOPE! That is MY business!"

Bob 'Idea Man' Hooey

One of the saddest challenges of Covid-19 were the thousands of people around the globe who could not access the internet or barely access it. I am sure someone is working to find a way to provide cost effective access in this time of challenge.

More than ever, we needed to reassess what business we were in, who were our potential clients, and how we could best reach and serve them despite these disruptive times.

More than ever, we needed to learn how to reach out and connect and communicate with those who are important to us: our families, our friends, our colleagues, our clients.

Those who take this seriously and adapt will emerge stronger, perhaps, totally redesigned, and restructured. And, perhaps more relevant and profitable as well. **This is our opportunity, our challenge as business leaders, to demonstrate our commitment to our clients, teams, suppliers, and communities.**

We can do it by working together! We can do it by sharing our lessons and encouragement in moving online and moving forward.

That is why I created PIVOT to Present.

Bob pictured here in China where he presented in Beijing (2017)

I reached out to some of my amazing colleagues in the speaking industry for their current tips, techniques, stories, and lessons learned as they pivoted to presenting and communicating on-line. I've compiled their contributions in this book, along with my own thoughts and experimentation.

Getting Started – a simple approach

Getting started online has gotten easier in the past couple of years. Zoom has always had a free program which can be used to learn the ropes before you invest in professional programs.

Zoom Personal Meeting – Free (*https://www.zoom.us/*)
Host up to 100 participants
40-minute maximum group meetings
Unlimited 1:1 Meetings

If you have a laptop, most of them have a microphone and camera so you're good to go, for now. As you move forward you can invest in reasonably priced HD cameras and plug in mics. But, for now you can experiment by hosting calls with family and friends to learn the program and become more proficient in leveraging it professionally. Zoom has some amazing demo videos to help you get started; invest your time to learn.

I have used Zoom for client interviews, and it worked great with my District leaders when I was a Region Advisor. I was comfortable with it, but still needed to learn how to present in this new medium. ***Jump in the water online is fine.*** 😊

Can you see me now?

One aspect critical to presenting online is adequate lighting. That doesn't mean you need to invest in expensive studio lighting; it does mean you need to use it well. Make sure your face is well lit with one or two lights in that direction. I use two LED goose neck lights on either side of my monitor facing each other which provide good lighting for my face. In fact, they give me a nice healthy look. You can also look at adding something as a back light if using a screen to eliminate shadows.

Play with your lighting until you determine what helps people be able to **see you clearly** and be able to read your facial expressions in this new medium. We've added some great articles on lighting in our resource section on-line.

A few reminders to effectively present on-line

- Block out what you are going to say, just like you would for a live presentation. Great visuals, interactive, well-paced.
- Practice, so you are comfortable with your platform choice.
- Tidy up your background so your audience isn't distracted.
- Make sure they can see your face – adequate lighting.
- Double check your connections and test your equipment.
- Camera level with your face – some say eye level.
- Minimize any potential distractions or interruptions.
- Sticky notes: next to your webcam works great so you avoid looking down at your notes on camera.
- Dress for the audience… no pjs or shorts please.
- Make eye contact by looking directly into the camera. Imagine you are speaking to that one person, because you actually are speaking to individuals on-line.

Apply these simple tips to help ensure you present effectively and garner your best impact on-line.

You will find some repetition in the ideas shared. These have been left for a simple reason: reinforcement of something that is true from the applied wisdom of many.

We have set up an online resource page as well and welcome submissions you feel might be of value to your fellow readers.
www.SuccessPublications.ca/PIVOT.html

Bob 'Idea Man' Hooey, *Creative Lead*
Certified Virtual Presenter

The Big Tech Reset

David is a tech guru as well as a CAPS colleague. Thanks my friend.

2020 has been an interesting year, so far. Many feel there was a big reset button pressed on everything in life. As the new normal is emerging, we are discovering communication with family, friends, and for business is taking new shape. Many people scrambled to get their technology back to a reasonable working level in terms of video conferencing capabilities. This means good quality video (webcam), solid audio (microphone), reliable connection (Internet), and decent bones running the communication software (fast laptop or desktop).

Zoom has become a verb implying connecting with people by video, though several are using it for audio only as well. Many wonder **which platform is the best**: Zoom vs Google Meet (Hangouts) vs Microsoft Teams vs Cisco WebEx vs Skype ...

Use the platform your clients/family/friends are most comfortable with. Good customer service in business and how you get new clients is by making things as easy as possible for them and solving their problems. Don't force your technology upon someone else if they seem apprehensive. Yes, we all think "our" solution is so easy, but many ***fear the unknown.*** This is one more roadblock for them becoming a potential new client or contact of yours.

When someone agrees to a virtual meeting, send them a calendar invite that includes the video link. Provide everything to them on a silver platter so it is as easy as possible. Ensure you are on time and you are professional. This includes what your own camera is viewing: good lightning, reduce background distractions, what you are wearing, the quality of your video and audio. Ensure your Internet connection does well for the video session and consider connecting your device with a wired ethernet cable to your Internet router instead of Wi-Fi. Make sure others in your household aren't watching Netflix at the moment which congests your connection to the Internet and will make your video & audio lower quality. Test any changes you make; this

is easy by having a quick session with a friend or colleague before your important meeting.

With the constant advancements in technology, it is recommended to **be part of a group such as a mastermind**. This trusted group of peers is great for asking questions, brainstorming, keeping up on latest tips & tricks, and giving feedback. They can be the ones who help recommend and test new technologies. Have a regular monthly Zoom session with your group that is always carved away in your calendar. For your first session, have everyone bring one single tip they would think everyone should know such as a website, an app, a gadget, or any life hack. Keep it brief and fun.

David Papp, *P.Eng. www.davidpapp.com Included with permission*

Certified Virtual Presenter/CVP

You may see this designation behind the names of some contributors; more as it becomes known. This is an indication that they have been tested (by e-Speakers) with a standardized on-line test to ensure they have the necessary equipment, skills, and expertise to present effectively in this exciting new medium.

This is a new designation created following the outbreak of COVID-19 around the globe. Our guess is it will be soon an industry standard in this new medium. **www.espeakers.com**

Zoom.com has amazing tutorials… use them!

Pro-Tip: Speaking Into A Black Hole

Ever felt like you were talking to a black hole and wondered if anyone even was listening? I did recently, when I was delivering some on-line training to Track and Field officials across Canada. The host asked everyone to turn off their video and audio to conserve band width. The silence was deafening.

As my husband says, it is very much like speaking on TV when you speak directly into the camera and hope there is someone viewing.

If you can, have someone in your viewing audience so you can see a bit of reaction. If that is not possible, perhaps put a picture next to your camera of people smiling or even laughing, so that you can get the energy from them.

Irene Gaudet, *www.VitrakCreative.com*

PRO-tip: How to get hired more often

"Every speaker needs to start with the basics to build a platform and client list. This can seem impossibly confusing and time consuming. It doesn't have to be. Here are four proven, no-cost strategies you need to repeat over and over if you want to grow long-term success:

- **Be an authority**: have a unique value proposition in a niche market. Be willing to continually refine this formula.
- **Publish** regular high-value content: blog, YouTube, SlideShare, articles. You are an expert – now you need to (continually) prove it.
- **Be of service**: help other speakers, send leads to bureaus, and share helpful advice freely. This isn't about good Karma – it will get you sales.
- **Be extraordinary** every time you present, keep promises, be easy to work with, get audience feedback. And make the event planner love you."

Hugh Culver, *CSP www.hughculver.com*

"It is not failure itself that holds you back; it is the fear of failure that paralyzes you."

Brian Tracy

Copyright and License Notes

Speaking for Success (10th edition) revised and expanded for 2023
Idea-rich techniques to master your message and power up your presentations

Bob 'Idea Man' Hooey, *DTM, PDG, CVP, Accredited Speaker*
2011 Spirit of CAPS recipient, Prolific author of 30 plus business and career success publications

Unattributed quotations are by Bob 'Idea Man' Hooey, CVP

Photos of Bob: Dov Friedmann, *www.photographybyDov.com*
Irene Gaudet, *www.vitrakcreative.com*
Frédéric Bélot, *www.fredericbelot.fr/fr*
Bonnie-Jean McAllister, *www.elantraphotography.com*

ISBN: 978-1-896737-93-5

Printed in the United States 10 9 8 7 6 5 4 3 2 1
1st edition 1998: **expanded 10th edition 2023**

Success Publications
Box 10, Egremont, AB T0A 0Z0
www.successpublications.ca
Creative office: 1-780-736-0009

Acknowledgements and Disclaimers

As is my custom, a very special dedication of this piece of myself, to the two people who meant the most to me, my folks **Ron and Marge Hooey**. Sadly, both my parents left this earthly realm in 1999. I still miss your encouragement and love. I was blessed with the two of you in my life.

To my inspiring wife, editor, and professional proofreader, **Irene Gaudet**, who loves, encourages, and supports me in my quest to continue sharing my **Ideas At Work!** across the world. Thank you seems so inadequate for your work in helping make my writing and my client service better!

My thanks to the many people who have encouraged me in my growth as a leader, speaker, and engaging trainer in each area of expertise including **Speaking for Success**.

- To my colleagues and friends in the National Speakers Association **(NSA)**, the Canadian Association of Professional Speakers **(CAPS)**, and the Global Speakers Federation **(GSF)** who continually challenge me to strive for success and increased excellence. To those speakers and leaders within our industry whose ideas and skills I have observed and shared in this publication.
- To my many **Toastmasters Accredited Speaker** colleagues, friends, and family around the world, to whom I owe an un-payable debt of gratitude for your investment, encouragement, and support when I was just starting down this path; and oh, so rough around the edges.
- To my great audiences, students, coaching clients, and readers across the globe who share their experiences and enjoyment of my work. Your positive and supportive feedback encourages me to keep working on additional programs and publications like this one. My experience with you creates the foundation for additional real-life experiences I can take from the stage to the page or the classroom.

- My thanks to a select few friends for your ongoing support and constructive abuse. You know who you are. ☺

We have not attempted to cite all the authorities and sources consulted in the preparation of this book. To do so would require much more space than is available. We have sought accurate attribution where possible. The list would include departments of various governments, libraries, industrial institutions, periodicals, and many individuals. Inspiration was drawn from many sources in the creation of **Speaking for Success**.

Disclaimer

LIMITS OF LIABILITY / DISCLAIMER OF WARRANTY:
The author and publisher of this book have used their best efforts in preparing this material. While every attempt has been made to verify information provided in this book, neither the author nor the publisher assumes any responsibility for any errors, omissions or inaccuracies. Graphics are royalty free or under license. Care has been taken to trace ownership of copyright material contained in this volume. The publisher will gladly receive information that will allow him to rectify any reference or credit line in subsequent editions.

Unattributed quotations are by Bob 'Idea Man' Hooey

The author and publisher make no representation or warranties with respect to the accuracy, applicability, fitness, or completeness of the contents of this program. They disclaim any warranties (expressed or implied), merchantability, or fitness for any purpose.

The author and publisher shall in no event be held liable for any loss or other damages, including but not limited to special, incidental, consequential, or other damages. As always, the advice of a competent legal, tax, accounting or other professional should be sought.

What Clients Say About Bob 'Idea Man' Hooey

As I travelled across North America, and more recently around the globe, sharing my **Ideas At Work!** I am fortunate to get feedback and comments from my audience. These comments come from people who have been touched, challenged, or simply enjoyed themselves in one of my sessions. The leveraged lessons as contained in **Speaking for Success** have allowed me to gain this positive and professionally satisfying response. If you are willing to apply yourself and practice and polish, you too can leave these kinds of impressions. **Enjoy the journey!**

"I still get comments from people about your presentation. ***Only a few speakers have left an impression that lasts that long.*** *You hit a spot with the tourism people."* **Janet Bell**, Yukon Economic Forums

"On very short notice Bob cleared his schedule and graciously presented at our meeting when the original Speaker was unable to attend. ***Last week Bob set the tone for our two-day leadership meeting and gave us all a motivational lift.*** His compassion and true interest in people were so clearly evident, making him very credible. He shared some great stories, has a wealth of experience and knowledge and it was a pleasure listening to him. His down-to-Earth style makes it easier to retain the information presented. He also followed up with additional info and handouts, cementing his message of building bridges, not walls. Fantastic job, Bob, and thanks again!" ***Barbara Afra Beler***, MBA, Senior Specialist Commercial Community, Alberta North, ***BMO Bank of Montreal***

"Thank you, Bob; it is ***always a pleasure to see a true professional at work.*** *You have made the name "Speaker" stand out as a truism - someone who encourages people to examine their lives and make adjustments. The personal stories you shared with your audience made such a great impression on everyone.* ***The comments indicated you hit people right where it is important - in their hearts.*** *Each of those in your audience took away a new feeling of personal success and encouragement."* **Sherry Knight**, Dimension Eleven Human Resources and Communications

"I have found ***Bob's attention to detail*** *and his ability to fine tune his seminars to match the time frame and needs of the audience to be a valuable asset to our educational program."* **Patsy Schell**, Executive Director Surrey Chamber of Commerce

"We greatly appreciate ***the energy and effort you put into researching and adapting your keynote to make it more meaningful to our member councils.*** *Early feedback from our delegates indicates that this year's convention was one of our most successful events yet, and we thank you for your contribution to this success."* **Larry Goodhope**, Executive Director Alberta Assoc. of Municipal Districts & Counties

"Without doubt, ***I have gained immeasurable self-assurance.*** *Bob, your patience and your encouragement has been much appreciated.* ***I strongly recommend your course to anyone looking for self-improvement and professional development.***" Jeannie Mura, Human Resources Chevron Canada

"I am pleased to recommend Bob 'Idea Man' Hooey to any organization looking for a charismatic, confident speaker and seminar leader. I have seen Bob in action on several occasions, and he is ALWAYS on! Bob has the ability to grab his audience's attention and keep it. Quite simply, ***if Bob is involved - your program or seminar is guaranteed to succeed.***" **Maurice Laving**, Coordinator Training and Development, London Drugs

"Great seeing you in Cancun and congratulations on a job well done. ***The seminar was a great success! Your humorous and conversational style was a tremendous asset.*** *It is my sincere hope that we can be associated again at future seminars."* **Donald MacPherson**, Attorney At Law, Phoenix, Arizona

"***What a great conference.*** *It was a great pleasure meeting with you at the Ritz Carlton, Cancun and I shall look forward to hopefully welcoming you and your family in Dublin, Ireland someday."* **A. Paul Ryan**, Petronva Corporation, Dublin, Ireland

"Dear Mr. Hooey: ***Thank you for elevating my Sales Team's knowledge during your sales management seminar in Tehran, Iran.*** I look forward to meeting you in person during your future seminars. Warm regards." **Mendi Ghaemi**, Managing Director, Bidar Group (Head office Egypt)

"On very short notice Bob cleared his schedule and graciously presented at our meeting when the original Speaker was unable to attend. ***Last week Bob set the tone for our two-day leadership meeting and gave us all a motivational lift.*** *His compassion and true interest in people were clearly evident, making him very credible. He shared some great stories, has a wealth of experience and knowledge and it was a pleasure listening to him. His down-to-Earth style makes it easier to retain the information presented. He also followed up with additional info and handouts, cementing his message of building bridges, not walls. Fantastic job, Bob, and thanks again!"*
Barbara Afra Beler*, MBA, Senior Specialist Commercial Community, Alberta North,* ***BMO Bank of Montreal***

Engage Bob for Your Leaders and Their Teams

"I have been so excited working with ***Bob Hooey****, as he has given inspiration and motivation to our leadership team members. Both at the Brick Warehouse – Alberta and more recently, here at Art Van Furniture – Michigan; with his years of experience in working with business executives and his humorous and delightful packaging of his material, he makes learning with Bob a real joy. But most importantly, anyone who comes in contact with his material is the better for it."*

Kim Yost, *retired CEO Art Van Furniture, former CEO The Brick*

Motivate your teams, your employees, and your leaders to *productively* grow and *profitably* succeed!

- **Protect** your conference investment - leverage your training dollars.
- **Enhance** your professional career and sell more products and services.
- **Equip** and motivate your leaders and their teams to grow and succeed, 'even' in tough times!
- **Leverage** your leadership to leave a significant legacy!

Call today to engage inspirational leadership keynote speaker, sales leaders' success coach, and employee development trainer, **Bob 'Idea Man' Hooey** and his innovative, audience based, results-focused, **Ideas At Work!** for your next company, convention, leadership, staff, sales, training, or association event. You might want to engage him as an executive speech coach too. **In Person or Virtually**, you'll be glad you did! **Call 1-780-736-0009 to connect with Bob 'Idea Man' Hooey, CVP today!**

We hope you've visited our special bonus page with video clips to help you enhance your presentations. Follow this link: **www.SuccessPublications.ca/Speaking-Tips.html**

Bob performing with The Passing Zone during the 2013 CAPS Foundation fundraiser in Vancouver, BC

I love what I do and the people I get to share my time and skills with around the globe. Over the past 29+ years, I have struggled at times to keep focused and positive as I travelled the globe sharing my **Ideas At Work!** Somehow, I found the energy to try again, to push myself to grow outside my comfort zone, and to explore the winner's zone. I trust this book will be a benefit in your quest to be a more impactful speaker and help you find and enhance your voice. The world needs more of you! I am so privileged to play my part in your quest.

A few bonus videos for your enjoyment and perhaps motivation too.

https://youtu.be/HRN0HyChtvg *Bob in Paris -European Speakers Summit*

https://youtu.be/-fAFD9mkUPo *Bob's demo video*

https://youtu.be/BA-sd_P96Jg *Bob at PSA Ireland sharing his Building Blocks for Speaking Success*

https://youtu.be/fhCKUM0z92o Bob answers audience questions at AFCP convention in Paris, France (2015)

What Colleagues Say About Bob…

I am humbled and inspired by the kind words from my colleagues in this business. Their encouragement helps me keep **Speaking for Success**!

"Bob Hooey is one of the best speakers, trainers and business consultants that I have ever met. We have worked together in training the top executives of billion- dollar companies, and received rave reviews… Bob Hooey and I have worked together for decades."
Brian Tracy, *Author, Speaker*

"Not only is Bob a trustful and highly professional expert, not only is he a fabulous and engaging speaker, but Bob is also one of the nicest men I have ever met. He combines the wisdom of experience with astounding vigor and charisma. I highly recommend him.
Elizabeth Grimaud, *AFCP (French Speakers Association)*

"I watched Bob Hooey deliver a speech in Cape Town, SA when he was feeling far less than 100%. The audience never knew. That's what a pro does. Shows up and delivers!"
Shep Hyken, *CSP, CPAE, Past President NSA*

***Bob 'Idea Man' Hooey** is a master-of-public speaking, not only in Canada, but internationally. Not only has he motivated, inspired, and energized tens of thousands of people in his audiences worldwide, but he also takes the time to work with aspiring and developing speakers to help them hone their skills and perfect their craft so they can be their very best on the platform and in the business. If you are interested in public speaking, or you are developing a career as a professional speaker, trainer, or keynoter, Bob's wisdom will help you get there.* **Sarah Elaine Eaton**, *Ph.D.*

Good news is always good! Congratulations on this wonderful achievement (Spirit of CAPS) - well deserved, I'm sure! And how gracious of you to "share" this award with so many others - you're a true leader and a real gentleman! **Chris Ford**, *DTM, Past International President (2007-2008) Toastmasters International*

Bob 'Idea Man' Hooey is a mentor to many and has done great things for CAPS Edmonton. Bob has also provided me with innovative ideas to help grow my business. His commitment to CAPS, the speaking profession, and professional speakers is admirable! It is a pleasure to recommend Bob. **Charmaine Hammond**, *Hammond International*

"We were thrilled when we secured Bob Hooey to speak at our annual convention in April this year (2015). Having heard so much about him over the years, I found him true to his reputation - **an absolute professional**, *keeping the client in contact and informed, sending through requirements early and confirming all that we needed from him. And then on the day, delivering a wonderful, fun and engaging presentation that both communicated Bob's message and fit in with our theme brilliantly. Should I have the opportunity in the future, I would love to work with Bob again."* **Charlotte Kemp**, *Convention Chair PSA SA 2015 Convention in Cape Town, SA*

If your company needs new and creative ideas, I highly recommend Canada's Ideaman, Bob Hooey. He has sincere passion for helping others to succeed and guiding them to reach their highest potential. You are leaving a legacy. Thank you.
Debra Kasowski, *Author of GPS Your Best Life*

Bob 'Idea Man' Hooey *is an exceptional speaker and facilitator who helps businesses and organizations grow profit and create effective teams. This leadership and sales expert has written more than a dozen books, travels the globe speaking to managers, corporations, and non-profits, increasing morale as well as profits. Bob is a leader within the speaking industry and is beloved by his peers for his mentorship, warmth and high skill. I highly recommend Bob as a speaker. He'll be the one your employees and conference attendees talk about.* **Shawne Duperon**, *CEO, ShawneTV (3-time Emmy award winner)*

I had the pleasure of hearing and watching Bob Hooey deliver a keynote speech several years ago when he gave a presentation at a Toastmasters International Convention. Bob impressed me greatly with his professionalism, energy, and ability to connect with his audience while giving them value. I heartily recommend this talented speaker and "Idea Farmer" to all who want to move to the next level. **Dilip Abayasekara**, *PIP, DTM, AS*

"I attended Speaking for Success in Edmonton. The mark of a true leader is someone who will lay down their own pride to teach all they know to their potential successors. To be taught by a man of his caliber was an honor whether you're a beginner like myself or a professional; the experience is well worth it! To Bob - it truly was an honor to meet you. Stay humble and enjoy the great success." **Samantha McLeod**

"I've known Bob for several years and follow his activities in business with interest. I originally met Bob when he spoke for a Rotary Leadership Institute and got to know him better when he came to Vladivostok, Russia to speak to our leadership. ***When you spoke, I thought you were one of us because you talked about our challenges just like yours.*** *You could understand the others, which makes you a great speaker!"* **Andrey Konyushok**, *Rotary International District 2225 Governor 2012-2013, far eastern Russia*

www.ingramcontent.com/pod-product-compliance
Lightning Source LLC
Chambersburg PA
CBHW071703210326
41597CB00017B/2307
* 9 7 8 1 8 9 6 7 3 7 9 3 5 *

www.ingramcontent.com/pod-product-compliance
Lightning Source LLC
Chambersburg PA
CBHW071704210326
41597CB00017B/2319
* 9 7 8 1 8 8 7 2 7 6 8 4 9 *